Photograph of Rooksnest from the rear.

# *Contents*

# List of Illustrations

Cover. Derwent Lees, *Pear Tree in Blossom*, 1913.

p. iii. Photograph of Rooksnest from the rear. By permission of the Provost and Fellows of King's College, Cambridge. Archives Centre, King's College, Cambridge. EMF/27/47.

p. xiv. Photograph of E. M. Forster, age 10, with his mother. By permission of the Provost and Fellows of King's College, Cambridge. Archives Centre, King's College, Cambridge. EMF/27/163.

p. 2. Title page of *Howards End*, first edition.

p. 284. The Embankment, 1900. National Media Museum/SSPL.

p. 334. Cover of *Votes for Women*, 13 June 1913.

p. 371. Charles Ricketts, illustration for *Daphnis and Chloe*. Tate, London/Art Resource.

# About Longman Cultural Editions

Inspired by the innovative *Longman Anthology of British Literature*, the Longman Cultural Editions are designed to illuminate the lively, ever variable intersections of literature, tradition, and culture. In each volume, a work or works of literary imagination gather new dimensions from materials that relate to informing traditions and debates, to contemporary conversations and controversies, and to later eras of reading and reaction. While the nature of the contexts varies from volume to volume, the reliable constants (in addition to handsome production and affordable pricing) are expert editing and helpful annotation throughout; a stimulating introduction; a table of dates to track composition, publication, and reception in relation to biographical, cultural, and historical events; illustrations guaranteed to spark conversation; and a guide for further browsing and study. Whether you are reading this volume along with the *Anthology*, or in a different or more specialized kind of course, or reading independently of any coursework, we hope you'll encounter much to stimulate your attention, curiosity, and pleasure.

SUSAN J. WOLFSON
General Editor, Longman Cultural Editions
Professor of English, Princeton University

# *About This Edition*

Helen and Margaret Schlegel, the sisters at the heart of *Howards End*, twice affirm the absolute priority of "personal relations." Such connections, they agree, are the "real life, for ever and ever," the "important thing for ever and ever" (pp. 22, 140). E. M. Forster seems to have thought so, too: twenty-eight years after the novel was published, he put faith in personal relationships at the head of a catalog of his beliefs. At the same time, part of the effect of *Howards End* is to show how intimate ties take form from broader social conditions, how they can be strained or strengthened by forces governing nations as well as families, by situations affecting people in the thousands, not just in twos and threes. In his later statement, Forster was quick to add that individual bonds furnish something "comparatively solid," not "absolutely solid," in "a world full of violence and cruelty" (*Two Cheers* 65).

When he was writing *Howards End*, the world certainly did not look as grim to most British people as it would in 1938. In 1909–10, World War I had yet to demonstrate that millions of Europeans could be killed in incomprehensibly horrific ways; Mussolini, Hitler, Franco, and Stalin had yet to illustrate that modern regimes could remain in power while dispensing with values once considered basic to civilization. The Edwardian era—which became the Georgian, technically speaking, on the death of Edward VII and the accession of George V in early 1910—was generally felt to be a period of prosperity in Britain, and new sources of comfort and entertainment (electric lights, motor cars, motion pictures) promised to make life more enjoyable, for the most fortunate, than it had ever been before. The stifling hold of Victorian convention was beginning to shake loose; fresh possibilities for life and thought were in the air. Some would remember it as a golden age.

Yet for all this sense of hope, the first decade of the twentieth century was rife with wariness about the state of Britain and of the world. Social investigators were calling attention to the appalling gap between the lifestyles of the affluent and the misery of the poor, spotlighting how a tiny fraction of the nation possessed an enormous portion of its wealth. Investigations of the health of the people, launched in the wake of surprising setbacks in the Boer War (1899–1902), were revealing the adverse effects of poor nutrition and squalid conditions at home and at work. Worry about Britain's ability to maintain its international preeminence was compounded by the commercial and military ascent of Germany and the vicissitudes of a morally dubious imperialism. And one of the great progressive dreams of the nineteenth century, the uniting of the various social classes through a commonly elevating public culture, seemed ever more elusive in spite of expanding public education and growing literacy.

To give a sense of the period's fascinating blend of optimism and anxiety, the Contexts section of this edition provides excerpts from key period writings on the condition of Britain, the Anglo-German rivalry, dilemmas of imperialism, and the role of culture in society. All figure significantly in *Howards End*, where rich confront poor, English heritage mixes with German, anti-imperialist sentiment meets colonial enterprise, and art-adoring intellectuals collide with cocky philistines. Forster's novel is lent further color by other issues Edwardians found pressing—transformations of the land (by new technologies and growing urban populations), rights and opportunities for women, changes in sexual mores, the future of liberalism, the nature of Englishness—and some of the Contexts documents address these topics as well. The pieces by Elizabeth Robins, Elizabeth von Arnim, Leonard Woolf, and Virginia Woolf, for example, speak to the situation of women, while the readings from von Arnim, George Meredith, Robert Louis Stevenson, Richard Jefferies, Edward Carpenter, and Goldsworthy Lowes Dickinson take up the question of human subjects' relationship to nature. To read the literature of Edwardian controversies is to see that the large questions of the day were not neatly partitioned from each other but powerfully inter-implicated. *Howards End* draws no small part of its force from such entanglements.

Other units in this volume illuminate the novel from other angles. A guide to money in the Edwardian era clarifies characters' economic status as well as propositions about wealth and charity voiced by various parties. A selection of early reviews offers a sense of what the first readers of Forster's many-faceted work found most arresting. Passages from the reading of the culture-hungry clerk, Leonard Bast, elucidate his predicament while unpacking allusions Forster's contemporaries would have recognized. An introduction gives a succinct account of Forster's life and the reception of *Howards End*; an afterword provides analysis of the work's social meanings; a table of dates presents biographical and historical contexts schematically. A guide to further reading, finally, tracks critical discussion of a novel that continues to be regarded as one of the most important books of its time.

## A Note on the Text

The version given here hews closely to the first edition, published in Britain by Edward Arnold in 1910. That text includes fewer errors and deviations from Forster's intentions than subsequent ones, and it seems best to provide readers of this Longman Cultural Edition an encounter as proximate as possible to that of the novel's first, admiring audiences. As in the first edition, initial words of chapters are capitalized and extra-long dashes appear when characters break off mid-sentence. Indentations in characters' letters are given as the first edition has them.

Where that edition obviously errs in spelling or punctuation, emendation has been made without remark. Otherwise, the text has been left unaltered, except for fifteen cases in which clear mistakes of diction, grammar, or reference have been corrected:

> at p. 55.10, "accuse" for "excuse" (first ed.)
> at p. 93.28, "footfall" for "football"
> at p. 101.28, "to be books" for "to books"
> at p. 122.22, "Wilcox" for "Wilson"
> at p. 172.16, "calling" for "call"
> at p. 178.4, "came" for "come"
> at p. 182.6, "began" for "begun"
> at pp. 189.2 and 189.12, "Pierpont" for "Pierpoint"
> at p. 196.1, "lain" for "laid"
> at p. 235.1, "out of the window" for "out of window"
> at p. 242.19, "her" for "them"
> at p. 253.5–6, "gravel, rubbish from" for "gravel rubbish on"
> at p. 260.20, "linked" for "lined"
> at p. 261.23, "shrank" for "shrunk"

Editorial footnotes sometimes pause over textual matters but are mainly designed to clarify allusions and usages.

This edition could not have come into existence without the extraordinary insight and good humor of Susan Wolfson or the meticulous care and endless good will of Rosie Ellis, Dianne Hall, Chrysta Meadowbrooke, and Courtney Bond. For access to the first edition of *Howards End* and for perfect cheer through many visits, the staff of Special Collections of the Milton S. Eisenhower Library at Johns Hopkins is gratefully acknowledged; for help with the first edition and numerous other period volumes, thanks are rendered to those at the George Peabody Library. For the illustrations, gratitude is due the Library of King's College, Cambridge; the Princeton University Library; the National Media Museum, Bradford; and the Tate Gallery. For patience, understanding, and support worthy of Forster's loveliest heroes and heroines, deepest thanks go, as ever and ever and ever, to Evelyn Schwarz and Chip Wass.

DOUGLAS MAO
Johns Hopkins University

Photograph of E. M. Forster, age 10, with his mother.

# Introduction

When *Howards End* was published in 1910, its thirty-one-year-old author already had three well-regarded novels and a number of short stories to his credit. He was not yet a literary celebrity, however; nor did E. M. Forster, known as Morgan to his friends, exhibit the magnetic presence or eerie sense of destiny that sometimes presages future renown. More likely to slip away in the midst of a conversation than to command a room, he often registered as drab, conventional, even prim (though his penetrating intelligence could flash forth disconcertingly), and his biography chimed with his manner. Choosing to live with an aging parent in the London suburb of Weybridge, he seemed to be continuing a personal history unmarked by adventurous flair. Yet that history does suggest why he was so comfortable writing fictions where women are the focal characters and why he should have been inclined to center one of his most ambitious stories on a house and an inheritance.

Born on 1 January 1879, Forster received his first important legacy before he was two: his father died, leaving the considerable sum of £7,000 behind. Thereafter, Morgan inhabited an atmosphere of intense feminine solicitude, his development watched closely by his mother, Lily, and an array of other relatives and friends. Preeminent among these was his father's forceful aunt Marianne Thornton, who nicknamed young Morgan "The Important One" and, on her death in 1887, left him £8,000 in trust. In his 1956 biography of "Aunt Monie," Forster calls this provision "the financial salvation" of his life. "Thanks to it," he explains, "I was able to go to Cambridge . . . . After Cambridge I was able to travel for a couple of years, and travelling inclined me to write" (*Marianne Thornton* 289).

When he was four, Morgan and his mother moved to a converted farmhouse called Rooksnest, north of Stevenage in the county of Hertfordshire; once occupied by a family named Howard, it became the model for Howards End. Like its literary double, Rooksnest had greengage trees, a glorious wych-elm, three floors of three rooms each on the front side, and a central hall out of which opened five doors, including one to the staircase (a door that, being difficult to detect at first, left visitors wondering how one reached the upper stories). Forster's feeling for the house clearly owed something to its idiosyncratic charms, but the bond may have been intensified by his sense of himself as its sole child. Although he had playmates in visiting relatives, the son of a farmer neighbor, and boys hired by his mother to tend the garden, there were no siblings. Nor, given Rooksnest's remove from city and town, were there other children of Forster's social class who could be regarded as sharers of his life at home. The house itself may thus have become the object of a special intimacy.

From eleven to fourteen, Forster boarded at a school in Sussex; then Lily lost the lease to Rooksnest and the two relocated to Tonbridge, in Kent, where he attended the Tonbridge School as one of a small number of nonresident students. Tonbridge's rough atmosphere was less than congenial to young Morgan, but he arrived at a stunning new appreciation of the possibilities of human companionship—and of human happiness—during his ensuing years at King's College, Cambridge. In that humane, stimulating, conversation-rich milieu, he found an existence where, as one biographer describes it, "things were valued for what they were in themselves, not for what use you could make of them" (Furbank 49). He also became friends with some extraordinary people, especially around the elite university discussion society to which he was elected in 1901, the Apostles. Other Apostles who became luminaries in British art and politics were the economist John Maynard Keynes, the art critic Roger Fry, and the writers Lytton Strachey and Leonard Woolf—all four of them later associated, as Forster was more tangentially, with the most famous intellectual coterie of the twentieth century, the Bloomsbury Group. Although Forster came to recognize blind spots in the Cambridge view of things, the mode of life there remained a kind of ideal for him, and he would gratefully renew his residence at King's, on an honorary fellowship, in 1946.

After graduation in 1901, Forster returned to living mainly with his mother, as he would until her death forty-four years later. But there were other pursuits for him in the period between Cambridge and *Howards End*. He traveled in Italy, Greece, and other parts of Europe; he worked on an edition of Virgil's *Aeneid* and had a love affair (not fully sexual and not very satisfying) with his Cambridge friend Hugh Meredith. He spent a few months in 1905 at Nassenheide,

Prussia, tutoring the children of the writer Elizabeth von Arnim; he gave lectures on Renaissance Florence all over England; and—an activity that textured his portrait of Leonard Bast in *Howards End*—he taught classes at the Working Men's College in London, where manual laborers, clerks, and others without access to the universities were offered a liberal (rather than vocational) education. These years also saw Forster quietly producing his short stories and novels, which surprised even his friends with their ingenuity, vitality, eloquence, and wit. He seems to have started thinking about the book that would become *Howards End* in mid-1908 and to have begun writing it soon after. He was able to show a draft to his publisher, Edward Arnold, in March 1910, and in October the novel appeared to glowing reviews.

Forster was a celebrity at last, but success brought him as much consternation as pleasure and may have inhibited his subsequent fiction writing: his next novel, *A Passage to India*, did not come out until 1924 and was the last to see print until his death in 1970. (*Maurice*, a homosexual love story, was released in 1971.) *Howards End* has, in any case, proven an overwhelming success with readers. By 1913 it had sold nearly 10,000 copies and by 1946 over a quarter of a million (Beauman 281); it had gone through over sixty impressions and editions by 1973 (Stallybrass, "Editor's Introduction" to *Manuscripts* xiv); it has never been out of print. Numerous other writers have rendered *Howards End* homage—Zadie Smith adapts key plot elements in *On Beauty* (2005), for example—and it is generally considered one of Forster's two masterpieces (*Passage* being the other).

Forster also remains one of the most famous English novelists of modern times. His reputation may have reached one high point in the middle of the twentieth century, when, thanks to his essays and radio broadcasts, he was regarded as a leading spokesman for liberal humanism, and humane values generally, in a troubled world. His stock may have dropped somewhat in succeeding years, when scholars and critics of early-twentieth-century literature reserved their highest esteem for James Joyce, Virginia Woolf, and other modernists whose formal innovations were more radical and dramatic. More recently, definitions of modernism have become more capacious, making it easier to appreciate the ways Forster *did* break new ground—in deft upendings of novelistic convention (the startlingly casual "One may as well begin with" that opens *Howards End*, for example); in lucidly understated challenges to received ideas; in characters whose very defiance of predictable destinies makes them seem truer to life.

Forster's popularity has also been enhanced by an efflorescence of interest in gay authors and by the success of film versions of his novels, especially *A Passage to India* (1984), *A Room with a View* (1985), *Maurice* (1987), and *Howards End* (1992). His formidable gifts as an analyst of human relationships would seem to guarantee all his novels a readership as long as people remain curious about each other. But the two works on which his fame has principally rested seem especially likely to captivate readers for years to come. In an era when globalization and the legacies of empire are so much a part of public consciousness, *A Passage to India* continues to encourage, perplex, and provoke audiences with its exploration of interactions across cultures. And there may be few books more compelling than *Howards End* for an age alert to the deepening chasm between affluence and poverty, the abyss of violence beneath culture's fragile lattices, and the breadth of possibilities that emerges with new—and old—modes of human connection.

# Table of Dates

EMF = Edward Morgan Forster.
Books whose authors are not named are by EMF.

| | |
|---|---|
| 1867 | Marianne Thornton (Monie), aunt of Edward Morgan Llewellyn Forster (Eddie), befriends Alice Clara Whichelo (Lily). |
| 1877 | Eddie and Lily marry. |
| 1879 | EMF, only child of Eddie and Lily, born on 1 January, one day before his parents' second wedding anniversary. |
| 1880 | Eddie dies of tuberculosis, leaving £7,000. |
| 1882 | Britain seizes control of the government of Egypt. |
| 1883 | EMF and Lily move to Rooksnest (in Stevenage, Hertfordshire), the model for Howards End. |
| 1884 | Cameroon established as a German colony in west-central Africa. |
| 1887 | Aunt Monie dies, leaving EMF £8,000. |
| 1890–93 | EMF attends Kent House boarding school in Eastbourne, Sussex. |
| 1891–1903 | Charles Booth publishes *Life and Labour of the People of London*. |
| 1893 | EMF and Lily move to Tonbridge, Kent. |
| 1893–97 | EMF attends the Tonbridge School as a day boy. |
| 1894 | Debussy's *Prélude à l'après-midi d'un faune* debuts in Paris on 22 December. |

| | |
|---|---|
| 1895 | Oscar Wilde's *Importance of Being Earnest* premiers in London on 14 February; Wilde convicted of gross indecency and sentenced to two years at hard labor on 25 May. |
| 1896 | A. E. Housman publishes *A Shropshire Lad.* |
| 1897 | First British-made automobiles produced by the Daimler Company. |
| 1897–1901 | EMF an undergraduate at King's College, Cambridge. |
| 1898 | Lily moves to Tunbridge Wells, Kent. |
| 1899 | Joseph Conrad publishes *Heart of Darkness.* |
| 1899–1902 | Second Boer War, commonly known as the Boer War, fought between British troops and Dutch settlers in southern Africa. |
| 1900–1901 | EMF makes first attempt at writing a novel. |
| 1901 | Nigeria becomes a British protectorate. |
| | Queen Victoria dies and Edward VII becomes king on 22 January. |
| | EMF elected to Cambridge Conversazione Society ("Apostles"). |
| | Benjamin Seebohm Rowntree publishes *Poverty, a Study of Town Life.* |
| 1901–2 | EMF and Lily travel in Italy and Austria. |
| 1901–9 | Theodore Roosevelt serves as President of the United States. |
| 1902 | Venezuelan Debt Crisis inspires Kipling's poem, "The Rowers." |
| 1902 | EMF begins teaching at the Working Men's College, London. |
| | J. A. Hobson publishes *Imperialism: A Study.* |
| 1903 | EMF travels to Greece on a King's College cruise. |
| | G. M. Trevelyan, Goldsworthy Lowes Dickinson, C. F. G. Masterman, and others found the liberal *Independent Review.* |

First story by EMF to see print, "Albergo Empedocle," published in December.

George Bernard Shaw publishes *Man and Superman*.

1904      EMF begins lecturing around England on Florentine history.

Report of government's Inter-Departmental Committee on Physical Deterioration details unhealthy condition of urban poor.

EMF travels in Wiltshire; at Figsbury Rings, meets lame shepherd boy whose wisdom inspires elements in *The Longest Journey*.

EMF and Lily move to Weybridge, Surrey.

1905      EMF at Nassenheide, Prussia, tutoring children of Elizabeth von Arnim.

*Where Angels Fear to Tread* published in October.

Women's Social and Political Union decides to use militant tactics in struggle for women's suffrage.

1906      EMF commences as Latin tutor of Syed Ross Masood, who becomes his friend and romantic object.

1907      *The Longest Journey* published in April.

EMF takes walking tour, commemorated in Oniton section of *Howards End*, in Wales and Shropshire.

Conrad publishes *The Secret Agent*; John Galsworthy publishes *The Country House*.

1908      First diary mention of novel that would become *Howards End* on 26 June.

*A Room with a View* published in October.

1909      EMF begins writing *Howards End*.

Masterman publishes *The Condition of England*; H. G. Wells publishes *Tono-Bungay*.

1910      *Howards End* published in October to strong reviews.

Roger Fry's pathbreaking exhibition, "Manet and the Post-Impressionists," opens in London in November.

EMF reads paper on "The Feminine Note in Literature" to the Friday Club in December, inaugurating closer ties with the Bloomsbury Group.

1911    *The Celestial Omnibus and Other Stories* published in spring.

Leonard Woolf returns from Ceylon.

L. T. Hobhouse publishes *Liberalism.*

1911–13    EMF works on *Arctic Summer*, never completed.

1912–13    EMF travels to India with Dickinson and Bob Trevelyan, elder brother of G. M.; visits Masood and sees Barabar Caves, a key inspiration for *A Passage to India.*

1913    D. H. Lawrence publishes *Sons and Lovers.*

1913–14    EMF writes *Maurice.*

1914    Egypt becomes a British protectorate.

1914–18    World War I.

1915    Virginia Woolf publishes *The Voyage Out.*

1915–19    EMF serves with Red Cross Wounded and Missing Bureau in Alexandria, Egypt.

1917    EMF begins romantic and sexual friendship with Egyptian tram conductor Mohammed el Adl.

1918    El Adl marries.

1919    British troops fire on unarmed crowd at Amritsar, India, killing hundreds.

1920    Indian National Congress, led by Mohandas Gandhi, declares policy of noncooperation with British.

1921–22    EMF serves as private secretary for the Maharaja of Dewas State Senior in India, visits Masood; on journey out and journey back, stops in Egypt to see El Adl.

1922    Britain issues declaration of Egyptian independence, though British troops remain in Egypt.

El Adl dies of tuberculosis.

Benito Mussolini becomes Prime Minister of Italy.

*Alexandria: A History and a Guide* published in December.

T. S. Eliot publishes *The Waste Land*; James Joyce publishes *Ulysses*; Virginia Woolf publishes *Jacob's Room*.

1923　*Pharos and Pharillon*, a second book about Alexandria, published in May by Leonard and Virginia Woolf's Hogarth Press.

1924　EMF's Aunt Laura dies, leaving him West Hackhurst, a house in Abinger Hammer, Surrey, designed by his father.

*A Passage to India* published in June to wide acclaim.

In "Mr. Bennett and Mrs. Brown," Virginia Woolf declares famously that "On or about December 1910 human nature changed."

1925　EMF and Lily move to West Hackhurst; EMF takes a flat in London.

1926　EMF purchases Piney Copse, a small wood near West Hackhurst.

1927　In March, EMF gives Clark Lectures at Cambridge, published in October as *Aspects of the Novel*.

1928　*The Eternal Moment and Other Stories* published in March.

EMF protests censorship of Radclyffe Hall's lesbian novel, *The Well of Loneliness*.

1930　EMF begins enduring relationship with Bob Buckingham.

1932　Bob marries May Hockey, though relationship with EMF continues.

EMF begins regular broadcasts on BBC radio.

1933　Adolf Hitler becomes Chancellor of Germany.

1934　*Goldsworthy Lowes Dickinson*, EMF's biography of his friend, published in April.

EMF becomes first president of National Council for Civil Liberties.

| | |
|---|---|
| 1935 | EMF heads British delegation to International Congress of Writers in Paris, gives speech on "Liberty in England." |
| 1936 | *Abinger Harvest*, important collection of essays, published in March. |
| 1938 | "What I Believe," key statement of basic personal principles, published in the *Nation*. |
| 1939–45 | World War II. |
| 1945 | Lily dies. |
| 1946 | EMF loses lease to site of West Hackhurst; elected Honorary Fellow of King's College, moves to Cambridge. |
| 1947 | EMF travels widely in United States. |
| | India gains independence from Great Britain. |
| 1949 | EMF refuses knighthood. |
| 1951 | *Two Cheers for Democracy*, collection of highly influential essays, published in November. |
| | *Billy Budd*, opera by Benjamin Britten with libretto by EMF and Eric Crozier, premiers in December. |
| 1953 | EMF made a Companion of Honour. |
| | *The Hill of Devi and Other Indian Writings* published in October. |
| 1956 | *Marianne Thornton*, EMF's biography of his relative and benefactor, published in May. |
| 1960 | Nigeria gains independence from Britain. |
| 1969 | EMF receives Order of Merit. |
| 1970 | EMF dies on 7 June at home of Bob and May Buckingham in Coventry, West Midlands. |
| 1971 | *Maurice* and *Albergo Empedocle and Other Writings* published. |
| 1972–2004 | Abinger Edition of EMF's works published. |
| 1992 | Film of *Howards End*, directed by James Ivory with screenplay by Ruth Prawer Jhabvala, released. |

# Howards End

*"Only connect . . ."*

# HOWARDS END

BY

## E. M. FORSTER

*"Only connect . . ."*

LONDON
EDWARD ARNOLD
1910

Title page of *Howards End*, first edition.

# CHAPTER I

ONE may as well begin with Helen's letters to her sister.

"HOWARDS END,
"*Tuesday.*

"DEAREST MEG,

"It isn't going to be what we expected. It is old and little, and altogether delightful—red brick. We can scarcely pack in as it is, and the dear knows what will happen when Paul (younger son) arrives tomorrow. From hall you go right or left into dining-room or drawing-room. Hall itself is practically a room. You open another door in it, and there are the stairs going up in a sort of tunnel to the first-floor. Three bedrooms in a row there, and three attics in a row above. That isn't all the house really, but it's all that one notices—nine windows as you look up from the front garden.

"Then there's a very big wych-elm—to the left as you look up—leaning a little over the house, and standing on the boundary between the garden and meadow. I quite love that tree already. Also ordinary elms, oaks—no nastier than ordinary oaks—pear-trees, apple-trees, and a vine. No silver birches, though. However, I must get on to my host and hostess. I only wanted to show that it isn't the least what we expected. Why did we settle that their house would be all gables and wiggles, and their garden all gamboge-coloured[1] paths? I believe simply because we associate them with expensive hotels—Mrs. Wilcox trailing in beautiful dresses down long corridors, Mr. Wilcox bullying porters, etc. We females are that unjust.

"I shall be back Saturday; will let you know train later. They are as angry as I am that you did not come too; really Tibby is too tiresome, he starts a new mortal disease every month. How could he have got hay fever in London? and even if he could, it seems hard that you should give up a visit to hear a schoolboy sneeze. Tell him that Charles Wilcox (the son who is here) has hay fever too, but he's brave, and gets quite cross when we inquire after it. Men like the Wilcoxes would do Tibby a power of good. But you won't agree, and I'd better change the subject.

"This long letter is because I'm writing before breakfast. Oh, the beautiful vine leaves! The house is covered with a vine. I looked out earlier, and Mrs. Wilcox was already in the garden. She evidently loves it. No wonder she sometimes looks tired. She was watching the large

[1]Bright yellow.

red poppies come out. Then she walked off the lawn to the meadow, whose corner to the right I can just see. Trail, trail, went her long dress over the sopping grass, and she came back with her hands full of the hay that was cut yesterday—I suppose for rabbits or something, as she kept on smelling it. The air here is delicious. Later on I heard the noise of croquet balls, and looked out again, and it was Charles Wilcox practising; they are keen on all games. Presently he started sneezing and had to stop. Then I hear more clicketing, and it is Mr. Wilcox practising, and then, 'a-tissue, a-tissue': he has to stop too. Then Evie comes out, and does some calisthenic exercises on a machine that is tacked on to a greengage[2]-tree—they put everything to use—and then she says 'a-tissue,' and in she goes. And finally Mrs. Wilcox reappears, trail, trail, still smelling hay and looking at the flowers. I inflict all this on you because once you said that life is sometimes life and sometimes only a drama, and one must learn to distinguish tother from which, and up to now I have always put that down as 'Meg's clever nonsense.' But this morning, it really does seem not life but a play, and it did amuse me enormously to watch the W's. Now Mrs. Wilcox has come in.

"I am going to wear [omission].[3] Last night Mrs. Wilcox wore an [omission], and Evie [omission]. So it isn't exactly a go-as-you-please place, and if you shut your eyes it still seems the wiggly hotel that we expected. Not if you open them. The dog-roses are too sweet. There is a great hedge of them over the lawn—magnificently tall, so that they fall down in garlands, and nice and thin at the bottom, so that you can see ducks through it and a cow. These belong to the farm, which is the only house near us. There goes the breakfast gong. Much love. Modified love to Tibby. Love to Aunt Juley; how good of her to come and keep you company, but what a bore. Burn this. Will write again Thursday.

"HELEN."

"HOWARDS END,
"*Friday.*

"DEAREST MEG,

"I am having a glorious time. I like them all. Mrs. Wilcox, if quieter than in Germany, is sweeter than ever, and I never saw anything like her steady unselfishness, and the best of it is that the others do not take advantage of her. They are the very happiest, jolliest family that you can imagine. I do really feel that we are making friends.

---

[2]Green-yellow plum.

[3]Suggests an editing of Helen's letter performed by the narrator.

The fun of it is that they think me a noodle,[4] and say so—at least, Mr. Wilcox does—and when that happens, and one doesn't mind, it's a pretty sure test, isn't it? He says the most horrid things about women's suffrage[5] so nicely, and when I said I believed in equality he just folded his arms and gave me such a setting down as I've never had. Meg, shall we ever learn to talk less? I never felt so ashamed of myself in my life. I couldn't point to a time when men had been equal, nor even to a time when the wish to be equal had made them happier in other ways. I couldn't say a word. I had just picked up the notion that equality is good from some book—probably from poetry, or you. Anyhow, it's been knocked into pieces, and, like all people who are really strong, Mr. Wilcox did it without hurting me. On the other hand, I laugh at them for catching hay fever. We live like fighting-cocks, and Charles takes us out every day in the motor—a tomb with trees in it, a hermit's house, a wonderful road that was made by the Kings of Mercia[6]—tennis—a cricket match—bridge—and at night we squeeze up in this lovely house. The whole clan's here now—it's like a rabbit warren. Evie is a dear. They want me to stop over Sunday—I suppose it won't matter if I do. Marvellous weather and the views marvellous—views westward to the high ground. Thank you for your letter. Burn this.

"Your affectionate

"HELEN."

"HOWARDS END,

"*Sunday.*

"Dearest, dearest Meg, —I do not know what you will say: Paul and I are in love—the younger son who only came here Wednesday."

## CHAPTER II

MARGARET glanced at her sister's note and pushed it over the breakfast-table to her aunt. There was a moment's hush, and then the flood-gates opened.

"I can tell you nothing, Aunt Juley. I know no more than you do. We met—we only met the father and mother abroad last spring. I

---

[4]Foolish person.

[5]Much discussed in the 19th c, the cause attracted more intense media attention after 1905, when the Women's Social and Political Union began using militant tactics. In 1918, Parliament granted voting rights to women over 30; in 1928, it made the age 21 (the same as for men).

[6]Medieval kingdom in central England; reached the height of its power in the 8th c.

know so little that I didn't even know their son's name. It's all so——"
She waved her hand and laughed a little.

"In that case it is far too sudden."

"Who knows, Aunt Juley, who knows?"

"But, Margaret dear, I mean, we mustn't be unpractical now that we've come to facts. It is too sudden, surely."

"Who knows!"

"But Margaret dear——"

"I'll go for her other letters," said Margaret. "No, I won't, I'll finish my breakfast. In fact, I haven't them. We met the Wilcoxes on an awful expedition that we made from Heidelberg to Speyer. Helen and I had got it into our heads that there was a grand old cathedral at Speyer—the Archbishop of Speyer was one of the seven electors—you know—'Speyer, Maintz, and Köln.' Those three sees once commanded the Rhine Valley and got it the name of Priest Street."[1]

"I still feel quite uneasy about this business, Margaret."

"The train crossed by a bridge of boats, and at first sight it looked quite fine. But oh, in five minutes we had seen the whole thing. The cathedral had been ruined, absolutely ruined, by restoration; not an inch left of the original structure. We wasted a whole day, and came across the Wilcoxes as we were eating our sandwiches in the public gardens. They too, poor things, had been taken in—they were actually stopping at Speyer—and they rather liked Helen insisting that they must fly with us to Heidelberg. As a matter of fact, they did come on next day. We all took some drives together. They knew us well enough to ask Helen to come and see them—at least, I was asked too, but Tibby's illness prevented me, so last Monday she went alone. That's all. You know as much as I do now. It's a young man out the unknown. She was to have come back Saturday, but put off till Monday, perhaps on account of—I don't know."

She broke off, and listened to the sounds of a London morning. Their house was in Wickham Place, and fairly quiet, for a lofty promontory of buildings separated it from the main thoroughfare. One had the sense of a backwater, or rather of an estuary, whose waters flowed in from the invisible sea, and ebbed into a profound silence while the

---

[1]The Holy Roman Empire's prince-electors chose its king. Through the 17th c there were seven electors, including the archbishops of Mainz, Trier, and Cologne (Köln). The Schlegels have apparently misremembered "Speyer" for Trier, about 100 miles away. The Speyer cathedral suffered various injuries over the centuries; its last major alteration before 1910 was a rebuilding of the front section in Romanesque style in 1854–58.

waves without were still beating. Though the promontory consisted of flats—expensive, with cavernous entrance halls, full of concierges and palms—it fulfilled its purpose, and gained for the older houses opposite a certain measure of peace. These, too, would be swept away in time, and another promontory would arise upon their site, as humanity piled itself higher and higher on the precious soil of London.

Mrs. Munt had her own method of interpreting her nieces. She decided that Margaret was a little hysterical, and was trying to gain time by a torrent of talk. Feeling very diplomatic, she lamented the fate of Speyer, and declared that never, never should she be so misguided as to visit it, and added of her own accord that the principles of restoration were ill understood in Germany. "The Germans," she said, "are too thorough, and this is all very well sometimes, but at other times it does not do."

"Exactly," said Margaret; "Germans are too thorough." And her eyes began to shine.

"Of course I regard you Schlegels as English," said Mrs. Munt hastily—"English to the backbone."

Margaret leaned forward and stroked her hand.

"And that reminds me—Helen's letter——"

"Oh yes, Aunt Juley, I am thinking all right about Helen's letter. I know—I must go down and see her. I am thinking about her all right. I am meaning to go down."

"But go with some plan," said Mrs. Munt, admitting into her kindly voice a note of exasperation. "Margaret, if I may interfere, don't be taken by surprise. What do you think of the Wilcoxes? Are they our sort? Are they likely[2] people? Could they appreciate Helen, who is to my mind a very special sort of person? Do they care about Literature and Art? That is most important when you come to think of it. Literature and Art. Most important. How old would the son be? She says 'younger son.' Would he be in a position to marry? Is he likely to make Helen happy? Did you gather——"

"I gathered nothing."

They began to talk at once.

"Then in that case——"

"In that case I can make no plans, don't you see."

"On the contrary——"

"I hate plans. I hate lines of action. Helen isn't a baby."

"Then in that case, my dear, why go down?"

---

[2]Promising or capable.

Margaret was silent. If her aunt could not see why she must go down, she was not going to tell her. She was not going to say "I love my dear sister; I must be near her at this crisis of her life." The affections are more reticent than the passions, and their expression more subtle. If she herself should ever fall in love with a man, she, like Helen, would proclaim it from the house-tops, but as she only loved a sister she used the voiceless language of sympathy.

"I consider you odd girls," continued Mrs. Munt, "and very wonderful girls, and in many ways far older than your years. But— you won't be offended?—frankly, I feel you are not up to this business. It requires an older person. Dear, I have nothing to call me back to Swanage." She spread out her plump arms. "I am all at your disposal. Let me go down to this house whose name I forget instead of you."

"Aunt Juley"—she jumped up and kissed her—"I must, must go to Howards End myself. You don't exactly understand, though I can never thank you properly for offering."

"I do understand," retorted Mrs. Munt, with immense confidence. "I go down in no spirit of interference, but to make inquiries. Inquiries are necessary. Now, I am going to be rude. You would say the wrong thing; to a certainty you would. In your anxiety for Helen's happiness you would offend the whole of these Wilcoxes by asking one of your impetuous questions—not that one minds offending them."

"I shall ask no questions. I have it in Helen's writing that she and a man are in love. There is no question to ask as long as she keeps to that. All the rest isn't worth a straw. A long engagement if you like, but inquiries, questions, plans, lines of action—no, Aunt Juley, no."

Away she hurried, not beautiful, not supremely brilliant, but filled with something that took the place of both qualities—something best described as a profound vivacity, a continual and sincere response to all that she encountered in her path through life.

"If Helen had written the same to me about a shop-assistant or a penniless clerk——"

"Dear Margaret, do come into the library and shut the door. Your good maids are dusting the banisters."

"—or if she had wanted to marry the man who calls for Carter Paterson,[3] I should have said the same." Then, with one of those turns that convinced her aunt that she was not mad really, and convinced observers of another type that she was not a barren theorist,

[3]Parcel-delivery company.

she added: "Though in the case of Carter Paterson I should want it to be a very long engagement indeed, I must say."

"I should think so," said Mrs. Munt; "and, indeed, I can scarcely follow you. Now, just imagine if you said anything of that sort to the Wilcoxes. I understand it, but most good people would think you mad. Imagine how disconcerting for Helen! What is wanted is a person who will go slowly, slowly in this business, and see how things are and where they are likely to lead to."

Margaret was down on[4] this.

"But you implied just now that the engagement must be broken off."

"I think probably it must; but slowly."

"Can you break an engagement off slowly?" Her eyes lit up. "What's an engagement made of, do you suppose? I think it's made of some hard stuff, that may snap, but can't break. It is different to the other ties of life. They stretch or bend. They admit of degree. They're different."

"Exactly so. But won't you let me just run down to Howards House, and save you all the discomfort? I will really not interfere, but I do so thoroughly understand the kind of thing you Schlegels want that one quiet look round will be enough for me."

Margaret again thanked her, again kissed her, and then ran upstairs to see her brother.

He was not so well.

The hay fever had worried him a good deal all night. His head ached, his eyes were wet, his mucous membrane, he informed her, in a most unsatisfactory condition. The only thing that made life worth living was the thought of Walter Savage Landor, from whose "Imaginary Conversations"[5] she had promised to read at frequent intervals during the day.

It was rather difficult. Something must be done about Helen. She must be assured that it is not a criminal offence to love at first sight. A telegram to this effect would be cold and cryptic, a personal visit seemed each moment more impossible. Now the doctor arrived, and said that Tibby was quite bad. Might it really be best to accept Aunt Juley's kind offer, and to send her down to Howards End with a note?

---

[4]Understood.

[5]Five volumes (1824–1829, with later additions) in which pairs of historical figures discuss literary, political, and philosophical questions.

Certainly Margaret was impulsive. She did swing rapidly from one decision to another. Running downstairs into the library, she cried: "Yes, I have changed my mind; I do wish that you would go."

There was a train from King's Cross[6] at eleven. At half-past ten Tibby, with rare self-effacement, fell asleep, and Margaret was able to drive her aunt to the station.

"You will remember, Aunt Juley, not to be drawn into discussing the engagement. Give my letter to Helen, and say whatever you feel yourself, but do keep clear of the relatives. We have scarcely got their names straight yet, and, besides, that sort of thing is so uncivilized and wrong."

"So uncivilized?" queried Mrs. Munt, fearing that she was losing the point of some brilliant remark.

"Oh, I used an affected word. I only meant would you please only talk the thing over with Helen."

"Only with Helen."

"Because——" But it was no moment to expound the personal nature of love. Even Margaret shrank from it, and contented herself with stroking her good aunt's hand, and with meditating, half sensibly and half poetically, on the journey that was about to begin from King's Cross.

Like many others who have lived long in a great capital, she had strong feelings about the various railway termini. They are our gates to the glorious and the unknown. Through them we pass out into adventure and sunshine, to them, alas! we return. In Paddington all Cornwall is latent and the remoter west; down the inclines of Liverpool Street lie fenlands and the illimitable Broads; Scotland is through the pylons of Euston; Wessex behind the poised chaos of Waterloo.[7] Italians realize this, as is natural; those of them who are so unfortunate as to serve as waiters in Berlin call the Anhalt Bahnhof the Stazione d'Italia, because by it they must return to their homes.[8] And he is a chilly Londoner who does not endow his stations with some personality, and extend to them, however shyly, the emotions of fear and love.

To Margaret—I hope that it will not set the reader against her—the station of King's Cross had always suggested Infinity. Its very situation—withdrawn a little behind the facile splendours of St. Pancras—implied a comment on the materialism of life. Those two great arches, colourless, indifferent, shouldering between them an unlovely clock,

---

[6]London station for lines north and east.

[7]Paddington, Liverpool, and the rest are London rail stations.

[8]The Anhalter Bahnhof in Berlin was known as the "Gateway to the South."

were fit portals for some eternal adventure, whose issue might be prosperous, but would certainly not be expressed in the ordinary language of prosperity. If you think this ridiculous, remember that it is not Margaret who is telling you about it; and let me hasten to add that they were in plenty of time for the train; that Mrs. Munt, though she took a second-class ticket, was put by the guard into a first (only two seconds on the train, one smoking and the other babies—one cannot be expected to travel with babies); and that Margaret, on her return to Wickham Place, was confronted with the following telegram:

"All over. Wish I had never written. Tell no one.—HELEN."

But Aunt Juley was gone—gone irrevocably, and no power on earth could stop her.

## CHAPTER III

MOST complacently did Mrs. Munt rehearse her mission. Her nieces were independent young women, and it was not often that she was able to help them. Emily's daughters had never been quite like other girls. They had been left motherless when Tibby was born, when Helen was five and Margaret herself but thirteen. It was before the passing of the Deceased Wife's Sister Bill,[1] so Mrs. Munt could without impropriety offer to go and keep house at Wickham Place. But her brother-in-law, who was peculiar and a German, had referred the question to Margaret, who with the crudity of youth had answered, 'No, they could manage much better alone.' Five years later Mr. Schlegel had died too, and Mrs. Munt had repeated her offer. Margaret, crude no longer, had been grateful and extremely nice, but the substance of her answer had been the same. "I must not interfere a third time," thought Mrs. Munt. However, of course she did. She learnt, to her horror, that Margaret, now of age,[2] was taking her money out of the old safe investments and putting it into Foreign Things, which always smash. Silence would have been criminal. Her own fortune was invested in Home Rails,[3] and most ardently did she beg her niece to imitate her. "Then we should be

---

[1]Bill repealing a controversial law (in force 1835–1907) that prevented a widower from marrying the sister of his deceased wife.

[2]Over 21, and thus legally able to do business.

[3]British railway companies.

together, dear." Margaret, out of politeness, invested a few hundreds in the Nottingham and Derby Railway, and though the Foreign Things did admirably and the Nottingham and Derby declined with the steady dignity of which only Home Rails are capable, Mrs. Munt never ceased to rejoice, and to say, "I did manage that, at all events. When the smash comes poor Margaret will have a nest-egg to fall back upon." This year Helen came of age, and exactly the same thing happened in Helen's case; she also would shift her money out of Consols,[4] but she, too, almost without being pressed, consecrated a fraction of it to the Nottingham and Derby Railway. So far so good, but in social matters their aunt had accomplished nothing. Sooner or later the girls would enter on the process known as throwing themselves away, and if they had delayed hitherto, it was only that they might throw themselves more vehemently in the future. They saw too many people at Wickham Place—unshaven musicians, an actress even, German cousins (one knows what foreigners are), acquaintances picked up at Continental hotels (one knows what they are too). It was interesting, and down at Swanage no one appreciated culture more than Mrs. Munt; but it was dangerous, and disaster was bound to come. How right she was, and how lucky to be on the spot when the disaster came!

The train sped northward, under innumerable tunnels. It was only an hour's journey, but Mrs. Munt had to raise and lower the window again and again. She passed through the South Welwyn Tunnel, saw light for a moment, and entered the North Welwyn Tunnel, of tragic fame.[5] She traversed the immense viaduct, whose arches span untroubled meadows and the dreamy flow of Tewin Water. She skirted the parks of politicians. At times the Great North Road[6] accompanied her, more suggestive of infinity than any railway, awakening, after a nap of a hundred years, to such life as is conferred by the stench of motor-cars, and to such culture as is implied by the advertisements of antibilious pills. To history, to tragedy, to the past, to the future, Mrs. Munt remained equally indifferent; hers but to concentrate on the end of her journey, and to rescue poor Helen from this dreadful mess.

The station for Howards End was at Hilton, one of the large villages that are strung so frequently along the North Road, and that

[4]"Consolidated Annuities," irredeemable government bonds.

[5]Scene of a fiery accident on the Great Northern Railway, 9–10 June 1866. Two people were killed.

[6]Major artery coursing from London to York and Edinburgh, much of it converted to automobile use in the 20th c.

owe their size to the traffic of coaching and pre-coaching days.[7] Being near London, it had not shared in the rural decay, and its long High Street had budded out right and left into residential estates. For about a mile a series of tiled and slated houses passed before Mrs. Munt's inattentive eyes, a series broken at one point by six Danish tumuli[8] that stood shoulder to shoulder along the highroad, tombs of soldiers. Beyond these tumuli habitations thickened, and the train came to a standstill in a tangle that was almost a town.

The station, like the scenery, like Helen's letters, struck an indeterminate note. Into which country will it lead, England or Suburbia? It was new, it had island platforms and a subway, and the superficial comfort exacted by business men. But it held hints of local life, personal intercourse, as even Mrs. Munt was to discover.

"I want a house," she confided to the ticket boy. "Its name is Howards Lodge. Do you know where it is?"

"Mr. Wilcox!" the boy called.

A young man in front of them turned round.

"She's wanting Howards End."

There was nothing for it but to go forward, though Mrs. Munt was too much agitated even to stare at the stranger. But remembering that there were two brothers, she had the sense to say to him, "Excuse me asking, but are you the younger Mr. Wilcox or the elder?"

"The younger. Can I do anything for you?"

"Oh, well"—she controlled herself with difficulty. "Really. Are you? I——" She moved away from the ticket boy and lowered her voice. "I am Miss Schlegel's aunt. I ought to introduce myself, oughtn't I? My name is Mrs. Munt."

She was conscious that he raised his cap and said quite coolly, "Oh, rather; Miss Schlegel is stopping with us. Did you want to see her?"

"Possibly——"

"I'll call you a cab. No; wait a mo." He thought. "Our motor's here. I'll run you up in it."

"That is very kind——"

"Not at all, if you'll just wait till they bring out a parcel from the office. This way."

"My niece is not with you by any chance?"

"No; I came over with my father. He has gone on north in your train. You'll see Miss Schlegel at lunch. You're coming up to lunch, I hope?"

[7]Time (prior to the start of the railway era in the mid-19th c) when the main way to convey passengers over long distances was by means of the large carriages known as coaches.

[8]Ancient burial mounds. Danish incursions into England began in the 9th c.

"I should like to come *up*," said Mrs. Munt, not committing herself to nourishment until she had studied Helen's lover a little more. He seemed a gentleman, but had so rattled her round that her powers of observation were numbed. She glanced at him stealthily. To a feminine eye there was nothing amiss in the sharp depressions at the corners of his mouth, nor in the rather box-like construction of his forehead. He was dark, clean-shaven, and seemed accustomed to command.

"In front or behind? Which do you prefer? It may be windy in front."

"In front if I may; then we can talk."

"But excuse me one moment—I can't think what they're doing with that parcel." He strode into the booking-office, and called with a new voice: "Hi! hi, you there! Are you going to keep me waiting all day? Parcel for Wilcox, Howards End. Just look sharp!" Emerging, he said in quieter tones: "This station's abominably organized; if I had my way, the whole lot of 'em should get the sack. May I help you in?"

"This is very good of you," said Mrs. Munt, as she settled herself into a luxurious cavern of red leather, and suffered her person to be padded with rugs and shawls. She was more civil than she had intended, but really this young man was very kind. Moreover, she was a little afraid of him: his self-possession was extraordinary. "Very good indeed," she repeated, adding: "It is just what I should have wished."

"Very good of you to say so," he replied, with a slight look of surprise, which, like most slight looks, escaped Mrs. Munt's attention. "I was just tooling my father over to catch the down train."

"You see, we heard from Helen this morning."

Young Wilcox was pouring in petrol, starting his engine, and performing other actions with which this story has no concern. The great car began to rock, and the form of Mrs. Munt, trying to explain things, sprang agreeably up and down among the red cushions. "The mater will be very glad to see you," he mumbled. "Hi! I say. Parcel. Parcel for Howards End. Bring it out. Hi!"

A bearded porter emerged with the parcel in one hand and an entry book in the other. With the gathering whir of the motor these ejaculations mingled: "Sign, must I? Why the—— should I sign after all this bother? Not even got a pencil on you? Remember next time I report you to the station-master. My time's of value, though yours mayn't be. Here"—here being a tip.

"Extremely sorry, Mrs. Munt."

"Not at all, Mr. Wilcox."

"And do you object to going through the village? It is rather a longer spin, but I have one or two commissions."

"I should love going through the village. Naturally I am very anxious to talk things over with you."

As she said this she felt ashamed, for she was disobeying Margaret's instructions. Only disobeying them in the letter, surely. Margaret had only warned her against discussing the incident with outsiders. Surely it was not 'uncivilized or wrong' to discuss it with the young man himself, since chance had thrown them together.

A reticent fellow, he made no reply. Mounting by her side, he put on gloves and spectacles, and off they drove, the bearded porter—life is a mysterious business—looking after them with admiration.

The wind was in their faces down the station road, blowing the dust into Mrs. Munt's eyes. But as soon as they turned into the Great North Road she opened fire. "You can well imagine," she said, "that the news was a great shock to us."

"What news?"

"Mr. Wilcox," she said frankly, "Margaret has told me everything—everything. I have seen Helen's letter."

He could not look her in the face, as his eyes were fixed on his work; he was travelling as quickly as he dared down the High Street. But he inclined his head in her direction, and said, "I beg your pardon; I didn't catch."

"About Helen. Helen, of course. Helen is a very exceptional person—I am sure you will let me say this, feeling towards her as you do—indeed, all the Schlegels are exceptional. I come in no spirit of interference, but it was a great shock."

They drew up opposite a draper's.[9] Without replying, he turned round in his seat, and contemplated the cloud of dust that they had raised in their passage through the village. It was settling again, but not all into the road from which he had taken it. Some of it had percolated through the open windows, some had whitened the roses and gooseberries of the wayside gardens, while a certain proportion had entered the lungs of the villagers. "I wonder when they'll learn wisdom and tar the roads," was his comment. Then a man ran out of the draper's with a roll of oilcloth, and off they went again.

"Margaret could not come herself, on account of poor Tibby, so I am here to represent her and to have a good talk."

"I'm sorry to be so dense," said the young man, again drawing up outside a shop. "But I still haven't quite understood."

"Helen, Mr. Wilcox—my niece and you."

[9]Fabric store.

He pushed up his goggles and gazed at her, absolutely bewildered. Horror smote her to the heart, for even she began to suspect that they were at cross-purposes, and that she had commenced her mission by some hideous blunder.

"Miss Schlegel and myself?" he asked, compressing his lips.

"I trust there has been no misunderstanding," quavered Mrs. Munt. "Her letter certainly read that way."

"What way?"

"That you and she——" She paused, then drooped her eyelids.

"I think I catch your meaning," he said stickily. "What an extraordinary mistake!"

"Then you didn't the least——" she stammered, getting blood-red in the face, and wishing she had never been born.

"Scarcely, as I am already engaged to another lady." There was a moment's silence, and then he caught his breath and exploded with, "Oh, good God! Don't tell me it's some silliness of Paul's."

"But you are Paul."

"I'm not."

"Then why did you say so at the station?"

"I said nothing of the sort."

"I beg your pardon, you did."

"I beg your pardon, I did not. My name is Charles."

"Younger" may mean son as opposed to father, or second brother as opposed to first. There is much to be said for either view, and later on they said it. But they had other questions before them now.

"Do you mean to tell me that Paul——"

But she did not like his voice. He sounded as if he was talking to a porter, and, certain that he had deceived her at the station, she too grew angry.

"Do you mean to tell me that Paul and your niece——"

Mrs. Munt—such is human nature—determined that she would champion the lovers. She was not going to be bullied by a severe young man. "Yes, they care for one another very much indeed," she said. "I dare say they will tell you about it by-and-by. We heard this morning."

And Charles clenched his fist and cried, "The idiot, the idiot, the little fool!"

Mrs. Munt tried to divest herself of her rugs. "If that is your attitude, Mr. Wilcox, I prefer to walk."

"I beg you will do no such thing. I take you up this moment to the house. Let me tell you the thing's impossible, and must be stopped."

Mrs. Munt did not often lose her temper, and when she did it was only to protect those whom she loved. On this occasion she blazed out. "I quite agree, sir. The thing is impossible, and I will come up and stop it. My niece is a very exceptional person, and I am not inclined to sit still while she throws herself away on those who will not appreciate her."

Charles worked his jaws.

"Considering she has only known your brother since Wednesday, and only met your father and mother at a stray hotel——"

"Could you possibly lower your voice? The shopman will overhear."

"Esprit de classe"—if one may coin the phrase[10]—was strong in Mrs. Munt. She sat quivering while a member of the lower orders deposited a metal funnel, a saucepan, and a garden squirt beside the roll of oilcloth.

"Right behind?"

"Yes, sir." And the lower orders vanished in a cloud of dust.

"I warn you: Paul hasn't a penny; it's useless."

"No need to warn us, Mr. Wilcox, I assure you. The warning is all the other way. My niece has been very foolish, and I shall give her a good scolding and take her back to London with me."

"He has to make his way out in Nigeria. He couldn't think of marrying for years, and when he does it must be a woman who can stand the climate, and is in other ways——Why hasn't he told us? Of course he's ashamed. He knows he's been a fool. And so he has—a damned fool."

She grew furious.

"Whereas Miss Schlegel has lost no time in publishing the news."

"If I were a man, Mr. Wilcox, for that last remark I'd box your ears. You're not fit to clean my niece's boots, to sit in the same room with her, and you dare—you actually dare—— I decline to argue with such a person."

"All I know is, she's spread the thing and he hasn't, and my father's away and I——"

"And all that I know is——"

"Might I finish my sentence, please?"

"No."

Charles clenched his teeth and sent the motor swerving all over the lane.

She screamed.

[10]From *esprit de corps* (French: group spirit).

So they played the game of Capping Families, a round of which is always played when love would unite two members of our race. But they played it with unusual vigour, stating in so many words that Schlegels were better than Wilcoxes, Wilcoxes better than Schlegels. They flung decency aside. The man was young, the woman deeply stirred; in both a vein of coarseness was latent. Their quarrel was no more surprising than are most quarrels—inevitable at the time, incredible afterwards. But it was more than usually futile. A few minutes, and they were enlightened. The motor drew up at Howards End, and Helen, looking very pale, ran out to meet her aunt.

"Aunt Juley, I have just had a telegram from Margaret; I—I meant to stop your coming. It isn't—it's over."

The climax was too much for Mrs. Munt. She burst into tears.

"Aunt Juley dear, don't. Don't let them know I've been so silly. It wasn't anything. Do bear up for my sake."

"Paul," cried Charles Wilcox, pulling his gloves off.

"Don't let them know. They are never to know."

"Oh, my darling Helen——"

"Paul! Paul!"

A very young man came out of the house.

"Paul, is there any truth in this?"

"I didn't—I don't——"

"Yes or no, man; plain question, plain answer. Did or didn't Miss Schlegel——"

"Charles dear," said a voice from the garden. "Charles, dear Charles, one doesn't ask plain questions. There aren't such things."

They were all silent. It was Mrs. Wilcox.

She approached just as Helen's letter had described her, trailing noiselessly over the lawn, and there was actually a wisp of hay in her hands. She seemed to belong not to the young people and their motor, but to the house, and to the tree that overshadowed it. One knew that she worshipped the past, and that the instinctive wisdom the past can alone bestow had descended upon her—that wisdom to which we give the clumsy name of aristocracy. High born she might not be. But assuredly she cared about her ancestors, and let them help her. When she saw Charles angry, Paul frightened, and Mrs. Munt in tears, she heard her ancestors say, "Separate those human beings who will hurt each other most. The rest can wait." So she did not ask questions. Still less did she pretend that nothing had happened, as a competent society hostess would have done. She said, "Miss Schlegel, would you take your aunt up to your room or to my room, whichever you think best. Paul, do find Evie, and tell her lunch for six, but I'm not sure whether we shall all be downstairs for it." And when they had obeyed her, she turned to her elder son, who still stood in the throbbing, stinking car, and smiled at him with tenderness, and without saying a word, turned away from him towards her flowers.

"Mother," he called, "are you aware that Paul has been playing the fool again?"

"It is all right, dear. They have broken off the engagement."

"Engagement——!"

"They do not love any longer, if you prefer it put that way," said Mrs. Wilcox, stooping down to smell a rose.

## CHAPTER IV

HELEN and her aunt returned to Wickham Place in a state of collapse, and for a little time Margaret had three invalids on her hands. Mrs. Munt soon recovered. She possessed to a remarkable degree the power of distorting the past, and before many days were over she had forgotten the part played by her own imprudence in the catastrophe. Even at the crisis she had cried, "Thank goodness, poor Margaret is saved this!" which during the journey to London evolved into, "It had to be gone through by someone," which in its turn ripened into the permanent form of "The one time I really did help Emily's girls was over the Wilcox business." But Helen was a more serious patient. New ideas had burst upon her like a thunder clap, and by them and by their reverberations she had been stunned.

The truth was that she had fallen in love, not with an individual, but with a family.

Before Paul arrived she had, as it were, been tuned up into his key. The energy of the Wilcoxes had fascinated her, had created new images of beauty in her responsive mind. To be all day with them in the open air, to sleep at night under their roof, had seemed the supreme joy of life, and had led to that abandonment of personality that is a possible prelude to love. She had liked giving in to Mr. Wilcox, or Evie, or Charles; she had liked being told that her notions of life were sheltered or academic; that Equality was nonsense, Votes for Women nonsense, Socialism nonsense, Art and Literature, except when conducive to strengthening the character, nonsense. One by one the Schlegel fetiches[1]

---

[1]Fetishes: here, cherished beliefs; more generally, objects of irrational psychological or religious devotion.

had been overthrown, and, though professing to defend them, she had rejoiced. When Mr. Wilcox said that one sound man of business did more good to the world than a dozen of your social reformers, she had swallowed the curious assertion without a gasp, and had leant back luxuriously among the cushions of his motor-car. When Charles said, "Why be so polite to servants? they don't understand it," she had not given the Schlegel retort of, "If they don't understand it, I do." No; she had vowed to be less polite to servants in the future. "I am swathed in cant," she thought, "and it is good for me to be stripped of it." And all that she thought or did or breathed was a quiet preparation for Paul. Paul was inevitable. Charles was taken up with another girl, Mr. Wilcox was so old, Evie so young, Mrs. Wilcox so different. Round the absent brother she began to throw the halo of Romance, to irradiate him with all the splendour of those happy days, to feel that in him she should draw nearest to the robust ideal. He and she were about the same age, Evie said. Most people thought Paul handsomer than his brother. He was certainly a better shot, though not so good at golf. And when Paul appeared, flushed with the triumph of getting through an examination, and ready to flirt with any pretty girl, Helen met him halfway, or more than halfway, and turned towards him on the Sunday evening.

He had been talking of his approaching exile in Nigeria, and he should have continued to talk of it, and allowed their guest to recover. But the heave of her bosom flattered him. Passion was possible, and he became passionate. Deep down in him something whispered, "This girl would let you kiss her; you might not have such a chance again."

That was "how it happened," or, rather, how Helen described it to her sister, using words even more unsympathetic than my own. But the poetry of that kiss, the wonder of it, the magic that there was in life for hours after it—who can describe that? It is so easy for an Englishman to sneer at these chance collisions of human beings. To the insular cynic and the insular moralist they offer an equal opportunity. It is so easy to talk of "passing emotion," and to forget how vivid the emotion was ere it passed. Our impulse to sneer, to forget, is at root a good one. We recognize that emotion is not enough, and that men and women are personalities capable of sustained relations, not mere opportunities for an electrical discharge. Yet we rate the impulse too highly. We do not admit that by collisions of this trivial sort the doors of heaven may be shaken open. To Helen, at all events, her life was to bring nothing more intense than the embrace of this boy who played no part in it. He had drawn her out of the house, where there was danger of surprise and light; he had led her by a path he knew, until they stood under the column of the vast wych-elm. A man in the darkness, he had whispered "I love you" when she was desiring love. In time his slender personality faded, the scene that he had evoked endured. In all the variable years that followed she never saw the like of it again.

"I understand," said Margaret—"at least, I understand as much as ever is understood of these things. Tell me now what happened on the Monday morning."

"It was over at once."

"How, Helen?"

"I was still happy while I dressed, but as I came downstairs I got nervous, and when I went into the dining-room I knew it was no good. There was Evie—I can't explain—managing the tea-urn, and Mr. Wilcox reading the 'Times.'"

"Was Paul there?"

"Yes; and Charles was talking to him about Stocks and Shares, and he looked frightened."

By slight indications the sisters could convey much to each other. Margaret saw horror latent in the scene, and Helen's next remark did not surprise her.

"Somehow, when that kind of man looks frightened it is too awful. It is all right for us to be frightened, or for men of another sort—father, for instance; but for men like that! When I saw all the others so placid, and Paul mad with terror in case I said the wrong thing, I felt for a moment that the whole Wilcox family was a fraud, just a wall of newspapers and motor-cars and golf-clubs, and that if it fell I should find nothing behind it but panic and emptiness."

"I don't think that. The Wilcoxes struck me as being genuine people, particularly the wife."

"No, I don't really think that. But Paul was so broad-shouldered; all kinds of extraordinary things made it worse, and I knew that it would never do—never. I said to him after breakfast, when the others were practising strokes, 'We rather lost our heads,' and he looked better at once, though frightfully ashamed. He began a speech about having no money to marry on, but it hurt him to make it, and I stopped him. Then he said, 'I must beg your pardon over this, Miss Schlegel; I can't think what came over me last night.' And I said, 'Nor what over me; never mind.' And then we parted—at least, until I remembered that I had written straight off to tell you the night before, and that frightened him again. I asked him to send a telegram for me, for he knew you would be coming or something; and he tried to get hold of the motor, but Charles and Mr. Wilcox wanted it to go to the station; and Charles offered to send the telegram for me, and then I had to say that the telegram was of no consequence, for Paul said Charles might read it, and though I wrote it out several times, he always said people would suspect something. He took it himself at last, pretending that he must walk down to get cartridges, and, what with one thing and the other, it was not handed in at the Post Office until too late. It was the most terrible morning. Paul disliked me more and more, and Evie talked cricket averages till I nearly screamed. I cannot think how I stood her all the other days. At last Charles and his father started for the station, and then came your telegram warning me that Aunt Juley was coming by that train, and Paul—oh, rather horrible— said that I had muddled it. But Mrs. Wilcox knew."

"Knew what?"

"Everything; though we neither of us told her a word, and had known all along, I think."

"Oh, she must have overheard you."

"I suppose so, but it seemed wonderful. When Charles and Aunt Juley drove up, calling each other names, Mrs. Wilcox stepped in from the garden and made everything less terrible. Ugh! but it has been a disgusting business. To think that——" She sighed.

"To think that because you and a young man meet for a moment, there must be all these telegrams and anger," supplied Margaret.

Helen nodded.

"I've often thought about it, Helen. It's one of the most interesting things in the world. The truth is that there is a great outer life that you and I have never touched—a life in which telegrams and anger count. Personal relations, that we think supreme, are not supreme there. There love means marriage settlements, death, death duties. So far I'm clear. But here my difficulty. This outer life, though obviously horrid, often seems the real one—there's grit in it. It does breed character. Do personal relations lead to sloppiness in the end?"

"Oh, Meg, that's what I felt, only not so clearly, when the Wilcoxes were so competent, and seemed to have their hands on all the ropes."

"Don't you feel it now?"

"I remember Paul at breakfast," said Helen quietly. "I shall never forget him. He had nothing to fall back upon. I know that personal relations are the real life, for ever and ever."

"Amen!"[2]

---

[2]The version of the Lord's Prayer most commonly recited by British Protestants concludes, "For thine is the kingdom, and the power, and the glory, for ever and ever. Amen."

So the Wilcox episode fell into the background, leaving behind it memories of sweetness and horror that mingled, and the sisters pursued the life that Helen had commended. They talked to each other and to other people, they filled the tall thin house at Wickham Place with those whom they liked or could befriend. They even attended public meetings. In their own fashion they cared deeply about politics, though not as politicians would have us care; they desired that public life should mirror whatever is good in the life within. Temperance, tolerance, and sexual equality were intelligible cries to them; whereas they did not follow our Forward Policy in Thibet[3] with the keen attention that it merits, and would at times dismiss the whole British Empire with a puzzled, if reverent, sigh. Not out of them are the shows of history erected: the world would be a grey, bloodless place were it entirely composed of Miss Schlegels. But the world being what it is, perhaps they shine out in it like stars.

A word on their origin. They were not "English to the backbone," as their aunt had piously asserted. But, on the other hand, they were not "Germans of the dreadful sort." Their father had belonged to a type that was more prominent in Germany fifty years ago than now. He was not the aggressive German, so dear to the English journalist, nor the domestic German, so dear to the English wit. If one classed him at all it would be as the countryman of Hegel and Kant,[4] as the idealist, inclined to be dreamy, whose Imperialism was the Imperialism of the air. Not that his life had been inactive. He had fought like blazes against Denmark, Austria, France. But he had fought without visualizing the results of victory. A hint of the truth broke on him after Sedan, when he saw the dyed moustaches of Napoleon going grey; another when he entered Paris, and saw the smashed windows of the Tuileries.[5] Peace came—it was all very immense, one had turned into an Empire—but he knew that some quality had vanished for which not all Alsace-Lorraine[6] could compensate

---

[3]Tibet. Starting in the 1820s, advocates of "forward" policy in Asia argued that in order to secure its imperial boundaries, Britain should extend its commercial, political, or military reach into new regions.

[4]Philosophers G. W. F. Hegel (1770–1831) and Immanuel Kant (1724–1804).

[5]Prussia, consolidating leadership of the German states, went to war with Denmark in 1864 and with Austria in 1866. The battle at Sedan, France (1–2 September 1870), in which France's Napoléon III was captured, was the turning point of the Franco-Prussian War of 1870–1871; Paris fell to the united German Empire on 28 January 1871. The centuries-old Tuileries Palace was Napoléon III's seat.

[6]Region ceded by France to the German Empire under the Treaty of Frankfurt, which ended the Franco-Prussian War.

him. Germany a commercial Power, Germany a naval Power, Germany with colonies here and a Forward Policy there, and legitimate aspirations in the other place, might appeal to others, and be fitly served by them; for his own part, he abstained from the fruits of victory, and naturalized himself in England. The more earnest members of his family never forgave him, and knew that his children, though scarcely English of the dreadful sort, would never be German to the backbone. He had obtained work in one of our provincial Universities, and there married Poor Emily (or Die Engländerin,[7] as the case may be), and as she had money, they proceeded to London, and came to know a good many people. But his gaze was always fixed beyond the sea. It was his hope that the clouds of materialism obscuring the Fatherland would part in time, and the mild intellectual light re-emerge. "Do you imply that we Germans are stupid, Uncle Ernst?" exclaimed a haughty and magnificent nephew. Uncle Ernst replied, "To my mind. You use the intellect, but you no longer care about it. That I call stupidity." As the haughty nephew did not follow, he continued, "You only care about the things that you can use, and therefore arrange them in the following order: Money, supremely useful; intellect, rather useful; imagination, of no use at all. No"—for the other had protested—"your Pan-Germanism[8] is no more imaginative than is our Imperialism over here. It is the vice of a vulgar mind to be thrilled by bigness, to think that a thousand square miles are a thousand times more wonderful than one square mile, and that a million square miles are almost the same as heaven. That is not imagination. No, it kills it. When their poets over here try to celebrate bigness they are dead at once, and naturally. Your poets too are dying, your philosophers, your musicians, to whom Europe has listened for two hundred years. Gone. Gone with the little courts that nurtured them—gone with Esterhaz and Weimar.[9] What? What's that? Your Universities? Oh yes, you have learned men, who collect more facts than do the learned men of England. They collect facts, and facts, and empires of facts. But which of them will rekindle the light within?"

---

[7]German: the Englishwoman.

[8]View that German-speaking people or predominantly German regions in Europe should be unified politically.

[9]The palace of Eszterháza, in Hungary, was a center of culture (especially music) built by Prince Nikolaus Esterházy in the late 18th c; its most famous artist-in-residence was the composer Franz Joseph Haydn (1732–1809). The ducal court at Weimar, Germany attracted artists and writers such as J. S. Bach (1685–1750), J. W. von Goethe (1749–1832), and Friedrich Schiller (1759–1805).

To all this Margaret listened, sitting on the haughty nephew's knee.

It was a unique education for the little girls. The haughty nephew would be at Wickham Place one day, bringing with him an even haughtier wife, both convinced that Germany was appointed by God to govern the world. Aunt Juley would come the next day, convinced that Great Britain had been appointed to the same post by the same authority. Were both these loud-voiced parties right? On one occasion they had met, and Margaret with clasped hands had implored them to argue the subject out in her presence. Whereat they blushed, and began to talk about the weather. "Papa" she cried—she was a most offensive child—"why will they not discuss this most clear question?" Her father, surveying the parties grimly, replied that he did not know. Putting her head on one side, Margaret then remarked, "To me one of two things is very clear; either God does not know his own mind about England and Germany, or else these do not know the mind of God." A hateful little girl, but at thirteen she had grasped a dilemma that most people travel through life without perceiving. Her brain darted up and down; it grew pliant and strong. Her conclusion was, that any human being lies nearer to the unseen than any organization, and from this she never varied.

Helen advanced along the same lines, though with a more irresponsible tread. In character she resembled her sister, but she was pretty, and so apt to have a more amusing time. People gathered round her more readily, especially when they were new acquaintances, and she did enjoy a little homage very much. When their father died and they ruled alone at Wickham Place, she often absorbed the whole of the company, while Margaret—both were tremendous talkers—fell flat. Neither sister bothered about this. Helen never apologized afterwards, Margaret did not feel the slightest rancour. But looks have their influence upon character. The sisters were alike as little girls, but at the time of the Wilcox episode their methods were beginning to diverge; the younger was rather apt to entice people, and, in enticing them, to be herself enticed; the elder went straight ahead, and accepted an occasional failure as part of the game.

Little need be premised about Tibby. He was now an intelligent man of sixteen, but dyspeptic and difficile.[10]

---

[10]Irritable (as if from digestive complaints) and difficult.

## CHAPTER V

It will be generally admitted that Beethoven's Fifth Symphony[1] is the most sublime noise that has ever penetrated into the ear of man. All sorts and conditions are satisfied by it. Whether you are like Mrs. Munt, and tap surreptitiously when the tunes come—of course, not so as to disturb the others—or like Helen, who can see heroes and shipwrecks in the music's flood; or like Margaret, who can only see the music; or like Tibby, who is profoundly versed in counterpoint, and holds the full score open on his knee; or like their cousin, Fräulein Mosebach, who remembers all the time that Beethoven is "echt Deutsch";[2] or like Fräulein Mosebach's young man, who can remember nothing but Fräulein Mosebach: in any case, the passion of your life becomes more vivid, and you are bound to admit that such a noise is cheap at two shillings.[3] It is cheap, even if you hear it in the Queen's Hall, dreariest music-room in London, though not as dreary as the Free Trade Hall, Manchester; and even if you sit on the extreme left of that hall, so that the brass bumps at you before the rest of the orchestra arrives, it is still cheap.

"Who is Margaret talking to?" said Mrs. Munt, at the conclusion of the first movement. She was again in London on a visit to Wickham Place.

Helen looked down the long line of their party, and said that she did not know.

"Would it be some young man or other whom she takes an interest in?"

"I expect so," Helen replied. Music enwrapped her, and she could not enter into the distinction that divides young men whom one takes an interest in from young men whom one knows.

"You girls are so wonderful in always having—— Oh dear! one mustn't talk."

For the Andante had begun—very beautiful, but bearing a family likeness to all the other beautiful Andantes that Beethoven had written, and, to Helen's mind, rather disconnecting the heroes and shipwrecks of the first movement from the heroes and goblins of the third. She heard the tune through once, and then her attention wandered, and she gazed at the audience, or the organ, or the ar-

---

[1]Completed in 1808.

[2]German: authentic German.

[3]See "Money," pp. 285–89.

chitecture. Much did she censure the attenuated Cupids who encircle the ceiling of the Queen's Hall, inclining each to each with vapid gesture, and clad in sallow pantaloons, on which the October sunlight struck. "How awful to marry a man like those Cupids!" thought Helen. Here Beethoven started decorating his tune, so she heard him through once more, and then she smiled at her cousin Frieda. But Frieda, listening to Classical Music, could not respond. Herr Liesecke, too, looked as if wild horses could not make him inattentive; there were lines across his forehead, his lips were parted, his pince-nez[4] at right angles to his nose, and he had laid a thick, white hand on either knee. And next to her was Aunt Juley, so British, and wanting to tap. How interesting that row of people was! What diverse influences had gone to the making! Here Beethoven, after humming and hawing with great sweetness, said "Heigho," and the Andante came to an end. Applause, and a round of "wunderschöning" and "pracht" volleying from the German contingent.[5] Margaret started talking to her new young man; Helen said to her aunt: "Now comes the wonderful movement: first of all the goblins, and then a trio of elephants dancing;" and Tibby implored the company generally to look out for the transitional passage on the drum.

"On the what, dear?"

"On the *drum*, Aunt Juley."

"No; look out for the part where you think you have done with the goblins and they come back," breathed Helen, as the music started with a goblin walking quietly over the universe, from end to end. Others followed him. They were not aggressive creatures; it was that that made them so terrible to Helen. They merely observed in passing that there was no such thing as splendour or heroism in the world. After the interlude of elephants dancing, they returned and made the observation for the second time. Helen could not contradict them, for, once at all events, she had felt the same, and had seen the reliable walls of youth collapse. Panic and emptiness! Panic and emptiness! The goblins were right.

Her brother raised his finger: it was the transitional passage on the drum.

---

[4]Eyeglasses that clip to the nose.

[5]"Pracht" means "splendor" in German; "wunderschön" means "very beautiful." In the manuscript of *Howards End*, Forster had, "a volume of what Helen called prachtvolleys" (29), which plays on "prachtvoll" or "splendid." Some editors thus think Forster intended, "a round of wunderschöning and prachtvolleying from the German contingent."

For, as if things were going too far, Beethoven took hold of the goblins and made them do what he wanted. He appeared in person. He gave them a little push, and they began to walk in major key instead of in a minor, and then—he blew with his mouth and they were scattered! Gusts of splendour, gods and demi-gods contending with vast swords, colour and fragrance broadcast on the field of battle, magnificent victory, magnificent death! Oh, it all burst before the girl, and she even stretched out her gloved hands as if it was tangible. Any fate was titanic; any contest desirable; conqueror and conquered would alike be applauded by the angels of the utmost stars.

And the goblins—they had not really been there at all? They were only the phantoms of cowardice and unbelief? One healthy human impulse would dispel them? Men like the Wilcoxes, or President Roosevelt,[6] would say yes. Beethoven knew better. The goblins really had been there. They might return—and they did. It was as if the splendour of life might boil over and waste to steam and froth. In its dissolution one heard the terrible, ominous note, and a goblin, with increased malignity, walked quietly over the universe from end to end. Panic and emptiness! Panic and emptiness! Even the flaming ramparts of the world might fall.

Beethoven chose to make all right in the end. He built the ramparts up. He blew with his mouth for the second time, and again the goblins were scattered. He brought back the gusts of splendour, the heroism, the youth, the magnificence of life and of death, and, amid vast roarings of a superhuman joy, he led his Fifth Symphony to its conclusion. But the goblins were there. They could return. He had said so bravely, and that is why one can trust Beethoven when he says other things.

Helen pushed her way out during the applause. She desired to be alone. The music summed up to her all that had happened or could happen in her career. She read it as a tangible statement, which could never be superseded. The notes meant this and that to her, and they could have no other meaning, and life could have no other meaning. She pushed right out of the building, and walked slowly down the outside staircase, breathing the autumnal air, and then she strolled home.

"Margaret," called Mrs. Munt, "is Helen all right?"

"Oh yes."

"She is always going away in the middle of a programme," said Tibby.

---

[6]Theodore Roosevelt, U.S. president 1901–1909, known for his masculine bravado.

"The music has evidently moved her deeply," said Fräulein Mosebach.

"Excuse me," said Margaret's young man, who had for some time been preparing a sentence, "but that lady has, quite inadvertently, taken my umbrella."

"Oh, good gracious me! —I am so sorry. Tibby, run after Helen."

"I shall miss the Four Serious Songs[7] if I do."

"Tibby love, you must go."

"It isn't of any consequence," said the young man, in truth a little uneasy about his umbrella.

"But of course it is. Tibby! Tibby!"

Tibby rose to his feet, and wilfully caught his person on the backs of the chairs. By the time he had tipped up the seat and had found his hat, and had deposited his full score in safety, it was "too late" to go after Helen. The Four Serious Songs had begun, and one could not move during their performance.

"My sister is so careless," whispered Margaret.

"Not at all," replied the young man; but his voice was dead and cold.

"If you would give me your address——"

"Oh, not at all, not at all;" and he wrapped his greatcoat over his knees.

Then the Four Serious Songs rang shallow in Margaret's ears. Brahms, for all his grumbling and grizzling, had never guessed what it felt like to be suspected of stealing an umbrella. For this fool of a young man thought that she and Helen and Tibby had been playing the confidence trick on him, and that if he gave his address they would break into his rooms some midnight or other and steal his walking-stick too. Most ladies would have laughed, but Margaret really minded, for it gave her a glimpse into squalor. To trust people is a luxury in which only the wealthy can indulge; the poor cannot afford it. As soon as Brahms had grunted himself out, she gave him her card[8] and said, "That is where we live; if you preferred, you could call for the umbrella after the concert, but I didn't like to trouble you when it has all been our fault."

His face brightened a little when he saw that Wickham Place was W.[9] It was sad to see him corroded with suspicion, and yet not daring to be impolite, in case these well-dressed people were honest after all.

---

[7]Songs by Johannes Brahms set to Biblical texts, first performed in 1896.

[8]Personal card (an implicit invitation to call).

[9]Postal code of an affluent part of London.

She took it as a good sign that he said to her, "It's a fine programme this afternoon, is it not?" for this was the remark with which he had originally opened, before the umbrella intervened.

"The Beethoven's fine," said Margaret, who was not a female of the encouraging type. "I don't like the Brahms, though, nor the Mendelssohn that came first—and ugh! I don't like this Elgar[10] that's coming."

"What, what?" called Herr Liesecke, overhearing. "The 'Pomp and Circumstance' will not be fine?"

"Oh, Margaret, you tiresome girl!" cried her aunt. "Here have I been persuading Herr Liesecke to stop for 'Pomp and Circumstance,' and you are undoing all my work. I am so anxious for him to hear what *we* are doing in music. Oh, you mustn't run down our English composers, Margaret."

"For my part, I have heard the composition at Stettin,"[11] said Fräulein Mosebach. "On two occasions. It is dramatic, a little."

"Frieda, you despise English music. You know you do. And English art. And English literature, except Shakespeare, and he's a German.[12] Very well, Frieda, you may go."

The lovers laughed and glanced at each other. Moved by a common impulse, they rose to their feet and fled from "Pomp and Circumstance."

"We have this call to pay in Finsbury Circus,[13] it is true," said Herr Liesecke, as he edged past her and reached the gangway just as the music started.

"Margaret——" loudly whispered by Aunt Juley. "Margaret, Margaret! Fräulein Mosebach has left her beautiful little bag behind her on the seat."

Sure enough, there was Frieda's reticule, containing her address book, her pocket dictionary, her map of London, and her money.

"Oh, what a bother—what a family we are! Fr-frieda!"

"Hush!" said all those who thought the music fine.

[10]English composer Edward Elgar's most famous works include the five *Pomp and Circumstance* marches (1901–1930).

[11]Now part of Poland, Stettin (Szczecin) on the Baltic coast was a major city of the German Empire in 1910.

[12]Many German Romantics (late 18th–early 19th c), including the translator A. W. Schlegel, championed the formal irregularity of Shakespeare's plays against the more rule-bound and classicizing drama of France. Some discerned a deep kinship between Shakespeare and German writing or ways of feeling.

[13]Square containing the oldest and largest public park in the City of London. (The historical heart of Greater London, the City was east of fashionable Westminster, which contained much of the "W" postcode.)

"But it's the number they want in Finsbury Circus——"

"Might I—couldn't I——" said the suspicious young man, and got very red.

"Oh, I would be so grateful."

He took the bag—money clinking inside it—and slipped up the gangway with it. He was just in time to catch them at the swing-door, and he received a pretty smile from the German girl and a fine bow from her cavalier. He returned to his seat up-sides with the world. The trust that they had reposed in him was trivial, but he felt that it cancelled his mistrust for them, and that probably he would not be "had" over his umbrella. This young man had been "had" in the past—badly, perhaps overwhelmingly—and now most of his energies went in defending himself against the unknown. But this afternoon—perhaps on account of music—he perceived that one must slack off occasionally, or what is the good of being alive? Wickham Place, W., though a risk, was as safe as most things, and he would risk it.

So when the concert was over and Margaret said, "We live quite near; I am going there now. Could you walk round with me, and we'll find your umbrella?" he said, "Thank you," peaceably, and followed her out of the Queen's Hall. She wished that he was not so anxious to hand[14] a lady downstairs, or to carry a lady's programme for her—his class was near enough her own for its manners to vex her. But she found him interesting on the whole—everyone interested the Schlegels on the whole at that time—and while her lips talked culture, her heart was planning to invite him to tea.

"How tired one gets after music!" she began.

"Do you find the atmosphere of Queen's Hall oppressive?"

"Yes, horribly."

"But surely the atmosphere of Covent Garden[15] is even more oppressive."

"Do you go there much?"

"When my work permits, I attend the gallery for the Royal Opera."

Helen would have exclaimed, "So do I. I love the gallery," and thus have endeared herself to the young man. Helen could do these things. But Margaret had an almost morbid horror of "drawing people out," of "making things go." She had been to the gallery at Covent Garden, but she did not "attend" it, preferring the more expensive seats; still less did she love it. So she made no reply.

[14]Gallantly offer one's hand to.

[15]Familiar name for the Royal Opera House in the Covent Garden district of London. The gallery held the least expensive seats.

"This year I have been three times—to 'Faust,' 'Tosca,' and——"
Was it 'Tannhouser' or 'Tannhoyser'? Better not risk the word.[16]

Margaret disliked "Tosca" and "Faust." And so, for one reason
and another, they walked on in silence, chaperoned by the voice of
Mrs. Munt, who was getting into difficulties with her nephew.

"I do in a *way* remember the passage, Tibby, but when every instrument is so beautiful, it is difficult to pick out one thing rather
than another. I am sure that you and Helen take me to the very nicest
concerts. Not a dull note from beginning to end. I only wish that our
German friends would have stayed till it finished."

"But surely you haven't forgotten the drum steadily beating on
the low C, Aunt Juley?" came Tibby's voice. "No one could. It's un-
mistakable."

"A specially loud part?" hazarded Mrs. Munt. "Of course I do
not go in for being musical," she added, the shot failing. "I only care
for music—a very different thing. But still I will say this for myself—
I do know when I like a thing and when I don't. Some people are the
same about pictures. They can go into a picture gallery—Miss Conder can—and say straight off what they feel, all round the wall. I
never could do that. But music is so different to pictures, to my mind.
When it comes to music I am as safe as houses, and I assure you,
Tibby, I am by no means pleased by everything. There was a thing—
something about a faun in French[17]—which Helen went into ec-
stasies over, but I thought it most tinkling and superficial, and said so,
and I held to my opinion too."

"Do you agree?" asked Margaret. "Do you think music is so different to pictures?"

"I—I should have thought so, kind of," he said.

"So should I. Now, my sister declares they're just the same. We
have great arguments over it. She says I'm dense; I say she's sloppy."
Getting under way, she cried: "Now, doesn't it seem absurd to you?
What *is* the good of the Arts if they're interchangeable? What *is* the
good of the ear if it tells you the same as the eye? Helen's one aim is
to translate tunes into the language of painting, and pictures into
the language of music. It's very ingenious, and she says several
pretty things in the process, but what's gained, I'd like to know?
Oh, it's all rubbish, radically false. If Monet's really Debussy, and

[16]Charles Gounod's *Faust* (1859); Giacomo Puccini's *Tosca* (1900); Wagner's
*Tannhäuser* (1845).

[17]Claude Debussy's groundbreaking, controversial *Prélude à l'après-midi d'un faune*
(1894).

Debussy's really Monet,[18] neither gentleman is worth his salt—
that's my opinion."

Evidently these sisters quarrelled.

"Now, this very symphony that we've just been having—she won't
let it alone. She labels it with meanings from start to finish; turns it
into literature. I wonder if the day will ever return when music will be
treated as music. Yet I don't know. There's my brother—behind us. He
treats music as music, and oh, my goodness! He makes me angrier
than anyone, simply furious. With him I daren't even argue."

An unhappy family, if talented.

"But, of course, the real villain is Wagner.[19] He has done more than
any man in the nineteenth century towards the muddling of the arts. I
do feel that music is in a very serious state just now, though extraordinarily interesting. Every now and then in history there do come these
terrible geniuses, like Wagner, who stir up all the wells of thought at
once. For a moment it's splendid. Such a splash as never was. But afterwards—such a lot of mud; and the wells—as it were, they communicate with each other too easily now, and not one of them will run quite
clear. That's what Wagner's done."

Her speeches fluttered away from the young man like birds. If only
he could talk like this, he would have caught the world. Oh, to acquire
culture! Oh, to pronounce foreign names correctly! Oh, to be well informed, discoursing at ease on every subject that a lady started! But it
would take one years. With an hour at lunch and a few shattered hours
in the evening, how was it possible to catch up with leisured women,
who had been reading steadily from childhood? His brain might be full
of names, he might have even heard of Monet and Debussy; the trouble
was that he could not string them together into a sentence, he could not
make them "tell," he could not quite forget about his stolen umbrella.
Yes, the umbrella was the real trouble. Behind Monet and Debussy the
umbrella persisted, with the steady beat of a drum. "I suppose my umbrella will be all right," he was thinking. "I don't really mind about it. I
will think about music instead. I suppose my umbrella will be all right."
Earlier in the afternoon he had worried about seats. Ought he to have
paid as much as two shillings? Earlier still he had wondered, "Shall I try
to do without a programme?" There had always been something to
worry him ever since he could remember, always something that dis-

---

[18]Claude Monet (1840–1926), French Impressionist painter. Debussy's music was often
called "Impressionist," though Debussy did not care to have the term applied to his work.

[19]Richard Wagner, German composer and champion of the *Gesamtkunstwerk* or total
work of art, which would synthesize music, poetry, visual art, and drama.

tracted him in the pursuit of beauty. For he did pursue beauty, and, therefore, Margaret's speeches did flutter away from him like birds.

Margaret talked ahead, occasionally saying, "Don't you think so? don't you feel the same?" And once she stopped, and said, "Oh, do interrupt me!" which terrified him. She did not attract him, though she filled him with awe. Her figure was meagre, her face seemed all teeth and eyes, her references to her sister and her brother were uncharitable. For all her cleverness and culture, she was probably one of those soulless, atheistical women who have been so shown up by Miss Corelli.[20] It was surprising (and alarming) that she should suddenly say, "I do hope that you'll come in and have some tea."

"I do hope that you'll come in and have some tea. We should be so glad. I have dragged you so far out of your way."

They had arrived at Wickham Place. The sun had set, and the backwater, in deep shadow, was filling with a gentle haze. To the right of the fantastic sky-line of the flats[21] towered black against the hues of evening; to the left the older houses raised a square-cut, irregular parapet against the grey. Margaret fumbled for her latchkey. Of course she had forgotten it. So, grasping her umbrella by its ferrule,[22] she leant over the area and tapped at the dining-room window.

"Helen! Let us in!"

"All right," said a voice.

"You've been taking this gentleman's umbrella."

"Taken a what?" said Helen, opening the door. "Oh, what's that? Do come in! How do you do?"

"Helen, you must not be so ramshackly. You took this gentleman's umbrella away from Queen's Hall, and he has had the trouble of coming round for it."

"Oh, I am so sorry!" cried Helen, all her hair flying. She had pulled off her hat as soon as she returned, and had flung herself into the big dining-room chair. "I do nothing but steal umbrellas. I am so very sorry! Do come in and choose one. Is yours a hooky or a nobbly? Mine's a nobbly—at least, I *think* it is."

The light was turned on, and they began to search the hall, Helen, who had abruptly parted with the Fifth Symphony, commenting with shrill little cries.

---

[20]Best-selling British novelist Marie Corelli (1855–1924), whose books would not have been considered serious literature by the Schlegels' set. Many of her novels have Christian themes but critique religious institutions.

[21]Apartments.

[22]Handle-band.

"Don't you talk, Meg! You stole an old gentleman's silk top-hat. Yes, she did, Aunt Juley. It is a positive fact. She thought it was a muff. Oh, heavens! I've knocked the In and Out card down. Where's Frieda? Tibby, why don't you ever—— No, I can't remember what I was going to say. That wasn't it, but do tell the maids to hurry tea up. What about this umbrella?" She opened it. "No, it's all gone along the seams. It's an appalling umbrella. It must be mine."

But it was not.

He took it from her, murmured a few words of thanks, and then fled, with the lilting step of the clerk.

"But if you will stop——" cried Margaret. "Now, Helen, how stupid you've been!"

"Whatever have I done?"

"Don't you see that you've frightened him away? I meant him to stop to tea. You oughtn't to talk about stealing or holes in an umbrella. I saw his nice eyes getting so miserable. No, it's not a bit of good now." For Helen had darted out into the street, shouting, "Oh, do stop!"

"I dare say it is all for the best," opined Mrs. Munt. "We know nothing about the young man, Margaret, and your drawing-room is full of very tempting little things."

But Helen cried: "Aunt Juley, how can you! You make me more and more ashamed. I'd rather he *had* been a thief and taken all the apostle spoons[23] than that I—— Well, I must shut the front-door, I suppose. One more failure for Helen."

"Yes, I think the apostle spoons could have gone as rent," said Margaret. Seeing that her aunt did not understand, she added: "You remember 'rent'? It was one of father's words—Rent to the ideal, to his own faith in human nature. You remember how he would trust strangers, and if they fooled him he would say, 'It's better to be fooled than to be suspicious'—that the confidence trick is the work of man, but the want-of-confidence-trick is the work of the devil."

"I remember something of the sort now," said Mrs. Munt, rather tartly, for she longed to add, "It was lucky that your father married a wife with money." But this was unkind, and she contented herself with, "Why, he might have stolen the little Ricketts[24] picture as well."

---

[23]Silver spoons, often given by sponsors at baptisms in the 15th–17th c, with handles ending in the figure of Jesus or an Apostle.

[24]English artist and illustrator Charles De Sousy Ricketts, 1866–1931. See illustration, p. 371.

"Better that he had," said Helen stoutly.

"No, I agree with Aunt Juley," said Margaret. "I'd rather mistrust people than lose my little Ricketts. There are limits."

Their brother, finding the incident commonplace, had stolen up-stairs to see whether there were scones for tea. He warmed the teapot—almost too deftly—rejected the Orange Pekoe that the par-lour-maid had provided, poured in five spoonfuls of a superior blend, filled up with really boiling water, and now called to the ladies to be quick or they would lose the aroma.

"All right, Auntie Tibby," called Helen, while Margaret, thoughtful again, said: "In a way, I wish we had a real boy in the house—the kind of boy who cares for men. It would make entertaining so much easier."

"So do I," said her sister. "Tibby only cares for cultured females singing Brahms." And when they joined him she said rather sharply: "Why didn't you make that young man welcome, Tibby? You must do the host a little, you know. You ought to have taken his hat and coaxed him into stopping, instead of letting him be swamped by screaming women."

Tibby sighed, and drew a long strand of hair over his forehead.

"Oh, it's no good looking superior. I mean what I say."

"Leave Tibby alone!" said Margaret, who could not bear her brother to be scolded.

"Here's the house a regular hen-coop!" grumbled Helen.

"Oh, my dear!" protested Mrs. Munt. "How can you say such dreadful things! The number of men you get here has always aston-ished me. If there is any danger it's the other way round."

"Yes, but it's the wrong sort of men, Helen means."

"No, I don't," corrected Helen. "We get the right sort of man, but the wrong side of him, and I say that's Tibby's fault. There ought to be a something about the house—an—I don't know what."

"A touch of the W.'s, perhaps?"

Helen put out her tongue.

"Who are the W.'s?" asked Tibby.

"The W.'s are things I and Meg and Aunt Juley know about and you don't, so there!"

"I suppose that ours is a female house," said Margaret, "and one must just accept it. No, Aunt Juley, I don't mean that this house is full of women. I am trying to say something much more clever. I mean that it was irrevocably feminine, even in father's time. Now I'm sure you understand! Well, I'll give you another example. It'll shock you, but I don't care. Suppose Queen Victoria gave a dinner-party, and that the guests had been Leighton, Millais, Swinburne, Rossetti, Meredith, Fitzgerald, etc.[25] Do you suppose that the atmosphere of that dinner would have been artistic? Heavens, no! The very chairs on which they sat would have seen to that. So with our house—it must be feminine, and all we can do is to see that it isn't effeminate. Just as another house that I can mention, but won't, sounded irrevocably masculine, and all its inmates can do is to see that it isn't brutal."

"That house being the W.s' house, I presume," said Tibby.

"You're not going to be told about the W.'s, my child," Helen cried, "so don't you think it. And on the other hand, I don't the least mind if you find out, so don't you think you've done anything clever, in either case. Give me a cigarette."

"You do what you can for the house," said Margaret. "The drawing-room reeks of smoke."

"If you smoked too, the house might suddenly turn masculine.[26] Atmosphere is probably a question of touch and go. Even at Queen Victoria's dinner-party—if something had been just a little different— perhaps if she'd worn a clinging Liberty tea-gown[27] instead of a magenta satin——"

"With an Indian shawl over her shoulders——"

"Fastened at the bosom with a Cairngorm[28]-pin——"

Bursts of disloyal laughter—you must remember that they are half German—greeted these suggestions, and Margaret said pensively, "How inconceivable it would be if the Royal Family cared about Art." And the conversation drifted away and away, and Helen's cigarette turned to a spot in the darkness, and the great flats opposite were sown with lighted windows, which vanished and were relit again, and vanished incessantly. Beyond them the thoroughfare roared gently—a tide that could never be quiet, while in the east, invisible behind the smokes of Wapping, the moon was rising.

---

[25]The pre-Raphaelite artists Frederic Leighton, J. E. Millais, and D. G. Rossetti anticipated the fin de siècle aesthetes in insisting on the priority of beauty and questioning some of the social conventions upheld by figures like the queen. Rossetti was also a poet; his fellow authors Algernon Charles Swinburne, George Meredith, and Edward FitzGerald were similarly devoted to the claims of art.

[26]In smoking, Helen marks herself a woman of advanced ideas. Women smokers were much discussed in the press by the 1890s but rarely seen in public before the end of World War I (Tinkler 17–18).

[27]Casual-fitting dress for daytime home entertaining; clothing by Liberty & Co. was associated with the aesthetic movement.

[28]Smoky quartz from Scotland's Cairngorm Mountains.

"That reminds me, Margaret. We might have taken that young man into the dining-room, at all events. Only the majolica[29] plate—and that is so firmly set in the wall. I am really distressed that he had no tea."

For that little incident had impressed the three women more than might be supposed. It remained as a goblin footfall, as a hint that all is not for the best in the best of all possible worlds,[30] and that beneath these superstructures of wealth and art there wanders an ill-fed boy, who has recovered his umbrella indeed, but who has left no address behind him, and no name.

## CHAPTER VI

WE are not concerned with the very poor. They are unthinkable, and only to be approached by the statistician or the poet. This story deals with gentlefolk, or with those who are obliged to pretend that they are gentlefolk.

The boy, Leonard Bast, stood at the extreme verge of gentility. He was not in the abyss, but he could see it, and at times people whom he knew had dropped in, and counted no more. He knew that he was poor, and would admit it: he would have died sooner than confess any inferiority to the rich. This may be splendid of him. But he was inferior to most rich people, there is not the least doubt of it. He was not as courteous as the average rich man, nor as intelligent, nor as healthy, nor as lovable. His mind and his body had been alike underfed, because he was poor, and because he was modern they were always craving better food. Had he lived some centuries ago, in the brightly coloured civilizations of the past, he would have had a definite status, his rank and his income would have corresponded. But in his day the angel of Democracy had arisen, enshadowing the classes with leathern wings, and proclaiming, "All men are equal—all men, that is to say, who possess umbrellas," and so he was obliged to assert gentility, lest he slipped into the abyss where nothing counts, and the statements of Democracy are inaudible.

As he walked away from Wickham Place, his first care was to prove that he was as good as the Miss Schlegels. Obscurely wounded in his pride, he tried to wound them in return. They were probably not ladies. Would real ladies have asked him to tea? They were cer-

[29]Brightly colored, tin-glazed earthenware in Italian Renaissance style. It became less fashionable around the end of the 19th c.

[30]The philosopher Gottfried Leibniz coined the phrase "best of all possible worlds" in his 1710 attempt at a theodicy (justification of God's ways); it was satirized by Voltaire in *Candide* (1759).

tainly ill-natured and cold. At each step his feeling of superiority increased. Would a real lady have talked about stealing an umbrella? Perhaps they were thieves after all, and if he had gone into the house they would have clapped a chloroformed handkerchief over his face. He walked on complacently as far as the Houses of Parliament. There an empty stomach asserted itself, and told him that he was a fool.

"Evening, Mr. Bast."

"Evening, Mr. Dealtry."

"Nice evening."

"Evening."

Mr. Dealtry, a fellow clerk, passed on, and Leonard stood wondering whether he would take the tram as far as a penny[1] would take him, or whether he would walk. He decided to walk—it is no good giving in, and he had spent money enough at Queen's Hall—and he walked over Westminster Bridge, in front of St. Thomas's Hospital, and through the immense tunnel that passes under the South-Western main line at Vauxhall. In the tunnel he paused and listened to the roar of the trains. A sharp pain darted through his head, and he was conscious of the exact form of his eye sockets. He pushed on for another mile, and did not slacken speed until he stood at the entrance of a road called Camelia Road, which was at present his home.

Here he stopped again, and glanced suspiciously to right and left, like a rabbit that is going to bolt into its hole. A block of flats, constructed with extreme cheapness, towered on either hand. Farther down the road two more blocks were being built, and beyond these an old house was being demolished to accommodate another pair. It was the kind of scene that may be observed all over London, whatever the locality—bricks and mortar rising and falling with the restlessness of the water in a fountain, as the city receives more and more men upon her soil. Camelia Road would soon stand out like a fortress, and command, for a little, an extensive view. Only for a little. Plans were out for the erection of flats in Magnolia Road also. And again a few years, and all the flats in either road might be pulled down, and new buildings, of a vastness at present unimaginable, might arise where they had fallen.

"Evening, Mr. Bast."

"Evening, Mr. Cunningham."

"Very serious thing this decline of the birth-rate in Manchester."

"I beg your pardon?"

---

[1] Singular of pence.

"Very serious thing this decline of the birth-rate in Manchester," repeated Mr. Cunningham, tapping the Sunday paper, in which the calamity in question had just been announced to him.

"Ah, yes," said Leonard, who was not going to let on that he had not bought a Sunday paper.

"If this kind of thing goes on the population of England will be stationary in 1960."

"You don't say so."

"I call it a very serious thing, eh?"

"Good-evening, Mr. Cunningham."

"Good-evening, Mr. Bast."

Then Leonard entered Block B of the flats, and turned, not up-stairs, but down, into what is known to house agents as a semi-base-ment, and to other men as a cellar. He opened the door, and cried "Hullo!" with the pseudo-geniality of the Cockney.[2] There was no re-ply. "Hullo!" he repeated. The sitting-room was empty, though the electric light had been left burning. A look of relief came over his face, and he flung himself into the armchair.

The sitting-room contained, besides the armchair, two other chairs, a piano, a three-legged table, and a cosy corner. Of the walls, one was occupied by the window, the other by a draped mantelshelf bristling with Cupids. Opposite the window was the door, and beside the door a bookcase, while over the piano there extended one of the masterpieces of Maud Goodman.[3] It was an amorous and not un-pleasant little hole when the curtains were drawn, and the lights turned on, and the gas-stove unlit. But it struck that shallow makeshift note that is so often heard in the modern dwelling-place. It had been too easily gained, and could be relinquished too easily.

As Leonard was kicking off his boots he jarred the three-legged table, and a photograph frame, honourably poised upon it, slid side-ways, fell off into the fireplace, and smashed. He swore in a colour-less sort of way, and picked the photograph up. It represented a young lady called Jacky, and had been taken at the time when young ladies called Jacky were often photographed with their mouths open. Teeth of dazzling whiteness extended along either of Jacky's jaws, and positively weighed her head sideways, so large were they and so numerous. Take my word for it, that smile was simply stunning, and

---

[2]Term for a lower-class Londoner (often disparaging, implying crudeness or vulgarity).

[3]The English painter Maude Goodman (1860–1938), disdained by art connoisseurs, was best known for depictions of sentimental domestic scenes.

it is only you and I who will be fastidious, and complain that true joy begins in the eyes, and that the eyes of Jacky did not accord with her smile, but were anxious and hungry.

Leonard tried to pull out the fragments of glass, and cut his fingers and swore again. A drop of blood fell on the frame, another followed, spilling over on to the exposed photograph. He swore more vigorously, and dashed to the kitchen, where he bathed his hands. The kitchen was the same size as the sitting room: through it was a bedroom. This completed his home. He was renting the flat furnished: of all the objects that encumbered it none were his own except the photograph frame, the Cupids, and the books.

"Damn, damn, damnation!" he murmured, together with such other words as he had learnt from older men. Then he raised his hand to his forehead and said, "Oh, damn it all——" which meant something different. He pulled himself together. He drank a little tea, black and silent, that still survived upon an upper shelf. He swallowed some dusty crumbs of a cake. Then he went back to the sitting-room, settled himself anew, and began to read a volume of Ruskin.[4]

'Seven miles to the north of Venice——'

How perfectly the famous chapter opens! How supreme its command of admonition and of poetry! The rich man is speaking to us from his gondola.

'Seven miles to the north of Venice the banks of sand which nearer the city rise little above low-water mark attain by degrees a higher level, and knit themselves at last into fields of salt morass, raised here and there into shapeless mounds, and intercepted by narrow creeks of sea.'

Leonard was trying to form his style on Ruskin: he understood him to be the greatest master of English Prose. He read forward steadily, occasionally making a few notes.

'Let us consider a little each of these characters in succession, and first (for of the shafts enough has been said already), what is very peculiar to this church—its luminousness.'

Was there anything to be learnt from this fine sentence? Could he adapt it to the needs of daily life? Could he introduce it, with modifications, when he next wrote a letter to his brother, the lay-reader?[5] For example—

---

[4]John Ruskin, influential social critic and art historian. Leonard is reading from *The Stones of Venice* (1851–1853); see pp. 300–04.

[5]Non-cleric licensed to conduct religious services.

'Let us consider a little each of these characters in succession, and first (for of the absence of ventilation enough has been said already), what is very peculiar to this flat—its obscurity.'

Something told him that the modifications would not do; and that something, had he known it, was the spirit of English Prose. 'My flat is dark as well as stuffy.' Those were the words for him.

And the voice in the gondola rolled on, piping melodiously of Effort and Self-Sacrifice, full of high purpose, full of beauty, full even of sympathy and the love of men, yet somehow eluding all that was actual and insistent in Leonard's life. For it was the voice of one who had never been dirty or hungry, and had not guessed successfully what dirt and hunger are.

Leonard listened to it with reverence. He felt that he was being done good to, and that if he kept on with Ruskin, and the Queen's Hall Concerts, and some pictures by Watts,[6] he would one day push his head out of the grey waters and see the universe. He believed in sudden conversion, a belief which may be right, but which is peculiarly attractive to a half-baked mind. It is the basis of much popular religion: in the domain of business it dominates the Stock Exchange, and becomes that "bit of luck" by which all successes and failures are explained. "If only I had a bit of luck, the whole thing would come straight. . . . He's got a most magnificent place down at Streatham and a 20 h.-p. Fiat,[7] but then, mind you, he's had luck. . . . I'm sorry the wife's so late, but she never has any luck over catching trains." Leonard was superior to these people; he did believe in effort and in a steady preparation for the change that he desired. But of a heritage that may expand gradually, he had no conception: he hoped to come to Culture suddenly, much as the Revivalist hopes to come to Jesus. Those Miss Schlegels had come to it; they had done the trick; their hands were upon the ropes, once and for all. And meanwhile, his flat was dark, as well as stuffy.

Presently there was a noise on the staircase. He shut up Margaret's card in the pages of Ruskin, and opened the door. A woman entered, of whom it is simplest to say that she was not respectable. Her appearance was awesome.[8] She seemed all strings and bell-pulls[9]—ribbons, chains, bead necklaces that clinked and caught— and a boa of azure feathers hung round her neck, with the ends

---

[6]George Frederic Watts (1817–1904), English Symbolist painter and sculptor.

[7]20-horsepower—an expensive car.

[8]Awe-inspiring.

[9]Handles attached to wires that ring bells.

uneven. Her throat was bare, wound with a double row of pearls, her arms were bare to the elbows, and might again be detected at the shoulder, through cheap lace. Her hat, which was flowery, resembled those punnets,[10] covered with flannel, which we sowed with mustard and cress in our childhood, and which germinated here yes, and there no. She wore it on the back of her head. As for her hair, or rather hairs, they are too complicated to describe, but one system went down her back, lying in a thick pad there, while another, created for a lighter destiny, rippled around her forehead. The face—the face does not signify. It was the face of the photograph, but older, and the teeth were not so numerous as the photographer had suggested, and certainly not so white. Yes, Jacky was past her prime, whatever that prime may have been. She was descending quicker than most women into the colourless years, and the look in her eyes confessed it.

"What ho!" said Leonard, greeting the apparition with much spirit, and helping it off with its boa.

Jacky, in husky tones, replied, "What ho!"

"Been out?" he asked. The question sounds superfluous, but it cannot have been really, for the lady answered, "No," adding, "Oh, I am so tired."

"You tired?"

"Eh?"

"I'm tired," said he, hanging the boa up.

"Oh, Len, I am so tired."

"I've been to that classical concert I told you about," said Leonard.

"What's that?"

"I came back as soon as it was over."

"Anyone been round to our place?" asked Jacky.

"Not that I've seen. I met Mr. Cunningham outside, and we passed a few remarks."

"What, not Mr. Cunningham?"

"Yes."

"Oh, you mean Mr. Cunningham."

"Yes. Mr. Cunningham."

"I've been out to tea at a lady friend's."

Her secret being at last given to the world, and the name of the lady-friend being even adumbrated, Jacky made no further experiments in the difficult and tiring art of conversation. She never had

[10]Small, light baskets for fruits or flowers.

been a great talker. Even in her photographic days she had relied upon her smile and her figure to attract, and now that she was—

"On the shelf,
On the shelf,
Boys, boys, I'm on the shelf,"

she was not likely to find her tongue. Occasional bursts of song (of which the above is an example) still issued from her lips, but the spoken word was rare.

She sat down on Leonard's knee, and began to fondle[11] him. She was now a massive woman of thirty-three, and her weight hurt him, but he could not very well say anything. Then she said, "Is that a book you're reading?" and he said, "That's a book," and drew it from her unreluctant grasp. Margaret's card fell out of it. It fell face downwards, and he murmured, "Bookmarker."

"Len——"

"What is it?" he asked, a little wearily, for she only had one topic of conversation when she sat upon his knee.

"You do love me?"

"Jacky, you know that I do. How can you ask such questions!"

"But you do love me, Len, don't you?"

"Of course I do."

A pause. The other remark was still due.

"Len——"

"Well? What is it?"

"Len, you will make it all right?"

"I can't have you ask me that again," said the boy, flaring up into a sudden passion. "I've promised to marry you when I'm of age, and that's enough. My word's my word. I've promised to marry you as soon as ever I'm twenty-one, and I can't keep on being worried. I've worries enough. It isn't likely I'd throw you over, let alone my word, when I've spent all this money. Besides, I'm an Englishman, and I never go back on my word. Jacky, do be reasonable. Of course I'll marry you. Only do stop badgering me."

"When's your birthday, Len?"

"I've told you again and again, the eleventh of November next. Now get off my knee a bit; someone must get supper, I suppose."

---

[11]Caress affectionately or with light flirtation.

Jacky went through to the bedroom, and began to see to her hat. This meant blowing at it with short sharp puffs. Leonard tidied up the sitting-room, and began to prepare their evening meal. He put a penny into the slot of the gas-meter, and soon the flat was reeking with metallic fumes. Somehow he could not recover his temper, and all the time he was cooking he continued to complain bitterly.

"It really is too bad when a fellow isn't trusted. It makes one feel so wild, when I've pretended to the people here that you're my wife— all right, all right, you *shall* be my wife—and I've bought you the ring to wear, and I've taken this flat furnished, and it's far more than I can afford, and yet you aren't content, and I've also not told the truth when I've written home." He lowered his voice. "He'd stop it." In a tone of horror, that was a little luxurious, he repeated: "My brother'd stop it. I'm going against the whole world, Jacky.

"That's what I am, Jacky. I don't take any heed of what anyone says. I just go straight forward, I do. That's always been my way. I'm not one of your weak knock-kneed chaps. If a woman's in trouble, I don't leave her in the lurch. That's not my street. No, thank you.

"I'll tell you another thing too. I care a good deal about improving myself by means of Literature and Art, and so getting a wider outlook. For instance, when you came in I was reading Ruskin's 'Stones of Venice.' I don't say this to boast, but just to show you the kind of man I am. I can tell you, I enjoyed that classical concert this afternoon."

To all his moods Jacky remained equally indifferent. When supper was ready—and not before—she emerged from the bedroom, saying: "But you do love me, don't you?"

They began with a soup square, which Leonard had just dissolved in some hot water. It was followed by the tongue—a freckled cylinder of meat, with a little jelly at the top, and a great deal of yellow fat at the bottom—ending with another square dissolved in water (jelly: pineapple), which Leonard had prepared earlier in the day. Jacky ate contentedly enough, occasionally looking at her man with those anxious eyes, to which nothing else in her appearance corresponded, and which yet seemed to mirror her soul. And Leonard managed to convince his stomach that it was having a nourishing meal.

After supper they smoked cigarettes and exchanged a few statements. She observed that her 'likeness' had been broken. He found occasion to remark, for the second time, that he had come straight back home after the concert at Queen's Hall. Presently she sat upon his knee. The inhabitants of Camelia Road tramped to and fro outside the window, just on a level with their heads, and the family in the flat on the ground-floor began to sing, "Hark, my soul, it is the Lord."[12]

"That tune fairly gives me the hump,"[13] said Leonard.

Jacky followed this, and said that, for her part, she thought it a lovely tune.

"No; I'll play you something lovely. Get up, dear, for a minute."

He went to the piano and jingled out a little Grieg.[14] He played badly and vulgarly, but the performance was not without its effect, for Jacky said she thought she'd be going to bed. As she receded, a new set of interests possessed the boy, and he began to think of what had been said about music by that odd Miss Schlegel—the one that twisted her face about so when she spoke. Then the thoughts grew sad and envious. There was the girl named Helen, who had pinched his umbrella, and the German girl who had smiled at him pleasantly, and Herr someone, and Aunt someone, and the brother—all, all with their hands on the ropes. They had all passed up that narrow, rich staircase at Wickham Place, to some ample room, whither he could never follow them, not if he read for ten hours a day. Oh, it was no good, this continual aspiration. Some are born cultured; the rest had better go in for whatever comes easy. To see life steadily and to see it whole was not for the likes of him.[15]

From the darkness beyond the kitchen a voice called, "Len?"

"You in bed?" he asked, his forehead twitching.

"M'm."

"All right."

Presently she called him again.

"I must clean my boots ready for the morning," he answered.

Presently she called him again.

"I rather want to get this chapter done."

"What?"

He closed his ears against her.

"What's that?"

"All right, Jacky, nothing; I'm reading a book."

"What?"

"What?" he answered, catching her degraded deafness.

[12]First line of the hymn "Lovest thou me?", lyrics by William Cowper (1731–1800).

[13]Vexes me, depresses me.

[14]Among the best-loved works of the Norwegian composer Edvard Grieg (1843–1907) are some short pieces for piano.

[15]In "To a Friend" (1849), Matthew Arnold (see pp. 365–69) wrote that the Greek tragedian Sophocles "saw life steadily, and saw it whole."

Presently she called him again.

Ruskin had visited Torcello by this time, and was ordering his gondoliers to take him to Murano. It occurred to him, as he glided over the whispering lagoons, that the power of Nature could not be shortened by the folly, nor her beauty altogether saddened by the misery, of such as Leonard.

## CHAPTER VII

"OH, Margaret," cried her aunt next morning, "such a most unfortunate thing has happened. I could not get you alone."

The most unfortunate thing was not very serious. One of the flats in the ornate block opposite had been taken furnished by the Wilcox family, "coming up, no doubt, in the hope of getting into London society." That Mrs. Munt should be the first to discover the misfortune was not remarkable, for she was so interested in the flats, that she watched their every mutation with unwearying care. In theory she despised them—they took away that old-world look—they cut off the sun—flats house a flashy type of person. But if the truth had been known, she found her visits to Wickham Place twice as amusing since Wickham Mansions had arisen, and would in a couple of days learn more about them than her nieces in a couple of months, or her nephew in a couple of years. She would stroll across and make friends with the porters, and inquire what the rents were, exclaiming for example: "What! a hundred and twenty for a basement? You'll never get it!" And they would answer: "One can but try, madam." The passenger lifts, the provision lifts, the arrangement for coals (a great temptation for a dishonest porter), were all familiar matters to her, and perhaps a relief from the politico-economical-æsthetic atmosphere that reigned at the Schlegels'.

Margaret received the information calmly, and did not agree that it would throw a cloud over poor Helen's life.

"Oh, but Helen isn't a girl with no interests," she explained. "She has plenty of other things and other people to think about. She made a false start with the Wilcoxes, and she'll be as willing as we are to have nothing more to do with them."

"For a clever girl, dear, how very oddly you do talk. Helen'll *have* to have something more to do with them, now that they're all opposite. She may meet that Paul in the street. She cannot very well not bow."

"Of course she must bow. But look here; let's do the flowers. I was going to say, the will to be interested in him has died, and what else matters? I look on that disastrous episode (over which you were so kind) as the killing of a nerve in Helen. It's dead, and she'll never be troubled with it again. The only things that matter are the things that interest one. Bowing, even calling and leaving cards, even a dinner-party—we can do all those things to the Wilcoxes, if they find it agreeable; but the other thing, the one important thing—never again. Don't you see?"

Mrs. Munt did not see, and indeed Margaret was making a most questionable statement—that any emotion, any interest once vividly aroused, can wholly die.

"I also have the honour to inform you that the Wilcoxes are bored with us. I didn't tell you at the time—it might have made you angry, and you had enough to worry you—but I wrote a letter to Mrs. W., and apologized for the trouble that Helen had given them. She didn't answer it."

"How very rude!"

"I wonder. Or was it sensible?"

"No, Margaret, most rude."

"In either case one can class it as reassuring."

Mrs. Munt sighed. She was going back to Swanage on the morrow, just as her nieces were wanting her most. Other regrets crowded upon her: for instance, how magnificently she would have cut[1] Charles if she had met him face to face. She had already seen him, giving an order to the porter—and very common he looked in a tall hat. But unfortunately his back was turned to her, and though she had cut his back, she could not regard this as a telling snub.

"But you will be careful, won't you?" she exhorted.

"Oh, certainly. Fiendishly careful."

"And Helen must be careful, too."

"Careful over what?" cried Helen, at that moment coming into the room with her cousin.

"Nothing," said Margaret, seized with a momentary awkwardness.

"Careful over what, Aunt Juley?"

Mrs. Munt assumed a cryptic air. "It is only that a certain family, whom we know by name but do not mention, as you said yourself last night after the concert, have taken the flat opposite from the Mathesons—where the plants are in the balcony."

Helen began some laughing reply, and then disconcerted them all by blushing. Mrs. Munt was so disconcerted that she exclaimed, "What, Helen, you don't mind them coming, do you?" and deepened the blush to crimson.

[1]Refused to acknowledge.

"Of course I don't mind," said Helen a little crossly. "It is that you and Meg are both so absurdly grave about it, when there's nothing to be grave about at all."

"I'm not grave," protested Margaret, a little cross in her turn.

"Well, you look grave; doesn't she, Frieda?"

"I don't feel grave, that's all I can say; you're going quite on the wrong tack."

"No, she does not feel grave," echoed Mrs. Munt. "I can bear witness to that. She disagrees——"

"Hark!" interrupted Fräulein Mosebach. "I hear Bruno entering the hall."

For Herr Liesecke was due at Wickham Place to call for the two younger girls. He was not entering the hall—in fact, he did not enter it for quite five minutes. But Frieda detected a delicate situation, and said that she and Helen had much better wait for Bruno down below, and leave Margaret and Mrs. Munt to finish arranging the flowers. Helen acquiesced. But, as if to prove that the situation was not delicate really, she stopped in the doorway and said:

"Did you say the Mathesons' flat, Aunt Juley? How wonderful you are! *I* never knew that the woman who laced too tightly's name was Matheson."

"Come, Helen," said her cousin.

"Go, Helen," said her aunt; and continued to Margaret almost in the same breath: "Helen cannot deceive me. She does mind."

"Oh, hush!" breathed Margaret. "Frieda'll hear you, and she can be so tiresome."

"She minds," persisted Mrs. Munt, moving thoughtfully about the room, and pulling the dead chrysanthemums out of the vases. "I knew she'd mind—and I'm sure a girl ought to! Such an experience! Such awful coarse-grained people! I know more about them than you do, which you forget, and if Charles had taken you that motor drive—well, you'd have reached the house a perfect wreck. Oh, Margaret, you don't know what you are in for. They're all bottled up against the drawing-room window. There's Mrs. Wilcox—I've seen her. There's Paul. There's Evie, who is a minx. There's Charles—I saw him to start with. And who would an elderly man with a moustache and a copper-coloured face be?"

"Mr. Wilcox, possibly."

"I knew it. And there's Mr. Wilcox."

"It's a shame to call his face copper colour," complained Margaret. "He has a remarkably good complexion for a man of his age."

Mrs. Munt, triumphant elsewhere, could afford to concede Mr. Wilcox his complexion. She passed on from it to the plan of campaign that her nieces should pursue in the future. Margaret tried to stop her.

"Helen did not take the news quite as I expected, but the Wilcox nerve is dead in her really, so there's no need for plans."

"It's as well to be prepared."

"No—it's as well not to be prepared."

"Why?"

"Because——"

Her thought drew being from the obscure borderland. She could not explain in so many words, but she felt that those who prepare for all the emergencies of life beforehand may equip themselves at the expense of joy. It is necessary to prepare for an examination, or a dinner-party, or a possible fall in the price of stock: those who attempt human relations must adopt another method, or fail. "Because I'd sooner risk it," was her lame conclusion.

"But imagine the evenings," exclaimed her aunt, pointing to the Mansions with the spout of the watering-can. "Turn the electric light on here or there, and it's almost the same room. One evening they may forget to draw their blinds down, and you'll see them; and the next, you yours, and they'll see you. Impossible to sit out on the balconies. Impossible to water the plants, or even speak. Imagine going out of the front-door, and they come out opposite at the same moment. And yet you tell me that plans are unnecessary, and you'd rather risk it."

"I hope to risk things all my life."

"Oh, Margaret, most dangerous."

"But after all," she continued with a smile, "there's never any great risk as long as you have money."

"Oh, shame! What a shocking speech!"

"Money pads the edges of things," said Miss Schlegel. "God help those who have none."

"But this is something quite new!" said Mrs. Munt, who collected new ideas as a squirrel collects nuts, and was especially attracted by those that are portable.

"New for me; sensible people have acknowledged it for years. You and I and the Wilcoxes stand upon money as upon islands. It is so firm beneath our feet that we forget its very existence. It's only when we see someone near us tottering that we realize all that an independent income means. Last night, when we were talking up here round the fire, I began to think that the very soul of the world is economic, and that the lowest abyss is not the absence of love, but the absence of coin."

"I call that rather cynical."

"So do I. But Helen and I, we ought to remember, when we are tempted to criticize others, that we are standing on these islands, and that most of the others are down below the surface of the sea. The poor cannot always reach those whom they want to love, and they can hardly ever escape from those whom they love no longer. We rich can. Imagine the tragedy last June, if Helen and Paul Wilcox had been poor people, and couldn't invoke railways and motor-cars to part them."

"That's more like Socialism," said Mrs. Munt suspiciously.

"Call it what you like. I call it going through life with one's hand spread open on the table. I'm tired of these rich people who pretend to be poor, and think it shows a nice mind to ignore the piles of money that keep their feet above the waves. I stand each year upon six hundred pounds, and Helen upon the same, and Tibby will stand upon eight,[2] and as fast as our pounds crumble away into the sea they are renewed—from the sea, yes, from the sea. And all our thoughts are the thoughts of six-hundred-pounders, and all our speeches; and because we don't want to steal umbrellas ourselves, we forget that below the sea people do want to steal them, and do steal them sometimes, and that what's a joke up here is down there reality——"

"There they go—there goes Fräulein Mosebach. Really, for a German she does dress charmingly. Oh——!"

"What is it?"

"Helen was looking up at the Wilcoxes' flat."

"Why shouldn't she?"

"I beg your pardon, I interrupted you. What was it you were saying about reality?"

"I had worked round to myself, as usual," answered Margaret in tones that were suddenly preoccupied.

"Do tell me this, at all events. Are you for the rich or for the poor?"

"Too difficult. Ask me another. Am I for poverty or for riches? For riches. Hurrah for riches!"

"For riches!" echoed Mrs. Munt, having, as it were, at last secured her nut.

"Yes. For riches. Money for ever!"

"So am I, and so, I am afraid, are most of my acquaintances at Swanage, but I am surprised that you agree with us."

[2]On these incomes, see "Money," pp. 285–89.

"Thank you so much, Aunt Juley. While I have talked theories, you have done the flowers."

"Not at all, dear. I wish you would let me help you in more important things."

"Well, would you be very kind? Would you come round with me to the registry office?[3] There's a housemaid who won't say yes but doesn't say no."

On their way thither they too looked up at the Wilcoxes' flat. Evie was in the balcony, "staring most rudely," according to Mrs. Munt. Oh yes, it was a nuisance, there was no doubt of it. Helen was proof against a passing encounter, but—— Margaret began to lose confidence. Might it reawake the dying nerve if the family were living close against her eyes? And Frieda Mosebach was stopping with them for another fortnight, and Frieda was sharp, abominably sharp, and quite capable of remarking, "You love one of the young gentlemen opposite, yes?" The remark would be untrue, but of the kind which, if stated often enough, may become true; just as the remark, 'England and Germany are bound to fight,' renders war a little more likely each time that it is made, and is therefore made the more readily by the gutter press of either nation.[4] Have the private emotions also their gutter press? Margaret thought so, and feared that good Aunt Juley and Frieda were typical specimens of it. They might, by continual chatter, lead Helen into a repetition of the desires of June. Into a repetition—they could not do more; they could not lead her into lasting love. They were—she saw it clearly—Journalism; her father, with all his defects and wrong-headedness, had been Literature, and had he lived, he would have persuaded his daughter rightly.

The registry office was holding its morning reception. A string of carriages filled the street. Miss Schlegel waited her turn, and finally had to be content with an insidious "temporary," being rejected by genuine housemaids on the ground of her numerous stairs. Her failure depressed her, and though she forgot the failure, the depression remained. On her way home she again glanced up at the Wilcoxes' flat, and took the rather matronly step of speaking about the matter to Helen.

"Helen, you must tell me whether this thing worries you."

"If what?" said Helen, who was washing her hands for lunch.

---

[3]Place to hire domestic help.

[4]In the years before World War I, the least reputable, most sensational British periodicals, or gutter press, worked to heighten public animosity against Germany.

"The W.s' coming."

"No, of course not."

"Really?"

"Really." Then she admitted that she was a little worried on Mrs. Wilcox's account; she implied that Mrs. Wilcox might reach backward into deep feelings, and be pained by things that never touched the other members of that clan. "I shan't mind if Paul points at our house and says, 'There lives the girl who tried to catch me.' But she might."

"If even that worries you, we could arrange something. There's no reason we should be near people who displease us or whom we displease, thanks to our money. We might even go away for a little."

"Well, I am going away. Frieda's just asked me to Stettin, and I shan't be back till after the New Year. Will that do? Or must I fly the country altogether? Really, Meg, what has come over you to make such a fuss?"

"Oh, I'm getting an old maid, I suppose. I thought I minded nothing, but really I—I should be bored if you fell in love with the same man twice and"—she cleared her throat—"you did go red, you know, when Aunt Juley attacked you this morning. I shouldn't have referred to it otherwise."

But Helen's laugh rang true, as she raised a soapy hand to heaven and swore that never, nowhere and nohow, would she again fall in love with any of the Wilcox family, down to its remotest collaterals.

## CHAPTER VIII

THE friendship between Margaret and Mrs. Wilcox, which was to develop so quickly and with such strange results, may perhaps have had its beginnings at Speyer, in the spring. Perhaps the elder lady, as she gazed at the vulgar, ruddy cathedral, and listened to the talk of Helen and her husband, may have detected in the other and less charming of the sisters a deeper sympathy, a sounder judgment. She was capable of detecting such things. Perhaps it was she who had desired the Miss Schlegels to be invited to Howards End, and Margaret whose presence she had particularly desired. All this is speculation: Mrs. Wilcox has left few clear indications behind her. It is certain that she came to call at Wickham Place a fortnight later, the very day that Helen was going with her cousin to Stettin.

"Helen!" cried Fräulein Mosebach in awestruck tones (she was now in her cousin's confidence)—"his mother has forgiven you!" And then, remembering that in England the new-comer ought not to call before she is called upon, she changed her tone from awe to disapproval, and opined that Mrs. Wilcox was "keine Dame."[1]

"Bother the whole family!" snapped Margaret. "Helen, stop giggling and pirouetting, and go and finish your packing. Why can't the woman leave us alone?"

"I don't know what I shall do with Meg," Helen retorted, collapsing upon the stairs. "She's got Wilcox and Box[2] upon the brain. Meg, Meg, I don't love the young gentleman; I don't love the young genterman, Meg, Meg. Can a body speak plainer?"

"Most certainly her love has died," asserted Fräulein Mosebach.

"Most certainly it has, Frieda, but that will not prevent me from being bored with the Wilcoxes if I return the call."

Then Helen simulated tears, and Fräulein Mosebach, who thought her extremely amusing, did the same. "Oh, boo hoo! boo hoo hoo! Meg's going to return the call, and I can't. 'Cos why? 'Cos I'm going to German-eye."

"If you are going to Germany, go and pack; if you aren't, go and call on the Wilcoxes instead of me."

"But, Meg, Meg, I don't love the young gentleman; I don't love the young—O lud, who's that coming down the stairs? I vow 'tis my brother. O crimini!"

A male—even such a male as Tibby—was enough to stop the foolery. The barrier of sex, though decreasing among the civilized, is still high, and higher on the side of women. Helen could tell her sister all, and her cousin much about Paul; she told her brother nothing. It was not prudishness, for she now spoke of "the Wilcox ideal" with laughter, and even with a growing brutality. Nor was it precaution, for Tibby seldom repeated any news that did not concern himself. It was rather the feeling that she betrayed a secret into the camp of men, and that, however trivial it was on this side of the barrier, it would become important on that. So she stopped, or rather began to fool on other subjects, until her long-suffering relatives drove her upstairs. Fräulein Mosebach followed her, but lingered to say heavily over the banisters to Margaret, "It is all right—she does not love the young man—he has not been worthy of her."

"Yes, I know; thanks very much."

"I thought I did right to tell you."

"Ever so many thanks."

---

[1]German: no lady.

[2]Playing on *Cox and Box* (1866), a popular comic opera (Stallybrass, "Notes," 357).

"What's that?" asked Tibby. No one told him, and he proceeded into the dining-room, to eat Elvas plums.[3]

That evening Margaret took decisive action. The house was very quiet, and the fog—we are in November now—pressed against the windows like an excluded ghost. Frieda and Helen and all their luggages had gone. Tibby, who was not feeling well, lay stretched on a sofa by the fire. Margaret sat by him, thinking. Her mind darted from impulse to impulse, and finally marshalled them all in review. The practical person, who knows what he wants at once, and generally knows nothing else, will accuse her of indecision. But this was the way her mind worked. And when she did act, no one could accuse her of indecision then. She hit out as lustily as if she had not considered the matter at all. The letter that she wrote Mrs. Wilcox glowed with the native hue of resolution. The pale cast of thought[4] was with her a breath rather than a tarnish, a breath that leaves the colours all the more vivid when it has been wiped away.

"DEAR MRS. WILCOX,

"I have to write something discourteous. It would be better if we did not meet. Both my sister and my aunt have given displeasure to your family, and, in my sister's case, the grounds for displeasure might recur. As far as I know, she no longer occupies her thoughts with your son. But it would not be fair, either to her or to you, if they met, and it is therefore right that our acquaintance, which began so pleasantly, should end.

"I fear that you will not agree with this; indeed, I know that you will not, since you have been good enough to call on us. It is only an instinct on my part, and no doubt the instinct is wrong. My sister would, undoubtedly, say that it is wrong. I write without her knowledge, and I hope that you will not associate her with my discourtesy.

"Believe me,
"Yours truly,
"M. J. SCHLEGEL."

Margaret sent this letter round by the post. Next morning she received the following reply by hand:

---

[3]Greengage plums from the Elvas region of Portugal, cooked in a sugar syrup.

[4]Soliloquizing on the halt of action by "conscience," Shakespeare's Hamlet murmurs that "the native hue of resolution / Is sicklied o'er with the pale cast of thought" (*Hamlet* 3.1)

"DEAR MISS SCHLEGEL,
"You should not have written me such a letter. I called to tell you
that Paul has gone abroad.

"RUTH WILCOX."

Margaret's cheeks burnt. She could not finish her breakfast. She
was on fire with shame. Helen had told her that the youth was
leaving England, but other things had seemed more important, and
she had forgotten. All her absurd anxieties fell to the ground, and
in their place arose the certainty that she had been rude to Mrs.
Wilcox. Rudeness affected Margaret like a bitter taste in the
mouth. It poisoned life. At times it is necessary, but woe to those
who employ it without due need. She flung on a hat and shawl, just
like a poor woman, and plunged into the fog, which still continued.
Her lips were compressed, the letter remained in her hand, and in
this state she crossed the street, entered the marble vestibule of the
flats, eluded the concierges, and ran up the stairs till she reached
the second-floor.

She sent in her name, and to her surprise was shown straight into
Mrs. Wilcox's bedroom.

"Oh, Mrs. Wilcox, I have made the baddest blunder. I am more,
more ashamed and sorry than I can say."

Mrs. Wilcox bowed gravely. She was offended, and did not pretend
to the contrary. She was sitting up in bed, writing letters on an invalid
table that spanned her knees. A breakfast tray was on another table beside her. The light of the fire, the light from the window, and the light of
a candle-lamp, which threw a quivering halo round her hands, combined to create a strange atmosphere of dissolution.

"I knew he was going to India in November, but I forgot."

"He sailed on the 17th for Nigeria, in Africa."

"I knew—I know. I have been too absurd all through. I am very
much ashamed."

Mrs. Wilcox did not answer.

"I am more sorry than I can say, and I hope that you will forgive
me."

"It doesn't matter, Miss Schlegel. It is good of you to have come
round so promptly."

"It does matter," cried Margaret. "I have been rude to you; and
my sister is not even at home, so there was not even that excuse."

"Indeed?"

"She has just gone to Germany."

"She gone as well," murmured the other. "Yes, certainly, it is quite safe—safe, absolutely, now."

"You've been worrying too!" exclaimed Margaret, getting more and more excited, and taking a chair without invitation. "How perfectly extraordinary! I can see that you have. You felt as I do; Helen mustn't meet him again."

"I did think it best."

"Now why?"

"That's a most difficult question," said Mrs. Wilcox, smiling, and a little losing her expression of annoyance. "I think you put it best in your letter—it was an instinct, which may be wrong."

"It wasn't that your son still——"

"Oh no; he often—my Paul is very young, you see."

"Then what was it?"

She repeated: "An instinct which may be wrong."

"In other words, they belong to types that can fall in love, but couldn't live together. That's dreadfully probable. I'm afraid that in nine cases out of ten Nature pulls one way and human nature another."

"These are indeed 'other words,'" said Mrs. Wilcox. "I had nothing so coherent in my head. I was merely alarmed when I knew that my boy cared for your sister."

"Ah, I have always been wanting to ask you. How *did* you know? Helen was so surprised when our aunt drove up, and you stepped forward and arranged things. Did Paul tell you?"

"There is nothing to be gained by discussing that," said Mrs. Wilcox after a moment's pause.

"Mrs. Wilcox, were you very angry with us last June? I wrote you a letter and you didn't answer it."

"I was certainly against taking Mrs. Matheson's flat. I knew it was opposite your house."

"But it's all right now?"

"I think so."

"You only think? You aren't sure? I do love these little muddles tidied up?"

"Oh yes, I'm sure," said Mrs. Wilcox, moving with uneasiness beneath the clothes. "I always sound uncertain over things. It is my way of speaking."

"That's all right, and I'm sure too."

Here the maid came in to remove the breakfast-tray. They were interrupted, and when they resumed conversation it was on more normal lines.

"I must say good-bye now—you will be getting up."

"No—please stop a little longer—I am taking a day in bed. Now and then I do."

"I thought of you as one of the early risers."

"At Howards End—yes; there is nothing to get up for in London."

"Nothing to get up for?" cried the scandalized Margaret. "When there are all the autumn exhibitions, and Ysaye playing in the afternoon![5] Not to mention people."

"The truth is, I am a little tired. First came the wedding, and then Paul went off, and, instead of resting yesterday, I paid a round of calls."

"A wedding?"

"Yes; Charles, my elder son, is married."

"Indeed!"

"We took the flat chiefly on that account, and also that Paul could get his African outfit. The flat belongs to a cousin of my husband's, and she most kindly offered it to us. So before the day came we were able to make the acquaintance of Dolly's people, which we had not yet done."

Margaret asked who Dolly's people were.

"Fussell. The father is in the Indian army—retired; the brother is in the army. The mother is dead."

So perhaps these were the "chinless sunburnt men" whom Helen had espied one afternoon through the window. Margaret felt mildly interested in the fortunes of the Wilcox family. She had acquired the habit on Helen's account, and it still clung to her. She asked for more information about Miss Dolly Fussell that was, and was given it in even, unemotional tones. Mrs. Wilcox's voice, though sweet and compelling, had little range of expression. It suggested that pictures, concerts, and people are all of small and equal value. Only once had it quickened—when speaking of Howards End.

"Charles and Albert Fussell have known one another some time. They belong to the same club, and are both devoted to golf. Dolly plays golf too, though I believe not so well, and they first met in a mixed foursome. We all like her, and are very much pleased. They were married on the 11th, a few days before Paul sailed. Charles was very anxious to have his brother as best man, so he made a great point of having it on the 11th. The Fussells would have preferred it after Christmas, but they were very nice about it. There is Dolly's photograph—in that double frame."

<hr>

[5]Belgian violinist Eugène Ysaÿe, 1858–1931. The autumn exhibitions were art shows held in that season at various venues.

"Are you quite certain that I'm not interrupting, Mrs. Wilcox?"

"Yes, quite."

"Then I will stay. I'm enjoying this."

Dolly's photograph was now examined. It was signed "For dear Mims," which Mrs. Wilcox interpreted as "the name she and Charles had settled that she should call me." Dolly looked silly, and had one of those triangular faces that so often prove attractive to a robust man. She was very pretty. From her Margaret passed to Charles, whose features prevailed opposite. She speculated on the forces that had drawn the two together till God parted them. She found time to hope that they would be happy.

"They have gone to Naples for their honeymoon."

"Lucky people!"

"I can hardly imagine Charles in Italy."

"Doesn't he care for travelling?"

"He likes travel, but he does see through foreigners so. What he enjoys most is a motor tour in England, and I think that would have carried the day if the weather had not been so abominable. His father gave him a car of his own for a wedding present, which for the present is being stored at Howards End."

"I suppose you have a garage there?"

"Yes. My husband built a little one only last month, to the west of the house, not far from the wych-elm, in what used to be the paddock for the pony."

The last words had an indescribable ring about them.

"Where's the pony gone?" asked Margaret after a pause.

"The pony? Oh, dead, ever so long ago."

"The wych-elm I remember. Helen spoke of it as a very splendid tree."

"It is the finest wych-elm in Hertfordshire. Did your sister tell you about the teeth?"

"No."

"Oh, it might interest you. There are pigs' teeth stuck into the trunk, about four feet from the ground. The country people put them in long ago, and they think that if they chew a piece of the bark, it will cure the toothache. The teeth are almost grown over now, and no one comes to the tree."

"I should. I love folklore and all festering superstitions."

"Do you think that the tree really did cure toothache, if one believed in it?"

"Of course it did. It would cure anything—once."

"Certainly I remember cases—you see I lived at Howards End long, long before Mr. Wilcox knew it. I was born there."

The conversation again shifted. At the time it seemed little more than aimless chatter. She was interested when her hostess explained that Howards End was her own property. She was bored when too minute an account was given of the Fussell family, of the anxieties of Charles concerning Naples, of the movements of Mr. Wilcox and Evie, who were motoring in Yorkshire. Margaret could not bear being bored. She grew inattentive, played with the photograph frame, dropped it, smashed Dolly's glass, apologized, was pardoned, cut her finger thereon, was pitied, and finally said she must be going—there was all the housekeeping to do, and she had to interview Tibby's riding-master.

Then the curious note was struck again.

"Good-bye, Miss Schlegel, good-bye. Thank you for coming. You have cheered me up."

"I'm so glad!"

"I—I wonder whether you ever think about yourself?"

"I think of nothing else," said Margaret, blushing, but letting her hand remain in that of the invalid.

"I wonder. I wondered at Heidelberg."

"*I'm* sure!"

"I almost think——"

"Yes?" asked Margaret, for there was a long pause—a pause that was somehow akin to the flicker of the fire, the quiver of the reading-lamp upon their hands, the white blur from the window; a pause of shifting and eternal shadows.

"I almost think you forget you're a girl."

Margaret was startled and a little annoyed. "I'm twenty-nine," she remarked. "That's not so wildly girlish."

Mrs. Wilcox smiled.

"What makes you say that? Do you mean that I have been gauche and rude?"

A shake of the head. "I only meant that I am fifty-one, and that to me, both of you—— Read it all in some book or other; I cannot put things clearly."

"Oh, I've got it—inexperience. I'm no better than Helen, you mean, and yet I presume to advise her."

"Yes. You have got it. Inexperience is the word."

"Inexperience," repeated Margaret, in serious yet buoyant tones. "Of course, I have everything to learn—absolutely every-

thing—just as much as Helen. Life's very difficult and full of sur-
prises. At all events, I've got as far as that. To be humble and kind,
to go straight ahead, to love people rather than pity them, to remember the submerged—well, one can't do all these things at once,
worse luck, because they're so contradictory. It's then that proportion comes in—to live by proportion. Don't *begin* with proportion.
Only prigs do that. Let proportion come in as a last resource, when
the better things have failed, and a deadlock—— Gracious me, I've
started preaching!"

"Indeed, you put the difficulties of life splendidly," said Mrs.
Wilcox, withdrawing her hand into the deeper shadows. "It is just
what I should have liked to say about them myself."

## CHAPTER IX

MRS. WILCOX cannot be accused of giving Margaret much information about life. And Margaret, on the other hand, has made a fair
show of modesty, and has pretended to an inexperience that she certainly did not feel. She had kept house for over ten years; she had en-
tertained, almost with distinction; she had brought up a charming
sister, and was bringing up a brother. Surely, if experience is attain-
able, she had attained it.

Yet the little luncheon-party that she gave in Mrs. Wilcox's honour was not a success. The new friend did not blend with the "one or
two delightful people" who had been asked to meet her, and the atmosphere was one of polite bewilderment. Her tastes were simple,
her knowledge of culture slight, and she was not interested in the
New English Art Club,[1] nor in the dividing-line between Journalism
and Literature, which was started as a conversational hare. The delightful people darted after it with cries of joy, Margaret leading them,
and not till the meal was half over did they realize that the principal
guest had taken no part in the chase. There was no common topic.
Mrs. Wilcox, whose life had been spent in the service of husband and
sons, had little to say to strangers who had never shared it, and whose
age was half her own. Clever talk alarmed her, and withered her delicate imaginings; it was the social counterpart of a motor-car, all jerks,
and she was a wisp of hay, a flower. Twice she deplored the weather,
twice criticized the train service on the Great Northern Railway. They

[1]Organization of artists founded in 1886 to counter the conservative Royal Academy
of Arts; strongly associated with Impressionism.

vigorously assented, and rushed on, and when she inquired whether there was any news of Helen, her hostess was too much occupied in placing Rothenstein[2] to answer. The question was repeated: "I hope that your sister is safe in Germany by now." Margaret checked herself and said "Yes, thank you; I heard on Tuesday." But the demon of vociferation was in her, and the next moment she was off again.

"Only on Tuesday, for they live right away at Stettin. Did you ever know anyone living at Stettin?"

"Never," said Mrs. Wilcox gravely, while her neighbour, a young man low down in the Education Office, began to discuss what people who lived at Stettin ought to look like. Was there such a thing as Stettininity? Margaret swept on.

"People at Stettin drop things into boats out of overhanging warehouses. At least, our cousins do, but aren't particularly rich. The town isn't interesting, except for a clock that rolls its eyes, and the view of the Oder, which truly is something special. Oh, Mrs. Wilcox, you would love the Oder! The river, or rather rivers—there seem to be dozens of them—are intense blue, and the plain they run through an intensest green."

"Indeed! That sounds like a most beautiful view, Miss Schlegel."

"So I say, but Helen, who will muddle things, says no, it's like music. The course of the Oder is to be like music. It's obliged to remind her of a symphonic poem. The part by the landing-stage is in B minor, if I remember rightly, but lower down things get extremely mixed. There is a slodgy theme in several keys at once, meaning mud-banks, and another for the navigable canal, and the exit into the Baltic is in C sharp major, pianissimo."

"What do the overhanging warehouses make of that?" asked the man, laughing.

"They make a great deal of it," replied Margaret, unexpectedly rushing off on a new track. "I think it's affectation to compare the Oder to music, and so do you, but the overhanging warehouses of Stettin take beauty seriously, which we don't, and the average Englishman doesn't, and despises all who do. Now don't say 'Germans have no taste,' or I shall scream. They haven't. But—but—such a tremendous but!—they take poetry seriously. They do take poetry seriously."

"Is anything gained by that?"

"Yes, yes. The German is always on the lookout for beauty. He may miss it through stupidity, or misinterpret it, but he is always asking beauty to enter his life, and I believe that in the end it will come.

[2]English painter and art critic William Rothenstein (1872–1945).

At Heidelberg I met a fat veterinary surgeon whose voice broke with sobs as he repeated some mawkish poetry. So easy for me to laugh— I, who never repeat poetry, good or bad, and cannot remember one fragment of verse to thrill myself with. My blood boils—well, I'm half German, so put it down to patriotism—when I listen to the tasteful contempt of the average islander for things Teutonic, whether they're Böcklin or my veterinary surgeon. 'Oh, Böcklin,' they say; 'he strains after beauty, he peoples Nature with gods too consciously.' Of course Böcklin strains, because he wants something—beauty and all the other intangible gifts that are floating about the world. So his landscapes don't come off, and Leader's do."

"I am not sure that I agree. Do you?" said he, turning to Mrs. Wilcox.

She replied: "I think Miss Schlegel puts everything splendidly"; and a chill fell on the conversation.

"Oh, Mrs. Wilcox, say something nicer than that. It's such a snub to be told you put things splendidly."

"I do not mean it as a snub. Your last speech interested me so much. Generally people do not seem quite to like Germany. I have long wanted to hear what is said on the other side."

"The other side? Then you do disagree. Oh, good! Give us your side."

"I have no side. But my husband"—her voice softened, the chill increased—"has very little faith in the Continent, and our children have all taken after him."

"On what grounds? Do they feel that the Continent is in bad form?"

Mrs. Wilcox had no idea; she paid little attention to grounds. She was not intellectual, nor even alert, and it was odd that, all the same, she should give the idea of greatness. Margaret, zigzagging with her friends over Thought and Art, was conscious of a personality that transcended their own and dwarfed their activities. There was no bitterness in Mrs. Wilcox; there was not even criticism; she was lovable, and no ungracious or uncharitable word had passed her lips. Yet she and daily life were out of focus: one or the other must show blurred. And at lunch she seemed more out of focus than usual, and nearer the line that divides daily life from a life that may be of greater importance.

"You will admit, though, that the Continent—it seems silly to speak of 'the Continent,' but really it is all more like itself than any part of it is like England. England is unique. Do have another jelly first. I was going to say that the Continent, for good or for evil, is interested in ideas. Its Literature and Art have what one might call the kink of the unseen about them, and this persists even through decadence and affectation. There is more liberty of action in England, but for liberty of thought go to bureaucratic Prussia. People will there discuss with humility vital questions that we here think ourselves too good to touch with tongs."

"I do not want to go to Prussia," said Mrs. Wilcox—"not even to see that interesting view that you were describing. And for discussing with humility I am too old. We never discuss anything at Howards End."

"Then you ought to!" said Margaret. "Discussion keeps a house alive. It cannot stand by bricks and mortar alone."

"It cannot stand without them," said Mrs. Wilcox, unexpectedly catching on to the thought, and rousing, for the first and last time, a faint hope in the breasts of the delightful people. "It cannot stand without them, and I sometimes think—— But I cannot expect your generation to agree, for even my daughter disagrees with me here."

"Never mind us or her. Do say!"

"I sometimes think that it is wiser to leave action and discussion to men."

There was a little silence.

"One admits that the arguments against the suffrage *are* extraordinarily strong," said a girl opposite, leaning forward and crumbling her bread.

"Are they? I never follow any arguments. I am only too thankful not to have a vote myself."

"We didn't mean the vote, though, did we?" supplied Margaret. "Aren't we differing on something much wider, Mrs. Wilcox? Whether women are to remain what they have been since the dawn of history; or whether, since men have moved forward so far, they too may move forward a little now. I say they may. I would even admit a biological change."

"I don't know, I don't know."

"I must be getting back to my overhanging warehouse," said the man. "They've turned disgracefully strict."

Mrs. Wilcox also rose.

"Oh, but come upstairs for a little. Miss Quested[3] plays. Do you like MacDowell?[4] Do you mind him only having two noises? If you must really go, I'll see you out. Won't you even have coffee?"

---

[3]Forster names a principal character in *A Passage to India* (1924) Adela Quested.
[4]American composer Edward MacDowell, 1860–1908.

They left the dining-room, closing the door behind them, and as Mrs. Wilcox buttoned up her jacket, she said: "What an interesting life you all lead in London!"

"No, we don't," said Margaret, with a sudden revulsion. "We lead the lives of gibbering monkeys. Mrs. Wilcox—really—— We have something quiet and stable at the bottom. We really have. All my friends have. Don't pretend you enjoyed lunch, for you loathed it, but forgive me by coming again, alone, or by asking me to you."

"I am used to young people," said Mrs. Wilcox, and with each word she spoke the outlines of known things grew dim. "I hear a great deal of chatter at home, for we, like you, entertain a great deal. With us it is more sport and politics, but—I enjoyed my lunch very much, Miss Schlegel, dear, and am not pretending, and only wish I could have joined in more. For one thing, I'm not particularly well just to-day. For another, you younger people move so quickly that it dazes me. Charles is the same, Dolly the same. But we are all in the same boat, old and young. I never forget that."

They were silent for a moment. Then, with a newborn emotion, they shook hands. The conversation ceased suddenly when Margaret re-entered the dining-room: her friends had been talking over her new friend, and had dismissed her as uninteresting.

## CHAPTER X

SEVERAL days passed.

Was Mrs. Wilcox one of the unsatisfactory people—there are many of them—who dangle intimacy and then withdraw it? They evoke our interests and affections, and keep the life of the spirit dawdling round them. Then they withdraw. When physical passion is involved, there is a definite name for such behaviour—flirting—and if carried far enough it is punishable by law. But no law—not public opinion even—punishes those who coquette with friendship, though the dull ache that they inflict, the sense of misdirected effort and exhaustion, may be as intolerable. Was she one of these?

Margaret feared so at first, for, with a Londoner's impatience, she wanted everything to be settled up immediately. She mistrusted the periods of quiet that are essential to true growth. Desiring to book Mrs. Wilcox as a friend, she pressed on the ceremony, pencil, as it were, in hand, pressing the more because the rest of the family were away, and the opportunity seemed favourable. But the elder woman would not be hurried. She refused to fit in with the Wickham Place set, or to reopen discussion of Helen and Paul, whom Margaret would have utilized as a short-cut. She took her time, or perhaps let time take her, and when the crisis did come all was ready.

The crisis opened with a message: would Miss Schlegel come shopping? Christmas was nearing, and Mrs. Wilcox felt behind-hand with the presents. She had taken some more days in bed, and must make up for lost time. Margaret accepted, and at eleven o'clock one cheerless morning they started out in a brougham.[1]

"First of all," began Margaret, "we must make a list and tick off the people's names. My aunt always does, and this fog may thicken up any moment. Have you any ideas?"

"I thought we would go to Harrod's or the Haymarket Stores,"[2] said Mrs. Wilcox rather hopelessly. "Everything is sure to be there. I am not a good shopper. The din is so confusing, and your aunt is quite right—one ought to make a list. Take my note-book, then, and write your own name at the top of the page."

"Oh, hooray!" said Margaret, writing it. "How very kind of you to start with me!" But she did not want to receive anything expensive. Their acquaintance was singular rather than intimate, and she divined that the Wilcox clan would resent any expenditure on outsiders; the more compact families do. She did not want to be thought a second Helen, who would snatch presents since she could not snatch young men, nor to be exposed, like a second Aunt Juley, to the insults of Charles. A certain austerity of demeanour was best, and she added: "I don't really want a Yuletide gift, though. In fact, I'd rather not."

"Why?"

"Because I've odd ideas about Christmas. Because I have all that money can buy. I want more people, but no more things."

"I should like to give you something worth your acquaintance, Miss Schlegel, in memory of your kindness to me during my lonely fortnight. It has so happened that I have been left alone, and you have stopped me from brooding. I am too apt to brood."

"If that is so," said Margaret, "if I have happened to be of use to you, which I didn't know, you cannot pay me back with anything tangible."

"I suppose not, but one would like to. Perhaps I shall think of something as we go about."

---

[1] A light, closed carriage seating two but sometimes having fold-away seating for two more.

[2] The Civil Service Stores (in the street known as the Haymarket) and Harrods were London department stores.

Her name remained at the head of the list, but nothing was written opposite it. They drove from shop to shop. The air was white, and when they alighted it tasted like cold pennies. At times they passed through a clot of grey. Mrs. Wilcox's vitality was low that morning, and it was Margaret who decided on a horse for this little girl, a golliwog[3] for that, for the rector's[4] wife a copper warming-tray. "We always give the servants money." "Yes, do you, yes, much easier," replied Margaret, but felt the grotesque impact of the unseen upon the seen, and saw issuing from a forgotten manger at Bethlehem this torrent of coins and toys. Vulgarity reigned. Public-houses, besides their usual exhortation against temperance reform, invited men to "Join our Christmas goose club"—one bottle of gin, etc., or two, according to subscription. A poster of a woman in tights heralded the Christmas pantomime,[5] and little red devils, who had come in again that year, were prevalent upon the Christmas-cards. Margaret was no morbid idealist. She did not wish this spate of business and self-advertisement checked. It was only the occasion of it that struck her with amazement annually. How many of these vacillating shoppers and tired shop-assistants realized that it was a divine event that drew them together? She realized it, though standing outside in the matter. She was not a Christian in the accepted sense; she did not believe that God had ever worked among us as a young artisan. These people, or most of them, believed it, and if pressed, would affirm it in words. But the visible signs of their belief were Regent Street or Drury Lane, a little mud displaced, a little money spent, a little food cooked, eaten, and forgotten. Inadequate. But in public who shall express the unseen adequately? It is private life that holds out the mirror to infinity; personal intercourse, and that alone, that ever hints at a personality beyond our daily vision.

"No, I do like Christmas on the whole," she announced. "In its clumsy way, it does approach Peace and Goodwill. But oh, it is clumsier every year."

"Is it? I am only used to country Christmases."

"We are usually in London, and play the game with vigour—carols at the Abbey, clumsy midday meal, clumsy dinner for the maids, followed by Christmas-tree and dancing of poor children, with songs

---

[3]Doll whose features suggest a grotesque caricature of a black person; named for a character in an 1895 children's book by Bertha and Florence Kate Upton.

[4]Local clergyman's.

[5]Popular entertainment built around familiar children's stories and featuring dance, slapstick, parodic songs, and celebrity entertainers.

from Helen. The drawing-room does very well for that. We put the tree in the powder-closet, and draw a curtain when the candles are lighted, and with the looking-glass behind it looks quite pretty. I wish we might have a powder-closet in our next house. Of course, the tree has to be very small, and the presents don't hang on it. No; the presents reside in a sort of rocky landscape made of crumpled brown paper."

"You spoke of your 'next house,' Miss Schlegel. Then are you leaving Wickham Place?"

"Yes, in two or three years, when the lease expires. We must."

"Have you been there long?"

"All our lives."

"You will be very sorry to leave it."

"I suppose so. We scarcely realize it yet. My father——" She broke off, for they had reached the stationery department of the Haymarket Stores, and Mrs. Wilcox wanted to order some private greeting cards.

"If possible, something distinctive," she sighed. At the counter she found a friend, bent on the same errand, and conversed with her insipidly, wasting much time. "My husband and our daughter are motoring." "Bertha too? Oh, fancy, what a coincidence!" Margaret, though not practical, could shine in such company as this. While they talked, she went through a volume of specimen cards, and submitted one for Mrs. Wilcox's inspection. Mrs. Wilcox was delighted—so original, words so sweet; she would order a hundred like that, and could never be sufficiently grateful. Then, just as the assistant was booking the order, she said: "Do you know, I'll wait. On second thoughts, I'll wait. There's plenty of time still, isn't there, and I shall be able to get Evie's opinion."

They returned to the carriage by devious paths; when they were in, she said, "But couldn't you get it renewed?"

"I beg your pardon?" asked Margaret.

"The lease, I mean."

"Oh, the lease! Have you been thinking of that all the time? How very kind of you!"

"Surely something could be done."

"No; values have risen too enormously. They mean to pull down Wickham Place, and build flats like yours."

"But how horrible!"

"Landlords are horrible."

Then she said vehemently: "It is monstrous, Miss Schlegel; it isn't right. I had no idea that this was hanging over you. I do pity you from the bottom of my heart. To be parted from your house, your father's house—it oughtn't to be allowed. It is worse than dying. I would rather die than——— Oh, poor girls! Can what they call civilization be right, if people mayn't die in the room where they were born? My dear, I am so sorry——"

Margaret did not know what to say. Mrs. Wilcox had been over-tired by the shopping, and was inclined to hysteria.

"Howards End was nearly pulled down once. It would have killed me."

"Howards End must be a very different house to ours. We are fond of ours, but there is nothing distinctive about it. As you saw, it is an ordinary London house. We shall easily find another."

"So you think."

"Again my lack of experience, I suppose!" said Margaret, easing away from the subject. "I can't say anything when you take up that line, Mrs. Wilcox. I wish I could see myself as you see me—foreshort-ened into a backfisch.[6] Quite the ingénue.[7] Very charming—wonder-fully well read for my age, but incapable——"

Mrs. Wilcox would not be deterred. "Come down with me to Howards End now," she said, more vehemently than ever. "I want you to see it. You have never seen it. I want to hear what you say about it, for you do put things so wonderfully."

Margaret glanced at the pitiless air and then at the tired face of her companion. "Later on I should love it," she continued, "but it's hardly the weather for such an expedition, and we ought to start when we're fresh. Isn't the house shut up, too?"

She received no answer. Mrs. Wilcox appeared to be annoyed.

"Might I come some other day?"

Mrs. Wilcox bent forward and tapped the glass. "Back to Wick-ham Place, please!" was her order to the coachman. Margaret had been snubbed.

"A thousand thanks, Miss Schlegel, for all your help."

"Not at all."

"It is such a comfort to get the presents off my mind—the Christ-mas-cards especially. I do admire your choice."

It was her turn to receive no answer. In her turn Margaret became annoyed.

"My husband and Evie will be back the day after to-morrow. That is why I dragged you out shopping to-day. I stayed in town chiefly to shop, but got through nothing, and now he writes that they

[6]Girl in her late teens.

[7]Innocent; also, the standard role of the unworldly girl in a play.

must cut their tour short, the weather is so bad, and the police-traps have been so bad—nearly as bad as in Surrey. Ours is such a careful chauffeur, and my husband feels it particularly hard that they should be treated like road-hogs."

"Why?"

"Well, naturally he—he isn't a road-hog."

"He was exceeding the speed-limit, I conclude. He must expect to suffer with the lower animals."

Mrs. Wilcox was silenced. In growing discomfort they drove homewards. The city seemed Satanic, the narrower streets oppressing like the galleries of a mine. No harm was done by the fog to trade, for it lay high, and the lighted windows of the shops were thronged with customers. It was rather a darkening of the spirit which fell back upon itself, to find a more grievous darkness within. Margaret nearly spoke a dozen times, but something throttled her. She felt petty and awkward, and her meditations on Christmas grew more cynical. Peace? It may bring other gifts, but is there a single Londoner to whom Christmas is peaceful? The craving for excitement and for elaboration has ruined that blessing. Goodwill? Had she seen any example of it in the hordes of purchasers? Or in herself? She had failed to respond to this invitation merely because it was a little queer and imaginative—she, whose birthright it was to nourish imagination! Better to have accepted, to have tired themselves a little by the journey, than coldly to reply, "Might I come some other day?" Her cynicism left her. There would be no other day. This shadowy woman would never ask her again.

They parted at the Mansions. Mrs. Wilcox went in after due civilities, and Margaret watched the tall, lonely figure sweep up the hall to the lift. As the glass doors closed on it she had the sense of an imprisonment. The beautiful head disappeared first, still buried in the muff; the long trailing skirt followed. A woman of undefinable rarity was going up heavenward, like a specimen in a bottle. And into what a heaven—a vault as of hell, sooty black, from which soots descended!

At lunch her brother, seeing her inclined for silence, insisted on talking. Tibby was not ill-natured, but from babyhood something drove him to do the unwelcome and the unexpected. Now he gave her a long account of the day-school that he sometimes patronized. The account was interesting, and she had often pressed him for it before, but she could not attend now, for her mind was focussed on the invisible. She discerned that Mrs. Wilcox, though a loving wife and mother, had only one passion in life—her house—and that the moment was solemn when she invited a friend to share this passion with her. To answer "another day" was to answer as a fool. "Another day" will do for brick and mortar, but not for the Holy of Holies into which Howards End had been transfigured. Her own curiosity was slight. She had heard more than enough about it in the summer. The nine windows, the vine, and the wych-elm had no pleasant connections for her, and she would have preferred to spend the afternoon at a concert. But imagination triumphed. While her brother held forth she determined to go, at whatever cost, and to compel Mrs. Wilcox to go, too. When lunch was over she stepped over to the flats.

Mrs. Wilcox had just gone away for the night.

Margaret said that it was of no consequence, hurried downstairs, and took a hansom to King's Cross. She was convinced that the escapade was important, though it would have puzzled her to say why. There was question of imprisonment and escape, and though she did not know the time of the train, she strained her eyes for St. Pancras' clock.[8]

Then the clock of King's Cross swung into sight, a second moon in that infernal sky, and her cab drew up at the station. There was a train for Hilton in five minutes. She took a ticket, asking in her agitation for a single. As she did so, a grave and happy voice saluted her and thanked her.

"I will come if I still may," said Margaret, laughing nervously.

"You are coming to sleep, dear, too. It is in the morning that my house is most beautiful. You are coming to stop. I cannot show you my meadow properly except at sunrise. These fogs"—she pointed at the station roof—"never spread far. I dare say they are sitting in the sun in Hertfordshire, and you will never repent joining them."

"I shall never repent joining you."

"It is the same."

They began the walk up the long platform. Far at its end stood the train, breasting the darkness without. They never reached it. Before imagination could triumph, there were cries of "Mother! mother!" and a heavy-browed girl darted out of the cloak-room and seized Mrs. Wilcox by the arm.

"Evie!" she gasped—"Evie, my pet——"

The girl called, "Father! I say! look who's here."

"Evie, dearest girl, why aren't you in Yorkshire?"

"No—motor smash—changed plans—father's coming."

"Why, Ruth!" cried Mr. Wilcox, joining them. "What in the name of all that's wonderful are you doing here, Ruth?"

[8]Prominent feature of St. Pancras Station (serving trains to the Midlands).

Mrs. Wilcox had recovered herself.

"Oh, Henry dear!—here's a lovely surprise—but let me intro-duce—but I think you know Miss Schlegel."

"Oh, yes," he replied, not greatly interested. "But how's yourself, Ruth?"

"Fit as a fiddle," she answered gaily.

"So are we, and so was our car, which ran A1 as far as Ripon, but there a wretched horse and cart which a fool of a driver——"

"Miss Schlegel, our little outing must be for another day."

"I was saying that this fool of a driver, as the policeman himself admits——"

"Another day, Mrs. Wilcox. Of course."

"—But as we've insured against third party risks, it won't so much matter——"

"—Cart and car being practically at right angles——"

The voices of the happy family rose high. Margaret was left alone. No one wanted her. Mrs. Wilcox walked out of King's Cross between her husband and her daughter, listening to both of them.

## CHAPTER XI

THE funeral was over. The carriages had rolled away through the soft mud, and only the poor remained. They approached to the newly-dug shaft and looked their last at the coffin, now almost hidden beneath the spadefuls of clay. It was their moment. Most of them were women from the dead woman's district, to whom black garments had been served out by Mr. Wilcox's orders. Pure curiosity had brought others. They thrilled with the excitement of a death, and of a rapid death, and stood in groups or moved between the graves, like drops of ink. The son of one of them, a wood-cutter, was perched high above their heads, pollarding[1] one of the churchyard elms. From where he sat he could see the village of Hilton, strung upon the North Road, with its accreting suburbs; the sunset beyond, scarlet and orange, winking at him beneath brows of grey; the church; the plantations; and behind him an unspoilt country of fields and farms. But he, too, was rolling the event luxuriously in his mouth. He tried to tell his mother down below all that he had felt when he saw the coffin approaching: how he could not leave his work, and yet did not like to go on with it; how he had almost slipped out of the tree, he was so upset; the rooks had

[1]Cutting back the branches of.

cawed, and no wonder—it was as if rooks knew too. His mother claimed the prophetic power herself—she had seen a strange look about Mrs. Wilcox for some time. London had done the mischief, said others. She had been a kind lady; her grandmother had been kind, too—a plainer person, but very kind. Ah, the old sort was dying out! Mr. Wilcox, he was a kind gentleman. They advanced to the topic again and again, dully, but with exaltation. The funeral of a rich person was to them what the funeral of Alcestis or Ophelia[2] is to the educated. It was Art; though remote from life, it enhanced life's values, and they witnessed it avidly.

The grave-diggers, who had kept up an undercurrent of disapproval—they disliked Charles; it was not a moment to speak of such things, but they did not like Charles Wilcox—the grave-diggers finished their work and piled up the wreaths and crosses above it. The sun set over Hilton: the grey brows of the evening flushed a little, and were cleft with one scarlet frown. Chattering sadly to each other, the mourners passed through the lych-gate[3] and traversed the chestnut avenues that led down to the village. The young wood-cutter stayed a little longer, poised above the silence and swaying rhythmically. At last the bough fell beneath his saw. With a grunt, he descended, his thoughts dwelling no longer on death, but on love, for he was mating. He stopped as he passed the new grave; a sheaf of tawny chrysanthemums had caught his eye. "They didn't ought to have coloured flowers at buryings," he reflected. Trudging on a few steps, he stopped again, looked furtively at the dusk, turned back, wrenched a chrysanthemum from the sheaf, and hid it in his pocket.

After him came silence absolute. The cottage that abutted on the churchyard was empty, and no other house stood near. Hour after hour the scene of the interment remained without an eye to witness it. Clouds drifted over it from the west; or the church may have been a ship, high-prowed, steering with all its company towards infinity. Towards morning the air grew colder, the sky clearer, the surface of the earth hard and sparkling above the prostrate dead. The wood-cutter, returning after a night of joy, reflected: "They lilies, they chrysants; it's a pity I didn't take them all."

Up at Howards End they were attempting breakfast. Charles and Evie sat in the dining-room, with Mrs. Charles. Their father, who

[2]In *Alcestis* (by Euripides, 5th c BCE), the title character agrees to die in place of her husband. Ophelia's funeral is the occasion of Hamlet's return to Denmark (*Hamlet*, 5.1).

[3]Roofed gateway to a churchyard.

could not bear to see a face, breakfasted upstairs. He suffered acutely. Pain came over him in spasms, as if it was physical, and even while he was about to eat, his eyes would fill with tears, and he would lay down the morsel untasted.

He remembered his wife's even goodness during thirty years. Not anything in detail—not courtship or early raptures—but just the unvarying virtue, that seemed to him a woman's noblest quality. So many women are capricious, breaking into odd flaws of passion or frivolity. Not so his wife. Year after year, summer and winter, as bride and mother, she had been the same, he had always trusted her. Her tenderness! Her innocence! The wonderful innocence that was hers by the gift of God. Ruth knew no more of worldly wickedness and wisdom than did the flowers in her garden, or the grass in her field. Her idea of business—"Henry, why do people who have enough money try to get more money?" Her idea of politics—"I am sure that if the mothers of various nations could meet, there would be no more wars." Her idea of religion—ah, this had been a cloud, but a cloud that passed. She came of Quaker stock, and he and his family, formerly Dissenters, were now members of the Church of England. The rector's sermons had at first repelled her, and she had expressed a desire for "a more inward light," adding, "not so much for myself as for baby" (Charles).[4] Inward light must have been granted, for he heard no complaints in later years. They brought up their three children without dispute. They had never disputed.

She lay under the earth now. She had gone, and as if to make her going the more bitter, had gone with a touch of mystery that was all unlike her. "Why didn't you tell me you knew of it?" he had moaned, and her faint voice had answered: "I didn't want to, Henry—I might have been wrong—and everyone hates illnesses." He had been told of the horror by a strange doctor, whom she had consulted during his absence from town. Was this altogether just? Without fully explaining, she had died. It was a fault on her part, and—tears rushed into his eyes—what a little fault! It was the only time she had deceived him in those thirty years.

He rose to his feet and looked out of the window, for Evie had come in with the letters, and he could meet no one's eye. Ah yes—she had been a good woman—she had been steady. He chose the word deliberately. To him steadiness included all praise.

[4]Dissenters, including members of the Religious Society of Friends (Quakers), were British Protestants not affiliated with the Church of England, the official state Church. The Quaker belief that the light of God is within each person shifts responsibility for salvation away from religious institutions and toward individuals.

He himself, gazing at the wintry garden, is in appearance a steady man. His face was not as square as his son's, and, indeed, the chin, though firm enough in outline, retreated a little, and the lips, ambiguous, were curtained by a moustache. But there was no external hint of weakness. The eyes, if capable of kindness and good-fellowship, if ruddy for the moment with tears, were the eyes of one who could not be driven. The forehead, too, was like Charles's. High and straight, brown and polished, merging abruptly into temples and skull, it had the effect of a bastion that protected his head from the world. At times it had the effect of a blank wall. He had dwelt behind it, intact and happy, for fifty years.

"The post's come, father," said Evie awkwardly.

"Thanks. Put it down."

"Has the breakfast been all right?"

"Yes, thanks."

The girl glanced at him and at it with constraint. She did not know what to do.

"Charles says do you want the 'Times'?"

"No, I'll read it later."

"Ring if you want anything, father, won't you?"

"I've all I want."

Having sorted the letters from the circulars, she went back to the dining-room.

"Father's eaten nothing," she announced, sitting down with wrinkled brows behind the tea-urn.

Charles did not answer, but after a moment he ran quickly upstairs, opened the door, and said: "Look here, father, you must eat, you know;" and having paused for a reply that did not come, stole down again. "He's going to read his letters first, I think," he said evasively; "I dare say he will go on with his breakfast afterwards." Then he took up the 'Times,' and for some time there was no sound except the clink of cup against saucer and of knife on plate.

Poor Mrs. Charles sat between her silent companions, terrified at the course of events, and a little bored. She was a rubbishy little creature, and she knew it. A telegram had dragged her from Naples to the death-bed of a woman whom she had scarcely known. A word from her husband had plunged her into mourning. She desired to mourn inwardly as well, but she wished that Mrs. Wilcox, since fated to die, could have died before the marriage, for then less would have been expected of her. Crumbling her toast, and too nervous to ask for the butter, she remained almost motionless, thankful only for this, that her father-in-law was having his breakfast upstairs.

At last Charles spoke. "They had no business to be pollarding those elms yesterday," he said to his sister.

"No indeed."

"I must make a note of that," he continued. "I am surprised that the rector allowed it."

"Perhaps it may not be the rector's affair."

"Whose else could it be?"

"The lord of the manor."

"Impossible."

"Butter, Dolly?"

"Thank you, Evie dear. Charles——"

"Yes, dear?"

"I didn't know one could pollard elms. I thought one only pollarded willows."

"Oh no, one can pollard elms."

"Then why oughtn't the elms in the churchyard to be pollarded?" Charles frowned a little, and turned again to his sister.

"Another point. I must speak to Chalkeley."

"Yes, rather; you must complain to Chalkeley."

"It's no good him saying he is not responsible for those men. He is responsible."

"Yes, rather."

Brother and sister were not callous. They spoke thus, partly because they desired to keep Chalkeley up to the mark—a healthy desire in its way—partly because they avoided the personal note in life. All Wilcoxes did. It did not seem to them of supreme importance. Or it may be as Helen supposed: they realized its importance, but were afraid of it. Panic and emptiness, could one glance behind. They were not callous, and they left the breakfast-table with aching hearts. Their mother never had come in to breakfast. It was in the other rooms, and especially in the garden, that they felt her loss most. As Charles went out to the garage, he was reminded at every step of the woman who had loved him and whom he could never replace. What battles he had fought against her gentle conservatism! How she had disliked improvements, yet how loyally she had accepted them when made! He and his father—what trouble they had had to get this very garage! With what difficulty had they persuaded her to yield them the paddock for it—the paddock that she loved more dearly than the garden itself! The vine—she had got her way about the vine. It still encumbered the south wall with its unproductive branches. And so with Evie, as she stood talking to the cook. Though she could take up her mother's work inside the house, just as the man could take it up without, she felt that something unique had fallen out of her life. Their grief, though less poignant than their father's, grew from deeper roots, for a wife may be replaced; a mother never.

Charles would go back to the office. There was little to do at Howards End. The contents of his mother's will had been long known to them. There were no legacies, no annuities, none of the posthumous bustle with which some of the dead prolong their activities. Trusting her husband, she had left him everything without reserve. She was quite a poor woman—the house had been all her dowry, and the house would come to Charles in time. Her watercolours Mr. Wilcox intended to reserve for Paul, while Evie would take the jewellery and lace. How easily she slipped out of life! Charles thought the habit laudable, though he did not intend to adopt it himself, whereas Margaret would have seen in it an almost culpable indifference to earthly fame. Cynicism—not the superficial cynicism that snarls and sneers, but the cynicism that can go with courtesy and tenderness—that was the note of Mrs. Wilcox's will. She wanted not to vex people. That accomplished, the earth might freeze over her for ever.

No, there was nothing for Charles to wait for. He could not go on with his honeymoon, so he would go up to London and work—he felt too miserable hanging about. He and Dolly would have the furnished flat while his father rested quietly in the country with Evie. He could also keep an eye on his own little house, which was being painted and decorated for him in one of the Surrey suburbs, and in which he hoped to instal himself soon after Christmas. Yes, he would go up after lunch in his new motor, and the town servants, who had come down for the funeral, would go up by train.

He found his father's chauffeur in the garage, said "Morning" without looking at the man's face, and, bending over the car, continued: "Hullo! my new car's been driven!"

"Has it, sir?"

"Yes," said Charles, getting rather red; "and whoever's driven it hasn't cleaned it properly, for there's mud on the axle. Take it off."

The man went for the cloths without a word. He was a chauffeur as ugly as sin—not that this did him disservice with Charles, who thought charm in a man rather rot, and had soon got rid of the little Italian beast with whom they had started.

"Charles——" His bride was tripping after him over the hoar-frost, a dainty black column, her little face and elaborate mourning hat forming the capital thereof.

"One minute, I'm busy. Well, Crane, who's been driving it, do you suppose?"

"Don't know, I'm sure, sir. No one's driven it since I've been back, but, of course, there's the fortnight I've been away with the other car in Yorkshire."

The mud came off easily.

"Charles, your father's down. Something's happened. He wants you in the house at once. Oh, Charles!"

"Wait, dear, wait a minute. Who had the key of the garage while you were away, Crane?"

"The gardener, sir."

"Do you mean to tell me that old Penny can drive a motor?"

"No, sir; no one's had the motor out, sir."

"Then how do you account for the mud on the axle?"

"I can't, of course, say for the time I've been in Yorkshire. No more mud now, sir."

Charles was vexed. The man was treating him as a fool, and if his heart had not been so heavy he would have reported him to his father. But it was not a morning for complaints. Ordering the motor to be round after lunch, he joined his wife, who had all the while been pouring out some incoherent story about a letter and a Miss Schlegel.

"Now, Dolly, I can attend to you. Miss Schlegel? What does she want?"

When people wrote a letter Charles always asked what they wanted. Want was to him the only cause of action. And the question in this case was correct, for his wife replied, "She wants Howards End."

"Howards End? Now, Crane, just don't forget to put on the Stepney wheel."[5]

"No, sir."

"Now, mind you don't forget, for I—— Come, little woman." When they were out of the chauffeur's sight he put his arm round her waist and pressed her against him. All his affection and half his attention—it was what he granted her throughout their happy married life.

"But you haven't listened, Charles——"

"What's wrong?"

"I keep on telling you—Howards End. Miss Schlegel's got it."

"Got what?" said Charles, unclasping her. "What the dickens are you talking about?"

[5]Spare wheel.

"Now, Charles, you promised not to say those naughty——"

"Look here, I'm in no mood for foolery. It's no morning for it either."

"I tell you—I keep on telling you—Miss Schlegel—she's got it—your mother's left it to her—and you've all got to move out!"

"*Howards End?*"

"*Howards End!*" she screamed, mimicking him, and as she did so Evie came dashing out of the shrubbery.

"Dolly, go back at once! My father's much annoyed with you. Charles"—she hit herself wildly—"come in at once to father. He's had a letter that's too awful."

Charles began to run, but checked himself, and stepped heavily across the gravel path. There the house was—the nine windows, the unprolific vine. He exclaimed, "Schlegels again!" and as if to complete chaos, Dolly said, "Oh no, the matron of the nursing home has written instead of her."

"Come in, all three of you!" cried his father, no longer inert. "Dolly, why have you disobeyed me?"

"Oh, Mr. Wilcox——"

"I told you not to go out to the garage. I've heard you all shouting in the garden. I won't have it. Come in."

He stood in the porch, transformed, letters in his hand.

"Into the dining-room, every one of you. We can't discuss private matters in the middle of all the servants. Here, Charles, here; read these. See what you make."

Charles took two letters, and read them as he followed the procession. The first was a covering note from the matron. Mrs. Wilcox had desired her, when the funeral should be over, to forward the enclosed. The enclosed—it was from his mother herself. She had written: "To my husband: I should like Miss Schlegel (Margaret) to have Howards End."

"I suppose we're going to have a talk about this?" he remarked, ominously calm.

"Certainly. I was coming out to you when Dolly——"

"Well, let's sit down."

"Come, Evie, don't waste time, sit down."

In silence they drew up to the breakfast-table. The events of yesterday—indeed, of this morning—suddenly receded into a past so remote that they seemed scarcely to have lived in it. Heavy breathings were heard. They were calming themselves. Charles, to steady them further, read the enclosure out loud: "A note in my mother's handwriting, in an envelope addressed to my father, sealed. Inside: 'I should like Miss Schlegel (Margaret) to have Howards End.' No date, no signature. Forwarded through the matron of that nursing home. Now, the question is——"

Dolly interrupted him. "But I say that note isn't legal. Houses ought to be done by a lawyer, Charles, surely."

Her husband worked his jaw severely. Little lumps appeared in front of either ear—a symptom that she had not yet learnt to respect, and she asked whether she might see the note. Charles looked at his father for permission, who said abstractedly, "Give it her." She seized it, and at once exclaimed: "Why, it's only in pencil! I said so. Pencil never counts."

"We know that it is not legally binding, Dolly," said Mr. Wilcox, speaking from out of his fortress. "We are aware of that. Legally, I should be justified in tearing it up and throwing it into the fire. Of course, my dear, we consider you as one of the family, but it will be better if you do not interfere with what you do not understand."

Charles, vexed both with his father and his wife, then repeated: "The question is——" He had cleared a space of the breakfast-table from plates and knives, so that he could draw patterns on the table-cloth. "The question is whether Miss Schlegel, during the fortnight we were all away, whether she unduly——" He stopped.

"I don't think that," said his father, whose nature was nobler than his son's.

"Don't think what?"

"That she would have—that it is a case of undue influence. No, to my mind the question is the—the invalid's condition at the time she wrote."

"My dear father, consult an expert if you like, but I don't admit it is my mother's writing."

"Why, you just said it was!" cried Dolly.

"Never mind if I did," he blazed out; "and hold your tongue."

The poor little wife coloured at this, and, drawing her handkerchief from her pocket, shed a few tears. No one noticed her. Evie was scowling like an angry boy. The two men were gradually assuming the manner of the committee-room. They were both at their best when serving on committees. They did not make the mistake of handling human affairs in the bulk, but disposed of them item by item, sharply. Caligraphy was the item before them now, and on it they turned their well-trained brains. Charles, after a little demur, accepted the writing as genuine, and they passed on to the next point. It is the best—perhaps the only—way of dodging emotion. They were the average human article, and had they considered the note as a whole it would have driven them miserable or mad. Considered item by item, the emotional content was minimized, and all went forward smoothly. The clock ticked, the coals blazed higher, and contended with the white radiance that poured in through the windows. Unnoticed, the sun occupied his sky, and the shadows of the tree stems, extraordinarily solid, fell like trenches of purple across the frosted lawn. It was a glorious winter morning. Evie's fox terrier, who had passed for white, was only a dirty grey dog now, so intense was the purity that surrounded him. He was discredited, but the blackbirds that he was chasing glowed with Arabian darkness, for all the conventional colouring of life had been altered. Inside, the clock struck ten with a rich and confident note. Other clocks confirmed it, and the discussion moved towards its close.

To follow it is unnecessary. It is rather a moment when the commentator should step forward. Ought the Wilcoxes to have offered their home to Margaret? I think not. The appeal was too flimsy. It was not legal; it had been written in illness, and under the spell of a sudden friendship; it was contrary to the dead woman's intentions in the past, contrary to her very nature, so far as that nature was understood by them. To them Howards End was a house: they could not know that to her it had been a spirit, for which she sought a spiritual heir. And—pushing one step farther in these mists—may they not have decided even better than they supposed? Is it credible that the possessions of the spirit can be bequeathed at all? Has the soul offspring? A wych-elm tree, a vine, a wisp of hay with dew on it—can passion for such things be transmitted where there is no bond of blood? No; the Wilcoxes are not to be blamed. The problem is too terrific, and they could not even perceive a problem. No; it is natural and fitting that after due debate they should tear the note up and throw it on to their dining-room fire. The practical moralist may acquit them absolutely. He who strives to look deeper may acquit them—almost. For one hard fact remains. They did neglect a personal appeal. The woman who had died did say to them, "Do this," and they answered, "We will not."

The incident made a most painful impression on them. Grief mounted into the brain and worked there disquietingly. Yesterday they had lamented: "She was a dear mother, a true wife: in our absence she neglected her health and died." To-day they thought: "She was not as true, as dear, as we supposed." The desire for a more inward light had found expression at last, the unseen had impacted on the seen, and all that they could say was "Treachery." Mrs. Wilcox had been treacherous to the family, to the laws of property, to her own written word. How did she expect Howards End to be conveyed to Miss Schlegel? Was her husband, to whom it legally belonged, to make it over to her as a free gift? Was the said Miss Schlegel to have a life interest in it, or to own it absolutely? Was there to be no compensation for the garage and other improvements that they had made under the assumption that all would be theirs some day? Treacherous! treacherous and absurd! When we think the dead both treacherous and absurd, we have gone far towards reconciling ourselves to their departure. That note, scribbled in pencil, sent through the matron, was unbusinesslike as well as cruel, and decreased at once the value of the woman who had written it.

"Ah, well!" said Mr. Wilcox, rising from the table. "I shouldn't have thought it possible."

"Mother couldn't have meant it," said Evie, still frowning.

"No, my girl, of course not."

"Mother believed so in ancestors too—it isn't like her to leave anything to an outsider, who'd never appreciate."

"The whole thing is unlike her," he announced. "If Miss Schlegel had been poor, if she had wanted a house, I could understand it a little. But she has a house of her own. Why should she want another? She wouldn't have any use for Howards End."

"That time may prove," murmured Charles.

"How?" asked his sister.

"Presumably she knows—mother will have told her. She got twice or three times into the nursing home. Presumably she is awaiting developments."

"What a horrid woman!" And Dolly, who had recovered, cried, "Why, she may be coming down to turn us out now!"

Charles put her right. "I wish she would," he said ominously. "I could then deal with her."

"So could I," echoed his father, who was feeling rather in the cold. Charles had been kind in undertaking the funeral arrangements and in telling him to eat his breakfast, but the boy as he grew up was a little dictatorial, and assumed the post of chairman too readily. "I could deal with her, if she comes, but she won't come. You're all a bit hard on Miss Schlegel."

"That Paul business was pretty scandalous, though."

"I want no more of the Paul business, Charles, as I said at the time, and besides, it is quite apart from this business. Margaret Schlegel has been officious and tiresome during this terrible week, and we have all suffered under her, but upon my soul she's honest. She's *not* in collusion with the matron. I'm absolutely certain of it.

Nor was she with the doctor, I'm equally certain of that. She did not hide anything from us, for up to that very afternoon she was as ignorant as we are. She, like ourselves, was a dupe——" He stopped for a moment. "You see, Charles, in her terrible pain your poor mother put us all in false positions. Paul would not have left England, you would not have gone to Italy, nor Evie and I into Yorkshire, if only we had known. Well, Miss Schlegel's position has been equally false. Take all in all, she has not come out of it badly."

Evie said: "But those chrysanthemums——"

"Or coming down to the funeral at all——" echoed Dolly.

"Why shouldn't she come down? She had the right to, and she stood far back among the Hilton women. The flowers—certainly we should not have sent such flowers, but they may have seemed the right thing to her, Evie, and for all you know they may be the custom in Germany."

"Oh, I forget she isn't really English," cried Evie. "That would explain a lot."

"She's a cosmopolitan," said Charles, looking at his watch. "I admit I'm rather down on cosmopolitans. My fault, doubtless. I cannot stand them, and a German cosmopolitan is the limit. I think that's about all, isn't it? I want to run down and see Chalkeley. A bicycle will do. And, by the way, I wish you'd speak to Crane some time. I'm certain he's had my new car out."

"Has he done it any harm?"

"No."

"In that case I shall let it pass. It's not worth while having a row."

Charles and his father sometimes disagreed. But they always parted with an increased regard for one another, and each desired no doughtier comrade when it was necessary to voyage for a little past the emotions. So the sailors of Ulysses voyaged past the Sirens, having first stopped one another's ears with wool.[6]

## CHAPTER XII

CHARLES need not have been anxious. Miss Schlegel had never heard of his mother's strange request. She was to hear of it in after years, when she had built up her life differently, and it was to fit into position as the headstone of the corner. Her mind was bent on other ques-

---

[6]In Book 12 of Homer's *Odyssey*, Odysseus (or Ulysses) has his crew members' ears plugged with wool to protect them from the Sirens' fatally alluring song.

tions now, and by her also it would have been rejected as the fantasy of an invalid.

She was parting from these Wilcoxes for the second time. Paul and his mother, ripple and great wave, had flowed into her life and ebbed out of it for ever. The ripple had left no traces behind: the wave had strewn at her feet fragments torn from the unknown. A curious seeker, she stood for a while at the verge of the sea that tells so little, but tells a little, and watched the outgoing of this last tremendous tide. Her friend had vanished in agony, but not, she believed, in degradation. Her withdrawal had hinted at other things besides disease and pain. Some leave our life with tears, others with an insane frigidity; Mrs. Wilcox had taken the middle course, which only rarer natures can pursue. She had kept proportion. She had told a little of her grim secret to her friends, but not too much; she had shut up her heart—almost, but not entirely. It is thus, if there is any rule, that we ought to die—neither as victim nor as fanatic, but as the seafarer who can greet with an equal eye the deep that he is entering, and the shore that he must leave.

The last word—whatever it would be—had certainly not been said in Hilton churchyard. She had not died there. A funeral is not death, any more than baptism is birth or marriage union. All three are the clumsy devices, coming now too late, now too early, by which Society would register the quick motions of man. In Margaret's eyes Mrs. Wilcox had escaped registration. She had gone out of life vividly, her own way, and no dust was so truly dust as the contents of that heavy coffin, lowered with ceremonial until it rested on the dust of the earth, no flowers so utterly wasted as the chrysanthemums that the frost must have withered before morning. Margaret had once said she "loved superstition." It was not true. Few women had tried more earnestly to pierce the accretions in which body and soul are enwrapped. The death of Mrs. Wilcox had helped her in her work. She saw a little more clearly than hitherto what a human being is, and to what he may aspire. Truer relationships gleamed. Perhaps the last word would be hope—hope even on this side of the grave.

Meanwhile, she could take an interest in the survivors. In spite of her Christmas duties, in spite of her brother, the Wilcoxes continued to play a considerable part in her thoughts. She had seen so much of them in the final week. They were not "her sort," they were often suspicious and stupid, and deficient where she excelled; but collision with them stimulated her, and she felt an interest that verged into liking, even for Charles. She desired to protect them, and often felt that they could protect her, excelling where she was deficient. Once past the rocks of emotion, they knew so well what to do, whom to send for; their hands were on all the ropes, they had grit as well as grittiness, and she valued grit enormously. They led a life that she could not attain to—the outer life of "telegrams and anger," which had detonated when Helen and Paul had touched in June, and had detonated again the other week. To Margaret this life was to remain a real force. She could not despise it, as Helen and Tibby affected to do. It fostered such virtues as neatness, decision, and obedience, virtues of the second rank, no doubt, but they have formed our civilization. They form character, too; Margaret could not doubt it: they keep the soul from becoming sloppy. How dare Schlegels despise Wilcoxes, when it takes all sorts to make a world?

"Don't brood too much," she wrote to Helen, "on the superiority of the unseen to the seen. It's true, but to brood on it is medieval. Our business is not to contrast the two, but to reconcile them."

Helen replied that she had no intention of brooding on such a dull subject. What did her sister take her for? The weather was magnificent. She and the Mosebachs had gone tobogganing on the only hill that Pomerania boasted. It was fun, but overcrowded, for the rest of Pomerania had gone there too. Helen loved the country, and her letter glowed with physical exercise and poetry. She spoke of the scenery, quiet, yet august; of the snow-clad fields, with their scampering herds of deer; of the river and its quaint entrance into the Baltic Sea; of the Oderberge,[1] only three hundred feet high, from which one slid all too quickly back into the Pomeranian plains, and yet these Oderberge were real mountains, with pine-forests, streams, and views complete. "It isn't size that counts so much as the way things are arranged." In another paragraph she referred to Mrs. Wilcox sympathetically, but the news had not bitten into her. She had not realized the accessories of death, which are in a sense more memorable than death itself. The atmosphere of precautions and recriminations, and in the midst a human body growing more vivid because it was in pain; the end of that body in Hilton churchyard; the survival of something that suggested hope, vivid in its turn against life's workaday cheerfulness; —all these were lost to Helen, who only felt that a pleasant lady could now be pleasant no longer. She returned to Wickham Place full of her own affairs—she had had another proposal—and Margaret, after a moment's hesitation, was content that this should be so.

The proposal had not been a serious matter. It was the work of Fräulein Mosebach, who had conceived the large and patriotic notion

[1]Mountains by the Oder River.

of winning back her cousins to the Fatherland by matrimony. England had played Paul Wilcox, and lost; Germany played Herr Förstmeister someone[2]—Helen could not remember his name. Herr Förstmeister lived in a wood, and, standing on the summit of the Oderberge, he had pointed out his house to Helen, or rather, had pointed out the wedge of pines in which it lay. She had exclaimed, "Oh, how lovely! That's the place for me!" and in the evening Frieda appeared in her bedroom. "I have a message, dear Helen," etc., and so she had, but had been very nice when Helen laughed; quite understood—a forest too solitary and damp—quite agreed, but Herr Förstmeister believed he had assurance to the contrary. Germany had lost, but with good-humour; holding the manhood of the world, she felt bound to win. "And there will even be someone for Tibby," concluded Helen. "There now, Tibby, think of that; Frieda is saving up a little girl for you, in pig-tails and white worsted stockings, but the feet of the stockings are pink, as if the little girl had trodden in strawberries. I've talked too much. My head aches. Now you talk."

Tibby consented to talk. He too was full of his own affairs, for he had just been up to try for a scholarship at Oxford. The men were down,[3] and the candidates had been housed in various colleges, and had dined in hall. Tibby was sensitive to beauty, the experience was new, and he gave a description of his visit that was almost glowing. The august and mellow University, soaked with the richness of the western counties that it has served for a thousand years, appealed at once to the boy's taste: it was the kind of thing he could understand, and he understood it all the better because it was empty. Oxford is— Oxford: not a mere receptacle for youth, like Cambridge. Perhaps it wants its inmates to love it rather than to love one another: such at all events was to be its effect on Tibby. His sisters sent him there that he might make friends, for they knew that his education had been cranky, and had severed him from other boys and men. He made no friends. His Oxford remained Oxford empty, and he took into life with him, not the memory of a radiance, but the memory of a colour scheme.

It pleased Margaret to hear her brother and sister talking. They did not get on overwell as a rule. For a few moments she listened to them, feeling elderly and benign. Then something occurred to her, and she interrupted:

"Helen, I told you about poor Mrs. Wilcox; that sad business?"

---

[2]A *Förstmeister* is a forester; *Herr* means Mister.
[3]Students were away on vacation.

"Yes."

"I have had a correspondence with her son. He was winding up the estate, and wrote to ask me whether his mother had wanted me to have anything. I thought it good of him, considering I knew her for so little. I said that she had once spoken of giving me a Christmas present, but we both forgot about it afterwards."

"I hope Charles took the hint."

"Yes—that is to say, her husband wrote later on, and thanked me for being a little kind to her, and actually gave me her silver vinaigrette.[4] Don't you think that is extraordinarily generous? It has made me like him very much. He hopes that this will not be the end of our acquaintance, but that you and I will go and stop with Evie some time in the future. I like Mr. Wilcox. He is taking up his work—rubber—it is a big business. I gather he is launching out rather. Charles is in it, too. Charles is married—a pretty little creature, but she doesn't seem wise. They took on the flat, but now they have gone off to a house of their own."

Helen, after a decent pause, continued her account of Stettin. How quickly a situation changes! In June she had been in a crisis; even in November she could blush and be unnatural; now it was January, and the whole affair lay forgotten. Looking back on the past six months, Margaret realized the chaotic nature of our daily life, and its difference from the orderly sequence that has been fabricated by historians. Actual life is full of false clues and sign-posts that lead nowhere. With infinite effort we nerve ourselves for a crisis that never comes. The most successful career must show a waste of strength that might have removed mountains, and the most unsuccessful is not that of the man who is taken unprepared, but of him who has prepared and is never taken. On a tragedy of that kind our national morality is duly silent. It assumes that preparation against danger is in itself a good, and that men, like nations, are the better for staggering through life fully armed. The tragedy of preparedness has scarcely been handled, save by the Greeks. Life is indeed dangerous, but not in the way morality would have us believe. It is indeed unmanageable, but the essence of it is not a battle. It is unmanageable because it is a romance, and its essence is romantic beauty.

Margaret hoped that for the future she would be less cautious, not more cautious, than she had been in the past.

---

[4]Small container for vinegar or smelling salts, held to the nose to block odors or revive the fainting.

# CHAPTER XIII

OVER two years passed, and the Schlegel household continued to lead its life of cultured, but not ignoble, ease, still swimming gracefully on the grey tides of London. Concerts and plays swept past them, money had been spent and renewed, reputations won and lost, and the city herself, emblematic of their lives, rose and fell in a continual flux, while her shallows washed more widely against the hills of Surrey and over the fields of Hertfordshire. This famous building had arisen, that was doomed. To-day Whitehall had been transformed: it would be the turn of Regent Street to-morrow. And month by month the roads smelt more strongly of petrol, and were more difficult to cross, and human beings heard each other speak with greater difficulty, breathed less of the air, and saw less of the sky. Nature withdrew: the leaves were falling by midsummer; the sun shone through dirt with an admired obscurity.

To speak against London is no longer fashionable. The Earth as an artistic cult has had its day, and the literature of the near future will probably ignore the country and seek inspiration from the town. One can understand the reaction. Of Pan and the elemental forces, the public has heard a little too much—they seem Victorian, while London is Georgian—and those who care for the earth with sincerity may wait long ere the pendulum swings back to her again.[1] Certainly London fascinates. One visualizes it as a tract of quivering grey, intelligent without purpose, and excitable without love; as a spirit that has altered before it can be chronicled; as a heart that certainly beats, but with no pulsation of humanity. It lies beyond everything: Nature, with all her cruelty, comes nearer to us than do these crowds of men. A friend explains himself: the earth is explicable—from her we came, and we must return to her. But who can explain Westminster Bridge Road or Liverpool Street in the morning—the city inhaling—or the same thoroughfares in the evening—the city exhaling her exhausted air? We reach in desperation beyond the fog, beyond the very stars, the voids of the universe are ransacked to justify the monster, and stamped with a human face. London is religion's opportunity—not the decorous religion of theologians, but anthropomorphic, crude. Yes, the continuous flow would be tolerable if a man of our own sort—not anyone pompous or tearful—were caring for us up in the sky.

---

[1]Pan was a goat-bodied woodland god in Greek mythology. "Georgian" refers to the new era of George V, whose reign began in 1910.

The Londoner seldom understands his city until it sweeps him, too, away from his moorings, and Margaret's eyes were not opened until the lease of Wickham Place expired. She had always known that it must expire, but the knowledge only became vivid about nine months before the event. Then the house was suddenly ringed with pathos. It had seen so much happiness. Why had it to be swept away? In the streets of the city she noted for the first time the architecture of hurry, and heard the language of hurry on the mouths of its inhabitants—clipped words, formless sentences, potted expressions of approval or disgust. Month by month things were stepping livelier, but to what goal? The population still rose, but what was the quality of the men born? The particular millionaire who owned the freehold of Wickham Place, and desired to erect Babylonian flats upon it—what right had he to stir so large a portion of the quivering jelly? He was not a fool—she had heard him expose Socialism—but true insight began just where his intelligence ended, and one gathered that this was the case with most millionaires. What right had such men—— But Margaret checked herself. That way lies madness. Thank goodness she, too, had some money, and could purchase a new home.

Tibby, now in his second year at Oxford, was down for the Easter vacation, and Margaret took the opportunity of having a serious talk with him. Did he at all know where he wanted to live? Tibby didn't know that he did know. Did he at all know what he wanted to do? He was equally uncertain, but when pressed remarked that he should prefer to be quite free of any profession. Margaret was not shocked, but went on sewing for a few minutes before she replied:

"I was thinking of Mr. Vyse. He never strikes me as particularly happy."

"Ye-es," said Tibby, and then held his mouth open in a curious quiver, as if he, too, had thought of Mr. Vyse, had seen round, through, over, and beyond Mr. Vyse, had weighed Mr. Vyse, grouped him, and finally dismissed him as having no possible bearing on the subject under discussion. That bleat of Tibby's infuriated Helen. But Helen was now down in the dining-room preparing a speech about political economy. At times her voice could be heard declaiming through the floor.

"But Mr. Vyse is rather a wretched, weedy man, don't you think? Then there's Guy. That was a pitiful business. Besides"—shifting to the general—"everyone is the better for some regular work."

Groans.

"I shall stick to it," she continued, smiling. "I am not saying it to educate you; it is what I really think. I believe that in the last century men have developed the desire for work, and they must not starve it. It's a new desire. It goes with a great deal that's bad, but in itself it's good, and I hope that for women, too, 'not to work' will soon become as shocking as 'not to be married' was a hundred years ago."

"I have no experience of this profound desire to which you allude," enunciated Tibby.

"Then we'll leave the subject till you do. I'm not going to rattle you round. Take your time. Only do think over the lives of the men you like most, and see how they've arranged them."

"I like Guy and Mr. Vyse most," said Tibby faintly, and leant so far back in his chair that he extended in a horizontal line from knees to throat.

"And don't think I'm not serious because I don't use the traditional arguments—making money, a sphere awaiting you, and so on—all of which are, for various reasons, cant." She sewed on. "I'm only your sister. I haven't any authority over you, and I don't want to have any. Just to put before you what I think the truth. You see"—she shook off the pince-nez to which she had recently taken—"in a few years we shall be the same age practically, and I shall want you to help me. Men are so much nicer than women."

"Labouring under such a delusion, why do you not marry?"

"I sometimes jolly well think I would if I got the chance."

"Has no body arst you?"

"Only ninnies."

"Do people ask Helen?"

"Plentifully."

"Tell me about them."

"No."

"Tell me about your ninnies, then."

"They were men who had nothing better to do," said his sister, feeling that she was entitled to score this point. "So take warning: you must work, or else you must pretend to work, which is what I do. Work, work, work if you'd save your soul and your body. It is honestly a necessity, dear boy. Look at the Wilcoxes, look at Mr. Pembroke. With all their defects of temper and understanding, such men give me more pleasure than many who are better equipped, and I think it is because they have worked regularly and honestly."

"Spare me the Wilcoxes," he moaned.

"I shall not. They are the right sort."

"Oh, goodness me, Meg!" he protested, suddenly sitting up, alert and angry. Tibby, for all his defects, had a genuine personality.

"Well, they're as near the right sort as you can imagine."

"No, no—oh, no!"

"I was thinking of the younger son, whom I once classed as a ninny, but who came back so ill from Nigeria. He's gone out there again, Evie Wilcox tells me—out to his duty."

'Duty' always elicited a groan.

"He doesn't want the money, it is work he wants, though it is beastly work—dull country, dishonest natives, an eternal fidget over fresh water and food. A nation who can produce men of that sort may well be proud. No wonder England has become an Empire."

"*Empire!*"

"I can't bother over results," said Margaret, a little sadly. "They are too difficult for me. I can only look at the men. An Empire bores me, so far, but I can appreciate the heroism that builds it up. London bores me, but what thousands of splendid people are labouring to make London——"

"What it is," he sneered.

"What it is, worse luck. I want activity without civilization. How paradoxical! Yet I expect that is what we shall find in heaven."

"And I," said Tibby, "want civilization without activity, which, I expect, is what we shall find in the other place."

"You needn't go as far as the other place, Tibbikins, if you want that. You can find it at Oxford."

"Stupid——"

"If I'm stupid, get me back to the house-hunting. I'll even live in Oxford if you like—North Oxford. I'll live anywhere except Bournemouth, Torquay, and Cheltenham. Oh yes, or Ilfracombe and Swanage and Tunbridge Wells and Surbiton and Bedford. There on no account."

"London, then."

"I agree, but Helen rather wants to get away from London. However, there's no reason we shouldn't have a house in the country and also a flat in town, provided we all stick together and contribute. Though of course—— Oh, how one does maunder on, and to think, to think of the people who are really poor. How do they live? Not to move about the world would kill me."

As she spoke, the door was flung open, and Helen burst in in a state of extreme excitement.

"Oh, my dears, what do you think? You'll never guess. A woman's been here asking me for her husband. Her *what?*" (Helen was fond of supplying her own surprise.) "Yes, for her husband, and it really is so."

"Not anything to do with Bracknell?" cried Margaret, who had lately taken on an unemployed of that name to clean the knives and boots.

"I offered Bracknell, and he was rejected. So was Tibby. (Cheer up, Tibby!) It's no one we know. I said, 'Hunt, my good woman; have a good look round, hunt under the tables, poke up the chimney, shake out the antimacassars.[2] Husband? husband?' Oh, and she so magnificently dressed and tinkling like a chandelier."

"Now, Helen, what did happen really?"

"What I say. I was, as it were, orating my speech. Annie opens the door like a fool, and shows a female straight in on me, with my mouth open. Then we began—very civilly. 'I want my husband, what I have reason to believe is here.' No—how unjust one is. She said 'whom,' not 'what.' She got it perfectly. So I said, 'Name, please?' and she said, 'Lan, Miss,' and there we were."

"Lan?"

"Lan or Len. We were not nice about our vowels. Lanoline."

"But what an extraordinary——"

"I said, 'My good Mrs. Lanoline, we have some grave misunderstanding here. Beautiful as I am, my modesty is even more remarkable than my beauty, and never, never has Mr. Lanoline rested his eyes on mine.'"

"I hope you were pleased," said Tibby.

"Of course," Helen squeaked. "A perfectly delightful experience. Oh, Mrs. Lanoline's a dear—she asked for a husband as if he was an umbrella. She mislaid him Saturday afternoon—and for a long time suffered no inconvenience. But all night, and all this morning her apprehensions grew. Breakfast didn't seem the same—no, no more did lunch, and so she strolled up to 2, Wickham Place as being the most likely place for the missing article."

"But how on earth——"

"Don't begin how on earthing. 'I know what I know,' she kept repeating, not uncivilly, but with extreme gloom. In vain I asked her what she did know. Some knew what others knew, and others didn't, and if they didn't, then others again had better be careful. Oh dear, she was incompetent! She had a face like a silkworm, and the dining-room reeks of orris-root.[3] We chatted pleasantly a little about husbands, and I wondered where hers was too, and advised her to go to

---

[2]Decorative protective coverings for the backs and arms of furniture. (Macassar was a hair oil used mainly by men.)

[3]Ingredient in perfume.

the police. She thanked me. We agreed that Mr. Lanoline's a notty, notty man, and hasn't no business to go on the lardy-da. But I think she suspected me up to the last. Bags I[4] writing to Aunt Juley about this. Now, Meg, remember—bags I."

"Bag it by all means," murmured Margaret, putting down her work. "I'm not sure that this is so funny, Helen. It means some horrible volcano smoking somewhere, doesn't it?"

"I don't think so—she doesn't really mind. The admirable creature isn't capable of tragedy."

"Her husband may be, though," said Margaret, moving to the window.

"Oh no, not likely. No one capable of tragedy could have married Mrs. Lanoline."

"Was she pretty?"

"Her figure may have been good once."

The flats, their only outlook, hung like an ornate curtain between Margaret and the welter of London. Her thoughts turned sadly to house-hunting. Wickham Place had been so safe. She feared, fantastically, that her own little flock might be moving into turmoil and squalor, into nearer contact with such episodes as these.

"Tibby and I have again been wondering where we'll live next September," she said at last.

"Tibby had better first wonder what he'll do," retorted Helen; and that topic was resumed, but with acrimony. Then tea came, and after tea Helen went on preparing her speech, and Margaret prepared one, too, for they were going out to a discussion society on the morrow. But her thoughts were poisoned. Mrs. Lanoline had risen out of the abyss, like a faint smell, a goblin footfall, telling of a life where love and hatred had both decayed.

## CHAPTER XIV

THE mystery, like so many mysteries, was explained. Next day, just as they were dressed to go out to dinner, a Mr. Bast called. He was a clerk in the employment of the Porphyrion Fire Insurance Company.[1] Thus much from his card. He had come "about the lady yesterday." Thus much from Annie, who had shown him into the dining-room.

---

[4] I have the first claim on.

---

[1] Named for Porphyrion, a giant killed by a thunderbolt from Zeus and an arrow from Zeus's son Heracles after he attempted to rape Zeus's wife Hera.

"Cheers, children!" cried Helen. "It's Mrs. Lanoline."

Tibby was interested. The three hurried downstairs, to find, not the gay dog they expected, but a young man, colourless, toneless, who had already the mournful eyes above a drooping moustache that are so common in London, and that haunt some streets of the city like accusing presences. One guessed him as the third generation, grandson to the shepherd or ploughboy whom civilization had sucked into the town; as one of the thousands who have lost the life of the body and failed to reach the life of the spirit. Hints of robustness survived in him, more than a hint of primitive good looks, and Margaret, noting the spine that might have been straight, and the chest that might have broadened, wondered whether it paid to give up the glory of the animal for a tail coat and a couple of ideas. Culture had worked in her own case, but during the last few weeks she had doubted whether it humanized the majority, so wide and so widening is the gulf that stretches between the natural and the philosophic man, so many the good chaps who are wrecked in trying to cross it. She knew this type very well—the vague aspirations, the mental dishonesty, the familiarity with the outsides of books. She knew the very tones in which he would address her. She was only unprepared for an example of her own visiting-card.

"You wouldn't remember giving me this, Miss Schlegel?" said he, uneasily familiar.

"No; I can't say I do."

"Well, that was how it happened, you see."

"Where did we meet, Mr. Bast? For the minute I don't remember."

"It was a concert at the Queen's Hall. I think you will recollect," he added pretentiously, "when I tell you that it included a performance of the Fifth Symphony of Beethoven."

"We hear the Fifth practically every time it's done, so I'm not sure—do you remember, Helen?"

"Was it the time the sandy cat walked round the balustrade?"

He thought not.

"Then I don't remember. That's the only Beethoven I ever remember specially."

"And you, if I may say so, took away my umbrella, inadvertently of course."

"Likely enough," Helen laughed, "for I steal umbrellas even oftener than I hear Beethoven. Did you get it back?"

"Yes, thank you, Miss Schlegel."

"The mistake arose out of my card, did it?" interposed Margaret.

"Yes, the mistake arose—it was a mistake."

"The lady who called here yesterday thought that you were calling too, and that she could find you?" she continued, pushing him forward, for, though he had promised an explanation, he seemed unable to give one.

"That's so, calling too—a mistake."

"Then why——?" began Helen, but Margaret laid a hand on her arm.

"I said to my wife," he continued more rapidly—"I said to Mrs. Bast, 'I have to pay a call on some friends,' and Mrs. Bast said to me, 'Do go.' While I was gone, however, she wanted me on important business, and thought I had come here, owing to the card, and so came after me, and I beg to tender my apologies, and hers as well, for any inconvenience we may have inadvertently caused you."

"No inconvenience," said Helen; "but I still don't understand."

An air of evasion characterized Mr. Bast. He explained again, but was obviously lying, and Helen didn't see why he should get off. She had the cruelty of youth. Neglecting her sister's pressure, she said, "I still don't understand. When did you say you paid this call?"

"Call? What call?" said he, staring as if her question had been a foolish one, a favourite device of those in mid-stream.

"This afternoon call."

"In the afternoon, of course!" he replied, and looked at Tibby to see how the repartee went. But Tibby, himself a repartee, was unsympathetic, and said, "Saturday afternoon or Sunday afternoon?"

"S—Saturday."

"Really!" said Helen; "and you were still calling on Sunday, when your wife came here. A long visit."

"I don't call that fair," said Mr. Bast, going scarlet and handsome. There was fight in his eyes. "I know what you mean, and it isn't so."

"Oh, don't let us mind," said Margaret, distressed again by odours from the abyss.

"It was something else," he asserted, his elaborate manner breaking down. "I was somewhere else to what you think, so there!"

"It was good of you to come and explain," she said. "The rest is naturally no concern of ours."

"Yes, but I want—I wanted—have you ever read 'The Ordeal of Richard Feverel'?"[2]

---

[2]Novel by George Meredith (1859); see pp. 304–07. The next works Leonard mentions are a novel by Robert Louis Stevenson (1885) and an anthology of writing on country travel (1899).

Margaret nodded.

"It's a beautiful book. I wanted to get back to the Earth, don't you see, like Richard does in the end. Or have you ever read Stevenson's 'Prince Otto'?"

Helen and Tibby groaned gently.

"That's another beautiful book. You get back to the Earth in that. I wanted——" He mouthed affectedly. Then through the mists of his culture came a hard fact, hard as a pebble. "I walked all the Saturday night," said Leonard. "I walked." A thrill of approval ran through the sisters. But culture closed in again. He asked whether they had ever read E. V. Lucas's "Open Road."

Said Helen, "No doubt it's another beautiful book, but I'd rather hear about your road."

"Oh, I walked."

"How far?"

"I don't know, nor for how long. It got too dark to see my watch."

"Were you walking alone, may I ask?"

"Yes," he said, straightening himself; "but we'd been talking it over at the office. There's been a lot of talk at the office lately about these things. The fellows there said one steers by the Pole Star, and I looked it up in the celestial atlas, but once out of doors everything gets so mixed——"

"Don't talk to me about the Pole Star," interrupted Helen, who was becoming interested. "I know its little ways. It goes round and round, and you go round after it."

"Well, I lost it entirely. First of all the street lamps, then the trees, and towards morning it got cloudy."

Tibby, who preferred his comedy undiluted, slipped from the room. He knew that this fellow would never attain to poetry, and did not want to hear him trying. Margaret and Helen remained. Their brother influenced them more than they knew: in his absence they were stirred to enthusiasm more easily.

"Where did you start from?" cried Margaret. "Do tell us more."

"I took the Underground to Wimbledon. As I came out of the office I said to myself, 'I must have a walk once in a way. If I don't take this walk now, I shall never take it.' I had a bit of dinner at Wimbledon, and then——"

"But not good country there, is it?"

"It was gas-lamps for hours. Still, I had all the night, and being out was the great thing. I did get into woods, too, presently."

"Yes, go on," said Helen.

"You've no idea how difficult uneven ground is when it's dark."

"Did you actually go off the roads?"

"Oh yes. I always meant to go off the roads, but the worst of it is that it's more difficult to find one's way."

"Mr. Bast, you're a born adventurer," laughed Margaret. "No professional athlete would have attempted what you've done. It's a wonder your walk didn't end in a broken neck. Whatever did your wife say?"

"Professional athletes never move without lanterns and compasses," said Helen. "Besides, they can't walk. It tires them. Go on."

"I felt like R. L. S. You probably remember how in 'Virginibus——'"[3]

"Yes, but the wood. This 'ere wood. How did you get out of it?"

"I managed one wood, and found a road the other side which went a good bit uphill. I rather fancy it was those North Downs, for the road went off into grass, and I got into another wood. That was awful, with gorse bushes. I did wish I'd never come, but suddenly it got light—just while I seemed going under one tree. Then I found a road down to a station, and took the first train I could back to London."

"But was the dawn wonderful?" asked Helen.

With unforgettable sincerity he replied, "No." The word flew again like a pebble from the sling. Down toppled all that had seemed ignoble or literary in his talk, down toppled tiresome R. L. S. and the "love of the earth" and his silk top-hat. In the presence of these women Leonard had arrived, and he spoke with a flow, an exultation, that he had seldom known.

"The dawn was only grey, it was nothing to mention——"

"Just a grey evening turned upside down. I know."

"—and I was too tired to lift up my head to look at it, and so cold too. I'm glad I did it, and yet at the time it bored me more than I can say. And besides—you can believe me or not as you choose—I was very hungry. That dinner at Wimbledon—I meant it to last me all night like other dinners. I never thought that walking would make such a difference. Why, when you're walking you want, as it were, a breakfast and luncheon and tea during the night as well, and I'd nothing but a packet of Woodbines.[4] Lord, I did feel bad! Looking back,

---

[3] *Virginibus Puerisque and Other Papers*, a collection of essays by Stevenson (1881); see pp. 308–12.

[4] Cigarettes.

it wasn't what you may call enjoyment. It was more a case of sticking to it. I did stick. I—I was determined. Oh, hang it all! what's the good—I mean, the good of living in a room for ever? There one goes on day after day, same old game, same up and down to town, until you forget there is any other game. You ought to see once in a way what's going on outside, if it's only nothing particular after all."

"I should just think you ought," said Helen, sitting on the edge of the table.

The sound of a lady's voice recalled him from sincerity, and he said: "Curious it should all come about from reading something of Richard Jefferies."[5]

"Excuse me, Mr. Bast, but you're wrong there. It didn't. It came from something far greater."

But she could not stop him. Borrow was imminent after Jefferies—Borrow, Thoreau, and sorrow.[6] R. L. S. brought up the rear, and the outburst ended in a swamp of books. No disrespect to these great names. The fault is ours, not theirs. They mean us to use them for sign-posts, and are not to blame if, in our weakness, we mistake the sign-post for the destination. And Leonard had reached the destination. He had visited the county of Surrey when darkness covered its amenities, and its cosy villas had re-entered ancient night. Every twelve hours this miracle happens, but he had troubled to go and see for himself. Within his cramped little mind dwelt something that was greater than Jefferies' books—the spirit that led Jefferies to write them; and his dawn, though revealing nothing but monotones, was part of the eternal sunrise that shows George Borrow Stonehenge.

"Then you don't think I was foolish?" he asked, becoming again the naïve and sweet-tempered boy for whom Nature had intended him.

"Heavens, no!" replied Margaret.

"Heaven help us if we do!" replied Helen.

"I'm very glad you say that. Now, my wife would never understand—not if I explained for days."

"No, it wasn't foolish!" cried Helen, her eyes aflame. "You've pushed back the boundaries; I think it splendid of you."

"You've not been content to dream as we have——"

"Though we have walked, too——"

---

[5] 19th-c English writer, known for his treatments of natural history and rural life; see pp. 312–15.

[6] 19th-c English travel writer George Henry Borrow; American Henry David Thoreau, most famous for *Walden* (1854). In British "received" pronunciation, "Thoreau" would take stress on the first syllable and thus rhyme with "Borrow" and "sorrow."

"I must show you a picture upstairs——"

Here the door-bell rang. The hansom had come to take them to their evening party.

"Oh, bother, not to say dash—I had forgotten we were dining out; but do, do, come round again and have a talk."

"Yes, you must—do," echoed Margaret.

Leonard, with extreme sentiment, replied: "No, I shall not. It's better like this."

"Why better?" asked Margaret.

"No, it is better not to risk a second interview. I shall always look back on this talk with you as one of the finest things in my life. Really. I mean this. We can never repeat. It has done me real good, and there we had better leave it."

"That's rather a sad view of life, surely."

"Things so often get spoiled."

"I know," flashed Helen, "but people don't."

He could not understand this. He continued in a vein which mingled true imagination and false. What he said wasn't wrong, but it wasn't right, and a false note jarred. One little twist, they felt, and the instrument might be in tune. One little strain, and it might be silent for ever. He thanked the ladies very much, but he would not call again. There was a moment's awkwardness, and then Helen said: "Go, then; perhaps you know best; but never forget you're better than Jefferies." And he went. Their hansom caught him up at the corner, passed with a waving of hands, and vanished with its accomplished load into the evening.

London was beginning to illuminate herself against the night. Electric lights sizzled and jagged in the main thoroughfares, gas-lamps in the side streets glimmered a canary gold or green. The sky was a crimson battlefield of spring, but London was not afraid. Her smoke mitigated the splendour, and the clouds down Oxford Street were a delicately painted ceiling, which adorned while it did not distract. She has never known the clear-cut armies of the purer air. Leonard hurried through her tinted wonders, very much part of the picture. His was a grey life, and to brighten it he had ruled off a few corners for romance. The Miss Schlegels—or, to speak more accurately, his interview with them—were to fill such a corner, nor was it by any means the first time that he had talked intimately to strangers. The habit was analogous to a debauch, an outlet, though the worst of outlets, for instincts that would not be denied. Terrifying him, it would beat down his suspicions and prudence until he was confiding secrets to people whom he had scarcely seen. It brought him many fears and some pleasant memories. Perhaps the keenest happiness he had ever known was during a railway journey to Cambridge, where a decent-mannered undergraduate had spoken to him. They had got into conversation, and gradually Leonard flung reticence aside, told some of his domestic troubles, and hinted at the rest. The undergraduate, supposing they could start a friendship, asked him to "coffee after hall,"[7] which he accepted, but afterwards grew shy, and took care not to stir from the commercial hotel where he lodged. He did not want Romance to collide with the Porphyrion, still less with Jacky, and people with fuller, happier lives are slow to understand this. To the Schlegels, as to the undergraduate, he was an interesting creature, of whom they wanted to see more. But they to him were denizens of Romance, who must keep to the corner he had assigned them, pictures that must not walk out of their frames.

His behaviour over Margaret's visiting-card had been typical. His had scarcely been a tragic marriage. Where there is no money and no inclination to violence tragedy cannot be generated. He could not leave his wife, and he did not want to hit her. Petulance and squalor was enough. Here "that card" had come in. Leonard, though furtive, was untidy, and left it lying about. Jacky found it, and then began, "What's that card, eh?" "Yes, don't you wish you knew what that card was?" "Len, who's Miss Schlegel?" etc. Months passed, and the card, now as a joke, now as a grievance, was handed about, getting dirtier and dirtier. It followed them when they moved from Camelia Road to Tulse Hill. It was submitted to third parties. A few inches of pasteboard, it became the battlefield on which the souls of Leonard and his wife contended. Why did he not say, "A lady took my umbrella, another gave me this that I might call for my umbrella"? Because Jacky would have disbelieved him? Partly, but chiefly because he was sentimental. No affection gathered round the card, but it symbolized the life of culture, that Jacky should never spoil. At night he would say to himself, "Well, at all events, she doesn't know about that card. Yah! done her there!"

Poor Jacky! she was not a bad sort, and had a great deal to bear. She drew her own conclusion—she was only capable of drawing one conclusion—and in the fulness of time she acted upon it. All the Friday Leonard had refused to speak to her, and had spent the evening observing the stars. On the Saturday he went up, as usual, to town, but he came not back Saturday night, nor Sunday morning, nor Sunday after-

---

[7]After the undergraduate had dined at his college.

noon. The inconvenience grew intolerable, and though she was now of a retiring habit, and shy of women, she went up to Wickham Place. Leonard returned in her absence. The card, the fatal card, was gone from the pages of Ruskin, and he guessed what had happened.

"Well?" he had exclaimed, greeting her with peals of laughter. "I know where you've been, but you don't know where I've been."

Jacky sighed, said, "Len, I do think you might explain," and resumed domesticity.

Explanations were difficult at this stage, and Leonard was too silly—or it is tempting to write, too sound a chap to attempt them. His reticence was not entirely the shoddy article that a business life promotes, the reticence that pretends that nothing is something, and hides behind the 'Daily Telegraph.' The adventurer, also, is reticent, and it is an adventure for a clerk to walk for a few hours in darkness. You may laugh at him, you who have slept nights out on the veldt, with your rifle beside you and all the atmosphere of adventure pat. And you also may laugh who think adventures silly. But do not be surprised if Leonard is shy whenever he meets you, and if the Schlegels rather than Jacky hear about the dawn.

That the Schlegels had not thought him foolish became a permanent joy. He was at his best when he thought of them. It buoyed him as he journeyed home beneath fading heavens. Somehow the barriers of wealth had fallen, and there had been—he could not phrase it—a general assertion of the wonder of the world. "My conviction," says the mystic, "gains infinitely the moment another soul will believe in it,"[8] and they had agreed that there was something beyond life's daily grey. He took off his top-hat and smoothed it thoughtfully. He had hitherto supposed the unknown to be books, literature, clever conversation, culture. One raised oneself by study, and got upsides with the world. But in that quick interchange a new light dawned. Was that "something" walking in the dark among the surburban hills?

He discovered that he was going bareheaded down Regent Street. London came back with a rush. Few were about at this hour, but all whom he passed looked at him with a hostility that was the more impressive because it was unconscious. He put his hat on. It was too big; his head disappeared like a pudding into a basin, the ears bending outwards at the touch of the curly brim. He wore it a little back-

---

[8]Thus is the 18th-c. German Romantic writer Novalis quoted in Thomas Carlyle's *On Heroes and Hero-Worship and the Heroic in History* (1841). Carlyle's translation of this line—from one of Novalis's famous "fragments"—also supplied the epigraph to Joseph Conrad's *Lord Jim* (1900).

wards, and its effect was greatly to elongate the face and to bring out the distance between the eyes and the moustache. Thus equipped, he escaped criticism. No one felt uneasy as he titupped[9] along the pavements, the heart of a man ticking fast in his chest.

## CHAPTER XV

THE sisters went out to dinner full of their adventure, and when they were both full of the same subject, there were few dinner-parties that could stand up against them. This particular one, which was all ladies, had more kick in it than most, but succumbed after a struggle. Helen at one part of the table, Margaret at the other, would talk of Mr. Bast and of no one else, and somewhere about the entrée their monologues collided, fell ruining, and became common property. Nor was this all. The dinner-party was really an informal discussion club; there was a paper after it, read amid coffee-cups and laughter in the drawing-room, but dealing more or less thoughtfully with some topic of general interest. After the paper came a debate, and in this debate Mr. Bast also figured, appearing now as a bright spot in civilization, now as a dark spot, according to the temperament of the speaker. The subject of the paper had been, "How ought I to dispose of my money?" the reader professing to be a millionaire on the point of death, inclined to bequeath her fortune for the foundation of local art galleries, but open to conviction from other sources. The various parts had been assigned beforehand, and some of the speeches were amusing. The hostess assumed the ungrateful rôle of 'the millionaire's eldest son,' and implored her expiring parent not to dislocate Society by allowing such vast sums to pass out of the family. Money was the fruit of self-denial, and the second generation had a right to profit by the self-denial of the first. What right had 'Mr. Bast' to profit? The National Gallery[1] was good enough for the likes of him. After property had had its say—a saying that is necessarily ungracious—the various philanthropists stepped forward. Something must be done for 'Mr. Bast': his conditions must be improved without impairing his independence; he must have a free library, or free tennis-courts; his rent must be paid in such a way that he did not know it was being paid; it must be made worth his while to join the Territorials;[2] he must be forcibly parted from his uninspiring wife, the money

[9]Capered.

---

[1]Major London museum, on Trafalgar Square.

[2]The British Army's volunteer reserve force, established in 1908.

going to her as compensation; he must be assigned a Twin Star, some member of the leisured classes who would watch over him ceaselessly (groans from Helen); he must be given food but no clothes, clothes but no food, a third-return ticket to Venice, without either food or clothes when he arrived there. In short, he might be given anything and every-thing so long as it was not the money itself.

And here Margaret interrupted.

"Order, order, Miss Schlegel!" said the reader of the paper. "You are here, I understand, to advise me in the interests of the Society for the Preservation of Places of Historic Interest or Natural Beauty. I cannot have you speaking out of your rôle. It makes my poor head go round, and I think you forget that I am very ill."

"Your head won't go round if only you'll listen to my argument," said Margaret. "Why not give him the money itself? You're supposed to have about thirty thousand a year."[3]

"Have I? I thought I had a million."

"Wasn't a million your capital? Dear me! we ought to have settled that. Still, it doesn't matter. Whatever you've got, I order you to give as many poor men as you can three hundred a year each."

"But that would be pauperizing them," said an earnest girl, who liked the Schlegels, but thought them a little unspiritual at times.

"Not if you gave them so much. A big windfall would not pau-perize a man. It is these little driblets, distributed among too many, that do the harm. Money's educational. It's far more educational than the things it buys." There was a protest. "In a sense," added Mar-garet, but the protest continued. "Well, isn't the most civilized thing going, the man who has learnt to wear his income properly?"

"Exactly what your Mr. Basts won't do."

"Give them a chance. Give them money. Don't dole them out poetry-books and railway-tickets like babies. Give them the wherewithal to buy these things. When your Socialism comes it may be different, and we may think in terms of commodities instead of cash. Till it comes give people cash, for it is the warp of civilization, whatever the woof may be.[4] The imagination ought to play upon money and realize it vividly, for it's the—the second most important thing in the world. It is so slurred over and hushed up, there is so little clear thinking—oh, political econ-omy, of course, but so few of us think clearly about our own private in-comes, and admit that independent thoughts are in nine cases out of

[3]On what this would mean, see "Money," pp. 285–89.

[4]The warp and the woof are the vertical and horizontal threads stretched on a loom in weaving; the warp is usually the stronger.

ten the result of independent means. Money: give Mr. Bast money, and don't bother about his ideals. He'll pick up those for himself."

She leant back while the more earnest members of the club began to misconstrue her. The female mind, though cruelly practical in daily life, cannot bear to hear ideals belittled in conversation, and Miss Schlegel was asked however she could say such dreadful things, and what it would profit Mr. Bast if he gained the whole world and lost his own soul. She answered, "Nothing, but he would not gain his soul until he had gained a little of the world." Then they said, "No, they did not believe it," and she admitted that an overworked clerk may save his soul in the superterrestrial sense, where the effort will be taken for the deed, but she denied that he will ever explore the spiritual resources of this world, will ever know the rarer joys of the body, or attain to clear and passionate intercourse with his fellows. Others had attacked the fabric of Society—Property, Interest, etc.; she only fixed her eyes on a few human beings, to see how, under present conditions, they could be made happier. Doing good to humanity was useless: the many-coloured efforts thereto spreading over the vast area like films and resulting in an universal grey. To do good to one, or, as in this case, to a few, was the utmost she dare hope for.

Between the idealists, and the political economists, Margaret had a bad time. Disagreeing elsewhere, they agreed in disowning her, and in keeping the administration of the millionaire's money in their own hands. The earnest girl brought forward a scheme of "personal supervision and mutual help," the effect of which was to alter poor people until they became exactly like people who were not so poor. The hostess pertinently remarked that she, as eldest son, might surely rank among the millionaire's legatees. Margaret weakly admitted the claim, and another claim was at once set up by Helen, who declared that she had been the millionaire's housemaid for over forty years, overfed and underpaid; was nothing to be done for her, so corpulent and poor? The millionaire then read out her last will and testament, in which she left the whole of her fortune to the Chancellor of the Exchequer.[5] Then she died. The serious parts of the discussion had been of higher merit than the playful—in a men's debate is the reverse more general?—but the meeting broke up hilariously enough, and a dozen happy ladies dispersed to their homes.

Helen and Margaret walked the earnest girl as far as Battersea Bridge Station, arguing copiously all the way. When she had gone they were conscious of an alleviation, and of the great beauty of the

[5]Head of the British Treasury.

evening. They turned back towards Oakley Street. The lamps and the plane-trees, following the line of the embankment, struck a note of dignity that is rare in English cities. The seats, almost deserted, were here and there occupied by gentlefolk in evening dress, who had strolled out from the houses behind to enjoy fresh air and the whisper of the rising tide. There is something continental about Chelsea Embankment. It is an open space used rightly, a blessing more frequent in Germany than here. As Margaret and Helen sat down, the city behind them seemed to be a vast theatre, an opera-house in which some endless trilogy was performing, and they themselves a pair of satisfied subscribers, who did not mind losing a little of the second act.

"Cold?"

"No."

"Tired?"

"Doesn't matter."

The earnest girl's train rumbled away over the bridge.

"I say, Helen——"

"Well?"

"Are we really going to follow up Mr. Bast?"

"I don't know."

"I think we won't."

"As you like."

"It's no good, I think, unless you really mean to know people. The discussion brought that home to me. We got on well enough with him in a spirit of excitement, but think of rational intercourse. We mustn't play at friendship. No, it's no good."

"There's Mrs. Lanoline, too," Helen yawned. "So dull."

"Just so, and possibly worse than dull."

"I should like to know how he got hold of your card."

"But he said—something about a concert and an umbrella——"

"Then did the card see the wife——"

"Helen, come to bed."

"No, just a little longer, it is so beautiful. Tell me; oh yes; did you say money is the warp of the world?"

"Yes."

"Then what's the woof?"

"Very much what one chooses," said Margaret. "It's something that isn't money—one can't say more."

"Walking at night?"

"Probably."

"For Tibby, Oxford?"

"It seems so."

"For you?"

"Now that we have to leave Wickham Place, I begin to think it's that. For Mrs. Wilcox it was certainly Howards End."

One's own name will carry immense distances. Mr. Wilcox, who was sitting with friends many seats away, heard his, rose to his feet, and strolled along towards the speakers.

"It is sad to suppose that places may ever be more important than people," continued Margaret.

"Why, Meg? They're so much nicer generally. I'd rather think of that forester's house in Pomerania than of the fat Herr Förstmeister who lived in it."

"I believe we shall come to care about people less and less, Helen. The more people one knows the easier it becomes to replace them. It's one of the curses of London. I quite expect to end my life caring most for a place."

Here Mr. Wilcox reached them. It was several weeks since they had met.

"How do you do?" he cried. "I thought I recognized your voices. Whatever are you both doing down here?"

His tones were protective. He implied that one ought not to sit out on Chelsea Embankment without a male escort. Helen resented this, but Margaret accepted it as part of the good man's equipment.

"What an age it is since I've seen you, Mr. Wilcox. I met Evie in the Tube, though, lately. I hope you have good news of your son."

"Paul?" said Mr. Wilcox, extinguishing his cigarette, and sitting down between them. "Oh, Paul's all right. We had a line from Madeira.[6] He'll be at work again by now."

"Ugh——" said Helen, shuddering from complex causes.

"I beg your pardon?"

"Isn't the climate of Nigeria too horrible?"

"Someone's got to go," he said simply. "England will never keep her trade overseas unless she is prepared to make sacrifices. Unless we get firm in West Africa, Ger—— untold complications may follow.[7] Now tell me all your news."

"Oh, we've had a splendid evening," cried Helen, who always woke up at the advent of a visitor. "We belong to a kind of club

---

[6]Archipelago in the northern Atlantic, ruled by Portugal.

[7]Anxieties about Germany's growing power (and encroachment on British imperial control) in Africa persisted in Britain in the years before World War I. See pp. 350–53.

that reads papers, Margaret and I—all women, but there is a discussion after. This evening it was on how one ought to leave one's money—whether to one's family, or to the poor, and if so how—oh, most interesting."

The man of business smiled. Since his wife's death he had almost doubled his income. He was an important figure at last, a reassuring name on company prospectuses, and life had treated him very well. The world seemed in his grasp as he listened to the River Thames, which still flowed inland from the sea. So wonderful to the girls, it held no mysteries for him. He had helped to shorten its long tidal trough by taking shares in the lock at Teddington, and if he and other capitalists thought good, some day it could be shortened again. With a good dinner inside him and an amiable but academic woman on either flank, he felt that his hands were on all the ropes of life, and that what he did not know could not be worth knowing.

"Sounds a most original entertainment!" he exclaimed, and laughed in his pleasant way. "I wish Evie would go to that sort of thing. But she hasn't the time. She's taken to breed Aberdeen terriers—jolly little dogs."

"I expect we'd better be doing the same, really."

"We pretend we're improving ourselves, you see," said Helen a little sharply, for the Wilcox glamour is not of the kind that returns, and she had bitter memories of the days when a speech such as he had just made would have impressed her favourably. "We suppose it a good thing to waste an evening once a fortnight over a debate, but, as my sister says, it may be better to breed dogs."

"Not at all. I don't agree with your sister. There's nothing like a debate to teach one quickness. I often wish I had gone in for them when I was a youngster. It would have helped me no end."

"Quickness——?"

"Yes. Quickness in argument. Time after time I've missed scoring a point because the other man has had the gift of the gab and I haven't. Oh, I believe in these discussions."

The patronizing tone, thought Margaret, came well enough from a man who was old enough to be their father. She had always maintained that Mr. Wilcox had a charm. In times of sorrow or emotion his inadequacy had pained her, but it was pleasant to listen to him now, and to watch his thick brown moustache and high forehead confronting the stars. But Helen was nettled. The aim of *their* debates she implied was Truth.

"Oh yes, it doesn't much matter what subject you take," said he.

Margaret laughed and said, "But this is going to be far better than the debate itself." Helen recovered herself and laughed too. "No, I won't go on," she declared. "I'll just put our special case to Mr. Wilcox."

"About Mr. Bast? Yes, do. He'll be more lenient to a special case."

"But, Mr. Wilcox, do first light another cigarette. It's this. We've just come across a young fellow, who's evidently very poor, and who seems interest———"

"What's his profession?"

"Clerk."

"What in?"

"Do you remember, Margaret?"

"Porphyrion Fire Insurance Company."

"Oh yes; the nice people who gave Aunt Juley a new hearth-rug. He seems interesting, in some ways very, and one wishes one could help him. He is married to a wife whom he doesn't seem to care for much. He likes books, and what one may roughly call adventure, and if he had a chance——— But he is so poor. He lives a life where all the money is apt to go on nonsense and clothes. One is so afraid that circumstances will be too strong for him and that he will sink. Well, he got mixed up in our debate. He wasn't the subject of it, but it seemed to bear on his point. Suppose a millionaire died, and desired to leave money to help such a man. How should he be helped? Should he be given three hundred pounds a year direct, which was Margaret's plan? Most of them thought this would pauperize him. Should he and those like him be given free libraries? I said 'No!' He doesn't want more books to read, but to read books rightly. My suggestion was he should be given something every year towards a summer holiday, but then there is his wife, and they said she would have to go too. Nothing seemed quite right! Now what do you think? Imagine that you were a millionaire, and wanted to help the poor. What would you do?"

Mr. Wilcox, whose fortune was not so very far below the standard indicated, laughed exuberantly. "My dear Miss Schlegel, I will not rush in where your sex has been unable to tread. I will not add another plan to the numerous excellent ones that have been already suggested. My only contribution is this: let your young friend clear out of the Porphyrion Fire Insurance Company with all possible speed."

"Why?" said Margaret.

He lowered his voice. "This is between friends. It'll be in the Receiver's hands[8] before Christmas. It'll smash," he added, thinking that she had not understood.

[8]Under the control of a court-appointed administrator due to financial distress.

"Dear me, Helen, listen to that. And he'll have to get another place!"

"*Will* have? Let him leave the ship before it sinks. Let him get one now."

"Rather than wait, to make sure?"

"Decidedly."

"Why's that?"

Again the Olympian laugh, and the lowered voice. "Naturally the man who's in a situation when he applies stands a better chance, is in a stronger position, than the man who isn't. It looks as if he's worth something. I know by myself—(this is letting you into the State secrets)—it affects an employer greatly. Human nature, I'm afraid."

"I hadn't thought of that," murmured Margaret, while Helen said, "Our human nature appears to be the other way round. We employ people because they're unemployed. The boot man, for instance."

"And how does he clean the boots?"

"Not well," confessed Margaret.

"There you are!"

"Then do you really advise us to tell this youth——?"

"I advise nothing," he interrupted, glancing up and down the Embankment, in case his indiscretion had been overheard. "I oughtn't to have spoken—but I happen to know, being more or less behind the scenes. The Porphyrion's a bad, bad concern—— Now, don't say I said so. It's outside the Tariff Ring."[9]

"Certainly I won't say. In fact, I don't know what that means."

"I thought an insurance company never smashed," was Helen's contribution. "Don't the others always run in and save them?"

"You're thinking of reinsurance," said Mr. Wilcox mildly. "It is exactly there that the Porphyrion is weak. It has tried to undercut,[10] has been badly hit by a long series of small fires, and it hasn't been able to reinsure. I'm afraid that public companies don't save one another for love."

"'Human nature,' I suppose," quoted Helen, and he laughed and agreed that it was. When Margaret said that she supposed that clerks, like everyone else, found it extremely difficult to get situations in these days, he replied, "Yes, extremely," and rose to rejoin his friends. He knew by his own office—seldom a vacant post, and hundreds of applicants for it; at present no vacant post.

---

[9]The Associated or Tariff Offices, a consortium of insurance companies (Stallybrass, "Notes," 360).

[10]Undersell competitors.

"And how's Howards End looking?" said Margaret, wishing to change the subject before they parted. Mr. Wilcox was a little apt to think one wanted to get something out of him.

"It's let."

"Really. And you wandering homeless in long-haired Chelsea? How strange are the ways of Fate!"

"No; it's let unfurnished. We've moved."

"Why, I thought of you both as anchored there for ever. Evie never told me."

"I dare say when you met Evie the thing wasn't settled. We only moved a week ago. Paul has rather a feeling for the old place, and we held on for him to have his holiday there; but, really, it is impossibly small. Endless drawbacks. I forget whether you've been up to it?"

"As far as the house, never."

"Well, Howards End is one of those converted farms. They don't really do, spend what you will on them. We messed away with a garage all among the wych-elm roots, and last year we enclosed a bit of the meadow and attempted a rockery. Evie got rather keen on Alpine plants. But it didn't do—no, it didn't do. You remember, or your sister will remember, the farm with those abominable guinea-fowls, and the hedge that the old woman never would cut properly, so that it all went thin at the bottom. And, inside the house, the beams—and the staircase through a door—picturesque enough, but not a place to live in." He glanced over the parapet cheerfully. "Full tide. And the position wasn't right either. The neighbourhood's getting suburban. Either be in London or out of it, I say; so we've taken a house in Ducie Street, close to Sloane Street, and a place right down in Shropshire—Oniton Grange.[11] Ever heard of Oniton? Do come and see us—right away from everywhere, up towards Wales."

"What a change!" said Margaret. But the change was in her own voice, which had become most sad. "I can't imagine Howards End or Hilton without you."

"Hilton isn't without us," he replied. "Charles is there still."

"Still?" said Margaret, who had not kept up with the Charles'. "But I thought he was still at Epsom. They were furnishing that Christmas—one Christmas. How everything alters! I used to admire Mrs. Charles from our windows very often. Wasn't it Epsom?"

"Yes, but they moved eighteen months ago. Charles, the good chap"—his voice dropped—"thought I should be lonely. I didn't want him to move, but he would, and took a house at the other end

[11]A grange is a house for a gentleman farmer.

of Hilton, down by the Six Hills. He had a motor, too. There they all are, a very jolly party—he and she and the two grandchildren."

"I manage other people's affairs so much better than they manage them themselves," said Margaret as they shook hands. "When you moved out of Howards End, I should have moved Mr. Charles Wilcox into it. I should have kept so remarkable a place in the family."

"So it is," he replied. "I haven't sold it, and don't mean to."

"No; but none of you are there."

"Oh, we've got a splendid tenant—Hamar Bryce, an invalid. If Charles ever wanted it—but he won't. Dolly is so dependent on modern conveniences. No, we have all decided against Howards End. We like it in a way, but now we feel that it is neither one thing nor the other. One must have one thing or the other."

"And some people are lucky enough to have both. You're doing yourself proud, Mr. Wilcox. My congratulations."

"And mine," said Helen.

"Do remind Evie to come and see us—two, Wickham Place. We shan't be there very long, either."

"You, too, on the move?"

"Next September," Margaret sighed.

"Everyone moving! Good-bye."

The tide had begun to ebb. Margaret leant over the parapet and watched it sadly. Mr. Wilcox had forgotten his wife, Helen her lover; she herself was probably forgetting. Everyone moving. Is it worth while attempting the past when there is this continual flux even in the hearts of men?

Helen roused her by saying: "What a prosperous vulgarian Mr. Wilcox has grown! I have very little use for him in these days. However, he did tell us about the Porphyrion. Let us write to Mr. Bast as soon as ever we get home, and tell him to clear out of it at once."

"Do; yes, that's worth doing. Let us."

"Let's ask him to tea."

## CHAPTER XVI

LEONARD accepted the invitation to tea next Saturday. But he was right; the visit proved a conspicuous failure.

"Sugar?" said Margaret.

"Cake?" said Helen. "The big cake or the little deadlies? I'm afraid you thought my letter rather odd, but we'll explain—we aren't odd, really—not affected, really. We're over-expressive: that's all."

As a lady's lap-dog Leonard did not excel. He was not an Italian, still less a Frenchman, in whose blood there runs the very spirit of persiflage[1] and of gracious repartee. His wit was the Cockney's; it opened no doors into imagination, and Helen was drawn up short by "The more a lady has to say, the better," administered waggishly.[2]

"Oh, yes," she said.

"Ladies brighten——"

"Yes, I know. The darlings are regular sunbeams. Let me give you a plate."

"How do you like your work?" interposed Margaret.

He, too, was drawn up short. He would not have these women prying into his work. They were Romance, and so was the room to which he had at last penetrated, with the queer sketches of people bathing upon its walls, and so were the very tea-cups, with their delicate borders of wild strawberries. But he would not let Romance interfere with his life. There is the devil to pay then.

"Oh, well enough," he answered.

"Your company is the Porphyrion, isn't it?"

"Yes, that's so"—becoming rather offended. "It's funny how things get round."

"Why funny?" asked Helen, who did not follow the workings of his mind. "It was written as large as life on your card, and considering we wrote to you there, and that you replied on the stamped paper——"

"Would you call the Porphyrion one of the big Insurance Companies?" pursued Margaret.

"It depends what you call big."

"I mean by big, a solid, well-established concern, that offers a reasonably good career to its employés."

"I couldn't say—some would tell you one thing and others another," said the employé uneasily. "For my own part"—he shook his head—"I only believe half I hear. Not that even; it's safer. Those clever ones come to the worse grief, I've often noticed. Ah, you can't be too careful."

He drank, and wiped his moustache, which was going to be one of those moustaches that always droop into tea-cups—more bother than they're worth, surely, and not fashionable either.

"I quite agree, and that's why I was curious to know: is it a solid, well-established concern?"

[1]Banter.

[2]Mischievously.

Leonard had no idea. He understood his own corner of the machine, but nothing beyond it. He desired to confess neither knowledge nor ignorance, and under these circumstances, another motion of the head seemed safest. To him, as to the British public, the Porphyrion was the Porphyrion of the advertisement—a giant, in the classical style, but draped sufficiently, who held in one hand a burning torch, and pointed with the other to St. Paul's[3] and Windsor Castle.[4] A large sum of money was inscribed below, and you drew your own conclusions. This giant caused Leonard to do arithmetic and write letters, to explain the regulations to new clients, and re-explain them to old ones. A giant was of an impulsive morality—one knew that much. He would pay for Mrs. Munt's hearthrug with ostentatious haste, a large claim he would repudiate quietly, and fight court by court. But his true fighting weight, his antecedents, his amours with other members of the commercial Pantheon[5]—all these were as uncertain to ordinary mortals as were the escapades of Zeus. While the gods are powerful, we learn little about them. It is only in the days of their decadence that a strong light beats into heaven.

"We were told the Porphyrion's no go," blurted Helen. "We wanted to tell you; that's why we wrote."

"A friend of ours did think that it is insufficiently reinsured," said Margaret.

Now Leonard had his clue. He must praise the Porphyrion. "You can tell your friend," he said, "that he's quite wrong."

"Oh, good!"

The young man coloured a little. In his circle to be wrong was fatal. The Miss Schlegels did not mind being wrong. They were genuinely glad that they had been misinformed. To them nothing was fatal but evil.

"Wrong, so to speak," he added.

"How 'so to speak'?"

"I mean I wouldn't say he's right altogether."

But this was a blunder. "Then he is right partly," said the elder woman, quick as lightning.

Leonard replied that everyone was right partly, if it came to that.

"Mr. Bast, I don't understand business, and I dare say my questions are stupid, but can you tell me what makes a concern 'right' or 'wrong'?"

---

[3]Cathedral of the Anglican Diocese of London, one of the city's most celebrated landmarks.

[4]Official residence of the royal family in Berkshire.

[5]Greek: all the gods (sometimes their temple).

Leonard sat back with a sigh.

"Our friend, who is also a business man, was so positive. He said before Christmas——"

"And advised you to clear out of it," concluded Helen. "But I don't see why he should know better than you do."

Leonard rubbed his hands. He was tempted to say that he knew nothing about the thing at all. But a commercial training was too strong for him. Nor could he say it was a bad thing, for this would be giving it away; nor yet that it was good, for this would be giving it away equally. He attempted to suggest that it was something between the two, with vast possibilities in either direction, but broke down under the gaze of four sincere eyes. And yet he scarcely distinguished between the two sisters. One was more beautiful and more lively, but "the Miss Schlegels" still remained a composite Indian god, whose waving arms and contradictory speeches were the product of a single mind.[6]

"One can but see," he remarked, adding, "as Ibsen says, 'things happen.'"[7] He was itching to talk about books and make the most of his romantic hour. Minute after minute slipped away, while the ladies, with imperfect skill, discussed the subject of reinsurance or praised their anonymous friend. Leonard grew annoyed—perhaps rightly. He made vague remarks about not being one of those who minded their affairs being talked over by others, but they did not take the hint. Men might have shown more tact. Women, however tactful elsewhere, are heavy-handed here. They cannot see why we should shroud our incomes and our prospects in a veil. "How much exactly have you, and how much do you expect to have next June?" And these were women with a theory, who held that reticence about money matters is absurd, and that life would be truer if each would state the exact size of the golden island upon which he stands, the exact stretch of warp over which he throws the woof that is not money. How can we do justice to the pattern otherwise?

And the precious minutes slipped away, and Jacky and squalor came nearer. At last he could bear it no longer, and broke in, reciting the names of books feverishly. There was a moment of piercing joy when Margaret said, "So *you* like Carlyle," and then the door opened, and "Mr. Wilcox, Miss Wilcox" entered, preceded by two prancing puppies.

---

[6]Many gods of Hinduism were represented as having multiple arms or heads.

[7]Controversial Norwegian dramatist Henrik Ibsen (1828–1906). Leonard may be misremembering *A Doll's House* (1879), in which Nora Helmer is ultimately disappointed in her hope that (as she puts it several times) a wonderful thing will happen.

"Oh, the dears! Oh, Evie, how too impossibly sweet!" screamed Helen, falling on her hands and knees.

"We brought the little fellows round," said Mr. Wilcox.

"I bred 'em myself."

"Oh, really! Mr. Bast, come and play with puppies."

"I've got to be going now," said Leonard sourly.

"But play with puppies a little first."

"This is Ahab, that's Jezebel," said Evie, who was one of those who name animals after the less successful characters of Old Testament history.[8]

"I've got to be going."

Helen was too much occupied with puppies to notice him.

"Mr. Wilcox, Mr. Ba—— Must you be really? Good-bye!"

"Come again," said Helen from the floor.

Then Leonard's gorge arose.[9] Why should he come again? What was the good of it? He said roundly: "No, I shan't; I knew it would be a failure."

Most people would have let him go. "A little mistake. We tried knowing another class—impossible." But the Schlegels had never played with life. They had attempted friendship, and they would take the consequences. Helen retorted, "I call that a very rude remark. What do you want to turn on me like that for?" and suddenly the drawing-room re-echoed to a vulgar row.[10]

"You ask me why I turn on you?"

"Yes."

"What do you want to have me here for?"

"To help you, you silly boy!" cried Helen. "And don't shout."

"*I* don't want your patronage. *I* don't want your tea. I was quite happy. What do you want to unsettle me for?" He turned to Mr. Wilcox. "I put it to this gentleman. I ask you, sir, am I to have my brain picked?"

Mr. Wilcox turned to Margaret with the air of humorous strength that he could so well command. "Are we intruding, Miss Schlegel? Can we be of any use, or shall we go?"

But Margaret ignored him.

[8]In Kings 1 and 2, Jezebel turns her husband, King Ahab, to the worship of the pagan god Baal. He dies in battle, his blood licked up by dogs; her body is devoured by dogs after she has been thrown from a window.

[9]In *Hamlet* V.1, the prince confronts the skull of his dead friend Yorick: "and now how abhorr'd in my imagination it is! my gorge rises at it."

[10]Noisy quarrel; rhymes with "cow."

"I'm connected with a leading insurance company, sir. I receive what I take to be an invitation from these—ladies" (he drawled the word). "I come, and it's to have my brain picked. I ask you, is it fair?"

"Highly unfair," said Mr. Wilcox, drawing a gasp from Evie, who knew that her father was becoming dangerous.

"There, you hear that? Most unfair, the gentleman says. There! Not content with"—pointing at Margaret—"you can't deny it." His voice rose: he was falling into the rhythm of a scene with Jacky. "But as soon as I'm useful it's a very different thing. 'Oh yes, send for him. Cross-question him. Pick his brains.' Oh yes. Now, take me on the whole, I'm a quiet fellow: I'm law-abiding, I don't wish any unpleasantness; but I—I——"

"You," said Margaret—"you—you——"

Laughter from Evie, as at a repartee.

"You are the man who tried to walk by the Pole star."

More laughter.

"You saw the sunrise."

Laughter.

"You tried to get away from the fogs that are stifling us all—away past books and houses to the truth. You were looking for a real home."

"I fail to see the connection," said Leonard, hot with stupid anger.

"So do I." There was a pause. "You were that last Sunday—you are this to-day. Mr. Bast! I and my sister have talked you over. We wanted to help you; we also supposed you might help us. We did not have you here out of charity—which bores us—but because we hoped there would be a connection between last Sunday and other days. What is the good of your stars and trees, your sunrise and the wind, if they do not enter into our daily lives? They have never entered into mine, but into yours, we thought——Haven't we all to struggle against life's daily greyness, against pettiness, against mechanical cheerfulness, against suspicion? I struggle by remembering my friends; others I have known by remembering some place—some beloved place or tree—we thought you one of these."

"Of course, if there's been any misunderstanding," mumbled Leonard, "all I can do is to go. But I beg to state——" He paused. Ahab and Jezebel danced at his boots and made him look ridiculous. "You were picking my brain for official information—I can prove it—I——" He blew his nose and left them.

"Can I help you now?" said Mr. Wilcox, turning to Margaret. "May I have one quiet word with him in the hall?"

"Helen, go after him—do anything—*anything*—to make the noodle understand."

Helen hesitated.

"But really——" said their visitor. "Ought she to?"

At once she went.

He resumed. "I would have chimed in, but I felt that you could polish him off for yourselves—I didn't interfere. You were splendid, Miss Schlegel—absolutely splendid. You can take my word for it, but there are very few women who could have managed him."

"Oh yes," said Margaret distractedly.

"Bowling him over with those long sentences was what fetched me," cried Evie.

"Yes, indeed," chuckled her father; "all that part about 'mechanical cheerfulness'—oh, fine!"

"I'm very sorry," said Margaret, collecting herself. "He's a nice creature really. I cannot think what set him off. It has been most unpleasant for you."

"Oh, *I* didn't mind." Then he changed his mood. He asked if he might speak as an old friend, and, permission given, said: "Oughtn't you really to be more careful?"

Margaret laughed, though her thoughts still strayed after Helen. "Do you realize that it's all your fault?" she said. "You're responsible."

"I?"

"This is the young man whom we were to warn against the Porphyrion. We warn him, and—look!"

Mr. Wilcox was annoyed. "I hardly consider that a fair deduction," he said.

"Obviously unfair," said Margaret. "I was only thinking how tangled things are. It's our fault mostly—neither yours nor his."

"Not his?"

"No."

"Miss Schlegel, you are too kind."

"Yes, indeed," nodded Evie, a little contemptuously.

"You behave much too well to people, and then they impose on you. I know the world and that type of man, and as soon as I entered the room I saw you had not been treating him properly. You must keep that type at a distance. Otherwise they forget themselves. Sad, but true. They aren't our sort, and one must face the fact."

"Ye-es."

"Do admit that we should never have had the outburst if he was a gentleman."

"I admit it willingly," said Margaret, who was pacing up and down the room. "A gentleman would have kept his suspicions to himself."

Mr. Wilcox watched her with a vague uneasiness.

"What did he suspect you of?"

"Of wanting to make money out of him."

"Intolerable brute! But how were you to benefit?"

"Exactly. How indeed! Just horrible, corroding suspicion. One touch of thought or of goodwill would have brushed it away. Just the senseless fear that does make men intolerable brutes."

"I come back to my original point. You ought to be more careful, Miss Schlegel. Your servants ought to have orders not to let such people in."

She turned to him frankly. "Let me explain exactly why we like this man, and want to see him again."

"That's your clever way of talking. I shall never believe you like him."

"I do. Firstly, because he cares for physical adventure, just as you do. Yes, you go motoring and shooting; he would like to go camping out. Secondly, he cares for something special *in* adventure. It is quickest to call that special something poetry——"

"Oh, he's one of that writer sort."

"No—oh no! I mean he may be, but it would be loathsome stuff. His brain is filled with the husks of books, culture—horrible; we want him to wash out his brain and go to the real thing. We want to show him how he may get upsides with life. As I said, either friends or the country, some"—she hesitated—"either some very dear person or some very dear place seems necessary to relieve life's daily grey, and to show that it is grey. If possible, one should have both."

Some of her words ran past Mr. Wilcox. He let them run past. Others he caught and criticized with admirable lucidity.

"Your mistake is this, and it is a very common mistake. This young bounder has a life of his own. What right have you to conclude it is an unsuccessful life, or, as you call it, 'grey'?"

"Because——"

"One minute. You know nothing about him. He probably has his own joys and interests—wife, children, snug little home. That's where we practical fellows"—he smiled—"are more tolerant than you intellectuals. We live and let live, and assume that things are jogging on fairly well elsewhere, and that the ordinary plain man may be trusted to look after his own affairs. I quite grant—I look at the faces of the clerks in my own office, and observe them to be dull, but I don't know what's going on beneath. So, by the way, with London. I have heard you rail against London, Miss Schlegel, and it seems a funny thing to say but I was very angry with you. What do you know about London? You only see civilization from the outside. I don't say in your case, but in too many cases that attitude leads to morbidity, discontent, and Socialism."

She admitted the strength of his position, though it undermined imagination. As he spoke, some outposts of poetry and perhaps of sympathy fell ruining, and she retreated to what she called her "second line"—to the special facts of the case.

"His wife is an old bore," she said simply. "He never came home last Saturday night because he wanted to be alone, and she thought he was with us."

"With *you?*"

"Yes." Evie tittered. "He hasn't got the cosy home that you assumed. He needs outside interests."

"Naughty young man!" cried the girl.

"Naughty?" said Margaret, who hated naughtiness more than sin. "When you're married, Miss Wilcox, won't you want outside interests?"

"He has apparently got them," put in Mr. Wilcox slyly.

"Yes, indeed, father."

"He was tramping in Surrey, if you mean that," said Margaret, pacing away rather crossly.

"Oh, I dare say!"

"Miss Wilcox, he was!"

"M-m-m-m!" from Mr. Wilcox, who thought the episode amusing, if risqué. With most ladies he would not have discussed it, but he was trading on Margaret's reputation as an emanicipated woman.

"He said so, and about such a thing he wouldn't lie."

They both began to laugh.

"That's where I differ from you. Men lie about their positions and prospects, but not about a thing of that sort."

He shook his head. "Miss Schlegel, excuse me, but I know the type."

"I said before—he isn't a type. He cares about adventures rightly. He's certain that our smug existence isn't all. He's vulgar and hysterical and bookish, but don't think that sums him up. There's manhood in him as well. Yes, that's what I'm trying to say. He's a real man."

As she spoke their eyes met, and it was as if Mr. Wilcox's defences fell. She saw back to the real man in him. Unwittingly she had touched his emotions. A woman and two men—they had formed the magic triangle of sex, and the male was thrilled to jealousy, in case the female was attracted by another male. Love, say the ascetics, reveals our shameful kinship with the beasts. Be it so: one can bear that; jealousy is the real shame. It is jealousy, not love, that connects us with the farm-yard intolerably, and calls up visions of two angry cocks and a complacent hen. Margaret crushed complacency down because she was civilized. Mr. Wilcox, uncivilized, continued to feel anger long after he had rebuilt his defences, and was again presenting a bastion to the world.

"Miss Schlegel, you're a pair of dear creatures, but you really *must* be careful in this uncharitable world. What does your brother say?"

"I forget."

"Surely he has some opinion?"

"He laughs, if I remember correctly."

"He's very clever, isn't he?" said Evie, who had met and detested Tibby at Oxford.

"Yes, pretty well—but I wonder what Helen's doing."

"She is very young to undertake this sort of thing," said Mr. Wilcox.

Margaret went out into the landing. She heard no sound, and Mr. Bast's topper[11] was missing from the hall.

"Helen!" she called.

"Yes!" replied a voice from the library.

"You in there?"

"Yes—he's gone some time."

Margaret went to her. "Why, you're all alone," she said.

"Yes—it's all right, Meg. Poor, poor creature——"

"Come back to the Wilcoxes and tell me later—Mr. W. much concerned, and slightly titillated."

"Oh, I've no patience with him. I hate him. Poor dear Mr. Bast! he wanted to talk literature, and we would talk business. Such a muddle of a man, and yet so worth pulling through. I like him extraordinarily."

"Well done," said Margaret, kissing her, "but come into the drawing-room now, and don't talk about him to the Wilcoxes. Make light of the whole thing."

Helen came and behaved with a cheerfulness that reassured their visitor—this hen at all events was fancy-free.

"He's gone with my blessing," she cried, "and now for puppies."

As they drove away, Mr. Wilcox said to his daughter:

"I am really concerned at the way those girls go on. They are as clever as you make 'em, but unpractical—God bless me! One of these days they'll go too far. Girls like that oughtn't to live alone in London. Until they marry, they ought to have someone to look after

[11]Top-hat.

them. We must look in more often—we're better than no one. You like them, don't you, Evie?"

Evie replied: "Helen's right enough, but I can't stand the toothy one. And I shouldn't have called either of them girls."

Evie had grown up handsome. Dark-eyed, with the glow of youth under sunburn, built firmly and firm-lipped, she was the best the Wilcoxes could do in the way of feminine beauty. For the present, puppies and her father were the only things she loved, but the net of matrimony was being prepared for her, and a few days later she was attracted to a Mr. Percy Cahill, an uncle of Mrs. Charles', and he was attracted to her.

## CHAPTER XVII

THE Age of Property holds bitter moments even for a proprietor. When a move is imminent, furniture becomes ridiculous, and Margaret now lay awake at nights wondering where, where on earth they and all their belongings would be deposited in September next. Chairs, tables, pictures, books, that had rumbled down to them through the generations, must rumble forward again like a slide of rubbish to which she longed to give the final push, and send toppling into the sea. But there were all their father's books—they never read them, but they were their father's, and must be kept. There was the marble-topped cheffonier[1]—their mother had set store by it, they could not remember why. Round every knob and cushion in the house sentiment gathered, a sentiment that was at times personal, but more often a faint piety to the dead, a prolongation of rites that might have ended at the grave.

It was absurd, if you came to think of it; Helen and Tibby came to think of it: Margaret was too busy with the house-agents. The feudal ownership of land did bring dignity, whereas the modern ownership of movables is reducing us again to a nomadic horde. We are reverting to the civilization of luggage, and historians of the future will note how the middle classes accreted possessions without taking root in the earth, and may find in this the secret of their imaginative poverty. The Schlegels were certainly the poorer for the loss of Wickham Place. It had helped to balance their lives, and almost to counsel them. Nor is their ground-landlord spiritually the richer. He has built flats on its site, his motor-cars grow swifter, his exposures of Socialism more trenchant. But he has spilt the precious distillation of the years, and no chemistry of his can give it back to society again.

[1]Cabinet similar to a sideboard.

Margaret grew depressed; she was anxious to settle on a house before they left town to pay their annual visit to Mrs. Munt. She enjoyed this visit, and wanted to have her mind at ease for it. Swanage, though dull, was stable, and this year she longed more than usual for its fresh air and for the magnificent downs that guard it on the north. But London thwarted her; in its atmosphere she could not concentrate. London only stimulates, it cannot sustain; and Margaret, hurrying over its surface for a house without knowing what sort of a house she wanted, was paying for many a thrilling sensation in the past. She could not even break loose from culture, and her time was wasted by concerts which it would be a sin to miss, and invitations which it would never do to refuse. At last she grew desperate; she resolved that she would go nowhere and be at home to no one until she found a house, and broke the resolution in half an hour.

Once she had humorously lamented that she had never been to Simpson's restaurant in the Strand.[2] Now a note arrived from Miss Wilcox, asking her to lunch there. Mr. Cahill was coming, and the three would have such a jolly chat, and perhaps end up at the Hippodrome.[3] Margaret had no strong regard for Evie, and no desire to meet her fiancé, and she was surprised that Helen, who had been far funnier about Simpson's, had not been asked instead. But the invitation touched her by its intimate tone. She must know Evie Wilcox better than she supposed, and declaring that she "simply must," she accepted.

But when she saw Evie at the entrance of the restaurant, staring fiercely at nothing after the fashion of athletic women, her heart failed her anew. Miss Wilcox had changed perceptibly since her engagement. Her voice was gruffer, her manner more downright, and she was inclined to patronize the more foolish virgin. Margaret was silly enough to be pained at this. Depressed at her isolation, she saw not only houses and furniture, but the vessel of life itself slipping past her, with people like Evie and Mr. Cahill on board.

There are moments when virtue and wisdom fail us, and one of them came to her at Simpson's in the Strand. As she trod the staircase, narrow, but carpeted thickly, as she entered the eating-room, where saddles of mutton were being trundled up to expectant clergymen, she had a strong, if erroneous, conviction of her own futility, and wished she had never come out of her backwater, where nothing happened except art and literature, and where no one ever got married or

---

[2]Known for traditional English food and décor since the mid-19th c.
[3]A large variety theater, opened in 1900.

succeeded in remaining engaged. Then came a little surprise. 'Father might be of the party—yes, father was.' With a smile of pleasure she moved forward to greet him, and her feeling of loneliness vanished.

"I thought I'd get round if I could," said he. "Evie told me of her little plan, so I just slipped in and secured a table. Always secure a table first. Evie, don't pretend you want to sit by your old father, because you don't. Miss Schlegel, come in my side, out of pity. My goodness, but you look tired! Been worrying round after your young clerks?"

"No, after houses," said Margaret, edging past him into the box. "I'm hungry, not tired; I want to eat heaps."

"That's good. What'll you have?"

"Fish pie," said she, with a glance at the menu.

"Fish pie! Fancy coming for fish pie to Simpson's. It's not a bit the thing to go for here."

"Go for something for me, then," said Margaret, pulling off her gloves. Her spirits were rising, and his reference to Leonard Bast had warmed her curiously.

"Saddle of mutton," said he after profound reflection; "and cider to drink. That's the type of thing. I like this place, for a joke, once in a way. It is so thoroughly Old English. Don't you agree?"

"Yes," said Margaret, who didn't. The order was given, the joint rolled up, and the carver, under Mr. Wilcox's direction, cut the meat where it was succulent, and piled their plates high. Mr. Cahill insisted on sirloin, but admitted that he had made a mistake later on. He and Evie soon fell into a conversation of the 'No, I didn't; yes, you did' type—conversation which, though fascinating to those who are engaged in it, neither desires nor deserves the attention of others.

"It's a golden rule to tip the carver. Tip everywhere's my motto."

"Perhaps it does make life more human."

"Then the fellows know one again. Especially in the East, if you tip, they remember you from year's end to year's end."

"Have you been in the East?"

"Oh, Greece and the Levant.[4] I used to go out for sport and business to Cyprus; some military society of a sort there. A few piastres,[5] properly distributed, help to keep one's memory green. But you, of course, think this shockingly cynical. How's your discussion society getting on? Any new Utopias lately?"

---

[4]Eastern Mediterranean.

[5]Units of currency used at various times in the Ottoman Empire and post-Ottoman Egypt, Lebanon, Palestine, Sudan, Syria, and Turkey.

"No, I'm house-hunting, Mr. Wilcox, as I've already told you once. Do you know of any houses?"

"Afraid I don't."

"Well, what's the point of being practical if you can't find two distressed females a house? We merely want a small house with large rooms, and plenty of them."

"Evie, I like that! Miss Schlegel expects me to turn house agent for her!"

"What's that, father?"

"I want a new home in September, and someone must find it. I can't."

"Percy, do you know of anything?"

"I can't say I do," said Mr. Cahill.

"How like you! You're never any good."

"Never any good. Just listen to her! Never any good. Oh, come!"

"Well, you aren't. Miss Schlegel, is he?"

The torrent of their love, having splashed these drops at Margaret, swept away on its habitual course. She sympathized with it now, for a little comfort had restored her geniality. Speech and silence pleased her equally, and while Mr. Wilcox made some preliminary inquiries about cheese, her eyes surveyed the restaurant, and admired its well-calculated tributes to the solidity of our past. Though no more Old English than the works of Kipling, it had selected its reminiscences so adroitly that her criticism was lulled, and the guests whom it was nourishing for imperial purposes bore the outer semblance of Parson Adams or Tom Jones.[6] Scraps of their talk jarred oddly on the ear. "Right you are! I'll cable out to Uganda this evening," came from the table behind. "Their Emperor wants war; well, let him have it," was the opinion of a clergyman. She smiled at such incongruities. "Next time," she said to Mr. Wilcox, "you shall come to lunch with me at Mr. Eustace Miles's."[7]

"With pleasure."

"No, you'd hate it," she said, pushing her glass towards him for some more cider. "It's all proteids and bodybuildings, and people come up to you and beg your pardon, but you have such a beautiful aura."

"A what?"

---

[6]Virtuous characters in Henry Fielding's novels *Joseph Andrews* (1742) and *Tom Jones* (1749). The views of Rudyard Kipling (1865–1936) on British patriotism and imperialism were complex and are still debated today; see pp. 347–49.

[7]Miles, a British tennis player and proponent of the physical culture movement, opened his vegetarian "restaurant with ideals" at Charing Cross in 1906. Proteids are proteins.

"Never heard of an aura? Oh, happy, happy man! I scrub at mine for hours. Nor of an astral plane?"[8]

He had heard of astral planes, and censured them.

"Just so. Luckily it was Helen's aura, not mine, and she had to chaperone it and do the politenesses. I just sat with my handkerchief in my mouth till the man went."

"Funny experiences seem to come to you two girls. No one's ever asked me about my—what d'ye call it? Perhaps I've not got one."

"You're bound to have one, but it may be such a terrible colour that no one dares mention it."

"Tell me, though, Miss Schlegel, do you really believe in the supernatural and all that?"

"Too difficult a question."

"Why's that? Gruyère or Stilton?"

"Gruyère, please."

"Better have Stilton."[9]

"Stilton. Because, though I don't believe in auras, and think Theosophy's only a halfway-house——"

"—Yet there may be something in it all the same," he concluded, with a frown.

"Not even that. It may be halfway in the wrong direction. I can't explain. I don't believe in all these fads, and yet I don't like saying that I don't believe in them."

He seemed unsatisfied, and said: "So you wouldn't give me your word that you *don't* hold with astral bodies and all the rest of it?"

"I could," said Margaret, surprised that the point was of any importance to him. "Indeed, I will. When I talked about scrubbing my aura, I was only trying to be funny. But why do you want this settled?"

"I don't know."

"Now, Mr. Wilcox, you do know."

"Yes, I am," "No, you're not," burst from the lovers opposite. Margaret was silent for a moment, and then changed the subject.

"How's your house?"

"Much the same as when you honoured it last week."

"I don't mean Ducie Street. Howards End, of course."

---

[8]The Theosophical Society, founded by Helena Petrovna Blavatsky and Henry Steel Olcott in 1875, promoted the ideas of an "astral plane" of the soul's existence and of "auras," energy fields emanating from people and things. Vegetarianism was often associated with belief systems, such as Theosophy, that turned on bodily or spiritual regeneration.

[9]An English cheese; Gruyère is Swiss.

"Why 'of course'?"

"Can't you turn out your tenant and let it to us? We're nearly demented."

"Let me think. I wish I could help you. But I thought you wanted to be in town. One bit of advice: fix your district, then fix your price, and then don't budge. That's how I got both Ducie Street and Oniton. I said to myself, 'I mean to be exactly here,' and I was, and Oniton's a place in a thousand."

"But I do budge. Gentlemen seem to mesmerize houses—cow them with an eye, and up they come, trembling. Ladies can't. It's the houses that are mesmerizing me. I've no control over the saucy things. Houses are alive. No?"

"I'm out of my depth," he said, and added: "Didn't you talk rather like that to your office boy?"

"Did I? —I mean I did, more or less. I talk the same way to everyone—or try to."

"Yes, I know. And how much do you suppose that he understood of it?"

"That's his lookout.[10] I don't believe in suiting my conversation to my company. One can doubtless hit upon some medium of exchange that seems to do well enough, but it's no more like the real thing than money is like food. There's no nourishment in it. You pass it to the lower classes, and they pass it back to you, and this you call 'social intercourse' or 'mutual endeavour,' when it's mutual priggishness if it's anything. Our friends at Chelsea don't see this. They say one ought to be at all costs intelligible, and sacrifice——"

"Lower classes," interrupted Mr. Wilcox, as it were thrusting his hand into her speech. "Well, you do admit that there are rich and poor. That's something."

Margaret could not reply. Was he incredibly stupid, or did he understand her better than she understood herself?

"You do admit that, if wealth was divided up equally, in a few years there would be rich and poor again just the same. The hard-working man would come to the top, the wastrel sink to the bottom."

"Everyone admits that."

"Your Socialists don't."

"My Socialists do. Yours mayn't; but I strongly suspect yours of being not Socialists, but ninepins,[11] which you have constructed for

[10]His problem (not mine).

[11]Propositions designed to be confuted easily (from the game whose object is to knock down nine wooden pins).

your own amusement. I can't imagine any living creature who would bowl over quite so easily."

He would have resented this had she not been a woman. But women may say anything—it was one of his holiest beliefs—and he only retorted, with a gay smile: "I don't care. You've made two damaging admissions, and I'm heartily with you in both."

In time they finished lunch, and Margaret, who had excused herself from the Hippodrome, took her leave. Evie had scarcely addressed her, and she suspected that the entertainment had been planned by the father. He and she were advancing out of their respective families towards a more intimate acquaintance. It had begun long ago. She had been his wife's friend, and, as such, he had given her that silver vinaigrette as a memento. It was pretty of him to have given that vinaigrette, and he had always preferred her to Helen—unlike most men. But the advance had been astonishing lately. They had done more in a week than in two years, and were really beginning to know each other.

She did not forget his promise to sample Eustace Miles, and asked him as soon as she could secure Tibby as his chaperon. He came, and partook of body-building dishes with humility.

Next morning the Schlegels left for Swanage. They had not succeeded in finding a new home.

## CHAPTER XVIII

As they were seated at Aunt Juley's breakfast-table at The Bays, parrying her excessive hospitality and enjoying the view of the bay, a letter came for Margaret and threw her into perturbation. It was from Mr. Wilcox. It announced an "important change" in his plans. Owing to Evie's marriage, he had decided to give up his house in Ducie Street, and was willing to let it on a yearly tenancy. It was a businesslike letter, and stated frankly what he would do for them and what he would not do. Also the rent. If they approved, Margaret was to come up *at once*—the words were underlined, as is necessary when dealing with women—and to go over the house with him. If they disapproved, a wire would oblige, as he should put it into the hands of an agent.

The letter perturbed, because she was not sure what it meant. If he liked her, if he had manœuvred to get her to Simpson's, might this be a manœuvre to get her to London, and result in an offer of marriage? She put it to herself as indelicately as possible, in the hope that her brain would cry, "Rubbish, you're a self-conscious fool!" But her brain only tingled a little and was silent, and for a time she sat gazing at the mincing waves, and wondering whether the news would seem strange to the others.

As soon as she began speaking, the sound of her own voice reassured her. There could be nothing in it. The replies also were typical, and in the burr of conversation her fears vanished.

"You needn't go though——" began her hostess.

"I needn't, but hadn't I better? It's really getting rather serious. We let chance after chance slip, and the end of it is we shall be bundled out bag and baggage into the street. We don't know what we *want*, that's the mischief with us——"

"No, we have no real ties," said Helen, helping herself to toast.

"Shan't I go up to town to-day, take the house if it's the least possible, and then come down by the afternoon train to-morrow, and start enjoying myself. I shall be no fun to myself or to others until this business is off my mind."

"But you won't do anything rash, Margaret?"

"There's nothing rash to do."

"Who *are* the Wilcoxes?" said Tibby, a question that sounds silly, but was really extremely subtle, as his aunt found to her cost when she tried to answer it. "I don't *manage* the Wilcoxes; I don't see where they come *in*."

"No more do I," agreed Helen. "It's funny that we just don't lose sight of them. Out of all our hotel acquaintances, Mr. Wilcox is the only one who has stuck. It is now over three years, and we have drifted away from far more interesting people in that time."

"Interesting people don't get one houses."

"Meg, if you start in your honest-English vein, I shall throw the treacle[1] at you."

"It's a better vein than the cosmopolitan," said Margaret, getting up. "Now, children, which is it to be? You know the Ducie Street house. Shall I say yes or shall I say no? Tibby love—which? I'm specially anxious to pin you both."

"It all depends what meaning you attach to the word 'possi——'"

"It depends on nothing of the sort. Say 'yes.'"

"Say 'no.'"

Then Margaret spoke rather seriously. "I think," she said, "that our race is degenerating. We cannot settle even this little thing; what will it be like when we have to settle a big one?"

"It will be as easy as eating," returned Helen.

[1]Molasses.

"I was thinking of father. How could he settle to leave Germany as he did, when he had fought for it as a young man, and all his feelings and friends were Prussian? How could he break loose with Patriotism and begin aiming at something else? It would have killed me. When he was nearly forty he could change countries and ideals—and we, at our age, can't change houses. It's humiliating."

"Your father may have been able to change countries," said Mrs. Munt with asperity, "and that may or may not be a good thing. But he could change houses no better than you can, in fact, much worse. Never shall I forget what poor Emily suffered in the move from Manchester."

"I knew it," cried Helen. "I told you so. It is the little things one bungles at. The big, real ones are nothing when they come."

"Bungle, my dear! You are too little to recollect—in fact, you weren't there. But the furniture was actually in the vans and on the move before the lease for Wickham Place was signed, and Emily took train with baby—who was Margaret then—and the smaller luggage for London, without so much as knowing where her new home would be. Getting away from that house may be hard, but it is nothing to the misery that we all went through getting you into it."

Helen, with her mouth full, cried:

"And that's the man who beat the Austrians, and the Danes, and the French, and who beat the Germans that were inside himself. And we're like him."

"Speak for yourself," said Tibby. "Remember that I am cosmopolitan, please."

"Helen may be right."

"Of course she's right," said Helen.

Helen might be right, but she did not go up to London. Margaret did that. An interrupted holiday is the worst of the minor worries, and one may be pardoned for feeling morbid when a business letter snatches one away from the sea and friends. She could not believe that her father had ever felt the same. Her eyes had been troubling her lately, so that she could not read in the train, and it bored her to look at the landscape, which she had seen but yesterday. At Southampton she "waved" to Frieda: Frieda was on her way down to join them at Swanage, and Mrs. Munt had calculated that their trains would cross. But Frieda was looking the other way, and Margaret travelled on to town feeling solitary and old-maidish. How like an old maid to fancy that Mr. Wilcox was courting her! She had once visited a spinster— poor, silly, and unattractive—whose mania it was that every man who approached her fell in love. How Margaret's heart had bled for the deluded thing! How she had lectured, reasoned, and in despair acquiesced! "I may have been deceived by the curate, my dear, but the young fellow who brings the midday post really is fond of me, and has, as a matter of fact——" It had always seemed to her the most hideous corner of old age, yet she might be driven into it herself by the mere pressure of virginity.

Mr. Wilcox met her at Waterloo[2] himself. She felt certain that he was not the same as usual; for one thing, he took offence at everything she said.

"This is awfully kind of you," she began, "but I'm afraid it's not going to do. The house has not been built that suits the Schlegel family."

"What! Have you come up determined not to deal?"

"Not exactly."

"Not exactly? In that case let's be starting."

She lingered to admire the motor, which was new, and a fairer creature than the vermilion giant that had borne Aunt Juley to her doom three years before.

"Presumably it's very beautiful," she said. "How do you like it, Crane?"

"Come, let's be starting," repeated her host. "How on earth did you know that my chauffeur was called Crane?"

"Why, I know Crane: I've been for a drive with Evie once. I know that you've got a parlourmaid called Milton. I know all sorts of things."

"Evie!" he echoed in injured tones. "You won't see her. She's gone out with Cahill. It's no fun, I can tell you, being left so much alone. I've got my work all day—indeed, a great deal too much of it—but when I come home in the evening, I tell you, I can't stand the house."

"In my absurd way, I'm lonely too," Margaret replied. "It's heartbreaking to leave one's old home. I scarcely remember anything before Wickham Place, and Helen and Tibby were born there. Helen says——"

"You, too, feel lonely?"

"Horribly. Hullo, Parliament's back!"

Mr. Wilcox glanced at Parliament contemptuously. The more important ropes of life lay elsewhere. "Yes, they are talking again," said he. "But you were going to say——"

"Only some rubbish about furniture. Helen says it alone endures while men and houses perish, and that in the end the world will be a desert of chairs and sofas—just imagine it! —rolling through infinity with no one to sit upon them."

[2]London rail station, serving lines to the southwest.

"Your sister always likes her little joke."

"She says 'Yes,' my brother says 'No,' to Ducie Street. It's no fun helping us, Mr. Wilcox, I assure you."

"You are not as unpractical as you pretend. I shall never believe it."

Margaret laughed. But she was—quite as unpractical. She could not concentrate on details. Parliament, the Thames, the irresponsive chauffeur, would flash into the field of house-hunting, and all demand some comment or response. It is impossible to see modern life steadily and see it whole, and she had chosen to see it whole. Mr. Wilcox saw steadily. He never bothered over the mysterious or the private. The Thames might run inland from the sea, the chauffeur might conceal all passion and philosophy beneath his unhealthy skin. They knew their own business, and he knew his.

Yet she liked being with him. He was not a rebuke, but a stimulus, and banished morbidity. Some twenty years her senior, he preserved a gift that she supposed herself to have already lost—not youth's creative power, but its self-confidence and optimism. He was so sure that it was a very pleasant world. His complexion was robust, his hair had receded but not thinned, the thick moustache and the eyes that Helen had compared to brandy-balls had an agreeable menace in them, whether they were turned towards the slums or towards the stars. Some day—in the millennium—there may be no need for his type. At present, homage is due to it from those who think themselves superior, and who possibly are.

"At all events you responded to my telegram promptly," he remarked.

"Oh, even I know a good thing when I see it."

"I'm glad you don't despise the goods of this world."

"Heavens, no! Only idiots and prigs do that."

"I am glad, very glad," he repeated, suddenly softening and turning to her, as if the remark had pleased him. "There is so much cant talked in would-be intellectual circles. I am glad you don't share it. Self-denial is all very well as a means of strengthening the character. But I can't stand those people who run down comforts. They have usually some axe to grind. Can you?"

"Comforts are of two kinds," said Margaret, who was keeping herself in hand—"those we can share with others, like fire, weather, or music; and those we can't—food, for instance. It depends."

"I mean reasonable comforts, of course. I shouldn't like to think that you——" He bent nearer; the sentence died unfinished. Margaret's head turned very stupid, and the inside of it seemed to revolve like the beacon in a lighthouse. He did not kiss her, for the hour was half-past twelve, and the car was passing by the stables of Buckingham Palace.

But the atmosphere was so charged with emotion that people only seemed to exist on her account, and she was surprised that Crane did not realize this, and turn round. Idiot though she might be, surely Mr. Wilcox was more—how should one put it? —more psychological than usual. Always a good judge of character for business purposes, he seemed this afternoon to enlarge his field, and to note qualities outside neatness, obedience, and decision.

"I want to go over the whole house," she announced when they arrived. "As soon as I get back to Swanage, which will be to-morrow afternoon, I'll talk it over once more with Helen and Tibby, and wire you 'yes' or 'no.'"

"Right. The dining-room." And they began their survey.

The dining-room was big, but over-furnished. Chelsea would have moaned aloud. Mr. Wilcox had eschewed those decorative schemes that wince, and relent, and refrain, and achieve beauty by sacrificing comfort and pluck. After so much self-colour and self-denial, Margaret viewed with relief the sumptuous dado, the frieze, the gilded wall-paper, amid whose foliage parrots sang. It would never do with her own furniture, but those heavy chairs, that immense sideboard loaded with presentation plate, stood up against its pressure like men. The room suggested men, and Margaret, keen to derive the modern capitalist from the warriors and hunters of the past, saw it as an ancient guest-hall, where the lord sat at meat among his thanes. Even the Bible—the Dutch Bible that Charles had brought back from the Boer War[3]—fell into position. Such a room admitted loot.

"Now the entrance-hall."

The entrance-hall was paved.

"Here we fellows smoke."

We fellows smoked in chairs of maroon leather. It was as if a motor-car had spawned. "Oh, jolly!" said Margaret, sinking into one of them.

"You do like it?" he said, fixing his eyes on her upturned face, and surely betraying an almost intimate note. "It's all rubbish not making oneself comfortable. Isn't it?"

"Ye-es. Semi-rubbish. Are those Cruikshanks?"

"Gillrays.[4] Shall we go on upstairs?"

"Does all this furniture come from Howards End?"

---

[3]The Second Boer War (1899–1902), against the Dutch-settled Boer republics of the Transvaal and the Orange Free State in southern Africa, ended in the subordination of both to British control.

[4]George Cruikshank (1792–1878) and James Gillray (1757–1815), celebrated caricaturists of British life and politics.

"The Howards End furniture has all gone to Oniton."

"Does—— However, I'm concerned with the house, not the furniture. How big is this smoking-room?"

"Thirty by fifteen. No, wait a minute. Fifteen and a half."

"Ah, well. Mr. Wilcox, aren't you ever amused at the solemnity with which we middle classes approach the subject of houses?"

They proceeded to the drawing-room. Chelsea managed better here. It was sallow and ineffective. One could visualize the ladies withdrawing to it, while their lords discussed life's realities below, to the accompaniment of cigars. Had Mrs. Wilcox's drawing-room looked thus at Howards End? Just as this thought entered Margaret's brain, Mr. Wilcox did ask her to be his wife, and the knowledge that she had been right so overcame her that she nearly fainted.

But the proposal was not to rank among the world's great love scenes.

"Miss Schlegel"—his voice was firm—"I have had you up on false pretences. I want to speak about a much more serious matter than a house."

Margaret almost answered: "I know——"

"Could you be induced to share my—is it probable——"

"Oh, Mr. Wilcox!" she interrupted, holding the piano and averting her eyes. "I see, I see. I will write to you afterwards if I may."

He began to stammer. "Miss Schlegel—Margaret—you don't understand."

"Oh yes! Indeed, yes!" said Margaret.

"I am asking you to be my wife."

So deep already was her sympathy, that when he said, "I am asking you to be my wife," she made herself give a little start. She must show surprise if he expected it. An immense joy came over her. It was indescribable. It had nothing to do with humanity, and most resembled the all-pervading happiness of fine weather. Fine weather is due to the sun, but Margaret could think of no central radiance here. She stood in his drawing-room happy, and longing to give happiness. On leaving him she realized that the central radiance had been love.

"You aren't offended, Miss Schlegel?"

"How could I be offended?"

There was a moment's pause. He was anxious to get rid of her, and she knew it. She had too much intuition to look at him as he struggled for possessions that money cannot buy. He desired comradeship and affection, but he feared them, and she, who had taught herself only to desire, and could have clothed the struggle with beauty, held back, and hesitated with him.

"Good-bye," she continued. "You will have a letter from me—I am going back to Swanage to-morrow."

"Thank you."

"Good-bye, and it's you I thank."

"I may order the motor round, mayn't I?"

"That would be most kind."

"I wish I had written instead. Ought I to have written?"

"Not at all."

"There's just one question——"

She shook her head. He looked a little bewildered, and they parted.

They parted without shaking hands: she had kept the interview, for his sake, in tints of the quietest grey. Yet she thrilled with happiness ere she reached her own house. Others had loved her in the past, if one may apply to their brief desires so grave a word, but those others had been "ninnies"—young men who had nothing to do, old men who could find nobody better. And she had often "loved," too, but only so far as the facts of sex demanded: mere yearnings for the masculine, to be dismissed for what they were worth, with a smile. Never before had her personality been touched. She was not young or very rich, and it amazed her that a man of any standing should take her seriously. As she sat trying to do accounts in her empty house, amidst beautiful pictures and noble books, waves of emotion broke, as if a tide of passion was flowing through the night air. She shook her head, tried to concentrate her attention, and failed. In vain did she repeat: "But I've been through this sort of thing before." She had never been through it; the big machinery, as opposed to the little, had been set in motion, and the idea that Mr. Wilcox loved, obsessed her before she came to love him in return.

She would come to no decision yet. "Oh, sir, this is so sudden"— that prudish phrase exactly expressed her when her time came. Premonitions are not preparation. She must examine more closely her own nature and his; she must talk it over judicially with Helen. It had been a strange love-scene—the central radiance unacknowledged from first to last. She, in his place, would have said "Ich liebe dich,"[5] but perhaps it was not his habit to open the heart. He might have done it if she had pressed him—as a matter of duty, perhaps; England expects every man to open his heart once; but the effort would have jarred him, and never, if she could avoid it, should he lose those defences that he had chosen to raise against the world. He must never be bothered

[5]German: "I love you."

with emotional talk, or with a display of sympathy. He was an elderly man now, and it would be futile and impudent to correct him.

Mrs. Wilcox strayed in and out, ever a welcome ghost; surveying the scene, thought Margaret, without one hint of bitterness.

## CHAPTER XIX

IF one wanted to show a foreigner England, perhaps the wisest course would be to take him to the final section of the Purbeck Hills, and stand him on their summit, a few miles to the east of Corfe. Then system after system of our island would roll together under his feet. Beneath him is the valley of the Frome, and all the wild lands that come tossing down from Dorchester, black and gold, to mirror their gorse in the expanses of Poole. The valley of the Stour is beyond, unaccountable stream, dirty at Blandford, pure at Wimborne—the Stour, sliding out of fat fields, to marry the Avon beneath the tower of Christchurch. The valley of the Avon—invisible, but far to the north the trained eye may see Clearbury Ring that guards it, and the imagination may leap beyond that on to Salisbury Plain itself, and beyond the Plain to all the glorious downs of Central England. Nor is Suburbia absent. Bournemouth's ignoble coast cowers to the right, heralding the pine-trees that mean, for all their beauty, red houses, and the Stock Exchange, and extend to the gates of London itself. So tremendous is the City's trail! But the cliffs of Freshwater it shall never touch, and the island will guard the Island's purity till the end of time. Seen from the west, the Wight is beautiful beyond all laws of beauty. It is as if a fragment of England floated forward to greet the foreigner—chalk of our chalk, turf of our turf, epitome of what will follow. And behind the fragment lies Southampton, hostess to the nations, and Portsmouth, a latent fire, and all around it, with double and treble collision of tides, swirls the sea. How many villages appear in this view! How many castles! How many churches, vanished or triumphant! How many ships, railways, and roads! What incredible variety of men working beneath that lucent sky to what final end! The reason fails, like a wave on the Swanage beach; the imagination swells, spreads, and deepens, until it becomes geographic and encircles England.

So Frieda Mosebach, now Frau Architect Liesecke, and mother to her husband's baby, was brought up to these heights to be impressed, and, after a prolonged gaze, she said that the hills were more swelling here than in Pomerania, which was true, but did not seem to Mrs. Munt apposite. Poole Harbour was dry, which led her to praise the absence of muddy foreshore at Friedrich Wilhelms Bad, Rügen, where beech-trees hang over the tideless Baltic, and cows may contemplate the brine. Rather unhealthy Mrs. Munt thought this would be, water being safer when it moved about.

"And your English lakes—Vindermere, Grasmere[1]—are they, then, unhealthy?"

"No, Frau Liesecke; but that is because they are fresh water, and different. Salt water ought to have tides, and go up and down a great deal, or else it smells. Look, for instance, at an aquarium."

"An aquarium! Oh, *Meesis* Munt, you mean to tell me that fresh aquariums stink less than salt? Why, then Victor, my brother-in-law, collected many tadpoles——"

"You are not to say 'stink,'" interrupted Helen; "at least, you may say it, but you must pretend you are being funny while you say it."

"Then 'smell.' And the mud of your Pool down there—does it not smell, or may I say 'stink, ha, ha'?"

"There always has been mud in Poole Harbour," said Mrs. Munt, with a slight frown. "The rivers bring it down, and a most valuable oyster-fishery depends upon it."

"Yes, that is so," conceded Frieda; and another international incident was closed.

"'Bournemouth is,'" resumed their hostess, quoting a local rhyme to which she was much attached—"'Bournemouth is, Poole was, and Swanage is to be the most important town of all and biggest of the three.' Now, Frau Liesecke, I have shown you Bournemouth, and I have shown you Poole, so let us walk backward a little, and look down again at Swanage."

"Aunt Juley, wouldn't that be Meg's train?"

A tiny puff of smoke had been circling the harbour, and now was bearing southwards towards them over the black and the gold.

"Oh, dearest Margaret, I do hope she won't be overtired."

"Oh, I do wonder—I do wonder whether she's taken the house."

"I hope she hasn't been hasty."

"So do I—oh, *so* do I."

"Will it be as beautiful as Wickham Place?" Frieda asked.

"I should think it would. Trust Mr. Wilcox for doing himself proud. All those Ducie Street houses are beautiful in their modern way, and I can't think why he doesn't keep on with it. But it's really for Evie that he went there, and now that Evie's going to be married——"

---

[1]Windermere and Grasmere, in the Lake District of northwestern England (famously associated with William Wordsworth and Romanticism's other Lake Poets, late 18th–early 19th c).

"Ah!"

"You've never seen Miss Wilcox, Frieda. How absurdly matrimonial you are!"

"But sister to that Paul?"

"Yes."

"And to that Charles," said Mrs. Munt with feeling. "Oh, Helen, Helen, what a time that was!"

Helen laughed. "Meg and I haven't got such tender hearts. If there's a chance of a cheap house, we go for it."

"Now look, Frau Liesecke, at my niece's train. You see, it is coming towards us—coming, coming; and, when it gets to Corfe, it will actually go *through* the downs, on which we are standing, so that, if we walk over, as I suggested, and look down on Swanage, we shall see it coming on the other side. Shall we?"

Frieda assented, and in a few minutes they had crossed the ridge and exchanged the greater view for the lesser. Rather a dull valley lay below, backed by the slope of the coastward downs. They were looking across the Isle of Purbeck and on to Swanage, soon to be the most important town of all, and ugliest of the three. Margaret's train reappeared as promised, and was greeted with approval by her aunt. It came to a standstill in the middle distance, and there it had been planned that Tibby should meet her, and drive her, and a tea-basket, up to join them.

"You see," continued Helen to her cousin, "the Wilcoxes collect houses as your Victor collects tadpoles. They have, one, Ducie Street; two, Howards End, where my great rumpus was; three, a country seat in Shropshire; four, Charles has a house in Hilton; and five, another near Epsom; and six, Evie will have a house when she marries, and probably a pied-à-terre in the country—which makes seven. Oh yes, and Paul a hut in Africa makes eight. I wish we could get Howards End. That was something like a dear little house! Didn't you think so, Aunt Juley?"

"I had too much to do, dear, to look at it," said Mrs. Munt, with a gracious dignity. "I had everything to settle and explain, and Charles Wilcox to keep in his place besides. It isn't likely I should remember much. I just remember having lunch in your bedroom."

"Yes, so do I. But, oh dear, dear, how dreadful it all seems! And in the autumn there began that anti-Pauline[2] movement—you, and Frieda, and Meg, and Mrs. Wilcox, all obsessed with the idea that I might yet marry Paul."

[2]Punning on theology opposed to St. Paul's doctrines.

"You yet may," said Frieda despondently.

Helen shook her head. "The Great Wilcox Peril will never return. If I'm certain of anything it's of that."

"One is certain of nothing but the truth of one's own emotions."

The remark fell damply on the conversation. But Helen slipped her arm round her cousin, somehow liking her the better for making it. It was not an original remark, nor had Frieda appropriated it passionately, for she had a patriotic rather than a philosophic mind. Yet it betrayed that interest in the universal which the average Teuton[3] possesses and the average Englishman does not. It was, however illogically, the good, the beautiful, the true, as opposed to the respectable, the pretty, the adequate. It was a landscape of Böcklin's beside a landscape of Leader's, strident and ill-considered, but quivering into supernatural life.[4] It sharpened idealism, stirred the soul. It may have been a bad preparation for what followed.

"Look!" cried Aunt Juley, hurrying away from generalities over the narrow summit of the down. "Stand where I stand, and you will see the pony-cart coming. I see the pony-cart coming."

They stood and saw the pony-cart coming. Margaret and Tibby were presently seen coming in it. Leaving the outskirts of Swanage, it drove for a little through the budding lanes, and then began the ascent.

"Have you got the house?" they shouted, long before she could possibly hear.

Helen ran down to meet her. The highroad passed over a saddle, and a track went thence at right angles along the ridge of the down.

"Have you got the house?"

Margaret shook her head.

"Oh, what a nuisance! So we're as we were?"

"Not exactly."

She got out, looking tired.

"Some mystery," said Tibby. "We are to be enlightened presently."

Margaret came close up to her and whispered that she had had a proposal of marriage from Mr. Wilcox.

Helen was amused. She opened the gate on to the downs so that her brother might lead the pony through. "It's just like a widower," she remarked. "They've cheek enough for anything, and invariably select one of their first wife's friends."

[3]German person (from the name of an ancient tribe).

[4]Arnold Böcklin (1827–1901), Swiss Symbolist painter known for his depictions of mythological figures and haunting, imaginary landscapes; Benjamin Williams Leader (1831–1923), English landscape painter.

Margaret's face flashed despair.

"That type——" She broke off with a cry. "Meg, not anything wrong with you?"

"Wait one minute," said Margaret, whispering always.

"But you've never conceivably—you've never——" She pulled herself together. "Tibby, hurry up through; I can't hold this gate indefinitely. Aunt Juley! I say, Aunt Juley, make the tea, will you, and Frieda; we've got to talk houses, and'll come on afterwards." And then, turning her face to her sister's, she burst into tears.

Margaret was stupefied. She heard herself saying, "Oh, really——" She felt herself touched with a hand that trembled.

"Don't," sobbed Helen, "don't, don't, Meg, don't!" She seemed incapable of saying any other word. Margaret, trembling herself, led her forward up the road, till they strayed through another gate on to the down.

"Don't, don't do such a thing! I tell you not to—don't! I know—don't!"

"What do you know?"

"Panic and emptiness," sobbed Helen. "Don't!"

Then Margaret thought, "Helen is a little selfish. I have never behaved like this when there has seemed a chance of her marrying." She said: "But we would still see each other very often, and you——"

"It's not a thing like that," sobbed Helen. And she broke right away and wandered distractedly upwards, stretching her hands towards the view and crying.

"What's happened to you?" called Margaret, following through the wind that gathers at sundown on the northern slopes of hills. "But it's stupid!" And suddenly stupidity seized her, and the immense landscape was blurred. But Helen turned back.

"Meg——"

"I don't know what's happened to either of us," said Margaret, wiping her eyes. "We must both have gone mad." Then Helen wiped hers, and they even laughed a little.

"Look here, sit down."

"All right; I'll sit down if you'll sit down."

"There. (One kiss.) Now, whatever, whatever is the matter?"

"I do mean what I said. Don't; it wouldn't do."

"Oh, Helen, stop saying 'don't'! It's ignorant. It's as if your head wasn't out of the slime. 'Don't' is probably what Mrs. Bast says all the day to Mr. Bast."

Helen was silent.

"Well?"

"Tell me about it first, and meanwhile perhaps I'll have got my head out of the slime."

"That's better. Well, where shall I begin? When I arrived at Waterloo—no, I'll go back before that, because I'm anxious you should know everything from the first. The 'first' was about ten days ago. It was the day Mr. Bast came to tea and lost his temper. I was defending him, and Mr. Wilcox became jealous about me, however slightly. I thought it was the involuntary thing, which men can't help any more than we can. You know—at least, I know in my own case—when a man has said to me, 'So-and-so's a pretty girl,' I am seized with a momentary sourness against So-and-so, and long to tweak her ear. It's a tiresome feeling, but not an important one, and one easily manages it. But it wasn't only this in Mr. Wilcox's case, I gather now."

"Then you love him?"

Margaret considered. "It is wonderful knowing that a real man cares for you," she said. "The mere fact of that grows more tremendous. Remember, I've known and liked him steadily for nearly three years."

"But loved him?"

Margaret peered into her past. It is pleasant to analyze feelings while they are still only feelings, and unembodied in the social fabric. With her arm round Helen, and her eyes shifting over the view, as if this county or that could reveal the secret of her own heart, she meditated honestly, and said, "No."

"But you will?"

"Yes," said Margaret, "of that I'm pretty sure. Indeed, I began the moment he spoke to me."

"And have settled to marry him?"

"I had, but am wanting a long talk about it now. What *is* it against him, Helen? You must try and say."

Helen, in her turn, looked outwards. "It is ever since Paul," she said finally.

"But what has Mr. Wilcox to do with Paul?"

"But he was there, they were all there that morning when I came down to breakfast, and saw that Paul was frightened—the man who loved me frightened and all his paraphernalia fallen, so that I knew it was impossible, because personal relations are the important thing for ever and ever, and not this outer life of telegrams and anger."

She poured the sentence forth in one breath, but her sister understood it, because it touched on thoughts that were familiar between them.

"That's foolish. In the first place, I disagree about the outer life. Well, we've often argued that. The real point is that there is the widest gulf between my love-making and yours. Yours was romance; mine will be prose. I'm not running it down—a very good kind of prose, but well considered, well thought out. For instance, I know all Mr. Wilcox's faults. He's afraid of emotion. He cares too much about success, too little about the past. His sympathy lacks poetry, and so isn't sympathy really. I'd even say"—she looked at the shining lagoons—"that, spiritually, he's not as honest as I am. Doesn't that satisfy you?"

"No, it doesn't," said Helen. "It makes me feel worse and worse. You must be mad."

Margaret made a movement of irritation.

"I don't intend him, or any man or any woman, to be all my life—good heavens, no! There are heaps of things in me that he doesn't, and shall never, understand."

Thus she spoke before the wedding ceremony and the physical union, before the astonishing glass shade had fallen that interposes between married couples and the world. She was to keep her independence more than do most women as yet. Marriage was to alter her fortunes rather than her character, and she was not far wrong in boasting that she understood her future husband. Yet he did alter her character—a little. There was an unforeseen surprise, a cessation of the winds and odours of life, a social pressure that would have her think conjugally.

"So with him," she continued. "There are heaps of things in him—more especially things that he does—that will always be hidden from me. He has all those public qualities which you so despise and enable all this——" She waved her hand at the landscape, which confirmed anything. "If Wilcoxes hadn't worked and died in England for thousands of years, you and I couldn't sit here without having our throats cut. There would be no trains, no ships to carry us literary people about in, no fields even. Just savagery. No—perhaps not even that. Without their spirit life might never have moved out of protoplasm. More and more do I refuse to draw my income and sneer at those who guarantee it. There are times when it seems to me——"

"And to me, and to all women. So one kissed Paul."

"That's brutal," said Margaret. "Mine is an absolutely different case. I've thought things out."

"It makes no difference thinking things out. They come to the same."

"Rubbish!"

There was a long silence, during which the tide returned into Poole Harbour. "One would lose something," murmured Helen, apparently to herself. The water crept over the mud-flats towards the gorse and the blackened heather. Branksea Island lost its immense foreshores, and became a sombre episode of trees. Frome was forced inward towards Dorchester, Stour against Wimborne, Avon towards Salisbury, and over the immense displacement the sun presided, leading it to triumph ere he sank to rest. England was alive, throbbing through all her estuaries, crying for joy through the mouths of all her gulls, and the north wind, with contrary motion, blew stronger against her rising seas. What did it mean? For what end are her fair complexities, her changes of soil, her sinuous coast? Does she belong to those who have moulded her and made her feared by other lands, or to those who have added nothing to her power, but have somehow seen her, seen the whole island at once, lying as a jewel in a silver sea,[5] sailing as a ship of souls, with all the brave world's fleet accompanying her towards eternity?

## CHAPTER XX

MARGARET had often wondered at the disturbance that takes place in the world's waters, when Love, who seems so tiny a pebble, slips in. Whom does Love concern beyond the beloved and the lover? Yet his impact deluges a hundred shores. No doubt the disturbance is really the spirit of the generations, welcoming the new generation, and chafing against the ultimate Fate, who holds all the seas in the palm of her hand. But Love cannot understand this. He cannot comprehend another's infinity; he is conscious only of his own—flying sunbeam, falling rose, pebble that asks for one quiet plunge below the fretting interplay of space and time. He knows that he will survive at the end of things, and be gathered by Fate as a jewel from the slime, and be handed with admiration round the assembly of the gods. "Men did produce this," they will say, and, saying, they will give men immortality. But meanwhile—what agitations meanwhile! The foundations of Property and Propriety are laid bare, twin rocks; Family Pride flounders to the surface, puffing and blowing, and refusing to be comforted; Theology, vaguely ascetic, gets up a nasty ground swell. Then the lawyers are aroused—cold

---

[5]Echoing John of Gaunt's praise of England as a "precious stone set in the silver sea," in Shakespeare's *Richard II*, 2.1.

brood—and creep out of their holes. They do what they can; they tidy up Property and Propriety, reassure Theology and Family Pride. Half-guineas[1] are poured on the troubled waters, the lawyers creep back, and, if all has gone well, Love joins one man and woman together in Matrimony.

Margaret had expected the disturbance, and was not irritated by it. For a sensitive woman she had steady nerves, and could bear with the incongruous and the grotesque; and, besides, there was nothing excessive about her love-affair. Good-humour was the dominant note of her relations with Mr. Wilcox, or, as I must now call him, Henry. Henry did not encourage romance, and she was no girl to fidget for it. An acquaintance had become a lover, might become a husband, but would retain all that she had noted in the acquaintance; and love must confirm an old relation rather than reveal a new one.

In this spirit she promised to marry him.

He was in Swanage on the morrow, bearing the engagement-ring. They greeted one another with a hearty cordiality that impressed Aunt Juley. Henry dined at The Bays, but had engaged a bedroom in the principal hotel: he was one of those men who know the principal hotel by instinct. After dinner he asked Margaret if she wouldn't care for a turn on the Parade. She accepted, and could not repress a little tremor; it would be her first real love scene. But as she put on her hat she burst out laughing. Love was so unlike the article served up in books: the joy, though genuine, was different; the mystery an unexpected mystery. For one thing, Mr. Wilcox still seemed a stranger.

For a time they talked about the ring; then she said:

"Do you remember the Embankment at Chelsea? It can't be ten days ago."

"Yes," he said, laughing. "And you and your sister were head and ears deep in some Quixotic[2] scheme. Ah well!"

"I little thought then, certainly. Did you?"

"I don't know about that; I shouldn't like to say."

"Why, was it earlier?" she cried. "Did you think of me this way earlier! How extraordinarily interesting, Henry! Tell me."

But Henry had no intention of telling. Perhaps he could not have told, for his mental states became obscure as soon as he had passed through them. He misliked the very word "interesting," connoting it

---

[1]The gold coins called guineas were minted only until 1813, but the term was used well into the twentieth century to indicate £1 plus 1s, especially in prices of luxury goods.

[2]Fancifully idealistic, from the Cervantes character Don Quixote.

with wasted energy and even with morbidity. Hard facts were enough for him.

"I didn't think of it," she pursued. "No; when you spoke to me in the drawing-room, that was practically the first. It was all so different from what it's supposed to be. On the stage, or in books, a proposal is—how shall I put it? —a full-blown affair, a kind of bouquet; it loses its literal meaning. But in life a proposal really is a proposal——"

"By the way——"

"—a suggestion, a seed," she concluded; and the thought flew away into darkness.

"I was thinking, if you didn't mind, that we ought to spend this evening in a business talk; there will be so much to settle."

"I think so too. Tell me, in the first place, how did you get on with Tibby?"

"With your brother?"

"Yes, during cigarettes."

"Oh, very well."

"I am so glad," she answered, a little surprised. "What did you talk about? Me, presumably."

"About Greece too."

"Greece was a very good card, Henry. Tibby's only a boy still, and one has to pick and choose subjects a little. Well done."

"I was telling him I have shares in a currant-farm near Calamata."[3]

"What a delightful thing to have shares in! Can't we go there for our honeymoon?"

"What to do?"

"To eat the currants. And isn't there marvellous scenery?"

"Moderately, but it's not the kind of place one could possibly go to with a lady."

"Why not?"

"No hotels."

"Some ladies do without hotels. Are you aware that Helen and I have walked alone over the Apennines,[4] with our luggage on our backs?"

"I wasn't aware, and, if I can manage it, you will never do such a thing again."

She said more gravely: "You haven't found time for a talk with Helen yet, I suppose?"

"No."

[3]Kalamata, city in southern Greece.
[4]Mountains stretching from the north to the south of Italy.

"Do, before you go. I am so anxious you two should be friends."

"Your sister and I have always hit it off," he said negligently. "But we're drifting away from our business. Let me begin at the beginning. You know that Evie is going to marry Percy Cahill."

"Dolly's uncle."

"Exactly. The girl's madly in love with him. A very good sort of fellow, but he demands—and rightly—a suitable provision with her. And in the second place, you will naturally understand, there is Charles. Before leaving town, I wrote Charles a very careful letter. You see, he has an increasing family and increasing expenses, and the I. and W. A. is nothing particular just now, though capable of development."

"Poor fellow!" murmured Margaret, looking out to sea, and not understanding.

"Charles being the elder son, some day Charles will have Howards End; but I am anxious, in my own happiness, not to be unjust to others."

"Of course not," she began, and then gave a little cry. "You mean money. How stupid I am! Of course not!"

Oddly enough, he winced a little at the word. "Yes. Money, since you put it so frankly. I am determined to be just to all—just to you, just to them. I am determined that my children shall have no case against me."

"Be generous to them," she said sharply. "Bother justice!"

"I am determined—and have already written to Charles to that effect——"

"But how much have you got?"

"What?"

"How much have you a year? I've six hundred."

"My income?"

"Yes. We must begin with how much you have, before we can settle how much you can give Charles. Justice, and even generosity, depend on that."

"I must say you're a downright young woman," he observed, patting her arm and laughing a little. "What a question to spring on a fellow!"

"Don't you know your income? Or don't you want to tell it me?"

"I——"

"That's all right"—now she patted him—"don't tell me. I don't want to know. I can do the sum just as well by proportion. Divide your income into ten parts. How many parts would you give to Evie, how many to Charles, how many to Paul?"

"The fact is, my dear, I hadn't any intention of bothering you with details. I only wanted to let you know that—well, that something must be done for the others, and you've understood me perfectly, so let's pass on to the next point."

"Yes, we've settled that," said Margaret, undisturbed by his strategic blunderings. "Go ahead; give away all you can, bearing in mind. I've a clear six hundred. What a mercy it is to have all this money about one."

"We've none too much, I assure you; you're marrying a poor man."

"Helen wouldn't agree with me here," she continued. "Helen daren't slang the rich, being rich herself, but she would like to. There's an odd notion, that I haven't yet got hold of, running about at the back of her brain, that poverty is somehow 'real.' She dislikes all organization, and probably confuses wealth with the technique of wealth. Sovereigns[5] in a stocking wouldn't bother her; cheques do. Helen is too relentless. One can't deal in her high-handed manner with the world."

"There's this other point, and then I must go back to my hotel and write some letters. What's to be done now about the house in Ducie Street?"

"Keep it on—at least, it depends. When do you want to marry me?"

She raised her voice, as too often, and some youths, who were also taking the evening air, overheard her. "Getting a bit hot, eh?" said one. Mr. Wilcox turned on them, and said sharply, "I say!" There was silence. "Take care I don't report you to the police." They moved away quietly enough, but were only biding their time, and the rest of the conversation was punctuated by peals of ungovernable laughter.

Lowering his voice and infusing a hint of reproof into it, he said: "Evie will probably be married in September. We could scarcely think of anything before then."

"The earlier the nicer, Henry. Females are not supposed to say such things, but the earlier the nicer."

"How about September for us too?" he asked, rather dryly.

"Right. Shall we go into Ducie Street ourselves in September? Or shall we try to bounce Helen and Tibby into it? That's rather an idea. They are so unbusinesslike, we could make them do anything by judicious management. Look here—yes. We'll do that. And we ourselves could live at Howards End or Shropshire."

He blew out his cheeks. "Heavens! how you women do fly round! My head's in a whirl. Point by point, Margaret. Howards End's impossible. I let it to Hamar Bryce on a three years' agreement last March. Don't you remember? Oniton. Well, that is much, much too far away to rely on entirely. You will be able to be down there entertaining a certain amount, but we must have a house within easy reach of Town. Only Ducie Street has huge drawbacks. There's a mews[6] behind."

Margaret could not help laughing. It was the first she had heard of the mews behind Ducie Street. When she was a possible tenant it had suppressed itself, not consciously, but automatically. The breezy Wilcox manner, though genuine, lacked the clearness of vision that is imperative for truth. When Henry lived in Ducie Street he remembered the mews; when he tried to let he forgot it; and if anyone had remarked that the mews must be either there or not, he would have felt annoyed, and afterwards have found some opportunity of stigmatizing the speaker as academic. So does my grocer stigmatize me when I complain of the quality of his sultanas,[7] and he answers in one breath that they are the best sultanas, and how can I expect the best sultanas at that price? It is a flaw inherent in the business mind, and Margaret may do well to be tender to it, considering all that the business mind has done for England.

"Yes, in summer especially, the mews is a serious nuisance. The smoking-room, too, is an abominable little den. The house opposite has been taken by operatic people. Ducie Street's going down, it's my private opinion."

"How sad! It's only a few years since they built those pretty houses."

"Shows things are moving. Good for trade."

"I hate this continual flux of London. It is an epitome of us at our worst—eternal formlessness; all the qualities, good, bad, and indifferent, streaming away—streaming, streaming for ever. That's why I dread it so. I mistrust rivers, even in scenery. Now, the sea——"

"High tide, yes."

"Hoy toid"—from the promenading youths.

"And these are the men to whom we give the vote," observed Mr. Wilcox, omitting to add that they were also the men to whom he gave work as clerks—work that scarcely encouraged them to grow into other men. "However, they have their own lives and interests. Let's get on."

He turned as he spoke, and prepared to see her back to The Bays. The business was over. His hotel was in the opposite direction, and if he accompanied her his letters would be late for the post. She implored him not to come, but he was obdurate.

[6]Row of stables.
[7]Small seedless raisins.

"A nice beginning, if your aunt saw you slip in alone!"

"But I always do go about alone. Considering I've walked over the Apennines, it's common sense. You will make me so angry. I don't the least take it as a compliment."

He laughed, and lit a cigar. "It isn't meant as a compliment, my dear. I just won't have you going about in the dark. Such people about too! It's dangerous."

"Can't I look after myself? I do wish——"

"Come along, Margaret; no wheedling."

A younger woman might have resented his masterly ways, but Margaret had too firm a grip of life to make a fuss. She was, in her own way, as masterly. If he was a fortress she was a mountain peak, whom all might tread, but whom the snows made nightly virginal. Disdaining the heroic outfit, excitable in her methods, garrulous, episodical, shrill, she misled her lover much as she had misled her aunt. He mistook her fertility for weakness. He supposed her "as clever as they make 'em," but no more, not realizing that she was penetrating to the depths of his soul, and approving of what she found there.

And if insight were sufficient, if the inner life were the whole of life, their happiness had been assured.

They walked ahead briskly. The parade and the road after it were well lighted, but it was darker in Aunt Juley's garden. As they were going up by the side-paths, through some rhododendrons, Mr. Wilcox, who was in front, said "Margaret" rather huskily, turned, dropped his cigar, and took her in his arms.

She was startled, and nearly screamed, but recovered herself at once, and kissed with genuine love the lips that were pressed against her own. It was their first kiss, and when it was over he saw her safely to the door and rang the bell for her, but disappeared into the night before the maid answered it. On looking back, the incident displeased her. It was so isolated. Nothing in their previous conversation had heralded it, and, worse still, no tenderness had ensued. If a man cannot lead up to passion he can at all events lead down from it, and she had hoped, after her complaisance,[8] for some interchange of gentle words. But he had hurried away as if ashamed, and for an instant she was reminded of Helen and Paul.

[8]Obligingness; deference.

## CHAPTER XXI

CHARLES had just been scolding his Dolly. She deserved the scolding, and had bent before it, but her head, though bloody, was unsubdued, and her chirrupings began to mingle with his retreating thunder.

"You've woken the baby. I knew you would. (Rum-ti-foo, Rackety-tackety-Tompkin!) I'm not responsible for what Uncle Percy does, nor for anybody else or anything, so there!"

"Who asked him while I was away? Who asked my sister down to meet him? Who sent them out in the motor day after day?"

"Charles, that reminds me of some poem."

"Does it indeed? We shall all be dancing to a very different music presently. Miss Schlegel has fairly got us on toast."

"I could simply scratch that woman's eyes out, and to say it's my fault is most unfair."

"It's your fault, and five months ago you admitted it."

"I didn't."

"You did."

"Tootle, tootle, playing on the pootle!" exclaimed Dolly, suddenly devoting herself to the child.

"It's all very well to turn the conversation, but father would never have dreamt of marrying as long as Evie was there to make him comfortable. But you must needs start match-making. Besides, Cahill's too old."

"Of course, if you're going to be rude to Uncle Percy——"

"Miss Schlegel always meant to get hold of Howards End, and, thanks to you, she's got it."

"I call the way you twist things round and make them hang together most unfair. You couldn't have been nastier if you'd caught me flirting. Could he, diddums?"

"We're in a bad hole, and must make the best of it. I shall answer the pater's[1] letter civilly. He's evidently anxious to do the decent thing. But I do not intend to forget these Schlegels in a hurry. As long as they're on their best behaviour—Dolly, are you listening?—we'll behave, too. But if I find them giving themselves airs, or monopolizing my father, or at all ill-treating him, or worrying him with their artistic beastliness, I intend to put my foot down, yes, firmly. Taking my mother's place! Heaven knows what poor old Paul will say when the news reaches him."

The interlude closes. It has taken place in Charles's garden at Hilton. He and Dolly are sitting in deck-chairs, and their motor is re-

---

[1]Father's (slang, from Latin: father).

garding them placidly from its garage across the lawn. A short-frocked edition of Charles also regards them placidly; a perambulator edition is squeaking; a third edition is expected shortly. Nature is turning out Wilcoxes in this peaceful abode, so that they may inherit the earth.

## CHAPTER XXII

MARGARET greeted her lord with peculiar tenderness on the morrow. Mature as he was, she might yet be able to help him to the building of the rainbow bridge that should connect the prose in us with the passion. Without it we are meaningless fragments, half monks, half beasts, unconnected arches that have never joined into a man. With it love is born, and alights on the highest curve, glowing against the grey, sober against the fire. Happy the man who sees from either aspect the glory of these outspread wings. The roads of his soul lie clear, and he and his friends shall find easy-going.

It was hard-going in the roads of Mr. Wilcox's soul. From boyhood he had neglected them. "I am not a fellow who bothers about my own inside." Outwardly he was cheerful, reliable, and brave; but within, all had reverted to chaos, ruled, so far as it was ruled at all, by an incomplete asceticism. Whether as boy, husband, or widower, he had always the sneaking belief that bodily passion is bad, a belief that is desirable only when held passionately. Religion had confirmed him. The words that were read aloud on Sunday to him and to other respectable men were the words that had once kindled the souls of St. Catharine and St. Francis[1] into a white-hot hatred of the carnal. He could not be as the saints and love the Infinite with a seraphic ardour, but he could be a little ashamed of loving a wife. 'Amabat, amare timebat.'[2] And it was here that Margaret hoped to help him.

It did not seem so difficult. She need trouble him with no gift of her own. She would only point out the salvation that was latent in his own soul, and in the soul of every man. Only connect! That was the whole of her sermon. Only connect the prose and the passion, and both will be exalted, and human love will be seen at its height. Live in fragments no longer. Only connect, and the beast and the monk, robbed of the isolation that is life to either, will die.

---

[1] St. Catherine of Alexandria (early 4th c) and St. Francis of Assisi (12th–13th c), both associated with chastity.

[2] Latin: "He loved, he was afraid to love."

Nor was the message difficult to give. It need not take the form of a good "talking." By quiet indications the bridge would be built and span their lives with beauty.

But she failed. For there was one quality in Henry for which she was never prepared, however much she reminded herself of it: his obtuseness. He simply did not notice things, and there was no more to be said. He never noticed that Helen and Frieda were hostile, or that Tibby was not interested in currant plantations; he never noticed the lights and shades that exist in the greyest conversation, the finger-posts, the milestones, the collisions, the illimitable views. Once—on another occasion—she scolded him about it. He was puzzled, but replied with a laugh: "My motto is Concentrate. I've no intention of frittering away my strength on that sort of thing." "It isn't frittering away the strength," she protested. "It's enlarging the space in which you may be strong." He answered: "You're a clever little woman, but my motto's Concentrate." And this morning he concentrated with a vengeance.

They met in the rhododendrons of yesterday. In the daylight the bushes were inconsiderable and the path was bright in the morning sun. She was with Helen, who had been ominously quiet since the affair was settled. "Here we all are!" she cried, and took him by one hand, retaining her sister's in the other.

"Here we are. Good-morning, Helen."

Helen replied, "Good-morning, Mr. Wilcox."

"Henry, she has had such a nice letter from the queer, cross boy. Do you remember him? He had a sad moustache, but the back of his head was young."

"I have had a letter too. Not a nice one—I want to talk it over with you:" for Leonard Bast was nothing to him now that she had given him her word; the triangle of sex was broken for ever.

"Thanks to your hint, he's clearing out of the Porphyrion."

"Not a bad business that Porphyrion," he said absently, as he took his own letter out of his pocket.

"Not a *bad*——" she exclaimed, dropping his hand. "Surely, on Chelsea Embankment——"

"Here's our hostess. Good-morning, Mrs. Munt. Fine rhododendrons. Good-morning, Frau Liesecke; we manage to grow flowers in England, don't we?"

"Not a *bad* business?"

"No. My letter's about Howards End. Bryce has been ordered abroad, and wants to sublet it. I am far from sure that I shall give him permission. There was no clause in the agreement. In my opinion, subletting is a mistake. If he can find me another tenant, whom I consider suitable, I may cancel the agreement. Morning, Schlegel. Don't you think that's better than subletting?"

Helen had dropped her hand now, and he had steered her past the whole party to the seaward side of the house. Beneath them was the bourgeois little bay, which must have yearned all through the centuries for just such a watering-place as Swanage to be built on its margin. The waves were colourless, and the Bournemouth steamer gave a further touch of insipidity, drawn up against the pier and hooting wildly for excursionists.

"When there is a sublet I find that damage——"

"Do excuse me, but about the Porphyrion. I don't feel easy— might I just bother you, Henry?"

Her manner was so serious that he stopped, and asked her a little sharply what she wanted.

"You said on Chelsea Embankment, surely, that it was a bad concern, so we advised this clerk to clear out. He writes this morning that he's taken our advice, and now you say it's not a bad concern."

"A clerk who clears out of any concern, good or bad, without securing a berth somewhere else first, is a fool, and I've no pity for him."

"He has not done that. He's going into a bank in Camden Town, he says. The salary's much lower, but he hopes to manage—a branch of Dempster's Bank. Is that all right?"

"Dempster! My goodness me, yes."

"More right than the Porphyrion?"

"Yes, yes, yes; safe as houses—safer."

"Very many thanks. I'm sorry—if you sublet——?"

"If he sublets, I shan't have the same control. In theory there should be no more damage done at Howards End; in practice there will be. Things may be done for which no money can compensate. For instance, I shouldn't want that fine wych-elm spoilt. It hangs—— Margaret, we must go and see the old place some time. It's pretty in its way. We'll motor down and have lunch with Charles."

"I should enjoy that," said Margaret bravely.

"What about next Wednesday?"

"Wednesday? No, I couldn't well do that. Aunt Juley expects us to stop here another week at least."

"But you can give that up now."

"Er—no," said Margaret, after a moment's thought.

"Oh, that'll be all right. I'll speak to her."

"This visit is a high solemnity. My aunt counts on it year after year. She turns the house upside down for us; she invites our special friends—she scarcely knows Frieda, and we can't leave her on her hands. I missed one day, and she would be so hurt if I didn't stay the full ten."

"But I'll say a word to her. Don't you bother."

"Henry, I won't go. Don't bully me."

"You want to see the house, though?"

"Very much—I've heard so much about it, one way or the other. Aren't there pigs' teeth in the wych-elm?"

"*Pigs' teeth?*"

"And you chew the bark for toothache."

"What a rum notion! Of course not!"

"Perhaps I have confused it with some other tree. There are still a great number of sacred trees in England, it seems."

But he left her to intercept Mrs. Munt, whose voice could be heard in the distance: to be intercepted himself by Helen.

"Oh, Mr. Wilcox, about the Porphyrion——" she began, and went scarlet all over her face.

"It's all right," called Margaret, catching them up. "Dempster's Bank's better."

"But I think you told us the Porphyrion was bad, and would smash before Christmas."

"Did I? It was still outside the Tariff Ring, and had to take rotten policies. Lately it came in—safe as houses now."

"In other words, Mr. Bast need never have left it."

"No, the fellow needn't."

"—and needn't have started life elsewhere at a greatly reduced salary."

"He only says 'reduced,'" corrected Margaret, seeing trouble ahead.

"With a man so poor, every reduction must be great. I consider it a deplorable misfortune."

Mr. Wilcox, intent on his business with Mrs. Munt, was going steadily on, but the last remark made him say: "What? What's that? Do you mean that I'm responsible?"

"You're ridiculous, Helen."

"You seem to think——" He looked at his watch. "Let me explain the point to you. It is like this. You seem to assume, when a business concern is conducting a delicate negotiation, it ought to keep the public informed stage by stage. The Porphyrion, according to you, was bound to say, 'I am trying all I can to get into the Tariff Ring. I am not sure that I shall succeed, but it is the only thing that will save me from insolvency, and I am trying.' My dear Helen——"

"Is that your point? A man who had little money has less—that's mine."

"I am grieved for your clerk. But it is all in the day's work. It's part of the battle of life."

"A man who had little money," she repeated, "has less, owing to us. Under these circumstances I do not consider 'the battle of life' a happy expression."

"Oh come, come!" he protested pleasantly. "You're not to blame. No one's to blame."

"Is no one to blame for anything?"

"I wouldn't say that, but you're taking it far too seriously. Who is this fellow?"

"We have told you about the fellow twice already," said Helen. "You have even met the fellow. He is very poor and his wife is an extravagant imbecile. He is capable of better things. We—we, the upper classes—thought we would help him from the height of our superior knowledge—and here's the result!"

He raised his finger. "Now, a word of advice."

"I require no more advice."

"A word of advice. Don't take up that sentimental attitude over the poor. See that she doesn't, Margaret. The poor are poor, and one's sorry for them, but there it is. As civilization moves forward, the shoe is bound to pinch in places, and it's absurd to pretend that anyone is responsible personally. Neither you, nor I, nor my informant, nor the man who informed him, nor the directors of the Porphyrion, are to blame for this clerk's loss of salary. It's just the shoe pinching—no one can help it; and it might easily have been worse."

Helen quivered with indignation.

"By all means subscribe to charities—subscribe to them largely—but don't get carried away by absurd schemes of Social Reform. I see a good deal behind the scenes, and you can take it from me that there is no Social Question—except for a few journalists who try to get a living out of the phrase. There are just rich and poor, as there always have been and always will be. Point me out a time when men have been equal——"

"I didn't say——"

"Point me out a time when desire for equality has made them happier. No, no. You can't. There always have been rich and poor. I'm no fatalist. Heaven forbid! But our civilization is moulded by great impersonal forces" (his voice grew complacent; it always did when he eliminated the personal), "and there always will be rich and poor. You can't deny it" (and now it was a respectful voice)—"and you can't deny that, in spite of all, the tendency of civilization has on the whole been upward."

"Owing to God, I suppose," flashed Helen.

He stared at her.

"You grab the dollars. God does the rest."

It was no good instructing the girl if she was going to talk about God in that neurotic modern way. Fraternal to the last, he left her for the quieter company of Mrs. Munt. He thought, "She rather reminds me of Dolly."

Helen looked out at the sea.

"Don't even discuss political economy with Henry," advised her sister. "It'll only end in a cry."

"But he must be one of those men who have reconciled science with religion," said Helen slowly. "I don't like those men. They are scientific themselves, and talk of the survival of the fittest, and cut down the salaries of their clerks, and stunt the independence of all who may menace their comfort, but yet they believe that somehow good—it is always that sloppy 'somehow'—will be the outcome, and that in some mystical way the Mr. Basts of the future will benefit because the Mr. Basts of to-day are in pain."

"He is such a man in theory. But oh, Helen, in theory!"

"But oh, Meg, what a theory!"

"Why should you put things so bitterly, dearie?"

"Because I'm an old maid," said Helen, biting her lip. "I can't think why I go on like this myself." She shook off her sister's hand and went into the house. Margaret, distressed at the day's beginning, followed the Bournemouth steamer with her eyes. She saw that Helen's nerves were exasperated by the unlucky Bast business beyond the bounds of politeness. There might at any minute be a real explosion, which even Henry would notice. Henry must be removed.

"Margaret!" her aunt called. "Magsy! It isn't true, surely, what Mr. Wilcox says, that you want to go away early next week?"

"Not 'want,'" was Margaret's prompt reply; "but there is so much to be settled, and I do want to see the Charles'."

"But going away without taking the Weymouth trip, or even the Lulworth?" said Mrs. Munt, coming nearer. "Without going once more up Nine Barrows Down?"

"I'm afraid so."

Mr. Wilcox rejoined her with, "Good! I did the breaking of the ice."

A wave of tenderness came over her. She put a hand on either shoulder, and looked deeply into the black, bright eyes. What was behind their competent stare? She knew, but was not disquieted.

## CHAPTER XXIII

MARGARET had no intention of letting things slide, and the evening before she left Swanage she gave her sister a thorough scolding. She censured her, not for disapproving of the engagement, but for throwing over her disapproval a veil of mystery. Helen was equally frank. "Yes," she said, with the air of one looking inwards, "there is a mystery. I can't help it. It's not my fault. It's the way life has been made." Helen in those days was over-interested in the subconscious self. She exaggerated the Punch and Judy aspect of life, and spoke of mankind as puppets, whom an invisible showman twitches into love and war. Margaret pointed out that if she dwelt on this she, too, would eliminate the personal. Helen was silent for a minute, and then burst into a queer speech, which cleared the air. "Go on and marry him. I think you're splendid; and if anyone can pull it off, you will." Margaret denied that there was anything to "pull off," but she continued: "Yes, there is, and I wasn't up to it with Paul. I can only do what's easy. I can only entice and be enticed. I can't, and won't, attempt difficult relations. If I marry, it will either be a man who's strong enough to boss me or whom I'm strong enough to boss. So I shan't ever marry, for there aren't such men. And Heaven help anyone whom I do marry, for I shall certainly run away from him before you can say 'Jack Robinson.' There! Because I'm uneducated. But you, you're different; you're a heroine."

"Oh, Helen! Am I? Will it be as dreadful for poor Henry as all that?"

"You mean to keep proportion, and that's heroic, it's Greek, and I don't see why it shouldn't succeed with you. Go on and fight with him and help him. Don't ask *me* for help, or even for sympathy. Henceforward I'm going my own way. I mean to be thorough, because thoroughness is easy. I mean to dislike your husband, and to tell him so. I mean to make no concessions to Tibby. If Tibby wants to live with me, he must lump me. I mean to love *you* more than ever. Yes, I do. You and I have built up something real, because it is purely spiritual. There's no veil of mystery over us. Unreality and mystery begin as soon as one touches the body. The popular view is, as usual, exactly the wrong one. Our bothers are over tangible things—money, husbands, house-hunting. But Heaven will work of itself."

Margaret was grateful for this expression of affection, and answered, "Perhaps." All vistas close in the unseen—no one doubts it—but Helen closed them rather too quickly for her taste. At every turn of speech one was confronted with reality and the absolute. Perhaps Margaret grew too old for metaphysics, perhaps Henry was weaning her from them, but she felt that there was something a little unbalanced in the mind that so readily shreds the visible. The business man who assumes that this life is everything, and the mystic who asserts that it is nothing, fail, on this side and on that, to hit the truth. "Yes, I see, dear; it's about halfway between," Aunt Juley had hazarded in earlier years. No; truth, being alive, was not halfway between anything. It was only to be found by continuous excursions into either realm, and though proportion is the final secret, to espouse it at the outset is to insure sterility.

Helen, agreeing here, disagreeing there, would have talked till midnight, but Margaret, with her packing to do, focussed the conversation on Henry. She might abuse Henry behind his back, but please would she always be civil to him in company? "I definitely dislike him, but I'll do what I can," promised Helen. "Do what you can with my friends in return."

This conversation made Margaret easier. Their inner life was so safe that they could bargain over externals in a way that would have been incredible to Aunt Juley, and impossible for Tibby or Charles. There are moments when the inner life actually "pays," when years of self-scrutiny, conducted for no ulterior motive, are suddenly of practical use. Such moments are still rare in the West; that they come at all promises a fairer future. Margaret, though unable to understand her sister, was assured against estrangement, and returned to London with a more peaceful mind.

The following morning, at eleven o'clock, she presented herself at the offices of the Imperial and West African Rubber Company. She was glad to go there, for Henry had implied his business rather than described it, and the formlessness and vagueness that one associates with Africa itself had hitherto brooded over the main sources of his wealth. Not that a visit to the office cleared things up. There was just the ordinary surface scum of ledgers and polished counters and brass bars that began and stopped for no possible reason, of electric-light globes blossoming in triplets, of little rabbit hutches faced with glass or wire, of little rabbits. And even when she penetrated to the inner depths, she found only the ordinary table and Turkey carpet, and though the map over the fireplace did depict a helping of West Africa, it was a very ordinary map. Another map hung opposite, on which the whole continent appeared, looking like a whale marked out for a blubber, and by its side was a door, shut, but Henry's voice came through it, dictating a "strong" letter. She might have been at the Porphyrion, or Dempster's Bank, or her own wine-merchant's. Everything seems just alike in these days. But perhaps she was seeing the Imperial side of the company rather than its West African, and Imperialism always had been one of her difficulties.

"One minute!" called Mr. Wilcox on receiving her name. He touched a bell, the effect of which was to produce Charles.

Charles had written his father an adequate letter—more adequate than Evie's, through which a girlish indignation throbbed. And he greeted his future stepmother with propriety.

"I hope that my wife—how do you do? —will give you a decent lunch," was his opening. "I left instructions, but we live in a rough-and-ready way. She expects you back to tea, too, after you have had a look at Howards End. I wonder what you'll think of the place. I wouldn't touch it with tongs myself. Do sit down! It's a measly little place."

"I shall enjoy seeing it," said Margaret, feeling, for the first time, shy.

"You'll see it at its worst, for Bryce decamped abroad last Monday without even arranging for a charwoman to clear up after him. I never saw such a disgraceful mess. It's unbelievable. He wasn't in the house a month."

"I've more than a little bone to pick with Bryce," called Henry from the inner chamber.

"Why did he go so suddenly?"

"Invalid type; couldn't sleep."

"Poor fellow!"

"Poor fiddlesticks!" said Mr. Wilcox, joining them. "He had the impudence to put up notice-boards without as much as saying with your leave or by your leave. Charles flung them down."

"Yes, I flung them down," said Charles modestly.

"I've sent a telegram after him, and a pretty sharp one, too. He, and he in person is responsible for the upkeep of that house for the next three years."

"The keys are at the farm; we wouldn't have the keys."

"Quite right."

"Dolly would have taken them, but I was in, fortunately."

"What's Mr. Bryce like?" asked Margaret.

But nobody cared. Mr. Bryce was the tenant, who had no right to sublet; to have defined him further was a waste of time. On his misdeeds they descanted profusely, until the girl who had been typing the strong letter came out with it. Mr. Wilcox added his signature. "Now we'll be off," said he.

A motor-drive, a form of felicity detested by Margaret, awaited her. Charles saw them in, civil to the last, and in a moment the offices of the Imperial and West African Rubber Company faded away. But it was not an impressive drive. Perhaps the weather was to blame, being grey and banked high with weary clouds. Perhaps Hertfordshire is scarcely intended for motorists. Did not a gentleman once motor so quickly through Westmoreland that he missed it? and if Westmoreland can be missed, it will fare ill with a county whose delicate structure particularly needs the attentive eye. Hertfordshire is England at its quietest, with little emphasis of river and hill; it is England meditative. If Drayton[1] were with us again to write a new edition of his incomparable poem, he would sing the nymphs of Hertfordshire as indeterminate of feature, with hair obfuscated by the London smoke. Their eyes would be sad, and averted from their fate towards the Northern flats, their leader not Isis or Sabrina, but the slowly flowing Lea.[2] No glory of raiment would be theirs, no urgency of dance; but they would be real nymphs.

The chauffeur could not travel as quickly as he had hoped, for the Great North Road was full of Easter traffic. But he went quite quick enough for Margaret, a poor-spirited creature, who had chickens and children on the brain.

"They're all right," said Mr. Wilcox. "They'll learn—like the swallows and the telegraph-wires."

"Yes, but, while they're learning——"

"The motor's come to stay," he answered. "One must get about. There's a pretty church—oh, you aren't sharp enough. Well, look out, if the road worries you—right outward at the scenery."

She looked at the scenery. It heaved and merged like porridge. Presently it congealed. They had arrived.

Charles's house on the left; on the right the swelling forms of the Six Hills. Their appearance in such a neighbourhood surprised her. They in-

---

[1]Michael Drayton's early 17th-c multi-volume poem *Poly-Olbion* celebrated English topography and history.

[2]The Isis is the Thames in Oxford; Sabrina is the Latin name for the Severn, which flows into England from Wales. The Lea runs through Hertfordshire.

terrupted the stream of residences that was thickening up towards Hilton. Beyond them she saw meadows and a wood, and beneath them she settled that soldiers of the best kind lay buried. She hated war and liked soldiers—it was one of her amiable inconsistencies.

But here was Dolly, dressed up to the nines, standing at the door to greet them, and here were the first drops of the rain. They ran in gaily, and after a long wait in the drawing-room, sat down to the rough-and-ready lunch, every dish in which concealed or exuded cream. Mr. Bryce was the chief topic of conversation. Dolly described his visit with the key, while her father-in-law gave satisfaction by chaffing[3] her and contradicting all she said. It was evidently the custom to laugh at Dolly. He chaffed Margaret, too, and Margaret, roused from a grave meditation, was pleased, and chaffed him back. Dolly seemed surprised, and eyed her curiously. After lunch the two children came down. Margaret disliked babies, but hit it off better with the two-year-old, and sent Dolly into fits of laughter by talking sense to him. "Kiss them now, and come away," said Mr. Wilcox. She came, but refused to kiss them: it was such hard luck on the little things, she said, and though Dolly proffered Chorly-worly and Porgly-woggles in turn, she was obdurate.

By this time it was raining steadily. The car came round with the hood up, and again she lost all sense of space. In a few minutes they stopped, and Crane opened the door of the car.

"What's happened?" asked Margaret.

"What do you suppose?" said Henry.

A little porch was close up against her face.

"Are we there already?"

"We are."

"Well, I never! In years ago it seemed so far away."

Smiling, but somehow disillusioned, she jumped out, and her impetus carried her to the front-door. She was about to open it, when Henry said: "That's no good; it's locked. Who's got the key?"

As he had himself forgotten to call for the key at the farm, no one replied. He also wanted to know who had left the front gate open, since a cow had strayed in from the road, and was spoiling the croquet lawn. Then he said rather crossly: "Margaret, you wait in the dry. I'll go down for the key. It isn't a hundred yards."

"Mayn't I come too?"

"No; I shall be back before I'm gone."

[3]Teasing.

Then the car turned away, and it was as if a curtain had risen. For the second time that day she saw the appearance of the earth.

There were the greengage-trees that Helen had once described, there the tennis lawn, there the hedge that would be glorious with dog-roses in June, but the vision now was of black and palest green. Down by the dell-hole[4] more vivid colours were awakening, and Lent lilies stood sentinel on its margin, or advanced in battalions over the grass. Tulips were a tray of jewels. She could not see the wych-elm tree, but a branch of the celebrated vine, studded with velvet knobs, had covered the porch. She was struck by the fertility of the soil; she had seldom been in a garden where the flowers looked so well, and even the weeds she was idly plucking out of the porch were intensely green. Why had poor Mr. Bryce fled from all this beauty? For she had already decided that the place was beautiful.

"Naughty cow! Go away!" cried Margaret to the cow, but without indignation.

Harder came the rain, pouring out of a windless sky, and spattering up from the notice-boards of the house-agents, which lay in a row on the lawn where Charles had hurled them. She must have interviewed Charles in another world—where one did have interviews. How Helen would revel in such a notion! Charles dead, all people dead, nothing alive but houses and gardens. The obvious dead, the intangible alive, and—no connection at all between them! Margaret smiled. Would that her own fancies were as clear-cut! Would that she could deal as high-handedly with the world! Smiling and sighing, she laid her hand upon the door. It opened. The house was not locked up at all.

She hesitated. Ought she to wait for Henry? He felt strongly about property, and might prefer to show her over himself. On the other hand, he had told her to keep in the dry, and the porch was beginning to drip. So she went in, and the draught from inside slammed the door behind.

Desolation greeted her. Dirty finger-prints were on the hall-windows, flue and rubbish on its unwashed boards. The civilization of luggage had been here for a month, and then decamped. Dining-room and drawing-room—right and left—were guessed only by their wall-papers. They were just rooms where one could shelter from the rain. Across the ceiling of each ran a great beam. The dining-room and hall revealed theirs openly, but the drawing-room's

---

[4]Depression or pit in the landscape. Furbank notes that at Rooksnest there was "a pond, which Lily [Forster's mother] had drained and which became known as the 'Dell'ole'" (17).

was match-boarded[5]—because the facts of life must be concealed from ladies? Drawing-room, dining-room, and hall—how petty the names sounded! Here were simply three rooms where children could play and friends shelter from the rain. Yes, and they were beautiful.

Then she opened one of the doors opposite—there were two—and exchanged wall-papers for whitewash. It was the servants' part, though she scarcely realized that: just rooms again, where friends might shelter. The garden at the back was full of flowering cherries and plums. Farther on were hints of the meadow and a black cliff of pines. Yes, the meadow was beautiful.

Penned in by the desolate weather, she recaptured the sense of space which the motor had tried to rob from her. She remembered again that ten square miles are not ten times as wonderful as one square mile, that a thousand square miles are not practically the same as heaven. The phantom of bigness, which London encourages, was laid for ever when she paced from the hall at Howards End to its kitchen and heard the rains run this way and that where the water-shed of the roof divided them.

Now Helen came to her mind, scrutinizing half Wessex from the ridge of the Purbeck Downs, and saying: "You will have to lose something." She was not so sure. For instance, she would double her kingdom by opening the door that concealed the stairs.

Now she thought of the map of Africa; of empires; of her father; of the two supreme nations, streams of whose life warmed her blood, but, mingling, had cooled her brain. She paced back into the hall, and as she did so the house reverberated.

"Is that you, Henry?" she called.

There was no answer, but the house reverberated again.

"Henry, have you got in?"

But it was the heart of the house beating, faintly at first, then loudly, martially. It dominated the rain.

It is the starved imagination, not the well-nourished, that is afraid. Margaret flung open the door to the stairs. A noise as of drums seemed to deafen her. A woman, an old woman, was descending, with figure erect, with face impassive, with lips that parted and said dryly:

"Oh! Well, I took you for Ruth Wilcox."

Margaret stammered: "I—— Mrs. Wilcox—I?"

[5]Covered with boards locking together to make a smooth surface.

"In fancy, of course—in fancy. You had her way of walking. Good-day." And the old woman passed out into the rain.

## CHAPTER XXIV

"It gave her quite a turn," said Mr. Wilcox, when retailing the incident to Dolly at tea-time. "None of you girls have any nerves, really. Of course, a word from me put it all right, but silly old Miss Avery—she frightened you, didn't she, Margaret? There you stood clutching a bunch of weeds. She might have said something, instead of coming down the stairs with that alarming bonnet on. I passed her as I came in. Enough to make the car shy. I believe Miss Avery goes in for being a character; some old maids do." He lit a cigarette. "It is their last resource. Heaven knows what she was doing in the place; but that's Bryce's business, not mine."

"I wasn't as foolish as you suggest," said Margaret. "She only startled me, for the house had been silent so long."

"Did you take her for a spook?" asked Dolly, for whom "spooks" and "going to church" summarized the unseen.

"Not exactly."

"She really did frighten you," said Henry, who was far from discouraging timidity in females. "Poor Margaret! And very naturally. Uneducated classes are so stupid."

"Is Miss Avery uneducated classes?" Margaret asked, and found herself looking at the decoration scheme of Dolly's drawing-room.

"She's just one of the crew at the farm. People like that always assume things. She assumed you'd know who she was. She left all the Howards End keys in the front lobby, and assumed that you'd seen them as you came in, that you'd lock up the house when you'd done, and would bring them on down to her. And there was her niece hunting for them down at the farm. Lack of education makes people very casual. Hilton was full of women like Miss Avery once."

"I shouldn't have disliked it, perhaps."

"Or Miss Avery giving me a wedding present," said Dolly.

Which was illogical but interesting. Through Dolly, Margaret was destined to learn a good deal.

"But Charles said I must try not to mind, because she had known his grandmother."

"As usual, you've got the story wrong, my good Dorothea."

"I mean great-grandmother—the one who left Mrs. Wilcox the house. Weren't both of them and Miss Avery friends when Howards End, too, was a farm?"

Her father-in-law blew out a shaft of smoke. His attitude to his dead wife was curious. He would allude to her, and hear her discussed, but never mentioned her by name. Nor was he interested in the dim, bucolic past. Dolly was—for the following reason.

"Then hadn't Mrs. Wilcox a brother—or was it an uncle? Anyhow, he popped the question, and Miss Avery, she said 'No.' Just imagine, if she'd said 'Yes,' she would have been Charles's aunt. (Oh, I say, that's rather good! 'Charlie's Aunt'! I must chaff him about that this evening.) And the man went out and was killed. Yes, I'm certain I've got it right now. Tom Howard—he was the last of them."

"I believe so," said Mr. Wilcox negligently.

"I say! Howards End—Howards Ended!" cried Dolly. "I'm rather on the spot this evening, eh?"

"I wish you'd ask whether Crane's ended."

"Oh, Mr. Wilcox, how *can* you?"

"Because, if he has had enough tea, we ought to go.—Dolly's a good little woman," he continued, "but a little of her goes a long way. I couldn't live near her if you paid me."

Margaret smiled. Though presenting a firm front to outsiders, no Wilcox could live near, or near the possessions of, any other Wilcox. They had the colonial spirit, and were always making for some spot where the white man might carry his burden unobserved. Of course, Howards End was impossible, so long as the younger couple were established in Hilton. His objections to the house were plain as daylight now.

Crane had had enough tea, and was sent to the garage, where their car had been trickling muddy water over Charles's. The downpour had surely penetrated the Six Hills by now, bringing news of our restless civilization. "Curious mounds," said Henry, "but in with you now; another time." He had to be up in London by seven—if possible, by six-thirty. Once more she lost the sense of space; once more trees, houses, people, animals, hills, merged and heaved into one dirtiness, and she was at Wickham Place.

Her evening was pleasant. The sense of flux which had haunted her all the year disappeared for a time. She forgot the luggage and the motor-cars, and the hurrying men who know so much and connect so little. She recaptured the sense of space, which is the basis of all earthly beauty, and, starting from Howards End, she attempted to realize England. She failed—visions do not come when we try, though they may come through trying. But an unexpected love of the island awoke in her, connecting on this side with the joys of the flesh, on that with the inconceivable. Helen and her father had known this love, poor Leonard Bast was groping after it, but it had been hidden from Margaret till this afternoon. It had certainly come through the house and old Miss Avery. Through them: the notion of "through" persisted; her mind trembled towards a conclusion which only the unwise have put into words. Then, veering back into warmth, it dwelt on ruddy bricks, flowering plum-trees, and all the tangible joys of spring.

Henry, after allaying her agitation, had taken her over his property, and had explained to her the use and dimensions of the various rooms. He had sketched the history of the little estate. "It is so unlucky," ran the monologue, "that money wasn't put into it about fifty years ago. Then it had four—five—times the land—thirty acres at least. One could have made something out of it then—a small park, or at all events shrubberies, and rebuilt the house farther away from the road. What's the good of taking it in hand now? Nothing but the meadow left, and even that was heavily mortgaged when I first had to do with things—yes, and the house too. Oh, it was no joke." She saw two women as he spoke, one old, the other young, watching their inheritance melt away. She saw them greet him as a deliverer. "Mismanagement did it—besides, the days for small farms are over. It doesn't pay—except with intensive cultivation. Small holdings, back to the land—ah! philanthropic bunkum. Take it as a rule that nothing pays on a small scale. Most of the land you see (they were standing at an upper window, the only one which faced west) belongs to the people at the Park—they made their pile over copper—good chaps. Avery's Farm, Sishe's—what they call the Common, where you see that ruined oak—one after the other fell in, and so did this, as near as is no matter." But Henry had saved it, without fine feelings or deep insight; but he had saved it, and she loved him for the deed. "When I had more control I did what I could: sold off the two and a half animals, and the mangy pony, and the superannuated tools; pulled down the outhouses; drained; thinned out I don't know how many guelderroses and elder-trees; and inside the house I turned the old kitchen into a hall, and made a kitchen behind where the dairy was. Garage and so on came later. But one could still tell it's been an old farm. And yet it isn't the place that would fetch one of your artistic crew." No, it wasn't; and if he did not quite understand it, the artistic crew would still less: it was English, and the wych-elm that she saw from the window was an English tree. No report had prepared her for its peculiar glory. It was neither warrior, nor lover, nor god; in none of these roles do the English excel. It was a comrade, bending over the house, strength and adventure in its roots, but in its utmost fingers tenderness, and the girth, that a dozen men could not have spanned, became in the end evanescent, till pale bud clusters seemed to float in the air. It was a comrade. House and tree transcended any similes of sex. Margaret thought of them now, and was to think of them through many a windy night and London day, but to compare either to man, to woman, always dwarfed the vision. Yet they kept within limits of the human. Their message was not of eternity, but of hope on this side of the grave. As she stood in the one, gazing at the other, truer relationship had gleamed.

Another touch, and the account of her day is finished. They entered the garden for a minute, and to Mr. Wilcox's surprise she was right. Teeth, pigs' teeth, could be seen in the bark of the wych-elm tree—just the white tips of them showing. "Extraordinary!" he cried. "Who told you?"

"I heard of it one winter in London," was her answer, for she, too, avoided mentioning Mrs. Wilcox by name.

## CHAPTER XXV

EVIE heard of her father's engagement when she was in for a tennis tournament, and her play went simply to pot. That she should marry and leave him had seemed natural enough; that he, left alone, should do the same was deceitful; and now Charles and Dolly said that it was all her fault. "But I never dreamt of such a thing," she grumbled. "Dad took me to call now and then, and made me ask her to Simpson's. Well, I'm altogether off dad." It was also an insult to their mother's memory; there they were agreed, and Evie had the idea of returning Mrs. Wilcox's lace and jewellery "as a protest." Against what it would protest she was not clear; but being only eighteen, the idea of renunciation appealed to her, the more as she did not care for jewellery or lace. Dolly then suggested that she and Uncle Percy should pretend to break off their engagement, and then perhaps Mr. Wilcox would quarrel with Miss Schlegel, and break off his; or Paul might be cabled for. But at this point Charles told them not to talk nonsense. So Evie settled to marry as soon as possible; it was no good hanging about with these Schlegels eyeing her. The date of her wedding was consequently put forward from September to August, and in the intoxication of presents she recovered much of her good-humour.

Margaret found that she was expected to figure at this function, and to figure largely; it would be such an opportunity, said Henry, for her to get to know his set. Sir James Bidder would be there, and all the Cahills and the Fussells, and his sister-in-law, Mrs. Warrington

Wilcox, had fortunately got back from her tour round the world. Henry she loved, but his set promised to be another matter. He had not the knack of surrounding himself with nice people—indeed, for a man of ability and virtue his choice had been singularly unfortunate; he had no guiding principle beyond a certain preference for mediocrity; he was content to settle one of the greatest things in life haphazard, and so, while his investments went right, his friends generally went wrong. She would be told, "Oh, So-and-so's a good sort—a thundering good sort," and find, on meeting him, that he was a brute or a bore. If Henry had shown real affection, she would have understood, for affection explains everything. But he seemed without sentiment. The "thundering good sort" might at any moment become "a fellow for whom I never did have much use, and have less now," and be shaken off cheerily into oblivion. Margaret had done the same as a schoolgirl. Now she never forgot anyone for whom she had once cared; she connected, though the connection might be bitter, and she hoped that some day Henry would do the same.

Evie was not to be married from Ducie Street. She had a fancy for something rural, and, besides, no one would be in London then, so she left her boxes for a few weeks at Oniton Grange, and her banns were duly published in the parish church, and for a couple of days the little town, dreaming between the ruddy hills, was roused by the clang of our civilization, and drew up by the roadside to let the motors pass. Oniton had been a discovery of Mr. Wilcox's—a discovery of which he was not altogether proud. It was up towards the Welsh border, and so difficult of access that he had concluded it must be something special. A ruined castle stood in the grounds. But having got there, what was one to do? The shooting was bad, the fishing indifferent, and womenfolk reported the scenery as nothing much. The place turned out to be in the wrong part of Shropshire, damn it, and though he never damned his own property aloud, he was only waiting to get it off his hands, and then to let fly. Evie's marriage was its last appearance in public. As soon as a tenant was found, it became a house for which he never had had much use, and had less now, and, like Howards End, faded into Limbo.

But on Margaret Oniton was destined to make a lasting impression. She regarded it as her future home, and was anxious to start straight with the clergy, etc., and, if possible, to see something of the local life. It was a market-town—as tiny a one as England possesses— and had for ages served that lonely valley, and guarded our marches[1]

---

[1]Borders; here, between England and Wales.

against the Kelt. In spite of the occasion, in spite of the numbing hilarity that greeted her as soon as she got into the reserved saloon[2] at Paddington, her senses were awake and watching, and though Oniton was to prove one of her innumerable false starts, she never forgot it, nor the things that happened there.

The London party only numbered eight—the Fussells, father and son, two Anglo-Indian ladies[3] named Mrs. Plynlimmon and Lady Edser, Mrs. Warrington Wilcox and her daughter, and, lastly, the little girl, very smart and quiet, who figures at so many weddings, and who kept a watchful eye on Margaret, the bride-elect. Dolly was absent—a domestic event detained her at Hilton; Paul had cabled a humorous message; Charles was to meet them with a trio of motors at Shrewsbury. Helen had refused her invitation; Tibby had never answered his. The management was excellent, as was to be expected with anything that Henry undertook; one was conscious of his sensible and generous brain in the background. They were his guests as soon as they reached the train; a special label for their luggage; a courier; a special lunch; they had only to look pleasant and, where possible, pretty. Margaret thought with dismay of her own nuptials—presumably under the management of Tibby. "Mr. Theobald Schlegel and Miss Helen Schlegel request the pleasure of Mrs. Plynlimmon's company on the occasion of the marriage of their sister Margaret." The formula was incredible, but it must soon be printed and sent, and though Wickham Place need not compete with Oniton, it must feed its guests properly, and provide them with sufficient chairs. Her wedding would either be ramshackly or bourgeois—she hoped the latter. Such an affair as the present, staged with a deftness that was almost beautiful, lay beyond her powers and those of her friends.

The low rich purr of a Great Western express is not the worst background for conversation, and the journey passed pleasantly enough. Nothing could have exceeded the kindness of the two men. They raised windows for some ladies, and lowered them for others, they rang the bell for the servant, they identified the colleges as the train slipped past Oxford, they caught books or bag-purses in the act of tumbling on to the floor. Yet there was nothing finicking about their politeness: it had the Public School touch,[4] and, though sedu-

[2]Luxuriously furnished rail car. London's Paddington station serves westbound trains.

[3]Family members of British civil servants in colonial India.

[4]The manner of elite male schools (especially Charterhouse, Eton, Harrow, Merchant Taylors', Rugby, Shrewsbury, St. Paul's, Westminster, and Winchester) where students were trained for university careers and public service.

lous, was virile. More battles than Waterloo have been won on our playing-fields,[5] and Margaret bowed to a charm of which she did not wholly approve, and said nothing when the Oxford colleges were identified wrongly. "Male and female created He them";[6] the journey to Shrewsbury confirmed this questionable statement, and the long glass saloon, that moved so easily and felt so comfortable, became a forcing-house[7] for the idea of sex.

At Shrewsbury came fresh air. Margaret was all for sight-seeing, and while the others were finishing their tea at the Raven, she annexed a motor and hurried over the astonishing city. Her chauffeur was not the faithful Crane, but an Italian, who dearly loved making her late. Charles, watch in hand, though with a level brow, was standing in front of the hotel when they returned. It was perfectly all right, he told her; she was by no means the last. And then he dived into the coffee-room, and she heard him say, "For God's sake, hurry the women up; we shall never be off," and Albert Fussell reply, "Not I; I've done my share," and Colonel Fussell opine that the ladies were getting them-selves up to kill. Presently Myra (Mrs. Warrington's daughter) ap-peared, and as she was his cousin, Charles blew her up[8] a little: she had been changing her smart travelling hat for a smart motor hat. Then Mrs. Warrington herself, leading the quiet child; the two Anglo-Indian ladies were always last. Maids, courier, heavy luggage, had al-ready gone on by a branch-line to a station nearer Oniton, but there were five hat-boxes and four dressing-bags to be packed, and five dust-cloaks to be put on, and to be put off at the last moment, because Charles declared them not necessary. The men presided over every-thing with unfailing good-humour. By half-past five the party was ready, and went out of Shrewsbury by the Welsh Bridge.

Shropshire had not the reticence of Hertfordshire. Though robbed of half its magic by swift movement, it still conveyed the sense of hills. They were nearing the buttresses that force the Severn east-ward and make it an English stream, and the sun, sinking over the Sentinels of Wales, was straight in their eyes. Having picked up an-other guest, they turned southward, avoiding the greater mountains,

---

[5]The Duke of Wellington, whose forces defeated Napoléon's at Waterloo in 1815, was popularly believed to have said that this battle "was won on the playing-fields of Eton."

[6]Genesis 1:27 (King James Version).

[7]Greenhouse (for "forcing" plants to maturity outside the normal growing season).

[8]Scolded her.

but conscious of an occasional summit, rounded and mild, whose colouring differed in quality from that of the lower earth, and whose contours altered more slowly. Quiet mysteries were in progress behind those tossing horizons: the West, as ever, was retreating with some secret which may not be worth the discovery, but which no practical man will ever discover.

They spoke of Tariff Reform.[9]

Mrs. Warrington was just back from the Colonies. Like many other critics of Empire, her mouth had been stopped with food, and she could only exclaim at the hospitality with which she had been received, and warn the Mother Country against trifling with young Titans. "They threaten to cut the painter,"[10] she cried, "and where shall we be then? Miss Schlegel, you'll undertake to keep Henry sound about Tariff Reform? It is our last hope."

Margaret playfully confessed herself on the other side, and they began to quote from their respective hand-books while the motor carried them deep into the hills. Curious these were, rather than impressive, for their outlines lacked beauty, and the pink fields on their summits suggested the handkerchiefs of a giant spread out to dry. An occasional outcrop of rock, an occasional wood, an occasional "forest," treeless and brown, all hinted at wildness to follow, but the main colour was an agricultural green. The air grew cooler; they had surmounted the last gradient, and Oniton lay below them with its church, its radiating houses, its castle, its river-girt peninsula. Close to the castle was a grey mansion, unintellectual but kindly, stretching with its grounds across the peninsula's neck—the sort of mansion that was built all over England in the beginning of the last century, while architecture was still an expression of the national character. That was the Grange, remarked Albert, over his shoulder, and then he jammed the brake on, and the motor slowed down and stopped. "I'm sorry," said he, turning round. "Do you mind getting out—by the door on the right. Steady on."

"What's happened?" asked Mrs. Warrington.

Then the car behind them drew up, and the voice of Charles was heard saying: "Get out the women at once." There was a concourse of males, and Margaret and her companions were hustled out and re-

---

[9]A scheme of protectionist agreements, supported by some Conservative politicians, designed to strengthen the Empire by giving the Dominions (self-governing colonies) an edge over other trading partners of Britain.

[10]Rope connecting a boat's bow to a dock or another craft.

ceived into the second car. What had happened? As it started off again, the door of a cottage opened, and a girl screamed wildly at them.

"What is it?" the ladies cried.

Charles drove them a hundred yards without speaking. Then he said: "It's all right. Your car just touched a dog."

"But stop!" cried Margaret, horrified.

"It didn't hurt him."

"Didn't really hurt him?" asked Myra.

"No."

"Do *please* stop!" said Margaret, leaning forward. She was standing up in the car, the other occupants holding her knees to steady her. "I want to go back, please."

Charles took no notice.

"We've left Mr. Fussell behind," said another; "and Angelo, and Crane."

"Yes, but no woman."

"I expect a little of"—Mrs. Warrington scratched her palm—"will be more to the point than one of us!"

"The insurance company see to that," remarked Charles, "and Albert will do the talking."

"I want to go back, though, I say!" repeated Margaret, getting angry.

Charles took no notice. The motor, loaded with refugees, continued to travel very slowly down the hill. "The men are there," chorused the others. "Men will see to it."

"The men *can't* see to it. Oh, this is ridiculous! Charles, I ask you to stop."

"Stopping's no good," drawled Charles.

"Isn't it?" said Margaret, and jumped straight out of the car.

She fell on her knees, cut her gloves, shook her hat over her ear. Cries of alarm followed her. "You've hurt yourself," exclaimed Charles, jumping after her.

"Of course I've hurt myself!" she retorted.

"May I ask what——"

"There's nothing to ask," said Margaret.

"Your hand's bleeding."

"I know."

"I'm in for a frightful row from the pater."

"You should have thought of that sooner, Charles."

Charles had never been in such a position before. It was a woman in revolt who was hobbling away from him, and the sight was too strange to leave any room for anger. He recovered himself when the others caught them up: their sort he understood. He commanded them to go back.

Albert Fussell was seen walking towards them.

"It's all right!" he called. "It wasn't a dog, it was a cat."

"There!" exclaimed Charles triumphantly. "It's only a rotten cat."

"Got room in your car for a little un? I cut as soon as I saw it wasn't a dog; the chauffeurs are tackling[11] the girl." But Margaret walked forward steadily. Why should the chauffeurs tackle the girl? Ladies sheltering behind men, men sheltering behind servants—the whole system's wrong, and she must challenge it.

"Miss Schlegel! 'Pon my word, you've hurt your hand."

"I'm just going to see," said Margaret. "Don't you wait, Mr. Fussell."

The second motor came round the corner. "It is all right, madam," said Crane in his turn. He had taken to calling her madam.

"What's all right? The cat?"

"Yes, madam. The girl will receive compensation for it."

"She was a very ruda girla," said Angelo from the third motor thoughtfully.

"Wouldn't you have been rude?"

The Italian spread out his hands, implying that he had not thought of rudeness, but would produce it if it pleased her. The situation became absurd. The gentlemen were again buzzing round Miss Schlegel with offers of assistance, and Lady Edser began to bind up her hand. She yielded, apologizing slightly, and was led back to the car, and soon the landscape resumed its motion, the lonely cottage disappeared, the castle swelled on its cushion of turf, and they had arrived. No doubt she had disgraced herself. But she felt their whole journey from London had been unreal. They had no part with the earth and its emotions. They were dust, and a stink, and cosmopolitan chatter, and the girl whose cat had been killed had lived more deeply than they.

"Oh, Henry," she exclaimed, "I have been so naughty," for she had decided to take up this line. "We ran over a cat. Charles told me not to jump out, but I would, and look!" She held out her bandaged hand. "Your poor Meg went such a flop."

Mr. Wilcox looked bewildered. In evening dress, he was standing to welcome his guests in the hall.

[11]Dealing with.

"Thinking it was a dog," added Mrs. Warrington.

"Ah, a dog's a companion!" said Colonel Fussell. "A dog'll remember you."

"Have you hurt yourself, Margaret?"

"Not to speak about; and it's my left hand."

"Well, hurry up and change."

She obeyed, as did the others. Mr. Wilcox then turned to his son.

"Now, Charles, what's happened?"

Charles was absolutely honest. He described what he believed to have happened. Albert had flattened out a cat, and Miss Schlegel had lost her nerve, as any woman might. She had been got safely into the other car, but when it was in motion had leapt out again, in spite of all that they could say. After walking a little on the road, she had calmed down and had said that she was sorry. His father accepted this explanation, and neither knew that Margaret had artfully prepared the way for it. It fitted in too well with their view of feminine nature. In the smoking-room, after dinner, the Colonel put forward the view that Miss Schlegel had jumped it out of devilry. Well he remembered as a young man, in the harbour of Gibraltar once, how a girl—a handsome girl, too—had jumped overboard for a bet. He could see her now, and all the lads overboard after her. But Charles and Mr. Wilcox agreed it was much more probably nerves in Miss Schlegel's case. Charles was depressed. That woman had a tongue. She would bring worse disgrace on his father before she had done with them. He strolled out on to the castle mound to think the matter over. The evening was exquisite. On three sides of him a little river whispered, full of messages from the west; above his head the ruins made patterns against the sky. He carefully reviewed their dealings with this family, until he fitted Helen, and Margaret, and Aunt Juley into an orderly conspiracy. Paternity had made him suspicious. He had two children to look after, and more coming, and day by day they seemed less likely to grow up rich men. "It is all very well," he reflected, "the pater saying that he will be just to all, but one can't be just indefinitely. Money isn't elastic. What's to happen if Evie has a family? And, come to that, so may the pater. There'll not be enough to go round, for there's none coming in, either through Dolly or Percy. It's damnable!" He looked enviously at the Grange, whose windows poured light and laughter. First and last, this wedding would cost a pretty penny. Two ladies were strolling up and down the garden terrace, and as the syllables "Imperialism" were wafted to his ears, he guessed that one of them was his aunt. She might have helped him, if she too had not had a family to provide for. "Everyone for himself," he repeated—a maxim which had cheered him in the past, but which rang grimly enough among the ruins of Oniton. He lacked his father's ability in business, and so had an ever higher regard for money; unless he could inherit plenty, he feared to leave his children poor.

As he sat thinking, one of the ladies left the terrace and walked into the meadow; he recognized her as Margaret by the white bandage that gleamed on her arm, and put out his cigar, lest the gleam should betray him. She climbed up the mound in zigzags, and at times stooped down, as if she was stroking the turf. It sounds absolutely incredible, but for a moment Charles thought that she was in love with him, and had come out to tempt him. Charles believed in temptresses, who are indeed the strong man's necessary complement, and having no sense of humour, he could not purge himself of the thought by a smile. Margaret, who was engaged to his father, and his sister's wedding-guest, kept on her way without noticing him, and he admitted that he had wronged her on this point. But what was she doing? Why was she stumbling about amongst the rubble and catching her dress in brambles and burrs? As she edged round the keep, she must have got to windward and smelt his cigar-smoke, for she exclaimed, "Hullo! Who's that?"

Charles made no answer.

"Saxon or Kelt?"[12] she continued, laughing in the darkness. "But it doesn't matter. Whichever you are, you will have to listen to me. I love this place. I love Shropshire. I hate London. I am glad that this will be my home. Ah, dear"—she was now moving back towards the house—"what a comfort to have arrived!"

"That woman means mischief," thought Charles, and compressed his lips. In a few minutes he followed her indoors, as the ground was getting damp. Mists were rising from the river, and presently it became invisible, though it whispered more loudly. There had been a heavy downpour in the Welsh hills.

## CHAPTER XXVI

NEXT morning a fine mist covered the peninsula. The weather promised well, and the outline of the castle mound grew clearer each moment that Margaret watched it. Presently she saw the keep, and the

---

[12]Ancient peoples from whom the English and the Welsh respectively trace their descent. Margaret playfully affects the voice of a frontier guard.

sun painted the rubble gold, and charged the white sky with blue. The shadow of the house gathered itself together, and fell over the garden. A cat looked up at her window and mewed. Lastly the river appeared, still holding the mists between its banks and its overhanging alders, and only visible as far as a hill, which cut off its upper reaches.

Margaret was fascinated by Oniton. She had said that she loved it, but it was rather its romantic tension that held her. The rounded Druids[1] of whom she had caught glimpses in her drive, the rivers hurrying down from them to England, the carelessly modelled masses of the lower hills, thrilled her with poetry. The house was insignificant, but the prospect from it would be an eternal joy, and she thought of all the friends she would have to stop in it, and of the conversion of Henry himself to a rural life. Society, too, promised favourably. The rector of the parish had dined with them last night, and she found that he was a friend of her father's, and so knew what to find in her. She liked him. He would introduce her to the town. While, on her other side, Sir James Bidder sat, repeating that she only had to give the word, and he would whip up the county families for twenty miles round. Whether Sir James, who was Garden Seeds,[2] had promised what he could perform, she doubted, but so long as Henry mistook them for the county families when they did call, she was content.

Charles and Albert Fussell now crossed the lawn. They were going for a morning dip, and a servant followed them with their bathing-dresses. She had meant to take a stroll herself before breakfast, but saw that the day was still sacred to men, and amused herself by watching their contretemps.[3] In the first place the key of the bathing-shed could not be found. Charles stood by the riverside with folded hands, tragical, while the servant shouted, and was misunderstood by another servant in the garden. Then came a difficulty about a spring-board,[4] and soon three people were running backwards and forwards over the meadow, with orders and counter orders and recriminations and apologies. If Margaret wanted to jump from a motor-car, she jumped; if Tibby thought paddling would benefit his ankles, he paddled; if a clerk desired adventure, he took a walk in the

---

[1]Hills in Wales and Shropshire; druids were ancient Celtic priests.

[2]Forster's ms. shows "tie-clips," then "boot-buttons," before settling on "Garden Seeds" (223). All indicate that Sir James's wealth derives from modern commercial enterprise and thus that he does not belong to the county families (nobility or gentry having ancestral seats in the area). "Seeds" plays nicely on promise versus performance.

[3]Mishaps (French: against the time).

[4]Diving board.

dark. But these athletes seemed paralyzed. They could not bathe without their appliances, though the morning sun was calling and the last mists were rising from the dimpling stream. Had they found the life of the body after all? Could not the men whom they despised as milksops beat them, even on their own ground?

She thought of the bathing arrangements as they should be in her day—no worrying of servants, no appliances, beyond good sense. Her reflections were disturbed by the quiet child, who had come out to speak to the cat, but was now watching her watch the men. She called, "Good-morning, dear," a little sharply. Her voice spread consternation. Charles looked round, and though completely attired in indigo blue, vanished into the shed, and was seen no more.

"Miss Wilcox is up——" the child whispered, and then became unintelligible.

"What's that?"

It sounded like, "——cut-yoke—sack-back—"

"I can't hear."

"—On the bed—tissue-paper——"

Gathering that the wedding-dress was on view, and that a visit would be seemly, she went to Evie's room. All was hilarity here. Evie, in a petticoat, was dancing with one of the Anglo-Indian ladies, while the other was adoring yards of white satin. They screamed, they laughed, they sang, and the dog barked.

Margaret screamed a little too, but without conviction. She could not feel that a wedding was so funny. Perhaps something was missing in her equipment.

Evie gasped: "Dolly is a rotter not to be here! Oh, we would rag just then!" Then Margaret went down to breakfast.

Henry was already installed; he ate slowly and spoke little, and was, in Margaret's eyes, the only member of their party who dodged emotion successfully. She could not suppose him indifferent either to the loss of his daughter or to the presence of his future wife. Yet he dwelt intact, only issuing orders occasionally—orders that promoted the comfort of his guests. He inquired after her hand; he set her to pour out the coffee and Mrs. Warrington to pour out the tea. When Evie came down there was a moment's awkwardness, and both ladies rose to vacate their places. "Burton," called Henry, "serve tea and coffee from the sideboard!" It wasn't genuine tact, but it was tact, of a sort—the sort that is as useful as the genuine, and saves even more situations at Board meetings. Henry treated a marriage like a funeral, item by item, never raising his eyes to the whole, and "Death, where is thy sting? Love, where is thy victory?"[5] one would exclaim at the close.

After breakfast she claimed a few words with him. It was always best to approach him formally. She asked for the interview, because he was going on to shoot grouse to-morrow, and she was returning to Helen in town.

"Certainly, dear," said he. "Of course, I have the time. What do you want?"

"Nothing."

"I was afraid something had gone wrong."

"No; I have nothing to say, but you may talk."

Glancing at his watch, he talked of the nasty curve at the lych-gate. She heard him with interest. Her surface could always respond to his without contempt, though all her deeper being might be yearning to help him. She had abandoned any plan of action. Love is the best, and the more she let herself love him, the more chance was there that he would set his soul in order. Such a moment as this, when they sat under fair weather by the walks of their future home, was so sweet to her that its sweetness would surely pierce to him. Each lift of his eyes, each parting of the thatched lip from the clean-shaven, must prelude the tenderness that kills the Monk and the Beast at a single blow. Disappointed a hundred times, she still hoped. She loved him with too clear a vision to fear his cloudiness. Whether he droned trivialities, as to-day, or sprang kisses on her in the twilight, she could pardon him, she could respond.

"If there is this nasty curve," she suggested, "couldn't we walk to the church? Not, of course, you and Evie; but the rest of us might very well go on first, and that would mean fewer carriages."

"One can't have ladies walking through the Market Square. The Fussells wouldn't like it; they were awfully particular at Charles's wedding. My—she—one of our party was anxious to walk, and certainly the church was just round the corner, and I shouldn't have minded; but the Colonel made a great point of it."

"You men shouldn't be so chivalrous," said Margaret thoughtfully.

"Why not?"

She knew why not, but said that she did not know. He then announced that, unless she had anything special to say, he must visit the wine-cellar, and they went off together in search of Burton. Though

---

[5]Paul, speaking of the resurrection of the dead, asks, "O death, where is thy sting? O grave, where is thy victory?" (1 Corinthians 15:55).

clumsy and a little inconvenient, Oniton was a genuine country-house. They clattered down flagged passages, looking into room after room, and scaring unknown maids from the performance of obscure duties. The wedding-breakfast must be in readiness when they came back from church, and tea would be served in the garden. The sight of so many agitated and serious people made Margaret smile, but she reflected that they were paid to be serious, and enjoyed being agitated. Here were the lower wheels of the machine that was tossing Evie up into nuptial glory. A little boy blocked their way with pig-pails. His mind could not grasp their greatness, and he said: "By your leave; let me pass, please." Henry asked him where Burton was. But the servants were so new that they did not know one another's names. In the still-room sat the band, who had stipulated for champagne as part of their fee, and who were already drinking beer. Scents of Araby came from the kitchen, mingled with cries. Margaret knew what had happened there, for it happened at Wickham Place. One of the wedding dishes had boiled over, and the cook was throwing cedar-shavings to hide the smell. At last they came upon the butler. Henry gave him the keys, and handed Margaret down the cellar-stairs. Two doors were unlocked. She, who kept all her wine at the bottom of the linen-cupboard, was astonished at the sight. "We shall never get through it!" she cried, and the two men were suddenly drawn into brotherhood, and exchanged smiles. She felt as if she had again jumped out of the car while it was moving.

Certainly Oniton would take some digesting. It would be no small business to remain herself, and yet to assimilate such an establishment. She must remain herself, for his sake as well as her own, since a shadowy wife degrades the husband whom she accompanies; and she must assimilate for reasons of common honesty, since she had no right to marry a man and make him uncomfortable. Her only ally was the power of Home. The loss of Wickham Place had taught her more than its possession. Howards End had repeated the lesson. She was determined to create new sanctities among these hills.

After visiting the wine-cellar, she dressed, and then came the wedding, which seemed a small affair when compared with the preparations for it. Everything went like one o'clock.[6] Mr. Cahill materialized out of space, and was waiting for his bride at the church door. No one dropped the ring or mispronounced the responses, or trod on Evie's train, or cried. In a few minutes the clergymen performed their duty, the register was signed, and they were back in their carriages,

[6]Perfectly smoothly.

negotiating the dangerous curve by the lych-gate. Margaret was convinced that they had not been married at all, and that the Norman church[7] had been intent all the time on other business.

There were more documents to sign at the house, and the breakfast to eat, and then a few more people dropped in for the garden party. There had been a great many refusals, and after all it was not a very big affair—not as big as Margaret's would be. She noted the dishes and the strips of red carpet, that outwardly she might give Henry what was proper. But inwardly she hoped for something better than this blend of Sunday church and fox-hunting. If only someone had been upset! But this wedding had gone off so particularly well—"quite like a Durbar"[8] in the opinion of Lady Edser, and she thoroughly agreed with her.

So the wasted day lumbered forward, the bride and bridegroom drove off, yelling with laughter, and for the second time the sun retreated towards the hills of Wales. Henry, who was more tired than he owned, came up to her in the castle meadow, and, in tones of unusual softness, said that he was pleased. Everything had gone off so well. She felt that he was praising her, too, and blushed; certainly she had done all she could with his intractable friends, and had made a special point of kowtowing to the men. They were breaking camp this evening: only the Warringtons and quiet child would stay the night, and the others were already moving towards the house to finish their packing. "I think it did go off well," she agreed. "Since I had to jump out of the motor, I'm thankful I lighted on my left hand. I am so very glad about it, Henry dear; I only hope that the guests at ours may be half as comfortable. You must all remember that we have no practical person among us, except my aunt, and she is not used to entertainments on a large scale."

"I know," he said gravely. "Under the circumstances, it would be better to put everything into the hands of Harrod's or Whiteley's,[9] or even to go to some hotel."

"You desire a hotel?"

"Yes, because—well, I mustn't interfere with you. No doubt you want to be married from your old home."

"My old home's falling into pieces, Henry. I only want my new. Isn't it a perfect evening——"

[7]Church in a style of Romanesque architecture developed by the Normans, who conquered England in the 11th c.

[8]Official ceremony, often lavish, held by a native prince demonstrating allegiance to the British crown or by a high British administrator in India.

[9]London department stores.

"The Alexandrina isn't bad——"

"The Alexandrina," she echoed, more occupied with the threads of smoke that were issuing from their chimneys, and ruling the sunlit slopes with parallels of grey.

"It's off Curzon Street."

"Is it? Let's be married from off Curzon Street."

Then she turned westward, to gaze at the swirling gold. Just where the river rounded the hill the sun caught it. Fairyland must lie above the bend, and its precious liquid was pouring towards them past Charles's bathing-shed. She gazed so long that her eyes were dazzled, and when they moved back to the house, she could not recognize the faces of people who were coming out of it. A parlour-maid was preceding them.

"Who are those people?" she asked.

"They're callers!" exclaimed Henry. "It's too late for callers."

"Perhaps they're town people who want to see the wedding presents."

"I'm not at home yet to townees."

"Well, hide among the ruins, and if I can stop them, I will."

He thanked her.

Margaret went forward, smiling socially. She supposed that these were unpunctual guests, who would have to be content with vicarious civility, since Evie and Charles were gone, Henry tired, and the others in their rooms. She assumed the airs of a hostess; not for long. For one of the group was Helen—Helen in her oldest clothes, and dominated by that tense, wounding excitement that had made her a terror in their nursery days.

"What is it?" she called. "Oh, what's wrong? Is Tibby ill?"

Helen spoke to her two companions, who fell back. Then she bore forward furiously.

"They're starving!" she shouted. "I found them starving!"

"Who? Why have you come?"

"The Basts."

"Oh, Helen!" moaned Margaret. "Whatever have you done now?"

"He has lost his place. He has been turned out of his bank. Yes, he's done for. We upper classes have ruined him, and I suppose you'll tell me it's the battle of life. Starving. His wife is ill. Starving. She fainted in the train."

"Helen, are you mad?"

"Perhaps. Yes. If you like, I'm mad. But I've brought them. I'll stand injustice no longer. I'll show up the wretchedness that lies under this luxury, this talk of impersonal forces, this cant about God doing what we're too slack to do ourselves."

"Have you actually brought two starving people from London to Shropshire, Helen?"

Helen was checked. She had not thought of this, and her hysteria abated. "There was a restaurant car on the train," she said.

"Don't be absurd. They aren't starving, and you know it. Now, begin from the beginning. I won't have such theatrical nonsense. How dare you! Yes, how dare you!" she repeated, as anger filled her, "bursting in to Evie's wedding in this heartless way. My goodness! but you've a perverted notion of philanthropy. Look"—she indicated the house—"servants, people out of the windows. They think it's some vulgar scandal, and I must explain, 'Oh no, it's only my sister screaming, and only two hangers-on of ours, whom she has brought here for no conceivable reason.'"

"Kindly take back that word 'hangers-on,'" said Helen, ominously calm.

"Very well," conceded Margaret, who for all her wrath was determined to avoid a real quarrel. "I, too, am sorry about them, but it beats me why you've brought them here, or why you're here yourself."

"It's our last chance of seeing Mr. Wilcox."

Margaret moved towards the house at this. She was determined not to worry Henry.

"He's going to Scotland. I know he is. I insist on seeing him."

"Yes, to-morrow."

"I knew it was our last chance."

"How do you do, Mr. Bast?" said Margaret, trying to control her voice. "This is an odd business. What view do you take of it?"

"There is Mrs. Bast, too," prompted Helen.

Jacky also shook hands. She, like her husband, was shy, and, furthermore, ill, and furthermore, so bestially stupid that she could not grasp what was happening. She only knew that the lady had swept down like a whirlwind last night, had paid the rent, redeemed the furniture, provided them with a dinner and a breakfast, and ordered them to meet her at Paddington next morning. Leonard had feebly protested, and when the morning came, had suggested that they shouldn't go. But she, half mesmerized, had obeyed. The lady had told them to, and they must, and their bed-sitting-room[10] had accordingly changed into Paddington, and Paddington into a railway

---

[10]Space functioning as both bedroom and sitting-room.

carriage, that shook, and grew hot, and grew cold, and vanished entirely, and reappeared amid torrents of expensive scent. "You have fainted," said the lady in an awe-struck voice. "Perhaps the air will do you good." And perhaps it had, for here she was, feeling rather better among a lot of flowers.

"I'm sure I don't want to intrude," began Leonard, in answer to Margaret's question. "But you have been so kind to me in the past in warning me about the Porphyrion that I wondered—why, I wondered whether——"

"Whether we could get him back into the Porphyrion again," supplied Helen. "Meg, this has been a cheerful business. A bright evening's work that was on Chelsea Embankment."

Margaret shook her head and returned to Mr. Bast.

"I don't understand. You left the Porphyrion because we suggested it was a bad concern, didn't you?"

"That's right."

"And went into a bank instead?"

"I told you all that," said Helen; "and they reduced their staff after he had been in a month, and now he's penniless, and I consider that we and our informant are directly to blame."

"I hate all this," Leonard muttered.

"I hope you do, Mr. Bast. But it's no good mincing matters. You have done yourself no good by coming here. If you intend to confront Mr. Wilcox, and to call him to account for a chance remark, you will make a very great mistake."

"I brought them. I did it all," cried Helen.

"I can only advise you to go at once. My sister has put you in a false position, and it is kindest to tell you so. It's too late to get to town, but you'll find a comfortable hotel in Oniton, where Mrs. Bast can rest, and I hope you'll be my guests there."

"That isn't what I want, Miss Schlegel," said Leonard. "You're very kind, and no doubt it's a false position, but you make me miserable. I seem no good at all."

"It's work he wants," interpreted Helen. "Can't you see?"

Then he said: "Jacky, let's go. We're more bother than we're worth. We're costing these ladies pounds and pounds already to get work for us, and they never will. There's nothing we're good enough to do."

"We would like to find you work," said Margaret rather conventionally. "We want to—I, like my sister. You're only down in your luck. Go to the hotel, have a good night's rest, and some day you shall pay me back the bill, if you prefer it."

But Leonard was near the abyss, and at such moments men see clearly. "You don't know what you're talking about," he said. "I shall never get work now. If rich people fail at one profession, they can try another. Not I. I had my groove, and I've got out of it. I could do one particular branch of insurance in one particular office well enough to command a salary, but that's all. Poetry's nothing, Miss Schlegel. One's thoughts about this and that are nothing. Your money, too, is nothing, if you'll understand me. I mean if a man over twenty once loses his own particular job, it's all over with him. I have seen it happen to others. Their friends gave them money for a little, but in the end they fall over the edge. It's no good. It's the whole world pulling. There always will be rich and poor."

He ceased. "Won't you have something to eat?" said Margaret. "I don't know what to do. It isn't my house, and though Mr. Wilcox would have been glad to see you at any other time—as I say, I don't know what to do, but I undertake to do what I can for you. Helen, offer them something. Do try a sandwich, Mrs. Bast."

They moved to a long table behind which a servant was still standing. Iced cakes, sandwiches innumerable, coffee, claret-cup,[11] champagne, remained almost intact: their overfed guests could do no more. Leonard refused. Jacky thought she could manage a little. Margaret left them whispering together, and had a few more words with Helen.

She said: "Helen, I like Mr. Bast. I agree that he's worth helping. I agree that we are directly responsible."

"No, indirectly. Via Mr. Wilcox."

"Let me tell you once for all that if you take up that attitude, I'll do nothing. No doubt you're right logically, and are entitled to say a great many scathing things about Henry. Only, I won't have it. So choose."

Helen looked at the sunset.

"If you promise to take them quietly to the George, I will speak to Henry about them—in my own way, mind; there is to be none of this absurd screaming about justice. I have no use for justice. If it was only a question of money, we could do it ourselves. But he wants work, and that we can't give him, but possibly Henry can."

"It's his duty to," grumbled Helen.

"Nor am I concerned with duty. I'm concerned with the characters of various people whom we know, and how, things being as they

---

[11]Punch made with claret (red Bordeaux wine).

are, things may be made a little better. Mr. Wilcox hates being asked favours: all business men do. But I am going to ask him, at the risk of a rebuff, because I want to make things a little better."

"Very well. I promise. You take it very calmly."

"Take them off to the George, then, and I'll try. Poor creatures! but they look tired." As they parted, she added: "I haven't nearly done with you, though, Helen. You have been most self-indulgent. I can't get over it. You have less restraint rather than more as you grow older. Think it over and alter yourself, or we shan't have happy lives."

She rejoined Henry. Fortunately he had been sitting down: these physical matters were important. "Was it townees?" he asked, greeting her with a pleasant smile.

"You'll never believe me," said Margaret, sitting down beside him. "It's all right now, but it was my sister."

"Helen here?" he cried, preparing to rise. "But she refused the invitation. I thought she despised weddings."

"Don't get up. She has not come to the wedding. I've bundled her off to the George."

Inherently hospitable, he protested.

"No; she has two of her protégés with her, and must keep with them."

"Let 'em all come."

"My dear Henry, did you see them?"

"I did catch sight of a brown bunch of a woman, certainly."

"The brown bunch was Helen, but did you catch sight of a sea-green and salmon bunch?"

"What! are they out beanfeasting?"[12]

"No; business. They wanted to see me, and later on I want to talk to you about them."

She was ashamed of her own diplomacy. In dealing with a Wilcox, how tempting it was to lapse from comradeship, and to give him the kind of woman that he desired! Henry took the hint at once, and said: "Why later on? Tell me now. No time like the present."

"Shall I?"

"If it isn't a long story."

"Oh, not five minutes; but there's a sting at the end of it, for I want you to find the man some work in your office."

"What are his qualifications?"

"I don't know. He's a clerk."

---

[12]Making merry. A beanfeast is an annual dinner given by employers to employees.

"How old?"

"Twenty-five, perhaps."

"What's his name?"

"Bast," said Margaret, and was about to remind him that they had met at Wickham Place, but stopped herself. It had not been a successful meeting.

"Where was he before?"

"Dempster's Bank."

"Why did he leave?" he asked, still remembering nothing.

"They reduced their staff."

"All right; I'll see him."

It was the reward of her tact and devotion through the day. Now she understood why some women prefer influence to rights. Mrs. Plynlimmon, when condemning suffragettes, had said: "The woman who can't influence her husband to vote the way she wants ought to be ashamed of herself." Margaret had winced, but she was influencing Henry now, and though pleased at her little victory, she knew that she had won it by the methods of the harem.

"I should be glad if you took him," she said, "but I don't know whether he's qualified."

"I'll do what I can. But, Margaret, this mustn't be taken as a precedent."

"No, of course—of course——"

"I can't fit in your protégés every day. Business would suffer."

"I can promise you he's the last. He—he's rather a special case."

"Protégés always are."

She let it stand at that. He rose with a little extra touch of complacency, and held out his hand to help her up. How wide the gulf between Henry as he was and Henry as Helen thought he ought to be! And she herself—hovering as usual between the two, now accepting men as they are, now yearning with her sister for Truth. Love and Truth—their warfare seems eternal. Perhaps the whole visible world rests on it, and if they were one, life itself, like the spirits when Prospero was reconciled to his brother, might vanish into air, into thin air.[13]

"Your protégé has made us late," said he. "The Fussells will just be starting."

---

[13]After Shakespeare's Prospero makes peace with his brother Antonio, usurper of his title, he releases his spirit-servant Ariel: "to the elements / Be free, and fare thou well!" (*The Tempest* 5.1.315–16).

On the whole she sided with men as they are. Henry would save the Basts as he had saved Howards End, while Helen and her friends were discussing the ethics of salvation. His was a slap-dash method, but the world has been built slap-dash, and the beauty of mountain and river and sunset may be but the varnish with which the unskilled artificer hides his joins. Oniton, like herself, was imperfect. Its apple-trees were stunted, its castle ruinous. It, too, had suffered in the border warfare between the Anglo-Saxon and the Kelt, between things as they are and as they ought to be. Once more the west was retreating, once again the orderly stars were dotting the eastern sky. There is certainly no rest for us on the earth. But there is happiness, and as Margaret descended the mound on her lover's arm, she felt that she was having her share.

To her annoyance, Mrs. Bast was still in the garden; the husband and Helen had left her there to finish her meal while they went to engage rooms. Margaret found this woman repellent. She had felt, when shaking her hand, an overpowering shame. She remembered the motive of her call at Wickham Place, and smelt again odours from the abyss—odours the more disturbing because they were involuntary. For there was no malice in Jacky. There she sat, a piece of cake in one hand, an empty champagne glass in the other, doing no harm to anybody.

"She's overtired," Margaret whispered.

"She's something else," said Henry. "This won't do. I can't have her in my garden in this state."

"Is she——" Margaret hesitated to add "drunk." Now that she was going to marry him, he had grown particular. He discountenanced risqué conversations now.

Henry went up to the woman. She raised her face, which gleamed in the twilight like a puff-ball.[14]

"Madam, you will be more comfortable at the hotel," he said sharply.

Jacky replied: "If it isn't Hen!"

"Ne crois pas que le mari lui ressemble," apologized Margaret. "Il est tout à fait différent."[15]

"Henry!" she repeated, quite distinctly.

Mr. Wilcox was much annoyed. "I can't congratulate you on your protégés," he remarked.

---

[14]Powder puff or dandelion seed-ball.

[15]"Don't think that the husband is like her. He's completely different." (Margaret assumes that the Basts don't understand French.)

"Hen, don't go. You do love me, dear, don't you?"

"Bless us, what a person!" sighed Margaret, gathering up her skirts.

Jacky pointed with her cake. "You're a nice boy, you are." She yawned. "There now, I love you."

"Henry, I am awfully sorry."

"And pray why?" he asked, and looked at her so sternly that she feared he was ill. He seemed more scandalized than the facts demanded.

"To have brought this down on you."

"Pray don't apologize."

The voice continued.

"Why does she call you 'Hen'?" said Margaret innocently. "Has she ever seen you before?"

"Seen Hen before!" said Jacky. "Who hasn't seen Hen? He's serving you like me, my dear. These boys! You wait—— Still we love 'em."

"Are you now satisfied?" Henry asked.

Margaret began to grow frightened. "I don't know what it is all about," she said. "Let's come in."

But he thought she was acting. He thought he was trapped. He saw his whole life crumbling. "Don't you indeed?" he said bitingly. "I do. Allow me to congratulate you on the success of your plan."

"This is Helen's plan, not mine."

"I now understand your interest in the Basts. Very well thought out. I am amused at your caution, Margaret. You are quite right—it was necessary. I am a man, and have lived a man's past. I have the honour to release you from your engagement."

Still she could not understand. She knew of life's seamy side as a theory; she could not grasp it as a fact. More words from Jacky were necessary—words unequivocal, undenied.

"So that——" burst from her, and she went indoors. She stopped herself from saying more.

"So what?" asked Colonel Fussell, who was getting ready to start in the hall.

"We were saying—Henry and I were just having the fiercest argument, my point being——" Seizing his fur coat from a footman, she offered to help him on. He protested, and there was a playful little scene.

"No, let me do that," said Henry, following.

"Thanks so much! You see—he has forgiven me!"

The Colonel said gallantly: "I don't expect there's much to forgive."

He got into the car. The ladies followed him after an interval. Maids, courier, and heavier luggage had been sent on earlier by the branch-line. Still chattering, still thanking their host and patronizing their future hostess, the guests were borne away.

Then Margaret continued: "So that woman has been your mistress?"

"You put it with your usual delicacy," he replied.

"When, please?"

"Why?"

"When, please?"

"Ten years ago."

She left him without a word. For it was not her tragedy: it was Mrs. Wilcox's.

## CHAPTER XXVII

HELEN began to wonder why she had spent a matter of eight pounds in making some people ill and others angry. Now that the wave of excitement was ebbing, and had left her, Mr. Bast, and Mrs. Bast stranded for the night in a Shropshire hotel, she asked herself what forces had made the wave flow. At all events, no harm was done. Margaret would play the game properly now, and though Helen disapproved of her sister's methods, she knew that the Basts would benefit by them in the long run.

"Mr. Wilcox is so illogical," she explained to Leonard, who had put his wife to bed, and was sitting with her in the empty coffee-room. "If we told him it was his duty to take you on, he might refuse to do it. The fact is, he isn't properly educated. I don't want to set you against him, but you'll find him a trial."

"I can never thank you sufficiently, Miss Schlegel," was all that Leonard felt equal to.

"I believe in personal responsibility. Don't you? And in personal everything. I hate—I suppose I oughtn't to say that—but the Wilcoxes are on the wrong tack surely. Or perhaps it isn't their fault. Perhaps the little thing that says 'I' is missing out of the middle of their heads, and then it's a waste of time to blame them. There's a nightmare of a theory that says a special race is being born which will rule the rest of us in the future just because it lacks the little thing that says 'I.' Had you heard that?"

"I get no time for reading."

"Had you thought it, then? That there are two kinds of people— our kind, who live straight from the middle of their heads, and the other kind who can't, because their heads have no middle? They can't say 'I.' They *aren't* in fact, and so they're supermen. Pierpont Morgan[1] has never said 'I' in his life."

Leonard roused himself. If his benefactress wanted intellectual conversation, she must have it. She was more important than his ruined past. "I never got on to Nietzsche," he said. "But I always understood that those supermen were rather what you may call egoists."[2]

"Oh, no, that's wrong," replied Helen. "No superman ever said 'I want,' because 'I want' must lead to the question, 'Who am I?' and so to Pity and to Justice. He only says 'want.' 'Want Europe,' if he's Napoleon; 'want wives,' if he's Bluebeard; 'want Botticelli,'[3] if he's Pierpont Morgan. Never the 'I'; and if you could pierce through him, you'd find panic and emptiness in the middle."

Leonard was silent for a moment. Then he said: "May I take it, Miss Schlegel, that you and I are both the sort that say 'I'?"

"Of course."

"And your sister too?"

"Of course," repeated Helen, a little sharply. She was annoyed with Margaret, but did not want her discussed. "All presentable people say 'I.'"

"But Mr. Wilcox—he is not perhaps——"

"I don't know that it's any good discussing Mr. Wilcox either."

"Quite so, quite so," he agreed. Helen asked herself why she had snubbed him. Once or twice during the day she had encouraged him to criticize, and then had pulled him up short. Was she afraid of him presuming? If so, it was disgusting of her.

But he was thinking the snub quite natural. Everything she did was natural, and incapable of causing offence. While the Miss Schlegels were together he had felt them scarcely human—a sort of admonitory whirligig.[4] But a Miss Schlegel alone was different. She was in Helen's case unmarried, in Margaret's about to be married, in neither case an echo of her sister. A light had fallen at last into this rich upper world,

[1]American financier John Pierpont (J. P.) Morgan (1837–1913), one of the world's wealthiest men.

[2]In *Thus Spoke Zarathustra* (1883–1885), Friedrich Nietzsche proposed that humans would be succeeded by a superior order of being he named the *Übermensch* (controversially translated as "superman").

[3]Europe-conquering Emperor, vanquished at Waterloo in 1815; wife-murderer of folklore; Italian Renaissance painter (*Primavera*; *The Birth of Venus*). In a 1902 book, the American writer Elbert Hubbard describes an unsuccessful attempt by Morgan to purchase a Botticelli from the art gallery at Yale University (58).

[4]Whirling toy or merry-go-round.

and he saw that it was full of men and women, some of whom were more friendly to him than others. Helen had become "his" Miss Schlegel, who scolded him and corresponded with him, and had swept down yesterday with grateful vehemence. Margaret, though not unkind, was severe and remote. He would not presume to help her, for instance. He had never liked her, and began to think that his original impression was true, and that her sister did not like her either. Helen was certainly lonely. She, who gave away so much, was receiving too little. Leonard was pleased to think that he could spare her vexation by holding his tongue and concealing what he knew about Mr. Wilcox. Jacky had announced her discovery when he fetched her from the lawn. After the first shock, he did not mind for himself. By now he had no illusions about his wife, and this was only one new stain on the face of a love that had never been pure. To keep perfection perfect, that should be his ideal, if the future gave him time to have ideals. Helen, and Margaret for Helen's sake, must not know.

Helen disconcerted him by turning the conversation to his wife. "Mrs. Bast—does she ever say 'I'?" she asked, half mischievously, and then, "Is she very tired?"

"It's better she stops in her room," said Leonard.

"Shall I sit up with her?"

"No, thank you; she does not need company."

"Mr. Bast, what kind of woman is your wife?"

Leonard blushed up to his eyes.

"You ought to know my ways by now. Does that question offend you?"

"No, oh no, Miss Schlegel, no."

"Because I love honesty. Don't pretend your marriage has been a happy one. You and she can have nothing in common."

He did not deny it, but said shyly: "I suppose that's pretty obvious; but Jacky never meant to do anybody any harm. When things went wrong, or I heard things, I used to think it was her fault, but, looking back, it's more mine. I needn't have married her, but as I have I must stick to her and keep her."

"How long have you been married?"

"Nearly three years."

"What did your people say?"

"They will not have anything to do with us. They had a sort of family council when they heard I was married, and cut us off altogether."

Helen began to pace up and down the room. "My good boy, what a mess!" she said gently. "Who are your people?"

He could answer this. His parents, who were dead, had been in trade; his sisters had married commercial travellers;[5] his brother was a lay-reader.

"And your grandparents?"

Leonard told her a secret that he had held shameful up to now. "They were just nothing at all," he said—"agricultural labourers and that sort."

"So! From which part?"

"Lincolnshire mostly, but my mother's father—he, oddly enough, came from these parts round here."

"From this very Shropshire. Yes, that is odd. My mother's people were Lancashire. But why do your brother and your sisters object to Mrs. Bast?"

"Oh, I don't know."

"Excuse me, you do know. I am not a baby. I can bear anything you tell me, and the more you tell the more I shall be able to help. Have they heard anything against her?"

He was silent.

"I think I have guessed now," said Helen very gravely.

"I don't think so, Miss Schlegel; I hope not."

"We must be honest, even over these things. I have guessed. I am frightfully, dreadfully sorry, but it does not make the least difference to me. I shall feel just the same to both of you. I blame, not your wife for these things, but men."

Leonard left it at that—so long as she did not guess the man. She stood at the window and slowly pulled up the blinds. The hotel looked over a dark square. The mists had begun. When she turned back to him her eyes were shining.

"Don't you worry," he pleaded. "I can't bear that. We shall be all right if I get work. If I could only get work—something regular to do. Then it wouldn't be so bad again. I don't trouble after books as I used. I can imagine that with regular work we should settle down again. It stops one thinking."

"Settle down to what?"

"Oh, just settle down."

"And that's to be life!" said Helen, with a catch in her throat. "How can you, with all the beautiful things to see and do—with music—with walking at night——"

"Walking is well enough when a man's in work," he answered. "Oh, I did talk a lot of nonsense once, but there's nothing like a

---

[5]Traveling salesmen.

bailiff[6] in the house to drive it out of you. When I saw him fingering my Ruskins and Stevensons, I seemed to see life straight real, and it isn't a pretty sight. My books are back again, thanks to you, but they'll never be the same to me again, and I shan't ever again think night in the woods is wonderful."

"Why not?" asked Helen, throwing up the window.

"Because I see one must have money."

"Well, you're wrong."

"I wish I was wrong, but—the clergyman—he has money of his own, or else he's paid; the poet or the musician—just the same; the tramp—he's no different. The tramp goes to the workhouse[7] in the end, and is paid for with other people's money. Miss Schlegel, the real thing's money, and all the rest is a dream."

"You're still wrong. You've forgotten Death."

Leonard could not understand.

"If we lived for ever, what you say would be true. But we have to die, we have to leave life presently. Injustice and greed would be the real thing if we lived for ever. As it is, we must hold to other things, because Death is coming. I love Death—not morbidly, but because He explains. He shows me the emptiness of Money. Death and Money are the eternal foes. Not Death and Life. Never mind what lies behind Death, Mr. Bast, but be sure that the poet and the musician and the tramp will be happier in it than the man who has never learnt to say, 'I am I.'"

"I wonder."

"We are all in a mist—I know, but I can help you this far—men like the Wilcoxes are deeper in the mist than any. Sane, sound Englishmen! building up empires, levelling all the world into what they call common sense. But mention Death to them and they're offended, because Death's really Imperial, and He cries out against them for ever."

"I am as afraid of Death as anyone."

"But not of the idea of Death."

"But what is the difference?"

"Infinite difference," said Helen, more gravely than before.

Leonard looked at her wondering, and had the sense of great things sweeping out of the shrouded night. But he could not receive them, because his heart was still full of little things. As the lost umbrella had spoilt the concert at Queen's Hall, so the lost situation was

---

[6]Sheriff's deputy who executes legal processes, including seizures for debt.

[7]Institution in which the poor were set to hard work and received meager food and lodging—generally considered a dreadful fate.

obscuring the diviner harmonies now. Death, Life and Materialism were fine words, but would Mr. Wilcox take him on as a clerk? Talk as one would, Mr. Wilcox was king of this world, the superman, with his own morality, whose head remained in the clouds.

"I must be stupid," he said apologetically.

While to Helen the paradox became clearer and clearer. 'Death destroys a man: the idea of Death saves him.'[8] Behind the coffins and the skeletons that stay the vulgar mind lies something so immense that all that is great in us responds to it. Men of the world may recoil from the charnel-house[9] that they will one day enter, but Love knows better. Death is his foe, but his peer, and in their age-long struggle the thews of Love have been strengthened, and his vision cleared, until there is no one who can stand against him.

"So never give in," continued the girl, and restated again and again the vague yet convincing plea that the Invisible lodges against the Visible. Her excitement grew as she tried to cut the rope that fastened Leonard to the earth. Woven of bitter experience, it resisted her. Presently the waitress entered and gave her a letter from Margaret. Another note, addressed to Leonard, was inside. They read them, listening to the murmurings of the river.

## CHAPTER XXVIII

FOR many hours Margaret did nothing; then she controlled herself, and wrote some letters. She was too bruised to speak to Henry; she could pity him, and even determine to marry him, but as yet all lay too deep in her heart for speech. On the surface the sense of his degradation was too strong. She could not command voice or look, and the gentle words that she forced out through her pen seemed to proceed from some other person.

"My dearest boy," she began, "this is not to part us. It is everything or nothing, and I mean it to be nothing. It happened long before we ever met, and even if it had happened since, I should be writing the same, I hope. I do understand."

But she crossed out "I do understand"; it struck a false note. Henry could not bear to be understood. She also crossed out, "It is

---

[8]In *The Life of Michelangelo Buonarroti* (1893), John Addington Symonds translates a passage from the great Renaissance artist as, "Marvellous is the operation of this thought of death, which, albeit death, by his nature, destroys all things, preserves and supports those who think on death, and defends them from all human passions" (310).

[9]Above-ground building or vault for storing bones.

everything or nothing." Henry would resent so strong a grasp of the situation. She must not comment; comment is unfeminine.

"I think that'll about do," she thought.

Then the sense of his degradation choked her. Was he worth all this bother? To have yielded to a woman of that sort was everything, yes, it was, and she could not be his wife. She tried to translate his temptation into her own language, and her brain reeled. Men must be different, even to want to yield to such a temptation. Her belief in comradeship was stifled, and she saw life as from that glass saloon on the Great Western, which sheltered male and female alike from the fresh air. Are the sexes really races, each with its own code of morality, and their mutual love a mere device of Nature to keep things going? Strip human intercourse of the proprieties, and is it reduced to this? Her judgment told her no. She knew that out of Nature's device we have built a magic that will win us immortality. Far more mysterious than the call of sex to sex is the tenderness that we throw into that call; far wider is the gulf between us and the farmyard than between the farmyard and the garbage that nourishes it. We are evolving, in ways that Science cannot measure, to ends that Theology dares not contemplate. "Men did produce one jewel," the gods will say, and, saying, will give us immortality. Margaret knew all this, but for the moment she could not feel it, and transformed the marriage of Evie and Mr. Cahill into a carnival of fools, and her own marriage—too miserable to think of that, she tore up the letter, and then wrote another:

"Dear Mr. Bast,

"I have spoken to Mr. Wilcox about you, as I promised, and am sorry to say that he has no vacancy for you.

"Yours truly,

"M. J. Schlegel."

She enclosed this in a note to Helen, over which she took less trouble than she might have done; but her head was aching, and she could not stop to pick her words:

"Dear Helen,

"Give him this. The Basts are no good. Henry found the woman drunk on the lawn. I am having a room got ready for you here, and will you please come round at once on getting this? The Basts are not at all the type we should trouble about. I may go round to them myself in the morning, and do anything that is fair.

"M."

In writing this, Margaret felt that she was being practical. Something might be arranged for the Basts later on, but they must be silenced for the moment. She hoped to avoid a conversation between the woman and Helen. She rang the bell for a servant, but no one answered it; Mr. Wilcox and the Warringtons were gone to bed, and the kitchen was abandoned to Saturnalia.[1] Consequently she went over to the George herself. She did not enter the hotel, for discussion would have been perilous, and, saying that the letter was important, she gave it to the waitress. As she recrossed the square she saw Helen and Mr. Bast looking out of the window of the coffee-room, and feared she was already too late. Her task was not yet over; she ought to tell Henry what she had done.

This came easily, for she saw him in the hall. The night wind had been rattling the pictures against the wall, and the noise had disturbed him.

"Who's there?" he called, quite the householder.

Margaret walked in and past him.

"I have asked Helen to sleep," she said. "She is best here; so don't lock the front-door."

"I thought someone had got in," said Henry.

"At the same time I told the man that we could do nothing for him. I don't know about later, but now the Basts must clearly go."

"Did you say that your sister is sleeping here, after all?"

"Probably."

"Is she to be shown up to your room?"

"I have naturally nothing to say to her; I am going to bed. Will you tell the servants about Helen? Could someone go to carry her bag?"

He tapped a little gong, which had been bought to summon the servants.

"You must make more noise than that if you want them to hear."

Henry opened a door, and down the corridor came shouts of laughter. "Far too much screaming there," he said, and strode towards it. Margaret went upstairs, uncertain whether to be glad that they had met, or sorry. They had behaved as if nothing had happened, and her deepest instincts told her that this was wrong. For his own sake, some explanation was due.

And yet—what could an explanation tell her? A date, a place, a few details, which she could imagine all too clearly. Now that the first shock was over, she saw that there was every reason to premise a

[1]Wild revelry; from the Roman festival of Saturn, in which even slaves participated.

Mrs. Bast. Henry's inner life had long lain open to her—his intellectual confusion, his obtuseness to personal influence, his strong but furtive passions. Should she refuse him because his outer life corresponded? Perhaps. Perhaps, if the dishonour had been done to her, but it was done long before her day. She struggled against the feeling. She told herself that Mrs. Wilcox's wrong was her own. But she was not a barren theorist. As she undressed, her anger, her regard for the dead, her desire for a scene, all grew weak. Henry must have it as he liked, for she loved him, and some day she would use her love to make him a better man.

Pity was at the bottom of her actions all through this crisis. Pity, if one may generalize, is at the bottom of woman. When men like us, it is for our better qualities, and however tender their liking, we dare not be unworthy of it, or they will quietly let us go. But unworthiness stimulates woman. It brings out her deeper nature, for good or for evil.

Here was the core of the question. Henry must be forgiven, and made better by love; nothing else mattered. Mrs. Wilcox, that unquiet yet kindly ghost, must be left to her own wrong. To her everything was in proportion now, and she, too, would pity the man who was blundering up and down their lives. Had Mrs. Wilcox known of his trespass? An interesting question, but Margaret fell asleep, tethered by affection, and lulled by the murmurs of the river that descended all the night from Wales. She felt herself at one with her future home, colouring it and coloured by it, and awoke to see, for the second time, Oniton Castle conquering the morning mists.

## CHAPTER XXIX

"HENRY dear——" was her greeting.

He had finished his breakfast, and was beginning the 'Times.' His sister-in-law was packing. She knelt by him and took the paper from him, feeling that it was unusually heavy and thick. Then, putting her face where it had been, she looked up in his eyes.

"Henry dear, look at me. No, I won't have you shirking. Look at me. There. That's all."

"You're referring to last evening," he said huskily. "I have released you from your engagement. I could find excuses, but I won't. No, I won't. A thousand times no. I'm a bad lot, and must be left at that."

Expelled from his old fortress, Mr. Wilcox was building a new one. He could no longer appear respectable to her, so he defended himself instead in a lurid past. It was not true repentance.

"Leave it where you will, boy. It's not going to trouble us: I know what I'm talking about, and it will make no difference."

"No difference?" he inquired. "No difference, when you find that I am not the fellow you thought?" He was annoyed with Miss Schlegel here. He would have preferred her to be prostrated by the blow, or even to rage. Against the tide of his sin flowed the feeling that she was not altogether womanly. Her eyes gazed too straight; they had read books that are suitable for men only. And though he had dreaded a scene, and though she had determined against one, there was a scene, all the same. It was somehow imperative.

"I am unworthy of you," he began. "Had I been worthy, I should not have released you from your engagement. I know what I am talking about. I can't bear to talk of such things. We had better leave it."

She kissed his hand. He jerked it from her, and, rising to his feet, went on: "You, with your sheltered life, and refined pursuits, and friends, and books, you and your sister, and women like you—I say, how can you guess the temptations that lie round a man?"

"It is difficult for us," said Margaret; "but if we are worth marrying, we do guess."

"Cut off from decent society and family ties, what do you suppose happens to thousands of young fellows overseas? Isolated. No one near. I know by bitter experience, and yet you say it makes 'no difference.'"

"Not to me."

He laughed bitterly. Margaret went to the sideboard and helped herself to one of the breakfast dishes. Being the last down, she turned out the spirit-lamp that kept them warm. She was tender, but grave. She knew that Henry was not so much confessing his soul as pointing out the gulf between the male soul and the female, and she did not desire to hear him on this point.

"Did Helen come?" she asked.

He shook his head.

"But that won't do at all, at all! We don't want her gossiping with Mrs. Bast."

"Good God! no!" he exclaimed, suddenly natural. Then he caught himself up. "Let them gossip. My game's up, though I thank you for your unselfishness—little as my thanks are worth."

"Didn't she send me a message or anything?"

"I heard of none."

"Would you ring the bell, please?"

"What to do?"

"Why, to inquire."

He swaggered up to it tragically, and sounded a peal. Margaret poured herself out some coffee. The butler came, and said that Miss Schlegel had slept at the George, so far as he had heard. Should he go round to the George?

"I'll go, thank you," said Margaret, and dismissed him.

"It is no good," said Henry. "Those things leak out; you cannot stop a story once it has started. I have known cases of other men—I despised them once, I thought that *I'm* different, *I* shall never be tempted. Oh, Margaret——" He came and sat down near her, improvising emotion. She could not bear to listen to him. "We fellows all come to grief once in our time. Will you believe that? There are moments when the strongest man—— 'Let him who standeth, take heed lest he fall.'[1] That's true, isn't it? If you knew all, you would excuse me. I was far from good influences—far even from England. I was very, very lonely, and longed for a woman's voice. That's enough. I have told you too much already for you to forgive me now."

"Yes, that's enough, dear."

"I have"—he lowered his voice—"I have been through hell."

Gravely she considered this claim. Had he? Had he suffered tortures of remorse, or had it been, "There! that's over. Now for respectable life again"? The latter, if she read him rightly. A man who has been through hell does not boast of his virility. He is humble and hides it, if, indeed, it still exists. Only in legend does the sinner come forth penitent, but terrible, to conquer pure woman by his resistless power. Henry was anxious to be terrible, but had not got it in him. He was a good average Englishman, who had slipped. The really culpable point—his faithlessness to Mrs. Wilcox—never seemed to strike him. She longed to mention Mrs. Wilcox.

And bit by bit the story was told her. It was a very simple story. Ten years ago was the time, a garrison town in Cyprus the place. Now and then he asked her whether she could possibly forgive him, and she answered, "I have already forgiven you, Henry." She chose her words carefully, and so saved him from panic. She played the girl, until he could rebuild his fortress and hide his soul from the world. When the butler came to clear away, Henry was in a very different mood—asked the fellow what he was in such a hurry for, complained of the noise last night in the servants' hall. Margaret looked intently at the butler. He, as a handsome young man, was faintly attractive to her as a woman—an attraction so faint as scarcely to be perceptible, yet the skies would have fallen if she had mentioned it to Henry.

[1]Adapting Paul's advice in 1 Corinthians 10:12 (King James Version).

On her return from the George the building operations were complete, and the old Henry fronted her, competent, cynical, and kind. He had made a clean breast, had been forgiven, and the great thing now was to forget his failure, and to send it the way of other unsuccessful investments. Jacky rejoined Howards End and Ducie Street, and the vermilion motor-car, and the Argentine Hard Dollars,[2] and all the things and people for whom he had never had much use, and had less now. Their memory hampered him. He could scarcely attend to Margaret, who brought back disquieting news from the George. Helen and her clients had gone.

"Well, let them go—the man and his wife, I mean, for the more we see of your sister the better."

"But they have gone separately—Helen very early, the Basts just before I arrived. They have left no message. They have answered neither of my notes. I don't like to think what it all means."

"What did you say in the notes?"

"I told you last night."

"Oh—ah—yes! Dear, would you like one turn in the garden?"

Margaret took his arm. The beautiful weather soothed her. But the wheels of Evie's wedding were still at work, tossing the guests outwards as deftly as they had drawn them in, and she could not be with him long. It had been arranged that they should motor to Shrewsbury, whence he would go north, and she back to London with the Warringtons. For a fraction of time she was happy. Then her brain recommenced.

"I am afraid there has been gossiping of some kind at the George. Helen would not have left unless she had heard something. I mismanaged that. It is wretched. I ought to have parted her from that woman at once."

"Margaret!" he exclaimed, loosing her arm impressively.

"Yes—yes, Henry?"

"I am far from a saint—in fact, the reverse—but you have taken me, for better or worse. Bygones must be bygones. You have promised to forgive me. Margaret, a promise is a promise. Never mention that woman again."

"Except for some practical reason—never."

"Practical! You practical!"

"Yes, I'm practical," she murmured, stooping over the mowing-machine and playing with the grass which trickled through her fingers like sand.

[2]Perhaps a bad speculation in the Argentine *peso fuerte* (hard dollar), in circulation until 1881, or a loss following the dramatic fall of the Argentine *peso* in 1891.

He had silenced her, but her fears made him uneasy. Not for the first time, he was threatened with blackmail. He was rich and supposed to be moral; the Basts knew that he was not, and might find it profitable to hint as much.

"At all events, you mustn't worry," he said. "This is a man's business." He thought intently. "On no account mention it to anybody."

Margaret flushed at advice so elementary, but he was really paving the way for a lie. If necessary he would deny that he had ever known Mrs. Bast, and prosecute her for libel. Perhaps he never had known her. Here was Margaret, who behaved as if he had not. There the house. Round them were half a dozen gardeners, clearing up after his daughter's wedding. All was so solid and spruce, that the past flew up out of sight like a spring-blind,[3] leaving only the last five minutes unrolled.

Glancing at these, he saw that the car would be round during the next five, and plunged into action. Gongs were tapped, orders issued, Margaret was sent to dress, and the housemaid to sweep up the long trickle of grass that she had left across the hall. As is Man to the Universe, so was the mind of Mr. Wilcox to the minds of some men—a concentrated light upon a tiny spot, a little Ten Minutes moving self-contained through its appointed years. No Pagan he, who lives for the Now, and may be wiser than all philosophers. He lived for the five minutes that have past, and the five to come; he had the business mind.

How did he stand now, as his motor slipped out of Oniton and breasted the great round hills? Margaret had heard a certain rumour, but was all right. She had forgiven him, God bless her, and he felt the manlier for it. Charles and Evie had not heard it, and never must hear. No more must Paul. Over his children he felt great tenderness, which he did not try to track to a cause: Mrs. Wilcox was too far back in his life. He did not connect her with the sudden aching love that he felt for Evie. Poor little Evie! he trusted that Cahill would make her a decent husband.

And Margaret? How did she stand?

She had several minor worries. Clearly her sister had heard something. She dreaded meeting her in town. And she was anxious about Leonard, for whom they certainly were responsible. Nor ought Mrs. Bast to starve. But the main situation had not altered. She still loved Henry. His actions, not his disposition, had disappointed her, and she could bear that. And she loved her future home. Standing up in the car, just where she had leapt from it two days before, she gazed back

---

[3]Roller window shade using a spring mechanism.

with deep emotion upon Oniton. Besides the Grange and the Castle keep, she could now pick out the church and the black-and-white gables of the George. There was the bridge, and the river nibbling its green peninsula. She could even see the bathing-shed, but while she was looking for Charles's new spring-board, the forehead of the hill rose up and hid the whole scene.

She never saw it again. Day and night the river flows down into England, day after day the sun retreats into the Welsh mountains, and the tower chimes, "See the Conquering Hero."[4] But the Wilcoxes have no part in the place, nor in any place. It is not their names that recur in the parish register. It is not their ghosts that sigh among the alders at evening. They have swept into the valley and swept out of it, leaving a little dust and a little money behind.

## CHAPTER XXX

TIBBY was now approaching his last year at Oxford. He had moved out of college, and was contemplating the Universe, or such portions of it as concerned him, from his comfortable lodgings in Long Wall. He was not concerned with much. When a young man is untroubled by passions and sincerely indifferent to public opinion, his outlook is necessarily limited. Tibby neither wished to strengthen the position of the rich nor to improve that of the poor, and so was well content to watch the elms nodding behind the mildly embattled parapets of Magdalen.[1] There are worse lives. Though selfish, he was never cruel; though affected in manner, he never posed. Like Margaret, he disdained the heroic equipment, and it was only after many visits that men discovered Schlegel to possess a character and a brain. He had done well in Mods,[2] much to the surprise of those who attended lectures and took proper exercise, and was now glancing disdainfully at Chinese in case he should some day consent to qualify as a Student Interpreter. To him thus employed Helen entered. A telegram had preceded her.

He noticed, in a distant way, that his sister had altered. As a rule he found her too pronounced, and had never come across this look of appeal, pathetic yet dignified—the look of a sailor who has lost everything at sea.

---

[4]"See, the Conqu'ring hero comes" is a chorus from G. F. Handel's 1747 oratorio *Judas Maccabaeus.*

[1]Tibby's lodgings would be across Longwall Street from Magdalen College.

[2]Moderations, examinations required in some courses of study at Oxford.

"I have come from Oniton," she began. "There has been a great deal of trouble there."

"Who's for lunch?" said Tibby, picking up the claret, which was warming in the hearth. Helen sat down submissively at the table. "Why such an early start?" he asked.

"Sunrise or something—when I could get away."

"So I surmise. Why?"

"I don't know what's to be done, Tibby. I am very much upset at a piece of news that concerns Meg, and do not want to face her, and I am not going back to Wickham Place. I stopped here to tell you this."

The landlady came in with the cutlets. Tibby put a marker in the leaves of his Chinese Grammar and helped them. Oxford—the Oxford of the vacation[3]—dreamed and rustled outside, and indoors the little fire was coated with grey where the sunshine touched it. Helen continued her odd story.

"Give Meg my love and say that I want to be alone. I mean to go to Munich or else Bonn."

"Such a message is easily given," said her brother.

"As regards Wickham Place and my share of the furniture, you and she are to do exactly as you like. My own feeling is that everything may just as well be sold. What does one want with dusty economic books, which have made the world no better, or with mother's hideous cheffoniers? I have also another commission for you. I want you to deliver a letter." She got up. "I haven't written it yet. Why shouldn't I post it, though?" She sat down again. "My head is rather wretched. I hope that none of your friends are likely to come in."

Tibby locked the door. His friends often found it in this condition. Then he asked whether anything had gone wrong at Evie's wedding.

"Not there," said Helen, and burst into tears.

He had known her hysterical—it was one of her aspects with which he had no concern—and yet these tears touched him as something unusual. They were nearer the things that did concern him, such as music. He laid down his knife and looked at her curiously. Then, as she continued to sob, he went on with his lunch.

The time came for the second course, and she was still crying. Apple Charlotte was to follow, which spoils by waiting. "Do you mind Mrs. Martlett coming in?" he asked, "or shall I take it from her at the door?"

"Could I bathe my eyes, Tibby?"

[3]Echoing "Oxford in the Vacation" (1820), a famous essay by Charles Lamb.

He took her to his bedroom, and introduced the pudding in her absence. Having helped himself, he put it down to warm in the hearth. His hand stretched towards the Grammar, and soon he was turning over the pages, raising his eyebrows scornfully, perhaps at human nature, perhaps at Chinese. To him thus employed Helen returned. She had pulled herself together, but the grave appeal had not vanished from her eyes.

"Now for the explanation," she said. "Why didn't I begin with it? I have found out something about Mr. Wilcox. He has behaved very wrongly indeed, and ruined two people's lives. It all came on me very suddenly last night; I am very much upset, and I do not know what to do. Mrs. Bast——"

"Oh, those people!"

Helen seemed silenced.

"Shall I lock the door again?"

"No, thanks, Tibbikins. You're being very good to me. I want to tell you the story before I go abroad. You must do exactly what you like—treat it as part of the furniture. Meg cannot have heard it yet, I think. But I cannot face her and tell her that the man she is going to marry has misconducted himself. I don't even know whether she ought to be told. Knowing as she does that I dislike him, she will suspect me, and think that I want to ruin her match. I simply don't know what to make of such a thing. I trust your judgment. What would you do?"

"I gather he has had a mistress," said Tibby.

Helen flushed with shame and anger. "And ruined two people's lives. And goes about saying that personal actions count for nothing, and there always will be rich and poor. He met her when he was trying to get rich out in Cyprus—I don't wish to make him worse than he is, and no doubt she was ready enough to meet him. But there it is. They met. He goes his way and she goes hers. What do you suppose is the end of such women?"

He conceded that it was a bad business.

"They end in two ways: Either they sink till the lunatic asylums and the workhouses are full of them, and cause Mr. Wilcox to write letters to the papers complaining of our national degeneracy, or else they entrap a boy into marriage before it is too late. She—I can't blame her."

"But this isn't all," she continued after a long pause, during which the landlady served them with coffee. "I come now to the business that took us to Oniton. We went all three. Acting on Mr. Wilcox's advice, the man throws up a secure situation and takes an insecure one, from which he is dismissed. There are certain excuses, but in the main Mr. Wilcox is to blame, as Meg herself admitted. It is only common justice that he should employ the man himself. But he meets the woman, and, like the cur that he is, he refuses, and tries to get rid of them. He makes Meg write. Two notes came from her late that evening—one for me, one for Leonard, dismissing him with barely a reason. I couldn't understand. Then it comes out that Mrs. Bast had spoken to Mr. Wilcox on the lawn while we left her to get rooms, and was still speaking about him when Leonard came back to her. This Leonard knew all along. He thought it natural he should be ruined twice. Natural! Could you have contained yourself?"

"It is certainly a very bad business," said Tibby.

His reply seemed to calm his sister. "I was afraid that I saw it out of proportion. But you are right outside it, and you must know. In a day or two—or perhaps a week—take whatever steps you think fit. I leave it in your hands."

She concluded her charge.

"The facts as they touch Meg are all before you," she added; and Tibby sighed and felt it rather hard that, because of his open mind, he should be empanelled to serve as a juror. He had never been interested in human beings, for which one must blame him, but he had had rather too much of them at Wickham Place. Just as some people cease to attend when books are mentioned, so Tibby's attention wandered when "personal relations" came under discussion. Ought Margaret to know what Helen knew the Basts to know? Similar questions had vexed him from infancy, and at Oxford he had learned to say that the importance of human beings has been vastly overrated by specialists. The epigram, with its faint whiff of the eighties, meant nothing. But he might have let it off now if his sister had not been ceaselessly beautiful.

"You see, Helen—have a cigarette—I don't see what I'm to do."

"Then there's nothing to be done. I dare say you are right. Let them marry. There remains the question of compensation."

"Do you want me to adjudicate that too? Had you not better consult an expert?"

"This part is in confidence," said Helen. "It has nothing to do with Meg, and do not mention it to her. The compensation—I do not see who is to pay it if I don't, and I have already decided on the minimum sum. As soon as possible I am placing it to your account, and when I am in Germany you will pay it over for me. I shall never forget your kindness, Tibbikins, if you do this."

"What is the sum?"

"Five thousand."

"Good God alive!" said Tibby, and went crimson.

"Now, what is the good of driblets? To go through life having done one thing—to have raised one person from the abyss: not these puny gifts of shillings and blankets—making the grey more grey. No doubt people will think me extraordinary."

"I don't care a damn what people think!" cried he, heated to unusual manliness of diction. "But it's half what you have."

"Not nearly half." She spread out her hands over her soiled skirt. "I have far too much, and we settled at Chelsea last spring that three hundred a year is necessary to set a man on his feet. What I give will bring in a hundred and fifty between two. It isn't enough."

He could not recover. He was not angry or even shocked, and he saw that Helen would still have plenty to live on. But it amazed him to think what haycocks[4] people can make of their lives. His delicate intonations would not work, and he could only blurt out that the five thousand pounds would mean a great deal of bother for him personally.

"I didn't expect you to understand me."

"I? I understand nobody."

"But you'll do it?"

"Apparently."

"I leave you two commissions, then. The first concerns Mr. Wilcox, and you are to use your discretion. The second concerns the money, and is to be mentioned to no one, and carried out literally. You will send a hundred pounds on account to-morrow."

He walked with her to the station, passing through those streets whose serried beauty never bewildered him and never fatigued. The lovely creature raised domes and spires into the cloudless blue, and only the ganglion of vulgarity round Carfax[5] showed how evanescent was the phantom, how faint its claim to represent England. Helen, rehearsing her commission, noticed nothing: the Basts were in her brain, and she retold the crisis in a meditative way, which might have made other men curious. She was seeing whether it would hold. He asked her once why she had taken the Basts right into the heart of Evie's wedding. She stopped like a frightened animal and said, "Does that seem to you so odd?" Her eyes, the hand laid on the mouth, quite haunted him, until they were absorbed into the fig-

---

[4]Literally, conical piles of hay.

[5]Crossroads considered the historical center of Oxford.

ure of St. Mary the Virgin, before whom he paused for a moment on the walk home.

It is convenient to follow him in the discharge of his duties. Margaret summoned him the next day. She was terrified at Helen's flight, and he had to say that she had called in at Oxford. Then she said: "Did she seem worried at any rumour about Henry?" He answered, "Yes." "I knew it was that!" she exclaimed. "I'll write to her." Tibby was relieved.

He then sent the cheque to the address that Helen gave him, and stated that later on he was instructed to forward five thousand pounds. An answer came back, very civil and quiet in tone—such an answer as Tibby himself would have given. The cheque was returned, the legacy refused, the writer being in no need of money. Tibby forwarded this to Helen, adding in the fulness of his heart that Leonard Bast seemed somewhat a monumental person after all. Helen's reply was frantic. He was to take no notice. He was to go down at once and say that she commanded acceptance. He went. A scurf of books and china ornaments awaited him. The Basts had just been evicted for not paying their rent, and had wandered no one knew whither. Helen had begun bungling with her money by this time, and had even sold out her shares in the Nottingham and Derby Railway. For some weeks she did nothing. Then she reinvested, and, owing to the good advice of her stockbrokers, became rather richer than she had been before.

## CHAPTER XXXI

HOUSES have their own ways of dying, falling as variously as the generations of men, some with a tragic roar, some quietly, but to an after-life in the city of ghosts, while from others—and thus was the death of Wickham Place—the spirit slips before the body perishes. It had decayed in the spring, disintegrating the girls more than they knew, and causing either to accost unfamiliar regions. By September it was a corpse, void of emotion, and scarcely hallowed by the memories of thirty years of happiness. Through its round-topped doorway passed furniture, and pictures, and books, until the last room was gutted and the last van had rumbled away. It stood for a week or two longer, open-eyed, as if astonished at its own emptiness. Then it fell. Navvies[1] came, and spilt it back into the grey. With their muscles and their beery good temper, they were not the worst of undertakers for a house which had always been human, and had not mistaken culture for an end.

[1]Manual laborers.

The furniture, with a few exceptions, went down into Hertford-shire, Mr. Wilcox having most kindly offered Howards End as a ware-house. Mr. Bryce had died abroad—an unsatisfactory affair—and as there seemed little guarantee that the rent would be paid regularly, he cancelled the agreement, and resumed possession himself. Until he relet the house, the Schlegels were welcome to stack their furniture in the garage and lower rooms. Margaret demurred, but Tibby accepted the offer gladly; it saved him from coming to any decision about the future. The plate and the more valuable pictures found a safer home in Lon-don, but the bulk of the things went country-ways, and were entrusted to the guardianship of Miss Avery.

Shortly before the move, our hero and heroine were married. They have weathered the storm, and may reasonably expect peace. To have no illusions and yet to love—what stronger surety can a woman find? She had seen her husband's past as well as his heart. She knew her own heart with a thoroughness that commonplace people believe impossi-ble. The heart of Mrs. Wilcox was alone hidden, and perhaps it is su-perstitious to speculate on the feelings of the dead. They were married quietly—really quietly, for as the day approached she refused to go through another Oniton. Her brother gave her away, her aunt, who was out of health, presided over a few colourless refreshments. The Wilcoxes were represented by Charles, who witnessed the marriage settlement, and by Mr. Cahill. Paul did send a cablegram. In a few minutes, and without the aid of music, the clergyman made them man and wife, and soon the glass shade had fallen that cuts off married couples from the world. She, a monogamist, regretted the cessation of some of life's innocent odours; he, whose instincts were polygamous, felt morally braced by the change, and less liable to the temptations that had assailed him in the past.

They spent their honeymoon near Innsbruck. Henry knew of a re-liable hotel there, and Margaret hoped for a meeting with her sister. In this she was disappointed. As they came south, Helen retreated over the Brenner, and wrote an unsatisfactory postcard from the shores of the Lake of Garda, saying that her plans were uncertain and had bet-ter be ignored. Evidently she disliked meeting Henry. Two months are surely enough to accustom an outsider to a situation which a wife has accepted in two days, and Margaret had again to regret her sister's lack of self-control. In a long letter she pointed out the need of charity in sexual matters: so little is known about them; it is hard enough for those who are personally touched to judge; then how futile must be the verdict of Society. "I don't say there is no standard, for that would destroy morality; only that there can be no standard until our impulses are classified and better understood." Helen thanked her for her kind letter—rather a curious reply. She moved south again, and spoke of wintering in Naples.

Mr. Wilcox was not sorry that the meeting failed. Helen left him time to grow skin over his wound. There were still moments when it pained him. Had he only known that Margaret was awaiting him—Margaret, so lively and intelligent, and yet so submissive—he would have kept himself worthier of her. Incapable of grouping the past, he confused the episode of Jacky with another episode that had taken place in the days of his bachelorhood. The two made one crop of wild oats, for which he was heartily sorry, and he could not see that those oats are of a darker stock which are rooted in another's dishonour. Unchastity and infidelity were as confused to him as to the Middle Ages, his only moral teacher. Ruth (poor old Ruth!) did not enter into his calculations at all, for poor old Ruth had never found him out.

His affection for his present wife grew steadily. Her cleverness gave him no trouble, and, indeed, he liked to see her reading poetry or something about social questions; it distinguished her from the wives of other men. He had only to call, and she clapped the book up and was ready to do what he wished. Then they would argue so jollily, and once or twice she had him in quite a tight corner, but as soon as he grew really serious, she gave in. Man is for war, woman for the recreation of the warrior, but he does not dislike it if she makes a show of fight. She cannot win in a real battle, having no muscles, only nerves. Nerves make her jump out of a moving motor-car, or refuse to be married fashionably. The warrior may well allow her to triumph on such occasions; they move not the imperishable plinth[2] of things that touch his peace.

Margaret had a bad attack of these nerves during the honeymoon. He told her—casually, as was his habit—that Oniton Grange was let. She showed her annoyance, and asked rather crossly why she had not been consulted.

"I didn't want to bother you," he replied. "Besides, I have only heard for certain this morning."

"Where are we to live?" said Margaret, trying to laugh. "I loved the place extraordinarily. Don't you believe in having a permanent home, Henry?"

He assured her that she misunderstood him. It is home life that distinguishes us from the foreigner. But he did not believe in a damp home.

[2]Column base.

"This is news. I never heard till this minute that Oniton was damp."

"My dear girl!"—he flung out his hand—"have you eyes? have you a skin? How could it be anything but damp in such a situation? In the first place, the Grange is on clay, and built where the castle moat must have been; then there's that detestable little river, steaming all night like a kettle. Feel the cellar walls; look up under the eaves. Ask Sir James or anyone. Those Shropshire valleys are notorious. The only possible place for a house in Shropshire is on a hill; but, for my part, I think the country is too far from London, and the scenery nothing special."

Margaret could not resist saying, "Why did you go there, then?"

"I—because——" He drew his head back and grew rather angry. "Why have we come to the Tyrol, if it comes to that? One might go on asking such questions indefinitely."

One might; but he was only gaining time for a plausible answer. Out it came, and he believed it as soon as it was spoken.

"The truth is, I took Oniton on account of Evie. Don't let this go any further."

"Certainly not."

"I shouldn't like her to know that she nearly let me in for a very bad bargain. No sooner did I sign the agreement than she got engaged. Poor little girl! She was so keen on it all, and wouldn't even wait to make proper inquiries about the shooting. Afraid it would get snapped up—just like all of your sex. Well, no harm's done. She has had her country wedding, and I've got rid of my house to some fellows who are starting a preparatory school."

"Where shall we live, then, Henry? I should enjoy living somewhere."

"I have not yet decided. What about Norfolk?"

Margaret was silent. Marriage had not saved her from the sense of flux. London was but a foretaste of this nomadic civilization which is altering human nature so profoundly, and throws upon personal relations a stress greater than they have ever borne before. Under cosmopolitanism, if it comes, we shall receive no help from the earth. Trees and meadows and mountains will only be a spectacle, and the binding force that they once exercised on character must be entrusted to Love alone. May Love be equal to the task!

"It is now what?" continued Henry. "Nearly October. Let us camp for the winter at Ducie Street, and look out for something in the spring."

"If possible, something permanent. I can't be as young as I was, for these alterations don't suit me."

"But, my dear, which would you rather have—alterations or rheumatism?"

"I see your point," said Margaret, getting up. "If Oniton is really damp, it is impossible, and must be inhabited by little boys. Only, in the spring, let us look before we leap. I will take warning by Evie, and not hurry you. Remember that you have a free hand this time. These endless moves must be bad for the furniture, and are certainly expensive."

"What a practical little woman it is! What's it been reading? Theo—theo—how much?"

"Theosophy."

So Ducie Street was her first fate—a pleasant enough fate. The house, being only a little larger than Wickham Place, trained her for the immense establishment that was promised in the spring. They were frequently away, but at home life ran fairly regularly. In the morning Henry went to the business, and his sandwich—a relic this of some prehistoric craving—was always cut by her own hand. He did not rely upon the sandwich for lunch, but liked to have it by him in case he grew hungry at eleven. When he had gone, there was the house to look after, and the servants to humanize, and several kettles of Helen's to keep on the boil. Her conscience pricked her a little about the Basts; she was not sorry to have lost sight of them. No doubt Leonard was worth helping, but being Henry's wife, she preferred to help someone else. As for theatres and discussion societies, they attracted her less and less. She began to "miss" new movements, and to spend her spare time rereading or thinking, rather to the concern of her Chelsea friends. They attributed the change to her marriage, and perhaps some deep instinct did warn her not to travel further from her husband than was inevitable. Yet the main cause lay deeper still; she had outgrown stimulants, and was passing from words to things. It was doubtless a pity not to keep up with Wedekind or John,[3] but some closing of the gates is inevitable after thirty, if the mind itself is to become a creative power.

## CHAPTER XXXII

SHE was looking at plans one day in the following spring—they had finally decided to go down into Sussex and build—when Mrs. Charles Wilcox was announced.

---

[3]Audiences were scandalized by the frank sexuality and violence in Frank Wedekind's plays *Spring Awakening, Earth Spirit,* and *Pandora's Box* (1891, 1895, 1904). Augustus John was a celebrated Welsh painter and turn-of-the-century London bohemian.

"Have you heard the news?" Dolly cried, as soon as she entered the room. "Charles is so ang—I mean he is sure you know about it, or, rather, that you don't know."

"Why, Dolly!" said Margaret, placidly kissing her. "Here's a surprise! How are the boys and the baby?"

Boys and the baby were well, and in describing a great row that there had been at the Hilton Tennis Club, Dolly forgot her news. The wrong people had tried to get in. The rector, as representing the older inhabitants, had said—Charles had said—the tax-collector had said—Charles had regretted not saying—and she closed the description with, "But lucky you, with four courts of your own at Midhurst."

"It will be very jolly," replied Margaret.

"Are those the plans? Does it matter me seeing them?"

"Of course not."

"Charles has never seen the plans."

"They have only just arrived. Here is the ground floor—no, that's rather difficult. Try the elevation. We are to have a good many gables and a picturesque sky-line."

"What makes it smell so funny?" said Dolly, after a moment's inspection. She was incapable of understanding plans or maps.

"I suppose the paper."

"And *which* way up is it?"

"Just the ordinary way up. That's the sky-line, and the part that smells strongest is the sky."

"Well, ask me another. Margaret—oh—what was I going to say? How's Helen?"

"Quite well."

"Is she never coming back to England? Everyone thinks it's awfully odd she doesn't."

"So it is," said Margaret, trying to conceal her vexation. She was getting rather sore on this point. "Helen is odd, awfully. She has now been away eight months."

"But hasn't she any address?"

"A poste restante[1] somewhere in Bavaria is her address. Do write her a line. I will look it up for you."

"No, don't bother. That's eight months she has been away, surely?"

"Exactly. She left just after Evie's wedding. It would be eight months."

---

[1] Post office.

"Just when baby was born, then?"

"Just so."

Dolly sighed, and stared enviously round the drawing-room. She was beginning to lose her brightness and good looks. The Charles' were not well off, for Mr. Wilcox, having brought up his children with expensive tastes, believed in letting them shift for themselves. After all, he had not treated them generously. Yet another baby was expected, she told Margaret, and they would have to give up the motor. Margaret sympathized, but in a formal fashion, and Dolly little imagined that the step-mother was urging Mr. Wilcox to make them a more liberal allowance. She sighed again, and at last the particular grievance was remembered. "Oh yes," she cried, "that is it: Miss Avery has been unpacking your packing-cases."

"Why has she done that? How unnecessary!"

"Ask another. I suppose you ordered her to."

"I gave no such orders. Perhaps she was airing the things. She did undertake to light an occasional fire."

"It was far more than an air," said Dolly solemnly. "The floor sounds covered with books. Charles sent me to know what is to be done, for he feels certain you don't know."

"Books!" cried Margaret, moved by the holy word. "Dolly, are you serious? Has she been touching our books?"

"Hasn't she, though! What used to be the hall's full of them. Charles thought for certain you knew of it."

"I am very much obliged to you, Dolly. What can have come over Miss Avery? I must go down about it at once. Some of the books are my brother's, and are quite valuable. She had no right to open any of the cases."

"I say she's dotty. She was the one that never got married, you know. Oh, I say, perhaps she thinks your books are wedding-presents to herself. Old maids are taken that way sometimes. Miss Avery hates us all like poison ever since her frightful dust-up with Evie."

"I hadn't heard of that," said Margaret. A visit from Dolly had its compensations.

"Didn't you know she gave Evie a present last August, and Evie returned it, and then—oh, goloshes! You never read such a letter as Miss Avery wrote."

"But it was wrong of Evie to return it. It wasn't like her to do such a heartless thing."

"But the present was so expensive."

"Why does that make any difference, Dolly?"

"Still, when it costs over five pounds—I didn't see it, but it was a lovely enamel pendant from a Bond Street[2] shop. You can't very well accept that kind of thing from a farm woman. Now, can you?"

"You accepted a present from Miss Avery when you were married."

"Oh, mine was old earthenware stuff—not worth a halfpenny. Evie's was quite different. You'd have to ask anyone to the wedding who gave you a pendant like that. Uncle Percy and Albert and father and Charles all said it was quite impossible, and when four men agree, what is a girl to do? Evie didn't want to upset the old thing, so thought a sort of joking letter best, and returned the pendant straight to the shop to save Miss Avery trouble."

"But Miss Avery said——"

Dolly's eyes grew round. "It was a perfectly awful letter. Charles said it was the letter of a madman. In the end she had the pendant back again from the shop and threw it into the duckpond."

"Did she give any reasons?"

"We think she meant to be invited to Oniton, and so climb into society."

"She's rather old for that," said Margaret pensively. "May not she have given the present to Evie in remembrance of her mother?"

"That's a notion. Give every one their due, eh? Well, I suppose I ought to be toddling. Come along Mr. Muff—you want a new coat, but I don't know who'll give it you, I'm sure;" and addressing her apparel with mournful humour, Dolly moved from the room.

Margaret followed her to ask whether Henry knew about Miss Avery's rudeness.

"Oh yes."

"I wonder, then, why he let me ask her to look after the house."

"But she's only a farm woman," said Dolly, and her explanation proved correct. Henry only censured the lower classes when it suited him. He bore with Miss Avery as with Crane—because he could get good value out of them. "I have patience with a man who knows his job," he would say, really having patience with the job, and not the man. Paradoxical as it may sound, he had something of the artist about him; he would pass over an insult to his daughter sooner than lose a good charwoman for his wife.

Margaret judged it better to settle the little trouble herself. Parties were evidently ruffled. With Henry's permission, she wrote a pleasant note to Miss Avery, asking her to leave the cases untouched. Then, at

[2]Home to fashionable London stores.

the first convenient opportunity, she went down herself, intending to repack her belongings and store them properly in the local warehouse: the plan had been amateurish and a failure. Tibby promised to accompany her, but at the last moment begged to be excused. So, for the second time in her life, she entered the house alone.

## CHAPTER XXXIII

THE day of her visit was exquisite, and the last of unclouded happiness that she was to have for many months. Her anxiety about Helen's extraordinary absence was still dormant, and as for a possible brush with Miss Avery—that only gave zest to the expedition. She had also eluded Dolly's invitation to luncheon. Walking straight up from the station, she crossed the village green and entered the long chestnut avenue that connects it with the church. The church itself stood in the village once. But it there attracted so many worshippers that the devil, in a pet, snatched it from its foundations, and poised it on an inconvenient knoll, three-quarters of a mile away. If this story is true, the chestnut avenue must have been planted by the angels. No more tempting approach could be imagined for the lukewarm Christian, and if he still finds the walk too long, the devil is defeated all the same, Science having built Holy Trinity, a Chapel of Ease, near the Charles', and roofed it with tin.

Up the avenue Margaret strolled slowly, stopping to watch the sky that gleamed through the upper branches of the chestnuts, or to finger the little horseshoes on the lower branches. Why has not England a great mythology? Our folklore has never advanced beyond daintiness, and the greater melodies about our country-side have all issued through the pipes of Greece. Deep and true as the native imagination can be, it seems to have failed here. It has stopped with the witches and the fairies. It cannot vivify one fraction of a summer field, or give names to half a dozen stars. England still waits for the supreme moment of her literature—for the great poet who shall voice her, or, better still, for the thousand little poets whose voices shall pass into our common talk.

At the church the scenery changed. The chestnut avenue opened into a road, smooth but narrow, which led into the untouched country. She followed it for over a mile. Its little hesitations pleased her. Having no urgent destiny, it strolled downhill or up as it wished, taking no trouble about the gradients, nor about the view, which nevertheless expanded. The great estates that throttle the south of Hertfordshire were less obtrusive here, and the appearance of the land was neither aristocratic nor suburban. To define it was difficult, but Margaret knew what it was not: it was not snobbish. Though its contours were slight, there was a touch of freedom in their sweep to which Surrey will never attain, and the distant brow of the Chilterns towered like a mountain. "Left to itself," was Margaret's opinion, "this county would vote Liberal." The comradeship, not passionate, that is our highest gift as a nation, was promised by it, as by the low brick farm where she called for the key.

But the inside of the farm was disappointing. A most finished young person received her. "Yes, Mrs. Wilcox; no, Mrs. Wilcox; oh yes, Mrs. Wilcox, auntie received your letter quite duly. Auntie has gone up to your little place at the present moment. Shall I send the servant to direct you?" Followed by: "Of course, auntie does not generally look after your place; she only does it to oblige a neighbour as something exceptional. It gives her something to do. She spends quite a lot of her time there. My husband says to me sometimes, 'Where's auntie?' I say, 'Need you ask? She's at Howards End.' Yes, Mrs. Wilcox. Mrs. Wilcox, could I prevail upon you to accept a piece of cake? Not if I cut it for you?"

Margaret refused the cake, but unfortunately this acquired her gentility in the eyes of Miss Avery's niece.

"I cannot let you go on alone. Now don't. You really mustn't. I will direct you myself if it comes to that. I must get my hat. Now"— roguishly—"Mrs. Wilcox, don't you move while I'm gone."

Stunned, Margaret did not move from the best parlour, over which the touch of art nouveau[1] had fallen. But the other rooms looked in keeping, though they conveyed the peculiar sadness of a rural interior. Here had lived an elder race, to which we look back with disquietude. The country which we visit at week-ends was really a home to it, and the graver sides of life, the deaths, the partings, the yearnings for love, have their deepest expression in the heart of the fields. All was not sadness. The sun was shining without. The thrush sang his two syllables on the budding guelder-rose. Some children were playing uproariously in heaps of golden straw. It was the presence of sadness at all that surprised Margaret, and ended by giving her a feeling of completeness. In these English farms, if anywhere, one might see life steadily and see it whole, group in one vision its transitoriness and its eternal youth, connect—connect without bitterness until all men are brothers. But her thoughts were interrupted by the return of Miss Avery's niece, and were so tranquillizing that she suffered the interruption gladly.

---

[1]Fin de siècle style characterized by curving lines and floral forms (French: new art).

It was quicker to go out by the back door, and, after due explanations, they went out by it. The niece was now mortified by innumerable chickens, who rushed up to her feet for food, and by a shameless
and maternal sow. She did not know what animals were coming to.
But her gentility withered at the touch of the sweet air. The wind was
rising, scattering the straw and ruffling the tails of the ducks as they
floated in families over Evie's pendant. One of those delicious gales of
spring, in which leaves still in bud seem to rustle, swept over the land
and then fell silent. "Georgie," sang the thrush. "Cuckoo," came
furtively from the cliff of pine-trees. "Georgie, pretty Georgie," and
the other birds joined in with nonsense. The hedge was a half-painted
picture which would be finished in a few days. Celandines grew on its
banks, lords and ladies and primroses in the defended hollows; the
wild rose-bushes, still bearing their withered hips, showed also the
promise of blossom. Spring had come, clad in no classical garb, yet
fairer than all springs; fairer even than she who walks through the
myrtles of Tuscany with the graces before her and the zephyr behind.[2]

The two women walked up the lane full of outward civility. But
Margaret was thinking how difficult it was to be earnest about furniture on such a day, and the niece was thinking about hats. Thus engaged, they reached Howards End. Petulant cries of "Auntie!"
severed the air. There was no reply, and the front door was locked.

"Are you sure that Miss Avery is up here?" asked Margaret.

"Oh yes, Mrs. Wilcox, quite sure. She is here daily."

Margaret tried to look in through the dining-room window, but the
curtain inside was drawn tightly. So with the drawing-room and the
hall. The appearance of these curtains was familiar, yet she did not remember them being there on her other visit: her impression was that
Mr. Bryce had taken everything away. They tried the back. Here again
they received no answer, and could see nothing; the kitchen-window
was fitted with a blind, while the pantry and scullery had pieces of
wood propped up against them, which looked ominously like the lids
of packing-cases. Margaret thought of her books, and she lifted up her
voice also. At the first cry she succeeded.

"Well, well!" replied someone inside the house. "If it isn't Mrs.
Wilcox come at last!"

"Have you got the key, auntie?"

"Madge, go away," said Miss Avery, still invisible.

"Auntie, it's Mrs. Wilcox——"

[2]Alluding to Botticelli's *Primavera* (c. 1478).

Margaret supported her. "Your niece and I have come together——"

"Madge, go away. This is no moment for your hat."

The poor woman went red. "Auntie gets more eccentric lately," she said nervously.

"Miss Avery!" called Margaret. "I have come about the furniture. Could you kindly let me in?"

"Yes, Mrs. Wilcox," said the voice, "of course." But after that came silence. They called again without response. They walked round the house disconsolately.

"I hope Miss Avery is not ill," hazarded Margaret.

"Well, if you'll excuse me," said Madge, "perhaps I ought to be leaving you now. The servants need seeing to at the farm. Auntie is so odd at times." Gathering up her elegancies, she retired defeated, and, as if her departure had loosed a spring, the front door opened at once.

Miss Avery said, "Well, come right in, Mrs. Wilcox!" quite pleasantly and calmly.

"Thank you so much," began Margaret, but broke off at the sight of an umbrella-stand. It was her own.

"Come right into the hall first," said Miss Avery. She drew the curtain, and Margaret uttered a cry of despair. For an appalling thing had happened. The hall was fitted up with the contents of the library from Wickham Place. The carpet had been laid, the big work-table drawn up near the window; the bookcases filled the wall opposite the fireplace, and her father's sword—this is what bewildered her particularly—had been drawn from its scabbard and hung naked amongst the sober volumes. Miss Avery must have worked for days.

"I'm afraid this isn't what we meant," she began. "Mr. Wilcox and I never intended the cases to be touched. For instance, these books are my brother's. We are storing them for him and for my sister, who is abroad. When you kindly undertook to look after things, we never expected you to do so much."

"The house has been empty long enough," said the old woman.

Margaret refused to argue. "I dare say we didn't explain," she said civilly. "It has been a mistake, and very likely our mistake."

"Mrs. Wilcox, it has been mistake upon mistake for fifty years. The house is Mrs. Wilcox's, and she would not desire it to stand empty any longer."

To help the poor decaying brain, Margaret said:

"Yes, Mrs. Wilcox's house, the mother of Mr. Charles."

"Mistake upon mistake," said Miss Avery. "Mistake upon mistake."

"Well, I don't know," said Margaret, sitting down in one of her own chairs. "I really don't know what's to be done." She could not help laughing.

The other said: "Yes, it should be a merry house enough."

"I don't know—I dare say. Well, thank you very much, Miss Avery. Yes, that's all right. Delightful."

"There is still the parlour." She went through the door opposite and drew a curtain. Light flooded the drawing-room and the drawing-room furniture from Wickham Place. "And the dining-room." More curtains were drawn, more windows were flung open to the spring. "Then through here——" Miss Avery continued passing and repassing through the hall. Her voice was lost, but Margaret heard her pulling up the kitchen blind. "I've not finished here yet," she announced, returning. "There's still a deal to do. The farm lads will carry your great wardrobes upstairs, for there is no need to go into expense at Hilton."

"It is all a mistake," repeated Margaret, feeling that she must put her foot down. "A misunderstanding. Mr. Wilcox and I are not going to live at Howards End."

"Oh, indeed. On account of his hay fever?"

"We have settled to build a new home for ourselves in Sussex, and part of this furniture—my part—will go down there presently." She looked at Miss Avery intently, trying to understand the kink in her brain. Here was no maundering old woman. Her wrinkles were shrewd and humorous. She looked capable of scathing wit and also of high but unostentatious nobility.

"You think that you won't come back to live here, Mrs. Wilcox, but you will."

"That remains to be seen," said Margaret, smiling. "We have no intention of doing so for the present. We happen to need a much larger house. Circumstances oblige us to give big parties. Of course, some day—one never knows, does one?"

Miss Avery retorted: "Some day! Tcha! tcha! Don't talk about some day. You are living here now."

"Am I?"

"You are living here, and have been for the last ten minutes, if you ask me."

It was a senseless remark, but with a queer feeling of disloyalty Margaret rose from her chair. She felt that Henry had been obscurely censured. They went into the dining-room, where the sunlight poured in upon her mother's cheffonier, and upstairs, where many an old god peeped from a new niche. The furniture fitted extraordinarily well. In the central room—over the hall, the room that Helen had slept in four years ago—Miss Avery had placed Tibby's old bassinette.

"The nursery," she said.

Margaret turned away without speaking.

At last everything was seen. The kitchen and lobby were still stacked with furniture and straw, but, as far as she could make out, nothing had been broken or scratched. A pathetic display of ingenuity! Then they took a friendly stroll in the garden. It had gone wild since her last visit. The gravel sweep was weedy, and grass had sprung up at the very jaws of the garage. And Evie's rockery was only bumps. Perhaps Evie was responsible for Miss Avery's oddness. But Margaret suspected that the cause lay deeper, and that the girl's silly letter had but loosed the irritation of years.

"It's a beautiful meadow," she remarked. It was one of those open-air drawing-rooms that have been formed, hundreds of years ago, out of the smaller fields. So the boundary hedge zigzagged down the hill at right angles, and at the bottom there was a little green annex—a sort of powder-closet for the cows.

"Yes, the maidy's well enough," said Miss Avery, "for those, that is, who don't suffer from sneezing." And she cackled maliciously. "I've seen Charlie Wilcox go out to my lads in hay time—oh, they ought to do this—they mustn't do that—he'd learn them to be lads. And just then the tickling took him. He has it from his father, with other things. There's not one Wilcox that can stand up against a field in June—I laughed fit to burst while he was courting Ruth."

"My brother gets hay fever too," said Margaret.

"This house lies too much on the land for them. Naturally, they were glad enough to slip in at first. But Wilcoxes are better than nothing, as I see you've found."

Margaret laughed.

"They keep a place going, don't they? Yes, it is just that."

"They keep England going, it is my opinion."

But Miss Avery upset her by replying: "Ay, they breed like rabbits. Well, well, it's a funny world. But He who made it knows what He wants in it, I suppose. If Mrs. Charlie is expecting her fourth, it isn't for us to repine."

"They breed and they also work," said Margaret, conscious of some invitation to disloyalty, which was echoed by the very breeze and by the songs of the birds. "It certainly is a funny world, but so long as men like my husband and his sons govern it, I think it'll never be a bad one—never really bad."

"No, better'n nothing," said Miss Avery, and turned to the wych-elm.

On their way back to the farm she spoke of her old friend much more clearly than before. In the house Margaret had wondered whether she quite distinguished the first wife from the second. Now she said: "I never saw much of Ruth after her grandmother died, but we stayed civil. It was a very civil family. Old Mrs. Howard never spoke against anybody, nor let anyone be turned away without food. Then it was never 'Trespassers will be prosecuted' in their land, but would people please not come in? Mrs. Howard was never created to run a farm."

"Had they no men to help them?" Margaret asked.

Miss Avery replied: "Things went on until there were no men."

"Until Mr. Wilcox came along," corrected Margaret, anxious that her husband should receive his dues.

"I suppose so; but Ruth should have married a—no disrespect to you to say this, for I take it you were intended to get Wilcox any way, whether she got him first or no."

"Whom should she have married?"

"A soldier!" exclaimed the old woman. "Some real soldier."

Margaret was silent. It was a criticism of Henry's character far more trenchant than any of her own. She felt dissatisfied.

"But that's all over," she went on. "A better time is coming now, though you've kept me long enough waiting. In a couple of weeks I'll see your lights shining through the hedge of an evening. Have you ordered in coals?"

"We are not coming," said Margaret firmly. She respected Miss Avery too much to humour her. "No. Not coming. Never coming. It has all been a mistake. The furniture must be repacked at once, and I am very sorry, but I am making other arrangements, and must ask you to give me the keys."

"Certainly, Mrs. Wilcox," said Miss Avery, and resigned her duties with a smile.

Relieved at this conclusion, and having sent her compliments to Madge, Margaret walked back to the station. She had intended to go to the furniture warehouse and give directions for removal, but the muddle had turned out more extensive than she expected, so she decided to consult Henry. It was as well that she did this. He was strongly against employing the local man whom he had previously recommended, and advised her to store in London after all.

But before this could be done an unexpected trouble fell upon her.

# CHAPTER XXXIV

IT was not unexpected entirely. Aunt Juley's health had been bad all the winter. She had had a long series of colds and coughs, and had been too busy to get rid of them. She had scarcely promised her niece "to really take my tiresome chest in hand," when she caught a chill and developed acute pneumonia. Margaret and Tibby went down to Swanage. Helen was telegraphed for, and that spring party that after all gathered in that hospitable house had all the pathos of fair memories. On a perfect day, when the sky seemed blue porcelain, and the waves of the discreet little bay beat gentlest of tattoes[1] upon the sand, Margaret hurried up through the rhododendrons, confronted again by the senselessness of Death. One death may explain itself, but it throws no light upon another: the groping inquiry must begin anew. Preachers or scientists may generalize, but we know that no generality is possible about those whom we love; not one heaven awaits them, not even one oblivion. Aunt Juley, incapable of tragedy, slipped out of life with odd little laughs and apologies for having stopped in it so long. She was very weak; she could not rise to the occasion, or realize the great mystery which all agree must await her; it only seemed to her that she was quite done up—more done up than ever before; that she saw and heard and felt less every moment; and that, unless something changed, she would soon feel nothing. Her spare strength she devoted to plans: could not Margaret take some steamer expeditions? were mackerel cooked as Tibby liked them? She worried herself about Helen's absence, and also that she should be the cause of Helen's return. The nurses seemed to think such interests quite natural, and perhaps hers was an average approach to the Great Gate. But Margaret saw Death stripped of any false romance; whatever the idea of Death may contain, the process can be trivial and hideous.

"Important—Margaret dear, take the Lulworth[2] when Helen comes."

"Helen won't be able to stop, Aunt Juley. She has telegraphed that she can only get away just to see you. She must go back to Germany as soon as you are well."

"How very odd of Helen! Mr. Wilcox——"

"Yes, dear?"

"Can he spare you?"

---

[1]Drumbeats.

[2]See ch. 22. Lulworth Cove, Lulworth Castle, and the villages of East Lulworth and West Lulworth lie west of Swanage in Dorset.

Henry wished her to come, and had been very kind. Yet again Margaret said so.

Mrs. Munt did not die. Quite outside her will, a more dignified power took hold of her and checked her on the downward slope. She returned, without emotion, as fidgety as ever. On the fourth day she was out of danger.

"Margaret—important," it went on: "I should like you to have some companion to take walks with. Do try Miss Conder."

"I have been a little walk with Miss Conder."

"But she is not really interesting. If only you had Helen."

"I have Tibby, Aunt Juley."

"No, but he has to do his Chinese. Some real companion is what you need. Really, Helen is odd."

"Helen is odd, very," agreed Margaret.

"Not content with going abroad, why does she want to go back there at once?"

"No doubt she will change her mind when she sees us. She has not the least balance."

That was the stock criticism about Helen, but Margaret's voice trembled as she made it. By now she was deeply pained at her sister's behaviour. It may be unbalanced to fly out of England, but to stop away eight months argues that the heart is awry as well as the head. A sick-bed could recall Helen, but she was deaf to more human calls; after a glimpse at her aunt, she would retire into her nebulous life behind some poste restante. She scarcely existed; her letters had become dull and infrequent; she had no wants and no curiosity. And it was all put down to poor Henry's account! Henry, long pardoned by his wife, was still too infamous to be greeted by his sister-in-law. It was morbid, and, to her alarm, Margaret fancied that she could trace the growth of morbidity back in Helen's life for nearly four years. The flight from Oniton; the unbalanced patronage of the Basts; the explosion of grief up on the Downs—all connected with Paul, an insignificant boy whose lips had kissed hers for a fraction of time. Margaret and Mrs. Wilcox had feared that they might kiss again. Foolishly: the real danger was reaction. Reaction against the Wilcoxes had eaten into her life until she was scarcely sane. At twenty-five she had an idée fixe.[3] What hope was there for her as an old woman?

The more Margaret thought about it the more alarmed she became. For many months she had put the subject away, but it was too

---

[3]Fixation (French: fixed idea).

big to be slighted now. There was almost a taint of madness. Were all Helen's actions to be governed by a tiny mishap, such as may happen to any young man or woman? Can human nature be constructed on lines so insignificant? The blundering little encounter at Howards End was vital. It propagated itself where graver intercourse lay barren; it was stronger than sisterly intimacy, stronger than reason or books. In one of her moods Helen had confessed that she still "enjoyed" it in a certain sense. Paul had faded, but the magic of his caress endured. And where there is enjoyment of the past there may also be reaction—propagation at both ends.

Well, it is odd and sad that our minds should be such seed-beds, and we without power to choose the seed. But man is an odd, sad creature as yet, intent on pilfering the earth, and heedless of the growths within himself. He cannot be bored about psychology. He leaves it to the specialist, which is as if he should leave his dinner to be eaten by a steam-engine. He cannot be bothered to digest his own soul. Margaret and Helen have been more patient, and it is suggested that Margaret has succeeded—so far as success is yet possible. She does understand herself, she has some rudimentary control over her own growth. Whether Helen has succeeded one cannot say.

The day that Mrs. Munt rallied Helen's letter arrived. She had posted it at Munich, and would be in London herself on the morrow. It was a disquieting letter, though the opening was affectionate and sane.

"DEAREST MEG,

"Give Helen's love to Aunt Juley. Tell her that I love, and have loved, her ever since I can remember. I shall be in London Thursday.

"My address will be care of the bankers. I have not yet settled on a hotel, so write or wire to me there and give me detailed news. If Aunt Juley is much better, or if, for a terrible reason, it would be no good my coming down to Swanage, you must not think it odd if I do not come. I have all sorts of plans in my head. I am living abroad at present, and want to get back as quickly as possible. Will you please tell me where our furniture is. I should like to take out one or two books; the rest are for you.

"Forgive me, dearest Meg. This must read like rather a tiresome letter, but all letters are from your loving

"HELEN."

It was a tiresome letter, for it tempted Margaret to tell a lie. If she wrote that Aunt Juley was still in danger her sister would come. Unhealthiness is contagious. We cannot be in contact with those who are in a morbid state without ourselves deteriorating. To "act for the best" might do Helen good, but would do herself harm, and, at the risk of disaster, she kept her colours flying a little longer. She replied that their aunt was much better, and awaited developments.

Tibby approved of her reply. Mellowing rapidly, he was a pleasanter companion than before. Oxford had done much for him. He had lost his peevishness, and could hide his indifference to people and his interest in food. But he had not grown more human. The years between eighteen and twenty-two, so magical for most, were leading him gently from boyhood to middle age. He had never known young-manliness, that quality which warms the heart till death, and gives Mr. Wilcox an imperishable charm. He was frigid, through no fault of his own, and without cruelty. He thought Helen wrong and Margaret right, but the family trouble was for him what a scene behind footlights is for most people. He had only one suggestion to make, and that was characteristic.

"Why don't you tell Mr. Wilcox?"

"About Helen?"

"Perhaps he has come across that sort of thing."

"He would do all he could, but——"

"Oh, you know best. But he is practical."

It was the student's belief in experts. Margaret demurred for one or two reasons. Presently Helen's answer came. She sent a telegram requesting the address of the furniture, as she would now return at once. Margaret replied, "Certainly not; meet me at the bankers at four." She and Tibby went up to London. Helen was not at the bankers, and they were refused her address. Helen had passed into chaos.

Margaret put her arm round her brother. He was all that she had left, and never had he seemed more unsubstantial.

"Tibby love, what next?"

He replied: "It is extraordinary."

"Dear, your judgment's often clearer than mine. Have you any notion what's at the back?"

"None, unless it's something mental."

"Oh—that!" said Margaret. "Quite impossible." But the suggestion had been uttered, and in a few minutes she took it up herself. Nothing else explained. And London agreed with Tibby. The mask fell off the city, and she saw it for what it really is—a caricature of infinity. The familiar barriers, the streets along which she moved, the houses between which she had made her little journeys for so many years, became negligible suddenly. Helen seemed one with grimy trees and the traffic and the slowly-flowing slabs of mud. She had accomplished a hideous act of renunciation and returned to the One. Margaret's own faith held firm. She knew the human soul will be merged, if it be merged at all, with the stars and the sea. Yet she felt that her sister had been going amiss for many years. It was symbolic the catastrophe should come now, on a London afternoon, while rain fell slowly.

Henry was the only hope. Henry was definite. He might know of some paths in the chaos that were hidden from them, and she determined to take Tibby's advice and lay the whole matter in his hands. They must call at his office. He could not well make it worse. She went for a few moments into St. Paul's, whose dome stands out of the welter so bravely, as if preaching the gospel of form. But within, St. Paul's is as its surroundings—echoes and whispers, inaudible songs, invisible mosaics, wet footmarks crossing and recrossing the floor. Si monumentum requiris, circumspice:[4] it points us back to London. There was no hope of Helen here.

Henry was unsatisfactory at first. That she had expected. He was overjoyed to see her back from Swanage, and slow to admit the growth of a new trouble. When they told him of their search, he only chaffed Tibby and the Schlegels generally, and declared that it was "just like Helen" to lead her relatives a dance.

"That is what we all say," replied Margaret. "But why should it be just like Helen? Why should she be allowed to be so queer, and to grow queerer?"

"Don't ask me. I'm a plain man of business. I live and let live. My advice to you both is, don't worry. Margaret, you've got black marks again under your eyes. You know that's strictly forbidden. First your aunt—then your sister. No, we aren't going to have it. Are we, Theobald?" He rang the bell. "I'll give you some tea, and then you go straight to Ducie Street. I can't have my girl looking as old as her husband."

"All the same, you have not quite seen our point," said Tibby.

Mr. Wilcox, who was in good spirits, retorted, "I don't suppose I ever shall." He leant back, laughing at the gifted but ridiculous family, while the fire flickered over the map of Africa. Margaret motioned to her brother to go on. Rather diffident, he obeyed her.

"Margaret's point is this," he said. "Our sister may be mad."

---

[4]Latin: "If you seek his monument, look around you"; the epitaph of architect Christopher Wren's tomb in St. Paul's.

Charles, who was working in the inner room, looked round.

"Come in, Charles," said Margaret kindly. "Could you help us at all? We are again in trouble."

"I'm afraid I cannot. What are the facts? We are all mad more or less, you know, in these days."

"The facts are as follows," replied Tibby, who had at times a pedantic lucidity. "The facts are that she has been in England for three days and will not see us. She has forbidden the bankers to give us her address. She refuses to answer questions. Margaret finds her letters colourless. There are other facts, but these are the most striking."

"She has never behaved like this before, then?" asked Henry.

"Of course not!" said his wife, with a frown.

"Well, my dear, how am I to know?"

A senseless spasm of annoyance came over her. "You know quite well that Helen never sins against affection," she said. "You must have noticed that much in her, surely."

"Oh yes; she and I have always hit it off together."

"No, Henry—can't you see?—I don't mean that."

She recovered herself, but not before Charles had observed her. Stupid and attentive, he was watching the scene.

"I was meaning that when she was eccentric in the past, one could trace it back to the heart in the long-run. She behaved oddly because she cared for someone, or wanted to help them. There's no possible excuse for her now. She is grieving us deeply, and that is why I am sure that she is not well. 'Mad' is too terrible a word, but she is not well. I shall never believe it. I shouldn't discuss my sister with you if I thought she was well—trouble you about her, I mean."

Henry began to grow serious. Ill-health was to him something perfectly definite. Generally well himself, he could not realize that we sink to it by slow gradations. The sick had no rights; they were outside the pale; one could lie to them remorselessly. When his first wife was seized, he had promised to take her down into Hertfordshire, but meanwhile arranged with a nursing-home instead. Helen, too, was ill. And the plan that he sketched out for her capture, clever and well-meaning as it was, drew its ethics from the wolf-pack.

"You want to get hold of her?" he said. "That's the problem, isn't it? She has got to see a doctor."

"For all I know she has seen one already."

"Yes, yes; don't interrupt." He rose to his feet and thought intently. The genial, tentative host disappeared, and they saw instead the man who had carved money out of Greece and Africa, and bought forests from the natives for a few bottles of gin. "I've got it," he said at last. "It's perfectly easy. Leave it to me. We'll send her down to Howards End."

"How will you do that?"

"After her books. Tell her that she must unpack them herself. Then you can meet her there."

"But, Henry, that's just what she won't let me do. It's part of her—whatever it is—never to see me."

"Of course you won't tell her you're going. When she is there, looking at the cases, you'll just stroll in. If nothing is wrong with her, so much the better. But there'll be the motor round the corner, and we can run her up to a specialist in no time."

Margaret shook her head. "It's quite impossible."

"Why?"

"It doesn't seem impossible to me," said Tibby; "it is surely a very tippy[5] plan."

"It is impossible, because——" She looked at her husband sadly. "It's not the particular language that Helen and I talk, if you see my meaning. It would do splendidly for other people, whom I don't blame."

"But Helen doesn't talk," said Tibby. "That's our whole difficulty. She won't talk your particular language, and on that account you think she's ill."

"No, Henry; it's sweet of you, but I couldn't."

"I see," he said; "you have scruples."

"I suppose so."

"And sooner than go against them you would have your sister suffer. You could have got her down to Swanage by a word, but you had scruples. And scruples are all very well. I am as scrupulous as any man alive, I hope; but when it is a case like this, when there is a question of madness——"

"I deny it's madness."

"You said just now——"

"It's madness when I say it, but not when you say it."

Henry shrugged his shoulders. "Margaret! Margaret!" he groaned. "No education can teach a woman logic. Now, my dear, my time is valuable. Do you want me to help you or not?"

"Not in that way."

"Answer my question. Plain question, plain answer. Do——"

Charles surprised them by interrupting. "Pater, we may as well keep Howards End out of it," he said.

[5]Clever.

"Why, Charles?"

Charles could give no reason; but Margaret felt as if, over tremendous distance, a salutation had passed between them.

"The whole house is at sixes and sevens," he said crossly. "We don't want any more mess."

"Who's 'we'?" asked his father. "My boy, pray, who's 'we'?"

"I am sure I beg your pardon," said Charles. "I appear always to be intruding."

By now Margaret wished she had never mentioned her trouble to her husband. Retreat was impossible. He was determined to push the matter to a satisfactory conclusion, and Helen faded as he talked. Her fair, flying hair and eager eyes counted for nothing, for she was ill, without rights, and any of her friends might hunt her. Sick at heart, Margaret joined in the chase. She wrote her sister a lying letter, at her husband's dictation; she said the furniture was all at Howards End, but could be seen on Monday next at 3 p.m., when a charwoman would be in attendance. It was a cold letter, and the more plausible for that. Helen would think she was offended. And on Monday next she and Henry were to lunch with Dolly, and then ambush themselves in the garden.

After they had gone, Mr. Wilcox said to his son: "I can't have this sort of behaviour, my boy. Margaret's too sweet-natured to mind, but I mind for her."

Charles made no answer.

"Is anything wrong with you, Charles, this afternoon?"

"No, pater; but you may be taking on a bigger business than you reckon."

"How?"

"Don't ask me."

## CHAPTER XXXV

ONE speaks of the moods of spring, but the days that are her true children have only one mood: they are all full of the rising and dropping of winds, and the whistling of birds. New flowers may come out, the green embroidery of the hedges increase, but the same heaven broods overhead, soft, thick, and blue, the same figures, seen and unseen, are wandering by coppice and meadow. The morning that Margaret had spent with Miss Avery, and the afternoon she set out to entrap Helen, were the scales of a single balance. Time might never have moved, rain never have fallen, and man alone, with his schemes and ailments, was troubling Nature until he saw her through a veil of tears.

She protested no more. Whether Henry was right or wrong, he was most kind, and she knew of no other standard by which to judge him. She must trust him absolutely. As soon as he had taken up a business, his obtuseness vanished. He profited by the slightest indications, and the capture of Helen promised to be staged as deftly as the marriage of Evie.

They went down in the morning as arranged, and he discovered that their victim was actually in Hilton. On his arrival he called at all the livery-stables in the village, and had a few minutes' serious conversation with the proprietors. What he said, Margaret did not know— perhaps not the truth; but news arrived after lunch that a lady had come by the London train, and had taken a fly[1] to Howards End.

"She was bound to drive," said Henry. "There will be her books."

"I cannot make it out," said Margaret for the hundredth time.

"Finish your coffee, dear. We must be off."

"Yes, Margaret, you know you must take plenty," said Dolly.

Margaret tried, but suddenly lifted her hand to her eyes. Dolly stole glances at her father-in-law which he did not answer. In the silence the motor came round to the door.

"You're not fit for it," he said anxiously. "Let me go alone. I know exactly what to do."

"Oh yes, I am fit," said Margaret, uncovering her face. "Only most frightfully worried. I cannot feel that Helen is really alive. Her letters and telegrams seem to have come from someone else. Her voice isn't in them. I don't believe your driver really saw her at the station. I wish I'd never mentioned it. I know that Charles is vexed. Yes, he is——" She seized Dolly's hand and kissed it. "There, Dolly will forgive me. There. Now we'll be off."

Henry had been looking at her closely. He did not like this breakdown.

"Don't you want to tidy yourself?" he asked.

"Have I time?"

"Yes, plenty."

She went to the lavatory by the front door, and as soon as the bolt slipped, Mr. Wilcox said quietly:

"Dolly, I'm going without her."

Dolly's eyes lit up with vulgar excitement. She followed him on tip-toe out to the car.

"Tell her I thought it best."

[1]One-horse, for-hire carriage.

"Yes, Mr. Wilcox, I see."

"Say anything you like. All right."

The car started well, and with ordinary luck would have got away. But Porgly-woggles, who was playing in the garden, chose this moment to sit down in the middle of the path. Crane, in trying to pass him, ran one wheel over a bed of wallflowers. Dolly screamed. Margaret, hearing the noise, rushed out hatless, and was in time to jump on the footboard. She said not a single word: he was only treating her as she had treated Helen, and her rage at his dishonesty only helped to indicate what Helen would feel against them. She thought, "I deserve it: I am punished for lowering my colours."[2] And she accepted his apologies with a calmness that astonished him.

"I still consider you are not fit for it," he kept saying.

"Perhaps I was not at lunch. But the whole thing is spread clearly before me now."

"I was meaning to act for the best."

"Just lend me your scarf, will you? This wind takes one's hair so."

"Certainly, dear girl. Are you all right now?"

"Look! My hands have stopped trembling."

"And have quite forgiven me? Then listen. Her cab should already have arrived at Howards End. (We're a little late, but no matter.) Our first move will be to send it down to wait at the farm, as, if possible, one doesn't want a scene before servants. A certain gentleman"—he pointed at Crane's back—"won't drive in, but will wait a little short of the front gate, behind the laurels. Have you still the keys of the house?"

"Yes."

"Well, they aren't wanted. Do you remember how the house stands?"

"Yes."

"If we don't find her in the porch, we can stroll round into the garden. Our object——"

Here they stopped to pick up the doctor.

"I was just saying to my wife, Mansbridge, that our main object is not to frighten Miss Schlegel. The house, as you know, is my property, so it should seem quite natural for us to be there. The trouble is evidently nervous—wouldn't you say so, Margaret?"

The doctor, a very young man, began to ask questions about Helen. Was she normal? Was there anything congenital or hereditary? Had anything occurred that was likely to alienate her from her family?

[2]A lowered flag signals surrender.

"Nothing," answered Margaret, wondering what would have happened if she had added: "Though she did resent my husband's immorality."

"She always was highly strung," pursued Henry, leaning back in the car as it shot past the church. "A tendency to spiritualism and those things, though nothing serious. Musical, literary, artistic, but I should say normal—a very charming girl."

Margaret's anger and terror increased every moment. How dare these men label her sister! What horrors lay ahead! What impertinences that shelter under the name of science! The pack was turning on Helen, to deny her human rights, and it seemed to Margaret that all Schlegels were threatened with her. "Were they normal?" What a question to ask! And it is always those who know nothing about human nature, who are bored by psychology and shocked by physiology, who ask it. However piteous her sister's state, she knew that she must be on her side. They would be mad together if the world chose to consider them so.

It was now five minutes past three. The car slowed down by the farm, in the yard of which Miss Avery was standing. Henry asked her whether a cab had gone past. She nodded, and the next moment they caught sight of it, at the end of the lane. The car ran silently like a beast of prey. So unsuspicious was Helen that she was sitting in the porch, with her back to the road. She had come. Only her head and shoulders were visible. She sat framed in the vine, and one of her hands played with the buds. The wind ruffled her hair, the sun glorified it; she was as she had always been.

Margaret was seated next to the door. Before her husband could prevent her, she slipped out. She ran to the garden gate, which was shut, passed through it, and deliberately pushed it in his face. The noise alarmed Helen. Margaret saw her rise with an unfamiliar movement, and, rushing into the porch, learnt the simple explanation of all their fears—her sister was with child.

"Is the truant all right?" called Henry.

She had time to whisper: "Oh, my darling——" The keys of the house were in her hand. She unlocked Howards End and thrust Helen into it. "Yes, all right," she said, and stood with her back to the door.

## CHAPTER XXXVI

"Margaret, you look upset!" said Henry.

Mansbridge had followed. Crane was at the gate, and the flyman had stood up on the box. Margaret shook her head at them; she could not speak any more. She remained clutching the keys, as if all their future depended on them. Henry was asking more questions. She shook her head again. His words had no sense. She heard him wonder why she had let Helen in. "You might have given me a knock with the gate," was another of his remarks. Presently she heard herself speaking. She, or someone for her, said "Go away." Henry came nearer. He repeated, "Margaret, you look upset again. My dear, give me the keys. What are you doing with Helen?"

"Oh, dearest, do go away, and I will manage it all."

"Manage what?"

He stretched out his hand for the keys. She might have obeyed if it had not been for the doctor.

"Stop that at least," she said piteously; the doctor had turned back, and was questioning the driver of Helen's cab. A new feeling came over her; she was fighting for women against men. She did not care about rights, but if men came into Howards End, it should be over her body.

"Come, this is an odd beginning," said her husband.

The doctor came forward now, and whispered two words to Mr. Wilcox—the scandal was out. Sincerely horrified, Henry stood gazing at the earth.

"I cannot help it," said Margaret. "Do wait. It's not my fault. Please all four of you to go away now."

Now the flyman was whispering to Crane.

"We are relying on you to help us, Mrs. Wilcox," said the young doctor. "Could you go in and persuade your sister to come out?"

"On what grounds?" said Margaret, suddenly looking him straight in the eyes.

Thinking it professional to prevaricate, he murmured something about a nervous breakdown.

"I beg your pardon, but it is nothing of the sort. You are not qualified to attend my sister, Mr. Mansbridge. If we require your services, we will let you know."

"I can diagnose the case more bluntly if you wish," he retorted.

"You could, but you have not. You are, therefore, not qualified to attend my sister."

"Come, come, Margaret!" said Henry, never raising his eyes. "This is a terrible business, an appalling business. It's doctor's orders. Open the door."

"Forgive me, but I will not."

"I don't agree."

Margaret was silent.

"This business is as broad as it's long," contributed the doctor. "We had better all work together. You need us, Mrs. Wilcox, and we need you."

"Quite so," said Henry.

"I do not need you in the least," said Margaret.

The two men looked at each other anxiously.

"No more does my sister, who is still many weeks from her confinement."

"Margaret, Margaret!"

"Well, Henry, send your doctor away. What possible use is he now?"

Mr. Wilcox ran his eye over the house. He had a vague feeling that he must stand firm and support the doctor. He himself might need support, for there was trouble ahead.

"It all turns on affection now," said Margaret. "Affection. Don't you see?" Resuming her usual methods, she wrote the word on the house with her finger. "Surely you see. I like Helen very much, you not so much. Mr. Mansbridge doesn't know her. That's all. And affection, when reciprocated, gives rights. Put that down in your notebook, Mr. Mansbridge. It's a useful formula."

Henry told her to be calm.

"You don't know what you want yourselves," said Margaret, folding her arms. "For one sensible remark I will let you in. But you cannot make it. You would trouble my sister for no reason. I will not permit it. I'll stand here all the day sooner."

"Mansbridge," said Henry in a low voice, "perhaps not now."

The pack was breaking up. At a sign from his master, Crane also went back into the car.

"Now, Henry, you," she said gently. None of her bitterness had been directed at him. "Go away now, dear. I shall want your advice later, no doubt. Forgive me if I have been cross. But, seriously, you must go."

He was too stupid to leave her. Now it was Mr. Mansbridge who called in a low voice to him.

"I shall soon find you down at Dolly's," she called, as the gate at last clanged between them. The fly moved out of the way, the motor backed, turned a little, backed again, and turned in the narrow road. A string of farm carts came up in the middle; but she waited through all, for there was no hurry. When all was over and the car had started, she opened the door. "Oh, my darling!" she said. "My darling, forgive me." Helen was standing in the hall.

## CHAPTER XXXVII

MARGARET bolted the door on the inside. Then she would have kissed her sister, but Helen, in a dignified voice, that came strangely from her, said:

"Convenient! You did not tell me that the books were unpacked. I have found nearly everything that I want."

"I told you nothing that was true."

"It has been a great surprise, certainly. Has Aunt Juley been ill?"

"Helen, you wouldn't think I'd invent that?"

"I suppose not," said Helen, turning away, and crying a very little. "But one loses faith in everything after this."

"We thought it was illness, but even then—— I haven't behaved worthily."

Helen selected another book.

"I ought not to have consulted anyone. What would our father have thought of me?"

She did not think of questioning her sister, nor of rebuking her. Both might be necessary in the future, but she had first to purge a greater crime than any that Helen could have committed—that want of confidence that is the work of the devil.

"Yes, I am annoyed," replied Helen. "My wishes should have been respected. I would have gone through this meeting if it was necessary, but after Aunt Juley recovered, it was not necessary. Planning my life, as I now have to do——"

"Come away from those books," called Margaret. "Helen, do talk to me."

"I was just saying that I have stopped living haphazard. One can't go through a great deal of——" she missed out the noun—"without planning one's actions in advance. I am going to have a child in June, and in the first place conversations, discussions, excitement, are not good for me. I will go through them if necessary, but only then. In the second place I have no right to trouble people. I cannot fit in with England as I know it. I have done something that the English never pardon. It would not be right for them to pardon it. So I must live where I am not known."

"But why didn't you tell me, dearest?"

"Yes," replied Helen judicially. "I might have, but decided to wait."

"I believe you would never have told me."

"Oh yes, I should. We have taken a flat in Munich."

Margaret glanced out of the window.

"By 'we' I mean myself and Monica. But for her, I am and have been and always wish to be alone."

"I have not heard of Monica."

"You wouldn't have. She's an Italian—by birth at least. She makes her living by journalism. I met her originally on Garda. Monica is much the best person to see me through."

"You are very fond of her, then."

"She has been extraordinarily sensible with me."

Margaret guessed at Monica's type—'Italiano Inglesiato'[1] they had named it: the crude feminist of the South, whom one respects but avoids. And Helen had turned to it in her need!

"You must not think that we shall never meet," said Helen, with a measured kindness. "I shall always have a room for you when you can be spared, and the longer you can be with me the better. But you haven't understood yet, Meg, and of course it is very difficult for you. This is a shock to you. It isn't to me, who have been thinking over our futures for many months, and they won't be changed by a slight contretemps, such as this. I cannot live in England."

"Helen, you've not forgiven me for my treachery. You *couldn't* talk like this to me if you had."

"Oh, Meg dear, why do we talk at all?" She dropped a book and sighed wearily. Then, recovering herself, she said: "Tell me, how is it that all the books are down here?"

"Series of mistakes."

"And a great deal of the furniture has been unpacked."

"All."

"Who lives here, then?"

"No one."

"I suppose you are letting it, though."

"The house is dead," said Margaret, with a frown. "Why worry on about it?"

"But I am interested. You talk as if I had lost all my interest in life. I am still Helen, I hope. Now this hasn't the feel of a dead house. The hall seems more alive even than in the old days, when it held the Wilcoxes' own things."

"Interested, are you? Very well, I must tell you, I suppose. My husband lent it on condition we—but by a mistake all our things were unpacked, and Miss Avery, instead of——" She stopped. "Look here,

[1]Italian: Anglicized Italian. Margaret uses the masculine form.

I can't go on like this. I warn you I won't. Helen, why should you be so miserably unkind to me, simply because you hate Henry?"

"I don't hate him now," said Helen. "I have stopped being a schoolgirl, and, Meg, once again, I'm not being unkind. But as for fitting in with your English life—no, put it out of your head at once. Imagine a visit from me at Ducie Street! It's unthinkable."

Margaret could not contradict her. It was appalling to see her quietly moving forward with her plans, not bitter or excitable, neither asserting innocence nor confessing guilt, merely desiring freedom and the company of those who would not blame her. She had been through— how much? Margaret did not know. But it was enough to part her from old habits as well as old friends.

"Tell me about yourself," said Helen, who had chosen her books, and was lingering over the furniture.

"There's nothing to tell."

"But your marriage has been happy, Meg?"

"Yes, but I don't feel inclined to talk."

"You feel as I do."

"Not that, but I can't."

"No more can I. It is a nuisance, but no good trying."

Something had come between them. Perhaps it was Society, which henceforward would exclude Helen. Perhaps it was a third life, already potent as a spirit. They could find no meeting-place. Both suffered acutely, and were not comforted by the knowledge that affection survived.

"Look here, Meg, is the coast clear?"

"You mean that you want to go away from me?"

"I suppose so—dear old lady! it isn't any use. I knew we should have nothing to say. Give my love to Aunt Juley and Tibby, and take more yourself than I can say. Promise to come and see me in Munich later."

"Certainly, dearest."

"For that is all we can do."

It seemed so. Most ghastly of all was Helen's common sense: Monica had been extraordinarily good for her.

"I am glad to have seen you and the things." She looked at the bookcase lovingly, as if she was saying farewell to the past.

Margaret unbolted the door. She remarked: "The car has gone, and here's your cab."

She led the way to it, glancing at the leaves and the sky. The spring had never seemed more beautiful. The driver, who was leaning on the gate, called out, "Please, lady, a message," and handed her Henry's visiting-card through the bars.

"How did this come?" she asked.

Crane had returned with it almost at once.

She read the card with annoyance. It was covered with instructions in domestic French. When she and her sister had talked she was to come back for the night to Dolly's. "Il faut dormir sur ce sujet."[2] While Helen was to be found "une comfortable chambre à l'hôtel."[3] The final sentence displeased her greatly until she remembered that the Charles' had only one spare room, and so could not invite a third guest.

"Henry would have done what he could," she interpreted.

Helen had not followed her into the garden. The door once open, she lost her inclination to fly. She remained in the hall, going from bookcase to table. She grew more like the old Helen, irresponsible and charming.

"This *is* Mr. Wilcox's house?" she inquired.

"Surely you remember Howards End?"

"Remember? I who remember everything! But it looks to be ours now."

"Miss Avery was extraordinary," said Margaret, her own spirits lightening a little. Again she was invaded by a slight feeling of disloyalty. But it brought her relief, and she yielded to it. "She loved Mrs. Wilcox, and would rather furnish her house with our things than think of it empty. In consequence here are all the library books."

"Not all the books. She hasn't unpacked the Art Books, in which she may show her sense. And we never used to have the sword here."

"The sword looks well, though."

"Magnificent."

"Yes, doesn't it?"

"Where's the piano, Meg?"

"I warehoused that in London. Why?"

"Nothing."

"Curious, too, that the carpet fits."

"The carpet's a mistake," announced Helen. "I know that we had it in London, but this floor ought to be bare. It is far too beautiful."

"You still have a mania for under-furnishing. Would you care to come into the dining-room before you start? There's no carpet there."

They went in, and each minute their talk became more natural.

"Oh, *what* a place for mother's cheffonier!" cried Helen.

---

[2]French: It's necessary to sleep on this subject.

[3]French: a comfortable room at the hotel. Henry inserts the English adjective instead of the proper French, *confortable*.

"Look at the chairs, though."

"Oh, look at them! Wickham Place faced north, didn't it?"

"North-west."

"Anyhow, it is thirty years since any of those chairs have felt the sun. Feel. Their dear little backs are quite warm."

"But why has Miss Avery made them set to partners? I shall just——"

"Over here, Meg. Put it so that anyone sitting will see the lawn."

Margaret moved a chair. Helen sat down in it.

"Ye-es. The window's too high."

"Try a drawing-room chair."

"No, I don't like the drawing-room so much. The beam has been match-boarded. It would have been so beautiful otherwise."

"Helen, what a memory you have for some things! You're perfectly right. It's a room that men have spoilt through trying to make it nice for women. Men don't know what we want——"

"And never will."

"I don't agree. In two thousand years they'll know."

"But the chairs show up wonderfully. Look where Tibby spilt the soup."

"Coffee. It was coffee surely."

Helen shook her head. "Impossible. Tibby was far too young to be given coffee at that time."

"Was father alive?"

"Yes."

"Then you're right and it must have been soup. I was thinking of much later—that unsuccessful visit of Aunt Juley's, when she didn't realize that Tibby had grown up. It was coffee then, for he threw it down on purpose. There was some rhyme, 'Tea, coffee—coffee, tea,' that she said to him every morning at breakfast. Wait a minute—how did it go?"

"I know—no, I don't. What a detestable boy Tibby was!"

"But the rhyme was simply awful. No decent person could have put up with it."

"Ah, that greengage tree," cried Helen, as if the garden was also part of their childhood. "Why do I connect it with dumbbells? And there come the chickens. The grass wants cutting. I love yellow-hammers——"[4]

Margaret interrupted her. "I have got it," she announced.

[4]European finches.

"'Tea, tea, coffee, tea,
Or chocolaritee.'

"That every morning for three weeks. No wonder Tibby was wild."
"Tibby is moderately a dear now," said Helen.
"There! I knew you'd say that in the end. Of course he's a dear."
A bell rang.
"Listen! what's that?"
Helen said, "Perhaps the Wilcoxes are beginning the siege."
"What nonsense—listen!"
And the triviality faded from their faces, though it left something behind—the knowledge that they never could be parted because their love was rooted in common things. Explanations and appeals had failed; they had tried for a common meeting-ground, and had only made each other unhappy. And all the time their salvation was lying round them—the past sanctifying the present; the present, with wild heart-throb, declaring that there would after all be a future, with laughter and the voices of children. Helen, still smiling, came up to her sister. She said, "It is always Meg." They looked into each other's eyes. The inner life had paid.
Solemnly the clapper tolled. No one was in the front. Margaret went to the kitchen, and struggled between packing-cases to the window. Their visitor was only a little boy with a tin can. And triviality returned.
"Little boy, what do you want?"
"Please, I am the milk."
"Did Miss Avery send you?" said Margaret, rather sharply.
"Yes, please."
"Then take it back and say we require no milk." While she called to Helen, "No, it's not the siege, but possibly an attempt to provision us against one."
"But I like milk," cried Helen. "Why send it away?"
"Do you? Oh, very well. But we've nothing to put it in, and he wants the can."
"Please, I'm to call in the morning for the can," said the boy.
"The house will be locked up then."
"In the morning would I bring eggs, too?"
"Are you the boy whom I saw playing in the stacks last week?"
The child hung his head.
"Well, run away and do it again."
"Nice little boy," whispered Helen. "I say, what's your name? Mine's Helen."

"Tom."

That was Helen all over. The Wilcoxes, too, would ask a child its name, but they never told their names in return.

"Tom, this one here is Margaret. And at home we've another called Tibby."

"Mine are lop-eareds," replied Tom, supposing Tibby to be a rabbit.

"You're a very good and rather a clever little boy. Mind you come again.—Isn't he charming?"

"Undoubtedly," said Margaret. "He is probably the son of Madge, and Madge is dreadful. But this place has wonderful powers."

"What do you mean?"

"I don't know."

"Because I probably agree with you."

"It kills what is dreadful and makes what is beautiful live."

"I do agree," said Helen, as she sipped the milk. "But you said that the house was dead not half an hour ago."

"Meaning that I was dead. I felt it."

"Yes, the house has a surer life than we, even if it was empty, and, as it is, I can't get over that for thirty years the sun has never shone full on our furniture. After all, Wickham Place was a grave. Meg, I've a startling idea."

"What is it?"

"Drink some milk to steady you."

Margaret obeyed.

"No, I won't tell you yet," said Helen, "because you may laugh or be angry. Let's go upstairs first and give the rooms an airing."

They opened window after window, till the inside, too, was rustling to the spring. Curtains blew, picture-frames tapped cheerfully. Helen uttered cries of excitement as she found this bed obviously in its right place, that in its wrong one. She was angry with Miss Avery for not having moved the wardrobes up. "Then one would see really." She admired the view. She was the Helen who had written the memorable letters four years ago. As they leant out, looking westward, she said: "About my idea. Couldn't you and I camp out in this house for the night?"

"I don't think we could well do that," said Margaret.

"Here are beds, tables, towels——"

"I know; but the house isn't supposed to be slept in, and Henry's suggestion was——"

"I require no suggestions. I shall not alter anything in my plans. But it would give me so much pleasure to have one night here with you. It will be something to look back on. Oh, Meg lovey, do let's!"

"But, Helen, my pet," said Margaret, "we can't without getting Henry's leave. Of course, he would give it, but you said yourself that you couldn't visit at Ducie Street now, and this is equally intimate."

"Ducie Street is his house. This is ours. Our furniture, our sort of people coming to the door. Do let us camp out, just one night, and Tom shall feed us on eggs and milk. Why not? It's a moon."

Margaret hesitated. "I feel Charles wouldn't like it," she said at last. "Even our furniture annoyed him, and I was going to clear it out when Aunt Juley's illness prevented me. I sympathize with Charles. He feels it's his mother's house. He loves it in rather an untaking way. Henry I could answer for—not Charles."

"I know he won't like it," said Helen. "But I am going to pass out of their lives. What difference will it make in the long run if they say, 'And she even spent the night at Howards End'?"

"How do you know you'll pass out of their lives? We have thought that twice before."

"Because my plans——"

"—which you change in a moment."

"Then because my life is great and theirs are little," said Helen, taking fire. "I know of things they can't know of, and so do you. We *know* that there's poetry. We *know* that there's death. They can only take them on hearsay. We know this is our house, because it feels ours. Oh, they may take the title-deeds and the doorkeys, but for this one night we are at home."

"It would be lovely to have you once more alone," said Margaret. "It may be a chance in a thousand."

"Yes, and we could talk." She dropped her voice. "It won't be a very glorious story. But under that wych-elm—honestly, I see little happiness ahead. Cannot I have this one night with you?"

"I needn't say how much it would mean to me."

"Then let us."

"It is no good hesitating. Shall I drive down to Hilton now and get leave?"

"Oh, we don't want leave."

But Margaret was a loyal wife. In spite of imagination and poetry—perhaps on account of them—she could sympathize with the technical attitude that Henry would adopt. If possible, she would be technical, too. A night's lodging—and they demanded no more—need not involve the discussion of general principles.

"Charles may say no," grumbled Helen.

"We shan't consult him."

"Go if you like; I should have stopped without leave."

It was the touch of selfishness, which was not enough to mar Helen's character, and even added to its beauty. She would have stopped without leave, and escaped to Germany the next morning. Margaret kissed her.

"Expect me back before dark. I am looking forward to it so much. It is like you to have thought of such a beautiful thing."

"Not a thing, only an ending," said Helen rather sadly; and the sense of tragedy closed in on Margaret again as soon as she left the house.

She was afraid of Miss Avery. It is disquieting to fulfil a prophecy, however superficially. She was glad to see no watching figure as she drove past the farm, but only little Tom, turning somersaults in the straw.

## CHAPTER XXXVIII

THE tragedy began quietly enough, and like many another talk, by the man's deft assertion of his superiority. Henry heard her arguing with the driver, stepped out and settled the fellow, who was inclined to be rude, and then led the way to some chairs on the lawn. Dolly, who had not been "told," ran out with offers of tea. He refused them, and ordered her to wheel baby's perambulator away, as they desired to be alone.

"But the diddums can't listen; he isn't nine months old," she pleaded.

"That's not what I was saying," retorted her father-in-law.

Baby was wheeled out of earshot, and did not hear about the crisis till later years. It was now the turn of Margaret.

"Is it what we feared?" he asked.

"It is."

"Dear girl," he began, "there is a troublesome business ahead of us, and nothing but the most absolute honesty and plain speech will see us through." Margaret bent her head. "I am obliged to question you on subjects we'd both prefer to leave untouched. As you know, I am not one of your Bernard Shaws who consider nothing sacred.[1] To speak as I must will pain me, but there are occasions—— We are husband and wife, not children. I am a man of the world, and you are a most exceptional woman."

All Margaret's senses forsook her. She blushed, and looked past him at the Six Hills, covered with spring herbage. Noting her colour, he grew still more kind.

---

[1] George Bernard Shaw (1856–1950), fearlessly controversial Irish essayist and dramatist.

"I see that you feel as I felt when—— My poor little wife! Oh, be brave! Just one or two questions, and I have done with you. Was your sister wearing a wedding-ring?"

Margaret stammered a "No."

There was an appalling silence.

"Henry, I really came to ask a favour about Howards End."

"One point at a time. I am now obliged to ask for the name of her seducer."

She rose to her feet and held the chair between them. Her colour had ebbed, and she was grey. It did not displease him that she should receive his question thus.

"Take your time," he counselled her. "Remember that this is far worse for me than for you."

She swayed; he feared she was going to faint. Then speech came, and she said slowly: "Seducer? No; I do not know her seducer's name."

"Would she not tell you?"

"I never even asked her who seduced her," said Margaret, dwelling on the hateful word thoughtfully.

"That is singular." Then he changed his mind. "Natural perhaps, dear girl, that you shouldn't ask. But until his name is known, nothing can be done. Sit down. How terrible it is to see you so upset! I knew you weren't fit for it. I wish I hadn't taken you."

Margaret answered, "I like to stand, if you don't mind, for it gives me a pleasant view of the Six Hills."

"As you like."

"Have you anything else to ask me, Henry?"

"Next you must tell me whether you have gathered anything. I have often noticed your insight, dear. I only wish my own was as good. You may have guessed something, even though your sister said nothing. The slightest hint would help us."

"Who is 'we'?"

"I thought it best to ring up Charles."

"That was unnecessary," said Margaret, growing warmer. "This news will give Charles disproportionate pain."

"He has at once gone to call on your brother."

"That too was unnecessary."

"Let me explain, dear, how the matter stands. You don't think that I and my son are other than gentlemen? It is in Helen's interests that we are acting. It is still not too late to save her name."

Then Margaret hit out for the first time. "Are we to make her seducer marry her?" she asked.

"If possible. Yes."

"But, Henry, suppose he turned out to be married already? One has heard of such cases."

"In that case he must pay heavily for his misconduct, and be thrashed within an inch of his life."

So her first blow missed. She was thankful of it. What had tempted her to imperil both of their lives? Henry's obtuseness had saved her as well as himself. Exhausted with anger, she sat down again, blinking at him as he told her as much as he thought fit. At last she said: "May I ask you my question now?"

"Certainly, my dear."

"To-morrow Helen goes to Munich——"

"Well, possibly she is right."

"Henry, let a lady finish. To-morrow she goes; to-night, with your permission, she would like to sleep at Howards End."

It was the crisis of his life. Again she would have recalled the words as soon as they were uttered. She had not led up to them with sufficient care. She longed to warn him that they were far more important than he supposed. She saw him weighing them, as if they were a business proposition.

"Why Howards End?" he said at last. "Would she not be more comfortable, as I suggested, at the hotel?"

Margaret hastened to give him reasons. "It is an odd request, but you know what Helen is and what women in her state are." He frowned, and moved irritably. "She has the idea that one night in your house would give her pleasure and do her good. I think she's right. Being one of those imaginative girls, the presence of all our books and furniture soothes her. This is a fact. It is the end of her girl-hood. Her last words to me were, 'A beautiful ending.'"

"She values the old furniture for sentimental reasons, in fact."

"Exactly. You have quite understood. It is her last hope of being with it."

"I don't agree there, my dear! Helen will have her share of the goods wherever she goes—possibly more than her share, for you are so fond of her that you'd give her anything of yours that she fancies, wouldn't you? and I'd raise no objection. I could under-stand it if it was her old home, because a home, or a house"—he changed the word, designedly; he had thought of a telling point—"because a house in which one has once lived becomes in a sort of way sacred, I don't know why. Associations and so on. Now Helen has no associations with Howards End, though I and Charles and

Evie have. I do not see why she wants to stay the night there. She will only catch cold."

"Leave it that you don't see," cried Margaret. "Call it fancy. But realize that fancy is a scientific fact. Helen is fanciful, and wants to."

Then he surprised her—a rare occurrence. He shot an unexpected bolt. "If she wants to sleep one night, she may want to sleep two. We shall never get her out of the house, perhaps."

"Well?" said Margaret, with the precipice in sight. "And suppose we don't get her out of the house? Would it matter? She would do no one any harm."

Again the irritated gesture.

"No, Henry," she panted, receding. "I didn't mean that. We will only trouble Howards End for this one night. I take her to London to-morrow——"

"Do you intend to sleep in a damp house, too?"

"She cannot be left alone."

"That's quite impossible! Madness. You must be here to meet Charles."

"I have already told you that your message to Charles was unnecessary, and I have no desire to meet him."

"Margaret—my Margaret——"

"What has this business to do with Charles? If it concerns me little, it concerns you less, and Charles not at all."

"As the future owner of Howards End," said Mr. Wilcox, arching his fingers, "I should say that it did concern Charles."

"In what way? Will Helen's condition depreciate the property?"

"My dear, you are forgetting yourself."

"I think you yourself recommended plain speaking."

They looked at each other in amazement. The precipice was at their feet now.

"Helen commands my sympathy," said Henry. "As your husband, I shall do all for her that I can, and I have no doubt that she will prove more sinned against than sinning. But I cannot treat her as if nothing has happened. I should be false to my position in society if I did."

She controlled herself for the last time. "No, let us go back to Helen's request," she said. "It is unreasonable, but the request of an unhappy girl. To-morrow she will go to Germany, and trouble society no longer. To-night she asks to sleep in your empty house—a house which you do not care about, and which you have not occupied for over a year. May she? Will you give my sister leave? Will you forgive her—as you hope to be forgiven, and as you have actually been forgiven? For-give her for one night only. That will be enough."

"As I have actually been forgiven——?"

"Never mind for the moment what I mean by that," said Mar-garet. "Answer my question."

Perhaps some hint of her meaning did dawn on him. If so, he blotted it out. Straight from his fortress he answered: "I seem rather unaccommodating, but I have some experience of life, and know how one thing leads to another. I am afraid that your sister had better sleep at the hotel. I have my children and the memory of my dear wife to consider. I am sorry, but see that she leaves my house at once."

"You mentioned Mrs. Wilcox."

"I beg your pardon?"

"A rare occurrence. In reply, may I mention Mrs. Bast?"

"You have not been yourself all day," said Henry, and rose from his seat with face unmoved. Margaret rushed at him and seized both his hands. She was transfigured.

"Not any more of this!" she cried. "You shall see the connection if it kills you, Henry! You have had a mistress—I forgave you. My sister has a lover—you drive her from the house. Do you see the connection? Stupid, hypocritical, cruel—oh, contemptible!—a man who insults his wife when she's alive and cants with her memory when she's dead. A man who ruins a woman for his pleasure, and casts her off to ruin other men. And gives bad financial advice, and then says he is not re-sponsible. These men are you. You can't recognize them, because you cannot connect. I've had enough of your unweeded kindness. I've spoilt you long enough. All your life you have been spoiled. Mrs. Wilcox spoiled you. No one has ever told what you are—muddled, criminally muddled. Men like you use repentance as a blind, so don't repent. Only say to yourself, 'What Helen has done, I've done.'"

"The two cases are different," Henry stammered. His real retort was not quite ready. His brain was still in a whirl, and he wanted a little longer.

"In what way different? You have betrayed Mrs. Wilcox, Helen only herself. You remain in society, Helen can't. You have had only pleasure, she may die. You have the insolence to talk to me of differences, Henry?"

Oh, the uselessness of it! Henry's retort came.

"I perceive you are attempting blackmail. It is scarcely a pretty weapon for a wife to use against her husband. My rule through life has been never to pay the least attention to threats, and I can only repeat what I said before: I do not give you and your sister leave to sleep at Howards End."

Margaret loosed his hands. He went into the house, wiping first one and then the other on his handkerchief. For a little she stood looking at the Six Hills, tombs of warriors, breasts of the spring. Then she passed out into what was now the evening.

## CHAPTER XXXIX

CHARLES and Tibby met at Ducie Street, where the latter was staying. Their interview was short and absurd. They had nothing in common but the English language, and tried by its help to express what neither of them understood. Charles saw in Helen the family foe. He had singled her out as the most dangerous of the Schlegels, and, angry as he was, looked forward to telling his wife how right he had been. His mind was made up at once: the girl must be got out of the way before she disgraced them farther. If occasion offered she might be married to a villain or, possibly, to a fool. But this was a concession to morality, it formed no part of his main scheme. Honest and hearty was Charles's dislike, and the past spread itself out very clearly before him; hatred is a skilful compositor. As if they were heads in a note-book, he ran through all the incidents of the Schlegels' campaign: the attempt to compromise his brother, his mother's legacy, his father's marriage, the introduction of the furniture, the unpacking of the same. He had not yet heard of the request to sleep at Howards End; that was to be their master-stroke and the opportunity for his. But he already felt that Howards End was the objective, and, though he disliked the house, was determined to defend it.

Tibby, on the other hand, had no opinions. He stood above the conventions: his sister had a right to do what she thought right. It is not difficult to stand above the conventions when we leave no hostages among them; men can always be more unconventional than women, and a bachelor of independent means need encounter no difficulties at all. Unlike Charles, Tibby had money enough; his ancestors had earned it for him, and if he shocked the people in one set of lodgings he had only to move into another. His was the Leisure without sympathy—an attitude as fatal as the strenuous: a little cold culture may be raised on it, but no art. His sisters had seen the family danger, and had never forgotten to discount the gold islets that raised them from the sea. Tibby gave all the praise to himself, and so despised the struggling and the submerged.

Hence the absurdity of the interview; the gulf between them was economic as well as spiritual. But several facts passed: Charles pressed for them with an impertinence that the undergraduate could not withstand. On what date had Helen gone abroad? To whom? (Charles was anxious to fasten the scandal on Germany.) Then, changing his tactics, he said roughly: "I suppose you realize that you are your sister's protector?"

"In what sense?"

"If a man played about with my sister, I'd send a bullet through him, but perhaps you don't mind."

"I mind very much," protested Tibby.

"Who d'ye suspect, then? Speak out, man. One always suspects someone."

"No one. I don't think so." Involuntarily he blushed. He had remembered the scene in his Oxford rooms.

"You are hiding something," said Charles. As interviews go, he got the best of this one. "When you saw her last, did she mention anyone's name? Yes or no!" he thundered, so that Tibby started.

"In my rooms she mentioned some friends, called the Basts——"

"Who are the Basts?"

"People—friends of hers at Evie's wedding."

"I don't remember. But, by great Scott! I do. My aunt told me about some tag-rag.[1] Was she full of them when you saw her? Is there a man? Did she speak of the man? Or—look here—have you had any dealings with him?"

Tibby was silent. Without intending it, he had betrayed his sister's confidence; he was not enough interested in human life to see where things will lead to. He had a strong regard for honesty, and his word, once given, had always been kept up to now. He was deeply vexed, not only for the harm he had done Helen, but for the flaw he had discovered in his own equipment.

"I see—you are in his confidence. They met at your rooms. Oh, what a family, what a family! God help the poor pater——"

And Tibby found himself alone.

## CHAPTER XL

LEONARD—he would figure at length in a newspaper report, but that evening he did not count for much. The foot of the tree was in shadow, since the moon was still hidden behind the house. But above,

---

[1]Riffraff.

to right, to left, down the long meadow the moonlight was streaming. Leonard seemed not a man, but a cause.

Perhaps it was Helen's way of falling in love—a curious way to Margaret, whose agony and whose contempt of Henry were yet imprinted with his image. Helen forgot people. They were husks that had enclosed her emotion. She could pity, or sacrifice herself, or have instincts, but had she ever loved in the noblest way, where man and woman, having lost themselves in sex, desire to lose sex itself in comradeship?

Margaret wondered, but said no word of blame. This was Helen's evening. Troubles enough lay ahead of her—the loss of friends and of social advantages, the agony, the supreme agony, of motherhood, which is even yet not a matter of common knowledge. For the present let the moon shine brightly and the breezes of the spring blow gently, dying away from the gale of the day, and let the earth, who brings increase, bring peace. Not even to herself dare she blame Helen. She could not assess her trespass by any moral code; it was everything or nothing. Morality can tell us that murder is worse than stealing, and group most sins in an order all must approve, but it cannot group Helen. The surer its pronouncements on this point, the surer may we be that morality is not speaking. Christ was evasive when they questioned Him. It is those that cannot connect who hasten to cast the first stone.

This was Helen's evening—won at what cost, and not to be marred by the sorrows of others. Of her own tragedy Margaret never uttered a word.

"One isolates," said Helen slowly. "I isolated Mr. Wilcox from the other forces that were pulling Leonard downhill. Consequently, I was full of pity, and almost of revenge. For weeks I had blamed Mr. Wilcox only, and so, when your letters came——"

"I need never have written them," sighed Margaret. "They never shielded Henry. How hopeless it is to tidy away the past, even for others!"

"I did not know that it was your own idea to dismiss the Basts."

"Looking back, that was wrong of me."

"Looking back, darling, I know that it was right. It is right to save the man whom one loves. I am less enthusiastic about justice now. But we both thought you wrote at his dictation. It seemed the last touch of his callousness. Being very much wrought up by this time—and Mrs. Bast was upstairs. I had not seen her, and had talked for a long time to Leonard—I had snubbed him for no reason, and that should have warned me I was in danger. So when the notes came I wanted us to go

to you for an explanation. He said that he guessed the explanation—
he knew of it, and you mustn't know. I pressed him to tell me. He said
no one must know; it was something to do with his wife. Right up to
the end we were Mr. Bast and Miss Schlegel. I was going to tell him
that he must be frank with me when I saw his eyes, and guessed that
Mr. Wilcox had ruined him in two ways, not one. I drew him to me. I
made him tell me. I felt very lonely myself. He is not to blame. He
would have gone on worshipping me. I want never to see him again,
though it sounds appalling. I wanted to give him money and feel finished. Oh, Meg, the little that is known about these things!"

She laid her face against the tree.

"The little, too, that is known about growth! Both times it was
loneliness, and the night, and panic afterwards. Did Leonard grow
out of Paul?"

Margaret did not speak for a moment. So tired was she that her
attention had actually wandered to the teeth—the teeth that had been
thrust into the tree's bark to medicate it. From where she sat she
could see them gleam. She had been trying to count them. "Leonard
is a better growth than madness," she said. "I was afraid that you
would react against Paul until you went over the verge."

"I did react until I found poor Leonard. I am steady now. I shan't
ever *like* your Henry, dearest Meg, or even speak kindly about him,
but all that blinding hate is over. I shall never rave against Wilcoxes
any more. I understand how you married him, and you will now be
very happy."

Margaret did not reply.

"Yes," repeated Helen, her voice growing more tender, "I do at
last understand."

"Except Mrs. Wilcox, dearest, no one understands our little
movements."

"Because in death—I agree."

"Not quite. I feel that you and I and Henry are only fragments of
that woman's mind. She knows everything. She is everything. She is
the house, and the tree that leans over it. People have their own deaths
as well as their own lives, and even if there is nothing beyond death,
we shall differ in our nothingness. I cannot believe that knowledge
such as hers will perish with knowledge such as mine. She knew about
realities. She knew when people were in love, though she was not in
the room. I don't doubt that she knew when Henry deceived her."

"Good-night, Mrs. Wilcox," called a voice.

"Oh, good-night, Miss Avery."

"Why should Miss Avery work for us?" Helen murmured.

"Why, indeed?"

Miss Avery crossed the lawn and merged into the hedge that divided it from the farm. An old gap, which Mr. Wilcox had filled up, had reappeared, and her track through the dew followed the path that he had turfed over, when he improved the garden and made it possible for games.

"This is not quite our house yet," said Helen. "When Miss Avery called, I felt we are only a couple of tourists."

"We shall be that everywhere, and for ever."

"But affectionate tourists——"

"But tourists who pretend each hotel is their home."

"I can't pretend very long," said Helen. "Sitting under this tree one forgets, but I know that to-morrow I shall see the moon rise out of Germany. Not all your goodness can alter the facts of the case. Unless you will come with me."

Margaret thought for a moment. In the past year she had grown so fond of England that to leave it was a real grief. Yet what detained her? No doubt Henry would pardon her outburst, and go on blustering and muddling into a ripe old age. But what was the good? She had just as soon vanish from his mind.

"Are you serious in asking me, Helen? Should I get on with your Monica?"

"You would not, but I am serious in asking you."

"Still, no more plans now. And no more reminiscences."

They were silent for a little. It was Helen's evening.

The present flowed by them like a stream. The tree rustled. It had made music before they were born, and would continue after their deaths, but its song was of the moment. The moment had passed. The tree rustled again. Their senses were sharpened, and they seemed to apprehend life. Life passed. The tree rustled again.

"Sleep now," said Margaret.

The peace of the country was entering into her. It has no commerce with memory, and little with hope. Least of all is it concerned with the hopes of the next five minutes. It is the peace of the present, which passes understanding. Its murmur came "now," and "now" once more as they trod the gravel, and "now," as the moonlight fell upon their father's sword. They passed upstairs, kissed, and amidst the endless iterations fell asleep. The house had enshadowed the tree at first, but as the moon rose higher the two disentangled, and were clear for a few moments at midnight. Margaret awoke and looked into the garden. How incomprehensible that Leonard Bast should have won her this night of peace! Was he also part of Mrs. Wilcox's mind?

## CHAPTER XLI

FAR different was Leonard's development. The months after Oniton, whatever minor troubles they might bring him, were all overshadowed by Remorse. When Helen looked back she could philosophize, or she could look into the future and plan for her child. But the father saw nothing beyond his own sin. Weeks afterwards, in the midst of other occupations, he would suddenly cry out, "Brute—you brute, I couldn't have——" and be rent into two people who held dialogues. Or brown rain would descend, blotting out faces and the sky. Even Jacky noticed the change in him. Most terrible were his sufferings when he awoke from sleep. Sometimes he was happy at first, but grew conscious of a burden hanging to him and weighing down his thoughts when they would move. Or little irons scorched his body. Or a sword stabbed him. He would sit at the edge of his bed, holding his heart and moaning, "Oh what *shall* I do, whatever *shall* I do?" Nothing brought ease. He could put distance between him and the trespass, but it grew in his soul.

Remorse is not among the eternal verities. The Greeks were right to dethrone her. Her action is too capricious, as though the Erinyes[1] selected for punishment only certain men and certain sins. And of all means to regeneration Remorse is surely the most wasteful. It cuts away healthy tissues with the poisoned. It is a knife that probes far deeper than the evil. Leonard was driven straight through its torments and emerged pure, but enfeebled—a better man, who would never lose control of himself again, but also a smaller man, who had less to control. Nor did purity mean peace. The use of the knife can become a habit as hard to shake off as passion itself, and Leonard continued to start with a cry out of dreams.

He built up a situation that was far enough from the truth. It never occurred to him that Helen was to blame. He forgot the intensity of their talk, the charm that had been lent him by sincerity, the magic of Oniton under darkness and of the whispering river. Helen loved the absolute. Leonard had been ruined absolutely, and had appeared to her as a man apart, isolated from the world. A real man, who cared

---

[1]In Greek mythology, female powers who avenge wrongdoing, especially the murder of kin.

for adventure and beauty, who desired to live decently and pay his way, who could have travelled more gloriously through life than the Juggernaut car that was crushing him. Memories of Evie's wedding had warped her, the starched servants, the yards of uneaten food, the rustle of overdressed women, motor-cars oozing grease on the gravel, rubbish from a pretentious band. She had tasted the lees[2] of this on her arrival: in the darkness, after failure, they intoxicated her. She and the victim seemed alone in a world of unreality, and she loved him absolutely, perhaps for half an hour.

In the morning she was gone. The note that she left, tender and hysterical in tone, and intended to be most kind, hurt her lover terribly. It was as if some work of art had been broken by him, some picture in the National Gallery slashed out of its frame. When he recalled her talents and her social position, he felt that the first passer-by had a right to shoot him down. He was afraid of the waitress and the porters at the railway-station. He was afraid at first of his wife, though later he was to regard her with a strange new tenderness, and to think, "There is nothing to choose between us, after all."

The expedition to Shropshire crippled the Basts permanently. Helen in her flight forgot to settle the hotel bill, and took their return tickets away with her; they had to pawn Jacky's bangles to get home, and the smash came a few days afterwards. It is true that Helen offered him five thousand pounds, but such a sum meant nothing to him. He could not see that the girl was desperately righting herself, and trying to save something out of the disaster, if it was only five thousand pounds. But he had to live somehow. He turned to his family, and degraded himself to a professional beggar. There was nothing else for him to do.

"A letter from Leonard," thought Blanche, his sister; "and after all this time." She hid it, so that her husband should not see, and when he had gone to his work read it with some emotion, and sent the prodigal a little money out of her dress allowance.

"A letter from Leonard!" said the other sister, Laura, a few days later. She showed it to her husband. He wrote a cruel, insolent reply, but sent more money than Blanche, so Leonard soon wrote to him again.

And during the winter the system was developed. Leonard realized that they need never starve, because it would be too painful for his relatives. Society is based on the family, and the clever wastrel can exploit this indefinitely. Without a generous thought on either side,

---

[2]Sediment at the bottom of a cup.

pounds and pounds passed. The donors disliked Leonard, and he grew to hate them intensely. When Laura censured his immoral marriage, he thought bitterly, "She minds that! What would she say if she knew the truth?" When Blanche's husband offered him work, he found some pretext for avoiding it. He had wanted work keenly at Oniton, but too much anxiety had shattered him, he was joining the unemployable. When his brother, the lay-reader, did not reply to a letter, he wrote again, saying that he and Jacky would come down to his village on foot. He did not intend this as blackmail. Still, the brother sent a postal order, and it became part of the system. And so passed his winter and his spring.

In the horror there are two bright spots. He never confused the past. He remained alive, and blessed are those who live, if it is only to a sense of sinfulness. The anodyne of muddledom, by which most men blur and blend their mistakes, never passed Leonard's lips—

> "And if I drink oblivion of a day,
> So shorten I the stature of my soul."[3]

It is a hard saying, and a hard man wrote it, but it lies at the root of all character.

And the other bright spot was his tenderness for Jacky. He pitied her with nobility now—not the contemptuous pity of a man who sticks to a woman through thick and thin. He tried to be less irritable. He wondered what her hungry eyes desired—nothing that she could express, or that he or any man could give her. Would she ever receive the justice that is mercy—the justice for by-products that the world is too busy to bestow? She was fond of flowers, generous with money, and not revengeful. If she had borne him a child he might have cared for her. Unmarried, Leonard would never have begged; he would have flickered out and died. But the whole of life is mixed. He had to provide for Jacky, and went down dirty paths that she might have a few feathers and the dishes of food that suited her.

One day he caught sight of Margaret and her brother. He was in St. Paul's. He had entered the cathedral partly to avoid the rain and partly to see a picture that had educated him in former years. But the light was bad, the picture ill placed, and Time and Judgment were inside him now. Death alone still charmed him, with her lap of poppies, on which all

---

[3]From sonnet XII of *Modern Love* (1852), George Meredith's 50-sonnet sequence about a crumbling marriage.

men shall sleep. He took one glance, and turned aimlessly away towards a chair. Then down the nave he saw Miss Schlegel and her brother. They stood in the fairway of passengers, and their faces were extremely grave. He was perfectly certain that they were in trouble about their sister.

Once outside—and he fled immediately—he wished that he had spoken to them. What was his life? What were a few angry words, or even imprisonment? He had done wrong—that was the true terror. Whatever they might know, he would tell them everything he knew. He re-entered St. Paul's. But they had moved in his absence, and had gone to lay their difficulties before Mr. Wilcox and Charles.

The sight of Margaret turned remorse into new channels. He desired to confess, and though the desire is proof of a weakened nature, which is about to lose the essence of human intercourse, it did not take an ignoble form. He did not suppose that confession would bring him happiness. It was rather that he yearned to get clear of the tangle. So does the suicide yearn. The impulses are akin, and the crime of suicide lies rather in its disregard for the feelings of those whom we leave behind. Confession need harm no one—it can satisfy that test—and though it was un-English, and ignored by our Anglican cathedral, Leonard had a right to decide upon it.

Moreover, he trusted Margaret. He wanted her hardness now. That cold, intellectual nature of hers would be just, if unkind. He would do whatever she told him, even if he had to see Helen. That was the supreme punishment she would exact. And perhaps she would tell him how Helen was. That was the supreme reward.

He knew nothing about Margaret, not even whether she was married to Mr. Wilcox, and tracking her out took several days. That evening he toiled through the wet to Wickham Place, where the new flats were now appearing. Was he also the cause of their move? Were they expelled from society on his account? Thence to a public library, but could find no satisfactory Schlegel in the directory. On the morrow he searched again. He hung about outside Mr. Wilcox's office at lunch time, and, as the clerks came out said: "Excuse me, sir, but is your boss married?" Most of them stared, some said, "What's that to you?" but one, who had not yet acquired reticence, told him what he wished. Leonard could not learn the private address. That necessitated more trouble with directories and tubes. Ducie Street was not discovered till the Monday, the day that Margaret and her husband went down on their hunting expedition to Howards End.

He called at about four o'clock. The weather had changed, and the sun shone gaily on the ornamental steps—black and white marble in triangles. Leonard lowered his eyes to them after ringing the bell. He felt in curious health: doors seemed to be opening and shutting inside his body, and he had been obliged to sleep sitting up in bed, with his back propped against the wall. When the parlourmaid came he could not see her face; the brown rain had descended suddenly.

"Does Mrs. Wilcox live here?" he asked.

"She's out," was the answer.

"When will she be back?"

"I'll ask," said the parlourmaid.

Margaret had given instructions that no one who mentioned her name should ever be rebuffed. Putting the door on the chain—for Leonard's appearance demanded this—she went through to the smoking-room, which was occupied by Tibby. Tibby was asleep. He had had a good lunch. Charles Wilcox had not yet rung him up for the distracting interview. He said drowsily: "I don't know. Hilton. Howards End. Who is it?"

"I'll ask, sir."

"No, don't bother."

"They have taken the car to Howards End," said the parlourmaid to Leonard.

He thanked her, and asked whereabouts that place was.

"You appear to want to know a good deal," she remarked. But Margaret had forbidden her to be mysterious. She told him against her better judgment that Howards End was in Hertfordshire.

"Is it a village, please?"

"Village! It's Mr. Wilcox's private house—at least, it's one of them. Mrs. Wilcox keeps her furniture there. Hilton is the village."

"Yes. And when will they be back?"

"Mr. Schlegel doesn't know. We can't know everything, can we?" She shut him out, and went to attend to the telephone, which was ringing furiously.

He loitered away another night of agony. Confession grew more difficult. As soon as possible he went to bed. He watched a patch of moonlight cross the floor of their lodging, and, as sometimes happens when the mind is overtaxed, he fell asleep for the rest of the room, but kept awake for the patch of moonlight. Horrible! Then began one of those disintegrating dialogues. Part of him said: "Why horrible? It's ordinary light from the moon." "But it moves." "So does the moon." "But it is a clenched fist." "Why not?" "But it is going to touch me." "Let it." And, seeming to gather motion, the patch ran up his blanket. Presently a blue snake appeared; then another, parallel to it. "Is there life in the moon?"

"Of course." "But I thought it was uninhabited." "Not by Time, Death, Judgment, and the smaller snakes." "Smaller snakes!" said Leonard indignantly and aloud. "What a notion!" By a rending effort of the will he woke the rest of the room up. Jacky, the bed, their food, their clothes on the chair, gradually entered his consciousness, and the horror vanished outwards, like a ring that is spreading through water.

"I say, Jacky, I'm going out for a bit."

She was breathing regularly. The patch of light fell clear of the striped blanket, and began to cover the shawl that lay over her feet. Why had he been afraid? He went to the window, and saw that the moon was descending through a clear sky. He saw her volcanoes, and the bright expanses that a gracious error has named seas. They paled, for the sun, who had lit them up, was coming to light the earth. Sea of Serenity, Sea of Tranquillity, Ocean of the Lunar Storms, merged into one lucent drop, itself to slip into the sempiternal dawn. And he had been afraid of the moon!

He dressed among the contending lights, and went through his money. It was running low again, but enough for a return ticket to Hilton. As it clinked Jacky opened her eyes.

"Hullo, Len! What ho, Len!"

"What ho, Jacky! see you again later."

She turned over and slept.

The house was unlocked, their landlord being a salesman at Covent Garden. Leonard passed out and made his way down to the station. The train, though it did not start for an hour, was already drawn up at the end of the platform, and he lay down in it and slept. With the first jolt he was in daylight; they had left the gateways of King's Cross, and were under blue sky. Tunnels followed, and after each the sky grew bluer, and from the embankment at Finsbury Park he had his first sight of the sun. It rolled along behind the eastern smokes—a wheel, whose fellow was the descending moon—and as yet it seemed the servant of the blue sky, not its lord. He dozed again. Over Tewin Water it was day. To the left fell the shadow of the embankment and its arches; to the right Leonard saw up into the Tewin Woods and towards the church, with its wild legend of immortality. Six forest trees—that is a fact—grow out of one of the graves in Tewin churchyard. The grave's occupant—that is the legend—is an atheist, who declared that if God existed, six forest trees would grow out of her grave. These things in Hertfordshire; and farther afield lay the house of a hermit—Mrs. Wilcox had known him—who barred himself up, and wrote prophecies, and gave all he had to the poor.

While, powdered in between, were the villas of business men, who saw life more steadily, though with the steadiness of the half-closed eye. Over all the sun was streaming, to all the birds were singing, to all the primroses were yellow, and the speedwell[4] blue, and the country, however they interpreted her, was uttering her cry of "now." She did not free Leonard yet, and the knife plunged deeper into his heart as the train drew up at Hilton. But remorse had become beautiful.

Hilton was asleep, or at the earliest, breakfasting. Leonard noticed the contrast when he stepped out of it into the country. Here men had been up since dawn. Their hours were ruled, not by a London office, but by the movements of the crops and the sun. That they were men of the finest type only the sentimentalist can declare. But they kept to the life of daylight. They are England's hope. Clumsily they carry forward the torch of the sun, until such time as the nation sees fit to take it up. Half clodhopper,[5] half board-school[6] prig, they can still throw back to a nobler stock, and breed yeomen.

At the chalk pit a motor passed him. In it was another type, whom Nature favours—the Imperial. Healthy, ever in motion, it hopes to inherit the earth. It breeds as quickly as the yeoman, and as soundly; strong is the temptation to acclaim it as a super-yeoman, who carries his country's virtue overseas. But the Imperialist is not what he thinks or seems. He is a destroyer. He prepares the way for cosmopolitanism, and though his ambitions may be fulfilled, the earth that he inherits will be grey.

To Leonard, intent on his private sin, there came the conviction of innate goodness elsewhere. It was not the optimism which he had been taught at school. Again and again must the drums tap, and the goblins stalk over the universe before joy can be purged of the superficial. It was rather paradoxical, and arose from his sorrow. Death destroys a man, but the idea of death saves him—that is the best account of it that has yet been given. Squalor and tragedy can beckon to all that is great in us, and strengthen the wings of love. They can beckon; it is not certain that they will, for they are not love's servants. But they can beckon, and the knowledge of this incredible truth comforted him.

As he approached the house all thought stopped. Contradictory notions stood side by side in his mind. He was terrified but happy,

[4]Small blue-flowering plant.
[5]Country laborer.
[6]Publicly funded institution created under the Elementary Education Act of 1870.

ashamed, but had done no sin. He knew the confession: "Mrs. Wilcox, I have done wrong," but sunrise had robbed its meaning, and he felt rather on a supreme adventure.

He entered a garden, steadied himself against a motor-car that he found in it, found a door open and entered a house. Yes, it would be very easy. From a room to the left he heard voices, Margaret's amongst them. His own name was called aloud, and a man whom he had never seen said, "Oh, is he there? I am not surprised. I now thrash him within an inch of his life."

"Mrs. Wilcox," said Leonard, "I have done wrong."

The man took him by the collar and cried, "Bring me a stick." Women were screaming. A stick, very bright, descended. It hurt him, not where it descended, but in the heart. Books fell over him in a shower. Nothing had sense.

"Get some water," commanded Charles, who had all through kept very calm. "He's shamming. Of course I only used the blade. Here, carry him out into the air."

Thinking that he understood these things, Margaret obeyed him. They laid Leonard, who was dead, on the gravel; Helen poured water over him.

"That's enough," said Charles.

"Yes, murder's enough," said Miss Avery, coming out of the house with the sword.

## CHAPTER XLII

WHEN Charles left Ducie Street he had caught the first train home, but had no inkling of the newest development until late at night. Then his father, who had dined alone, sent for him, and in very grave tones inquired for Margaret.

"I don't know where she is, pater," said Charles. "Dolly kept back dinner nearly an hour for her."

"Tell me when she comes in."

Another hour passed. The servants went to bed, and Charles visited his father again, to receive further instructions. Mrs. Wilcox had still not returned.

"I'll sit up for her as late as you like, but she can hardly be coming. Isn't she stopping with her sister at the hotel?"

"Perhaps," said Mr. Wilcox thoughtfully—"perhaps."

"Can I do anything for you, sir?"

"Not to-night, my boy."

Mr. Wilcox liked being called sir. He raised his eyes and gave his son more open a look of tenderness than he usually ventured. He saw Charles as little boy and strong man in one. Though his wife had proved unstable his children were left to him.

After midnight he tapped on Charles's door. "I can't sleep," he said. "I had better have a talk with you and get it over."

He complained of the heat. Charles took him out into the garden, and they paced up and down in their dressing-gowns. Charles became very quiet as the story unrolled; he had known all along that Margaret was as bad as her sister.

"She will feel differently in the morning," said Mr. Wilcox, who had of course said nothing about Mrs. Bast. "But I cannot let this kind of thing continue without comment. I am morally certain that she is with her sister at Howards End. The house is mine—and, Charles, it will be yours—and when I say that no one is to live there, I mean that no one is to live there. I won't have it." He looked angrily at the moon. "To my mind this question is connected with something far greater, the rights of property itself."

"Undoubtedly," said Charles.

Mr. Wilcox linked his arm in his son's, but somehow liked him less as he told him more. "I don't want you to conclude that my wife and I had anything of the nature of a quarrel. She was only over-wrought, as who would not be? I shall do what I can for Helen, but on the understanding that they clear out of the house at once. Do you see? That is a sine qua non."[1]

"Then at eight to-morrow I may go up in the car?"

"Eight or earlier. Say that you are acting as my representative, and, of course, use no violence, Charles."

On the morrow, as Charles returned, leaving Leonard dead upon the gravel, it did not seem to him that he had used violence. Death was due to heart disease. His stepmother herself had said so, and even Miss Avery had acknowledged that he only used the flat of the sword. On his way through the village he informed the police, who thanked him, and said there must be an inquest. He found his father in the garden shading his eyes from the sun.

"It has been pretty horrible," said Charles gravely. "They were there, and they had the man up there with them too."

"What—what man?"

"I told you last night. His name was Bast."

---

[1] A non-negotiable point, an essential (Latin: without which not).

"My God! is it possible?" said Mr. Wilcox. "In your mother's house! Charles, in your mother's house!"

"I know, pater. That was what I felt. As a matter of fact, there is no need to trouble about the man. He was in the last stages of heart disease, and just before I could show him what I thought of him he went off. The police are seeing about it at this moment."

Mr. Wilcox listened attentively.

"I got up there—oh, it couldn't have been more than half-past seven. The Avery woman was lighting a fire for them. They were still upstairs. I waited in the drawing-room. We were all moderately civil and collected, though I had my suspicions. I gave them your message, and Mrs. Wilcox said, 'Oh yes, I see; yes,' in that way of hers."

"Nothing else?"

"I promised to tell you, 'with her love,' that she was going to Germany with her sister this evening. That was all we had time for."

Mr. Wilcox seemed relieved.

"Because by then I suppose the man got tired of hiding, for suddenly Mrs. Wilcox screamed out his name. I recognized it, and I went for him in the hall. Was I right, pater? I thought things were going a little too far."

"Right, my dear boy? I don't know. But you would have been no son of mine if you hadn't. Then did he just—just—crumple up as you said?" He shrank from the simple word.

"He caught hold of the bookcase, which came down over him. So I merely put the sword down and carried him into the garden. We all thought he was shamming. However, he's dead right enough. Awful business!"

"Sword?" cried his father, with anxiety in his voice. "What sword? Whose sword?"

"A sword of theirs."

"What were you doing with it?"

"Well, didn't you see, pater, I had to snatch up the first thing handy. I hadn't a riding-whip or stick. I caught him once or twice over the shoulders with the flat of their old German sword."

"Then what?"

"He pulled over the bookcase, as I said, and fell," said Charles, with a sigh. It was no fun doing errands for his father, who was never quite satisfied.

"But the real cause was heart disease? Of that you're sure?"

"That or a fit. However, we shall hear more than enough at the inquest on such unsavoury topics."

They went into breakfast. Charles had a racking headache, consequent on motoring before food. He was also anxious about the future, reflecting that the police must detain Helen and Margaret for the inquest and ferret the whole thing out. He saw himself obliged to leave Hilton. One could not afford to live near the scene of a scandal—it was not fair on one's wife. His comfort was that the pater's eyes were opened at last. There would be a horrible smash up, and probably a separation from Margaret; then they would all start again, more as they had been in his mother's time.

"I think I'll go round to the police-station," said his father when breakfast was over.

"What for?" cried Dolly, who had still not been "told."

"Very well, sir. Which car will you have?"

"I think I'll walk."

"It's a good half-mile," said Charles, stepping into the garden. "The sun's very hot for April. Shan't I take you up, and then, perhaps, a little spin round by Tewin?"

"You go on as if I didn't know my own mind," said Mr. Wilcox fretfully. Charles hardened his mouth. "You young fellows' one idea is to get into a motor. I tell you, I want to walk: I'm very fond of walking."

"Oh, all right; I'm about the house if you want me for anything. I thought of not going up to the office to-day, if that is your wish."

"It is, indeed, my boy," said Mr. Wilcox, and laid a hand on his sleeve.

Charles did not like it; he was uneasy about his father, who did not seem himself this morning. There was a petulant touch about him—more like a woman. Could it be that he was growing old? The Wilcoxes were not lacking in affection; they had it royally, but they did not know how to use it. It was the talent in the napkin,[2] and, for a warm-hearted man, Charles had conveyed very little joy. As he watched his father shuffling up the road, he had a vague regret—a wish that something had been different somewhere—a wish (though he did not express it thus) that he had been taught to say "I" in his youth. He meant to make up for Margaret's defection, but knew that his father had been very happy with her until yesterday. How had she done it? By some dishonest trick, no doubt—but how?

---

[2]In the Parable of the Talents (Matthew 25:14–30), a master entrusts talents (measures of money) to three servants while away; on returning, he rebukes the servant who buried his talent in the ground instead of putting it into circulation. In another rendering (Luke 19:12–27), the foolish servant hides the talent in a piece of cloth ("napkin" in the King James Version).

Mr. Wilcox reappeared at eleven, looking very tired. There was to be an inquest on Leonard's body to-morrow, and the police required his son to attend.

"I expected that," said Charles. "I shall naturally be the most important witness there."

## CHAPTER XLIII

OUT of the turmoil and horror that had begun with Aunt Juley's illness and was not even to end with Leonard's death, it seemed impossible to Margaret that healthy life should re-emerge. Events succeeded in a logical, yet senseless, train. People lost their humanity, and took values as arbitrary as those in a pack of playing-cards. It was natural that Henry should do this and cause Helen to do that, and then think her wrong for doing it; natural that she herself should think him wrong; natural that Leonard should want to know how Helen was, and come, and Charles be angry with him for coming—natural, but unreal. In this jangle of causes and effects what had become of their true selves? Here Leonard lay dead in the garden, from natural causes; yet life was a deep, deep river, death a blue sky, life was a house, death a wisp of hay, a flower, a tower, life and death were anything and everything, except this ordered insanity, where the king takes the queen, and the ace the king. Ah, no; there was beauty and adventure behind, such as the man at her feet had yearned for; there was hope this side of the grave; there were truer relationships beyond the limits that fetter us now. As a prisoner looks up and sees stars beckoning, so she, from the turmoil and horror of those days, caught glimpses of the diviner wheels.

And Helen, dumb with fright, but trying to keep calm for the child's sake, and Miss Avery, calm, but murmuring tenderly, "No one ever told the lad he'll have a child"—they also reminded her that horror is not the end. To what ultimate harmony we tend she did not know, but there seemed great chance that a child would be born into the world, to take the great chances of beauty and adventure that the world offers. She moved through the sunlit garden, gathering narcissi, crimson-eyed and white. There was nothing else to be done; the time for telegrams and anger was over, and it seemed wisest that the hands of Leonard should be folded on his breast and be filled with flowers. Here was the father; leave it at that. Let Squalor be turned into Tragedy, whose eyes are the stars, and whose hands hold the sunset and the dawn.

And even the influx of officials, even the return of the doctor, vulgar and acute, could not shake her belief in the eternity of beauty. Science explained people, but could not understand them. After long centuries among the bones and muscles it might be advancing to knowledge of the nerves, but this would never give understanding. One could open the heart to Mr. Mansbridge and his sort without discovering its secrets to them, for they wanted everything down in black and white, and black and white was exactly what they were left with.

They questioned her closely about Charles. She never suspected why. Death had come, and the doctor agreed that it was due to heart disease. They asked to see her father's sword. She explained that Charles's anger was natural, but mistaken. Miserable questions about Leonard followed, all of which she answered unfalteringly. Then back to Charles again. "No doubt Mr. Wilcox may have induced death," she said; "but if it wasn't one thing it would have been another, as you yourselves know." At last they thanked her, and took the sword and the body down to Hilton. She began to pick up the books from the floor.

Helen had gone to the farm. It was the best place for her, since she had to wait for the inquest. Though, as if things were not hard enough, Madge and her husband had raised trouble; they did not see why they should receive the offscourings of Howards End. And, of course, they were right. The whole world was going to be right, and amply avenge any brave talk against the conventions. "Nothing matters," the Schlegels had said in the past, "except one's self-respect and that of one's friends." When the time came, other things mattered terribly. However, Madge had yielded, and Helen was assured of peace for one day and night, and to-morrow she would return to Germany.

As for herself, she determined to go too. No message came from Henry; perhaps he expected her to apologize. Now that she had time to think over her own tragedy, she was unrepentant. She neither forgave him for his behaviour nor wished to forgive him. Her speech to him seemed perfect. She would not have altered a word. It had to be uttered once in a life, to adjust the lopsidedness of the world. It was spoken not only to her husband, but to thousands of men like him—a protest against the inner darkness in high places that comes with a commercial age. Though he would build up his life without hers, she could not apologize. He had refused to connect, on the clearest issue that can be laid before a man, and their love must take the consequences.

No, there was nothing more to be done. They had tried not to go over the precipice but perhaps the fall was inevitable. And it comforted her to think that the future was certainly inevitable: cause and effect would go jangling forward to some goal doubtless, but to none that she could imagine. At such moments the soul retires within, to float upon the bosom of a deeper stream, and has communion with the dead, and sees the world's glory not diminished, but different in kind to what she has supposed. She alters her focus until trivial things are blurred. Margaret had been tending this way all the winter. Leonard's death brought her to the goal. Alas! that Henry should fade away as reality emerged, and only her love for him should remain clear, stamped with his image like the cameos we rescue out of dreams.

With unfaltering eye she traced his future. He would soon present a healthy mind to the world again, and what did he or the world care if he was rotten at the core? He would grow into a rich, jolly old man, at times a little sentimental about women, but emptying his glass with anyone. Tenacious of power, he would keep Charles and the rest dependent, and retire from business reluctantly and at an advanced age. He would settle down—though she could not realize this. In her eyes Henry was always moving and causing others to move, until the ends of the earth met. But in time he must get too tired to move, and settle down. What next? The inevitable word. The release of the soul to its appropriate Heaven.

Would they meet in it? Margaret believed in immortality for herself. An eternal future had always seemed natural to her. And Henry believed in it for himself. Yet, would they meet again? Are there not rather endless levels beyond the grave, as the theory that he had censured teaches? And his level, whether higher or lower, could it possibly be the same as hers?

Thus gravely meditating, she was summoned by him. He sent up Crane in the motor. Other servants passed like water, but the chauffeur remained, though impertinent and disloyal. Margaret disliked Crane, and he knew it.

"Is it the keys that Mr. Wilcox wants?" she asked.

"He didn't say, madam."

"You haven't any note for me?"

"He didn't say, madam."

After a moment's thought she locked up Howards End. It was pitiable to see in it the stirrings of warmth that would be quenched for ever. She raked out the fire that was blazing in the kitchen, and spread the coals in the gravelled yard. She closed the windows and drew the curtains. Henry would probably sell the place now.

She was determined not to spare him, for nothing new had happened as far as they were concerned. Her mood might never have altered from yesterday evening. He was standing a little outside Charles's gate, and motioned the car to stop. When his wife got out he said hoarsely: "I prefer to discuss things with you outside."

"It will be more appropriate in the road, I am afraid," said Margaret. "Did you get my message?"

"What about?"

"I am going to Germany with my sister. I must tell you now that I shall make it my permanent home. Our talk last night was more important than you have realized. I am unable to forgive you and am leaving you."

"I am extremely tired," said Henry, in injured tones. "I have been walking about all the morning, and wish to sit down."

"Certainly, if you will consent to sit on the grass."

The Great North Road should have been bordered all its length with glebe.[1] Henry's kind had filched most of it. She moved to the scrap opposite, wherein were the Six Hills. They sat down on the farther side, so that they could not be seen by Charles or Dolly.

"Here are your keys," said Margaret. She tossed them towards him. They fell on the sunlit slope of grass, and he did not pick them up.

"I have something to tell you," he said gently.

She knew this superficial gentleness, this confession of hastiness, that was only intended to enhance her admiration of the male.

"I don't want to hear it," she replied. "My sister is going to be ill. My life is going to be with her now. We must manage to build up something, she and I and her child."

"Where are you going?"

"Munich. We start after the inquest, if she is not too ill."

"After the inquest?"

"Yes."

"Have you realized what the verdict at the inquest will be?"

"Yes, heart disease."

"No, my dear; manslaughter."

Margaret drove her fingers through the grass. The hill beneath her moved as if it was alive.

"Manslaughter," repeated Mr. Wilcox. "Charles may go to prison. I dare not tell him. I don't know what to do—what to do. I'm broken—I'm ended."

---

[1]Cultivated land belonging to a church, or cultivated land generally.

No sudden warmth arose in her. She did not see that to break him was her only hope. She did not enfold the sufferer in her arms. But all through that day and the next a new life began to move. The verdict was brought in. Charles was committed for trial. It was against all reason that he should be punished, but the law, being made in his image, sentenced him to three years' imprisonment. Then Henry's fortress gave way. He could bear no one but his wife, he shambled up to Margaret afterwards and asked her to do what she could with him. She did what seemed easiest—she took him down to recruit[2] at Howards End.

## CHAPTER XLIV

TOM'S father was cutting the big meadow. He passed again and again amid whirring blades and sweet odours of grass, encompassing with narrowing circles the sacred centre of the field. Tom was negotiating with Helen.

"I haven't any idea," she replied. "Do you suppose baby may, Meg?"

Margaret put down her work and regarded them absently. "What was that?" she asked.

"Tom wants to know whether baby is old enough to play with hay?"

"I haven't the least notion," answered Margaret, and took up her work again.

"Now, Tom, baby is not to stand; he is not to lie on his face; he is not to lie so that his head wags; he is not to be teased or tickled; and he is not to be cut into two or more pieces by the cutter. Will you be as careful as all that?"

Tom held out his arms.

"That child is a wonderful nursemaid," remarked Margaret.

"He is fond of baby. That's why he does it!" was Helen's answer. "They're going to be lifelong friends."

"Starting at the ages of six and one?"

"Of course. It will be a great thing for Tom."

"It may be a greater thing for baby."

Fourteen months had passed, but Margaret still stopped at Howards End. No better plan had occurred to her. The meadow was being recut, the great red poppies were reopening in the garden. July would follow with the little red poppies among the wheat, August with the cutting of the wheat. These little events would become part of

[2]Get his health back.

her year after year. Every summer she would fear lest the well should give out, every winter lest the pipes should freeze; every westerly gale might blow the wych-elm down and bring the end of all things, and so she could not read or talk during a westerly gale. The air was tranquil now. She and her sister were sitting on the remains of Evie's rockery, where the lawn merged into the field.

"What a time they all are!" said Helen. "What can they be doing inside?" Margaret, who was growing less talkative, made no answer. The noise of the cutter came intermittently, like the breaking of waves. Close by them a man was preparing to scythe out one of the dell-holes.

"I wish Henry was out to enjoy this," said Helen. "This lovely weather and to be shut up in the house! It's very hard."

"It has to be," said Margaret. "The hay-fever is his chief objection against living here, but he thinks it worth while."

"Meg, is or isn't he ill? I can't make out."

"Not ill. Eternally tired. He has worked very hard all his life, and noticed nothing. Those are the people who collapse when they do notice a thing."

"I suppose he worries dreadfully about his part of the tangle."

"Dreadfully. That is why I wish Dolly had not come, too, to-day. Still, he wanted them all to come. It has to be."

"Why does he want them?"

Margaret did not answer.

"Meg, may I tell you something? I like Henry."

"You'd be odd if you didn't," said Margaret.

"I usen't to."

"Usen't!" She lowered her eyes a moment to the black abyss of the past. They had crossed it, always excepting Leonard and Charles. They were building up a new life, obscure, yet gilded with tranquillity. Leonard was dead; Charles had two years more in prison. One usen't always to see clearly before that time. It was different now.

"I like Henry because he does worry."

"And he likes you because you don't."

Helen sighed. She seemed humiliated, and buried her face in her hands. After a time she said: "About love," a transition less abrupt than it appeared.

Margaret never stopped working.

"I mean a woman's love for a man. I supposed I should hang my life on to that once, and was driven up and down and about as if something was worrying through me. But everything is peaceful now; I seem cured. That Herr Förstmeister, whom Frieda keeps writing about, must be a noble character, but he doesn't see that I shall never marry him or anyone. It isn't shame or mistrust of myself. I simply couldn't. I'm ended. I used to be so dreamy about a man's love as a girl, and think that for good or evil love must be the great thing. But it hasn't been; it has been itself a dream. Do you agree?"

"I do not agree. I do not."

"I ought to remember Leonard as my lover," said Helen, stepping down into the field. "I tempted him, and killed him, and it is surely the least I can do. I would like to throw out all my heart to Leonard on such an afternoon as this. But I cannot. It is no good pretending. I am forgetting him." Her eyes filled with tears. "How nothing seems to match—how, my darling, my precious——" She broke off. "Tommy!"

"Yes, please?"

"Baby's not to try and stand.—There's something wanting in me. I see you loving Henry, and understanding him better daily, and I know that death wouldn't part you in the least. But I——Is it some awful appalling, criminal defect?"

Margaret silenced her. She said: "It is only that people are far more different than is pretended. All over the world men and women are worrying because they cannot develop as they are supposed to develop. Here and there they have the matter out, and it comforts them. Don't fret yourself, Helen. Develop what you have; love your child. I do not love children. I am thankful to have none. I can play with their beauty and charm, but that is all—nothing real, not one scrap of what there ought to be. And others—others go farther still, and move outside humanity altogether. A place, as well as a person, may catch the glow. Don't you see that all this leads to comfort in the end? It is part of the battle against sameness. Differences—eternal differences, planted by God in a single family, so that there may always be colour; sorrow perhaps, but colour in the daily grey. Then I can't have you worrying about Leonard. Don't drag in the personal when it will not come. Forget him."

"Yes, yes, but what has Leonard got out of life?"

"Perhaps an adventure."

"Is that enough?"

"Not for us. But for him."

Helen took up a bunch of grass. She looked at the sorrel, and the red and white and yellow clover, and the quaker grass, and the daisies, and the bents[1] that composed it. She raised it to her face.

[1]Stiff grass.

"Is it sweetening yet?" asked Margaret.

"No, only withered."

"It will sweeten to-morrow."

Helen smiled. "Oh, Meg, you are a person," she said. "Think of the racket and torture this time last year. But now I couldn't stop unhappy if I tried. What a change—and all through you!"

"Oh, we merely settled down. You and Henry learnt to understand one another and to forgive, all through the autumn and the winter."

"Yes, but who settled us down?"

Margaret did not reply. The scything had begun, and she took off her pince-nez to watch it.

"You!" cried Helen. "You did it all, sweetest, though you're too stupid to see. Living here was your plan—I wanted you; he wanted you; and everyone said it was impossible, but you knew. Just think of our lives without you, Meg—I and baby with Monica, revolting by theory, he handed about from Dolly to Evie. But you picked up the pieces, and made us a home. Can't it strike you—even for a moment—that your life has been heroic? Can't you remember the two months after Charles's arrest, when you began to act, and did all?"

"You were both ill at the time," said Margaret. "I did the obvious things. I had two invalids to nurse. Here was a house, ready furnished and empty. It was obvious. I didn't know myself it would turn into a permanent home. No doubt I have done a little towards straightening the tangle, but things that I can't phrase have helped me."

"I hope it will be permanent," said Helen, drifting away to other thoughts.

"I think so. There are moments when I feel Howards End peculiarly our own."

"All the same, London's creeping."

She pointed over the meadow—over eight or nine meadows, but at the end of them was a red rust.

"You see that in Surrey and even Hampshire now," she continued. "I can see it from the Purbeck Downs. And London is only part of something else, I'm afraid. Life's going to be melted down, all over the world."

Margaret knew that her sister spoke truly. Howards End, Oniton, the Purbeck Downs, the Oderberge, were all survivals, and the melting-pot was being prepared for them. Logically, they had no right to be alive. One's hope was in the weakness of logic. Were they possibly the earth beating time?

"Because a thing is going strong now, it need not go strong for ever," she said. "This craze for motion has only set in during the last hundred years. It may be followed by a civilization that won't be a movement, because it will rest on the earth. All the signs are against it now, but I can't help hoping, and very early in the morning in the garden I feel that our house is the future as well as the past."

They turned and looked at it. Their own memories coloured it now, for Helen's child had been born in the central room of the nine. Then Margaret said, "Oh, take care—!" for something moved behind the window of the hall, and the door opened.

"The conclave's breaking at last. I'll go."

It was Paul.

Helen retreated with the children far into the field. Friendly voices greeted her. Margaret rose, to encounter a man with a heavy black moustache.

"My father has asked for you," he said with hostility.

She took her work and followed him.

"We have been talking business," he continued, "but I dare say you knew all about it beforehand."

"Yes, I did."

Clumsy of movement—for he had spent all his life in the saddle—Paul drove his foot against the paint of the front door. Mrs. Wilcox gave a little cry of annoyance. She did not like anything scratched; she stopped in the hall to take Dolly's boa and gloves out of a vase.

Her husband was lying in a great leather chair in the dining-room, and by his side, holding his hand rather ostentatiously, was Evie. Dolly, dressed in purple, sat near the window. The room was a little dark and airless; they were obliged to keep it like this until the carting of the hay. Margaret joined the family without speaking; the five of them had met already at tea, and she knew quite well what was going to be said. Averse to wasting her time, she went on sewing. The clock struck six.

"Is this going to suit everyone?" said Henry in a weary voice. He used the old phrases, but their effect was unexpected and shadowy. "Because I don't want you all coming here later on and complaining that I have been unfair."

"It's apparently got to suit us," said Paul.

"I beg your pardon, my boy. You have only to speak, and I will leave the house to you instead."

Paul frowned ill-temperedly, and began scratching at his arm. "As I've given up the outdoor life that suited me, and I have come home to look after the business, it's no good my settling down here," he said at last. "It's not really the country, and it's not the town."

"Very well. Does my arrangement suit you, Evie?"

"Of course, Father."

"And you, Dolly?"

Dolly raised her faded little face, which sorrow could wither but not steady. "Perfectly splendidly," she said. "I thought Charles wanted it for the boys, but last time I saw him he said no, because we cannot possibly live in this part of England again. Charles says we ought to change our name, but I cannot think what to, for Wilcox just suits Charles and me, and I can't think of any other name."

There was a general silence. Dolly looked nervously round, fearing that she had been inappropriate. Paul continued to scratch his arm.

"Then I leave Howards End to my wife absolutely," said Henry. "And let every one understand that; and after I am dead let there be no jealousy and no surprise."

Margaret did not answer. There was something uncanny in her triumph. She, who had never expected to conquer anyone, had charged straight through these Wilcoxes and broken up their lives.

"In consequence, I leave my wife no money," said Henry. "That is her own wish. All that she would have had will be divided among you. I am also giving you a great deal in my lifetime, so that you may be independent of me. That is her wish, too. She also is giving away a great deal of money. She intends to diminish her income by half during the next ten years; she intends when she dies to leave the house to her—to her nephew, down in the field. Is all that clear? Does everyone understand?"

Paul rose to his feet. He was accustomed to natives, and a very little shook him out of the Englishman. Feeling manly and cynical, he said: "Down in the field? Oh, come! I think we might have had the whole establishment, piccaninnies[2] included."

Mrs. Cahill whispered: "Don't, Paul. You promised you'd take care." Feeling a woman of the world, she rose and prepared to take her leave.

Her father kissed her. "Good-bye, old girl," he said; "don't you worry about me."

"Good-bye, dad."

Then it was Dolly's turn. Anxious to contribute, she laughed nervously, and said: "Good-bye, Mr. Wilcox. It does seem curious

---

[2]Racist term for young black children.

that Mrs. Wilcox should have left Margaret Howards End, and yet she get it, after all."

From Evie came a sharply-drawn breath. "Good-bye," she said to Margaret, and kissed her.

And again and again fell the word, like the ebb of a dying sea.

"Good-bye."

"Good-bye, Dolly."

"So long, father."

"Good-bye, my boy; always take care of yourself."

"Good-bye, Mrs. Wilcox."

"Good-bye."

Margaret saw their visitors to the gate. Then she returned to her husband and laid her head in his hands. He was pitiably tired. But Dolly's remark had interested her. At last she said: "Could you tell me, Henry, what was that about Mrs. Wilcox having left me Howards End?"

Tranquilly he replied: "Yes, she did. But that is a very old story. When she was ill and you were so kind to her she wanted to make you some return, and, not being herself at the time, scribbled 'Howards End' on a piece of paper. I went into it thoroughly, and, as it was clearly fanciful, I set it aside, little knowing what my Margaret would be to me in the future."

Margaret was silent. Something shook her life in its inmost recesses, and she shivered.

"I didn't do wrong, did I?" he asked, bending down.

"You didn't, darling. Nothing has been done wrong."

From the garden came laughter. "Here they are at last!" exclaimed Henry, disengaging himself with a smile. Helen rushed into the gloom, holding Tom by one hand and carrying her baby on the other. There were shouts of infectious joy.

"The field's cut!" Helen cried excitedly—"the big meadow! We've seen to the very end, and it'll be such a crop of hay as never!"

*Weybridge*, 1908–1910.

# *Afterword*

*Howards End* does not seem to have started out as a rumination on the present and future of England. A diary entry for 26 June 1908 suggests that Forster began, instead, with people and a story:

> Idea for another novel shaping. In a prelude Helen goes to stop with the Wilcoxes, gets engaged to the son & breaks it off immediately, for her instinct sees the spiritual cleavage between the families. Mrs Wilcox dies, and some 2 years later Margaret gets engaged to the widower, a man impeccable publicly. They are accosted by a prostitute. M., because she understands & is great, marries him. The wrong thing to do. He, because he is little, cannot bear to be understood, & goes to the bad. He is frank, kind, & attractive. But he dreads ideas. (quoted in Stallybrass, "Editor's Introduction" to *Howards End* vii)

Here we find marital complexities but nothing about imperial commerce, temperamental differences but not income hierarchies, wrong guesses about a man but no forecasts of a nomadic civilization. Yet it is easy to see how there could evolve from this core a novel that asks, as the famous critic Lionel Trilling put it in 1943, "Who shall inherit England?" (118). The diary entry already envisions a divide between two kinds of people, great souls who embrace ideas and narrower ones who dislike them, and hints that the difference will be played out as a "cleavage" between clans. From here, it is a short step to the opposition between Schlegels passionate about culture, intellect, and the "the inner life," on the one hand, and Wilcoxes focused on commerce, money, and material eminence, on the other. Even had Forster adhered more austerely to his initial sketch, the result might have joined the ranks of "condition of England novels," as social-problem fictions had been called since the middle of the nineteenth century. What keys *Howards End* to the particular question of who shall inherit England is its adaptation of another time-tested staple, the inheritance plot. Everything sweeps toward the disposition of a house (estate, structure, dynasty, way of life) that implies England as a whole.

Even the barest outline of Forster's life up to the writing of *Howards End* suggests, as noted in the introduction, why he might have chosen to build a story around a house, a will, and the perspective of intelligent women. Less immediately evident, perhaps, is what led him to center the narrative on a tension between culture and commerce. Supported by legacies, he never had to choose between the pecuniary chanciness of a writer's career and a more reliable line of work, nor did his life at Rooksnest, Cambridge, and Weybridge mandate much contact with the business world. What in Forster's experience might have led to the Wilcoxes' vigorous emergence in his imagination?

One factor, no doubt, was an awareness—shared by most of those privileged to live on inheritances—that interest income did not simply fall from the sky. (The narrator of *Howards End* is at pains to note that the Schlegel sisters invest wisely.) But a more important element lay in the outlook of the liberal intellectuals with whom Forster most closely identified. As the biographer P. N. Furbank notes, the Cambridge of Forster's day was averse to acknowledging the role of those involved in commerce in the nation's maintenance: the old snobbery of the aristocracy toward the merchant class had been replaced by a prejudice that "it was scholars and civil servants, not business men, who ran Britain" (50). At the same time, Forster's set believed that living honestly meant subjecting all one's ideas, especially those that might be clung to for comfort or convenience, to rigorous scrutiny. With such convictions, and a typically liberal alertness to the economic grounding of social phenomena, Forster was primed to confront the dependence of cultivated existence on the machinery of industry, finance, and trade. When Margaret protests to her aunt that she's "tired of these rich people who pretend to be poor, and think it shows a nice mind to ignore the piles of money that keep their feet above the waves," (p. 51), she vents a sentiment many of Forster's friends would have endorsed.

*Howards End* does not, then, simply set good, curious, cultured Schlegels against bad, greedy, vulgar Wilcoxes (or for that matter anemic, useless, hypocritical Schlegels against active, productive, honest Wilcoxes). Rather, it probes the tender point that the development of heart and mind permitted by civilization owes a great deal to less sensitive people, not to say deeds from which the civilized might recoil. Forster was far from the only writer of the day to ponder this circumstance. In *Cantos* 8–11, first published in 1923, Ezra Pound pays homage to Sigismondo Malatesta, a fifteenth-century Italian warlord and mercenary who was also a patron of the arts (and whom Forster would mention in more than one of his later essays). In "Ancestral Houses," from the same year, William Butler Yeats imagines the refined milieu of the great country house coming to birth when, long ago, "Some violent bitter man, some powerful man / Called architect and artist in, that they, / Bitter and violent men, might rear in stone / The sweetness that all longed for night and day, / The gentleness none there had ever known" (200). Margaret Schlegel herself considers that Wilcox virtues, though "of the second rank, no doubt, . . . have formed our civilization" (p. 85) and later lectures Helen,

> If Wilcoxes hadn't worked and died in England for thousands of years, you and I couldn't sit here without having our throats cut. There would be no trains, no ships to carry us literary people about in, no fields even. Just savagery. No—perhaps not even that. Without their spirit life might never have moved out of protoplasm. More and more do I refuse to draw my income and sneer at those who guarantee it. (p. 141).

Forster's confrontation with culture's less agreeable debts goes much further than this speech of Margaret's, however. It also encompasses Helen's point that the Wilcoxes owe their success partly to the exploitation of others. Leonard Bast, already poor, has been made poorer by Helen and Margaret's transmission of some bad advice from Henry; told of this turn, Henry chalks it all up to "the battle of life." "The poor are poor," he insists, "and one's sorry for them, but there it is. As civilization moves forward, the shoe is bound to pinch in places, and it's absurd to pretend that anyone is responsible personally" (pp. 154–55). In the wake of this evasion of blame, Helen complains, "I don't like those men. They are scientific themselves, and talk of the survival of the fittest, and cut down the salaries of their clerks, . . . but yet they believe that somehow good—it is always that sloppy 'somehow'—will be the outcome, and that in some mystical way the Mr. Basts of the future will benefit because the Mr. Basts of to-day are in pain" (p. 155). The rub of Helen's account is this: if Schlegelian comfort depends on Wilcoxian business, as Margaret has insisted, then the gentle life of the Schlegels too is implicated in the abuse of the Leonards of the world (including those injured by imperial ventures such as the Wilcoxes' rubber firm).

The Wilcox way of "panic and emptiness" and "telegrams and anger" (pp. 21–22) cannot be the right one, therefore, but the Schlegel way is burdened by problems of its own. Who, then, deserves to inherit England? By positioning the memorable cries of "Schlegels were better than Wilcoxes, Wilcoxes better than Schlegels" so early in his novel (p. 18), Forster invites readers to guess that the answer will be one or the other, or both. Yet by the end of the narrative another candidate has emerged. Sharing Howards End with Margaret, Helen, and Henry is a child who will eventually inherit the house—and whose father is Leonard Bast.

Might Forster therefore be proposing a destiny in which the nation belongs to workers as well as intellectuals and business people? One point in support of this inference is that although the Schlegels, Wilcoxes, and Basts are all technically middle class—Forster would begin a well-known 1926 essay by remarking the "essentially middle-class" character of the English (*Abinger Harvest* 3)—they call to mind the old triad of aristocracy, bourgeoisie, and proletariat. Living on inheritances, the Schlegels evoke the gentry even though they have less money than the Wilcoxes; the Wilcoxes embody the active, entrepreneurial middle classes whose dominance was clinched by the industrial revolution; the Basts, in their precarious poverty, suggest all those at the lower end of the social scale. In giving all three a share of a house that Margaret sees as "the future as well as the past" (p. 271), Forster could be limning a reconciliation among the tiers of Britain's enduring class hierarchy.

Yet such a conclusion suppresses some crucial complications. One is that *Howards End* is best described as surveying the destinies not of three classes of people but of four. This becomes clearer when one takes Forster's previous novels into account, since all of them give a prominent place to figures one critic has named "noble peasants" (Olson 389)—characters who live close to nature and who, in their profound authenticity and native goodness, suggest the best humanity has to offer. Forster's devotion to this kind of person emerges most vividly at the end of *The Longest Journey* (1907): there, Stephen Wonham, on whom "the sun and the wind had worked . . . daily ever since he was born," rests with his daughter on the Wiltshire downs and reflects that "century after century, his thoughts and passions would triumph in England" (96–97, 308–09). The heroine of *A Room with a View* (1908), Lucy Honeychurch, chooses the right mate in marrying George Emerson, a young man who presses the claims of nature and the body in spite of his education and regards himself as dressed enough to appear among ladies when he stands "[b]arefoot, bare-chested, radiant and personable against the shadowy woods" (152). Gino Carella, the principal noble peasant in *Where Angels Fear to Tread* (1905), is less appealing, but seen with his infant son he too inspires awe in the most perceptive of the novel's characters. "The man was majestic; he was a part of Nature" (136), thinks Caroline Abbott, just as Margaret Schlegel muses how Ruth Wilcox, so much in communion with the earth, "give[s] the idea of greatness" (p. 63). Similar souls in *Howards End* include Miss Avery, young Tom, and even Leonard Bast—who breaks with convention by walking through the woods all night, whose grandparents were "agricultural labourers," and in whom survive "[h]ints of robustness . . . , more than a hint of primitive good looks" (pp. 191, 94).

In the earlier novels, characters elevated by nature are often set off against others compromised by culture. Stephen Wonham seems the rightful bearer of England's future in part because he does not suffer from the weaknesses of his Cambridge-educated half-brother, Rickie Elliott (the hero for most of the novel); another foil to Stephen is the monstrous Mrs. Failing, who mistakes her peevish cruelty for modern cleverness and whose "attitude toward Nature was severely aesthetic": "If she liked a ploughed field, it was only as a spot of colour—not also as a hint of the endless strength of the earth" (110). In *A Room with a View*, George's rival for Lucy's hand is the fastidious Cecil Vyse, perhaps the same Mr. Vyse whom Margaret Schlegel describes as "rather a wretched, weedy man" (p. 89). In *Where Angels Fear to Tread*, Gino's opposite number is Philip Herriton, another weak-willed (though sometimes insightful) aesthete.

With *Howards End*, Forster departs from this pattern. Though Tibby bespeaks the dangers of an overwrought intellectualism, his highly cultured sisters attract readers' sympathy throughout the novel—and prove ascendant at the close. Helen, restored to England, is the mother of the heir-designate of Howards End, while Margaret, "who had never expected to conquer anyone, had charged straight through these Wilcoxes and broken up their lives" (p. 272).

Yet Forster makes it doubtful that Margaret and Helen stand for culture alone when they obtain this victory. At the lunch held in her honor in chapter 9, Ruth Wilcox has trouble keeping up with the sparkling conversation, yet she exudes a significance beside which the talk of Margaret's bright young guests seems flimsy: "She was not intellectual, nor even alert, and it was odd that, all the same, she should give the idea of greatness. Margaret, zigzagging with her friends over Thought and Art, was conscious of a personality that transcended their own and dwarfed their activities" (p. 63). After her marriage, Margaret starts to turn away from "theatres and discussion societies," to "'miss' new movements," to "spend her spare time re-reading or thinking"—which, the narrator suggests, is no loss (p. 210). The last scene finds her sewing and watching farmers at work, her preeminent concern not the life of the mind but the safety of house and meadow. And along the way, a profound affinity with Ruth, if not a spiritual possession, has grown more and more pronounced. She duplicates Ruth's "way of walking," according to Miss Avery (p. 163); she has assumed the dead woman's habit of caressing the earth and vegetation; she has become a Mrs. Wilcox herself by marrying Henry; and, against all probability, she has inherited the house Ruth wanted her to have. Forster includes nothing to contradict, and much to support, the sensation Margaret describes to Helen as they sit beneath the wych-elm: "I feel that you and I and Henry are only fragments of that woman's mind. She knows everything. She is everything. She is the house, and the tree that leans over it. . . . She knew about realities" (p. 250).

A novel's conclusion, especially if improbable and happy, can often be read as embodying its author's desires—as a realization in the fictional world of what the author would like for the real one. Margaret's "uncanny . . . triumph" (p. 272) solicits such an interpretation unabashedly. Whether one takes that victory to be sheer happenstance or the fruit of supernatural intervention by Ruth, it suggests a hope, on Forster's part, that the future will belong to people in whom the best of culture fuses with something even more crucial, feeling for the earth. (The same is true in *The Longest Journey*, where Stephen is a reader as well as a rustic, and in *A Room with a View*, where George blends naturalness with intellection.) The roots of such a hope can certainly be traced to Forster's history: having grown up a coddled, intellectual child amid farmers and groundskeepers, he found himself, in adulthood, attracted philosophically and sexually to men who seemed at ease with their bodies and in tune with the land. His ideal seems to merge what he admired in such people with what he liked in himself and his more erudite friends.

But the dream of uniting nature and culture, innocence and sophistication, was not just Forster's personal idiosyncrasy. It was the motor of a long literary and philosophical tradition. In the pastoral mode—which stretched back to Forster's favorite classical poet, Theocritus (Beauman 78), and encompassed writers such as Virgil and Edmund Spenser—simple herdsmen recite beautifully wrought poetry, thus playing out a fantasy in which high art issues from artless souls. In the late eighteenth and early nineteenth centuries, cultivated persons' longing for the authenticity of those closest to nature was explored by Romantic writers such as Jean-Jacques Rousseau, William Wordsworth, Friedrich Schiller, and the brothers August Wilhelm and Friedrich Schlegel. (The last may have seemed an attractive source for Margaret and Helen's surname thanks to their high ideals, passion for art, and marriages to intellectually formidable women.) In the early twentieth century, strains of the pastoral problem lingered in analyses such as György Lukács *Theory of the Novel*

(1916), which discerned the essence of the novel form in a split between humans and world unfelt by the ancient Greeks, and Oswald Spengler's *Decline of the West* (1918), which found the essence of late Western civilization in a drive to dominate nature through technology.

Not three classes of people but four: should we say, then, that the hopeful conclusion of *Howards End* finds noble peasants sharing England's destiny with intellectuals, business people, and workers? The problem with such a judgment is that it does not quite capture the harshness in Margaret's "uncanny triumph." While the Schlegel sisters, Tom, baby, and (presumably) Miss Avery are comfortably in possession of Howards End, the Wilcoxes have been routed, and the Basts (apart from Leonard's continuation in his child) have vanished. Henry is no longer a confident patriarch but a dependent shadow; the younger Wilcoxes have given up their claims to the place (in exchange for other compensations, to be sure); Leonard is dead; and Jacky's fate goes unrecorded. What, then, is the true share of money-makers and wage-earners in the future Forster imagines? How does he conceive of their place in society?

Earlier passages in the novel furnish some guidance. At the end of a paragraph on Margaret's dawning affection for Henry, the narrator comments, "Some day—in the millennium—there may be no need for his type. At present, homage is due to it from those who think themselves superior, and who possibly are" (p. 131). The two sentences may at first seem a model of ambivalence, denigrating the Wilcox type ("there may be no need") only to elevate it ("homage is due . . . from those who think themselves superior") and then denigrate it again ("and who possibly are"). Examined more closely, however, they yield a coherent, if unexpected, claim: although the Wilcoxes may be needed for a long time to come, the world when finally perfected will have no use for them. The statement thus does not contradict, but does add an unsettling shading to, Margaret's opinion that "If Wilcoxes hadn't worked and died in England for thousands of years, you and I couldn't sit here without having our throats cut." It also jibes with a conversation in chapter 33, in which Miss Avery—who had been friends with Ruth Howard before the latter became Ruth Wilcox—acknowledges that Henry saved Howards End from utter ruin. Margaret is "anxious that her husband should receive his dues," but her interlocutor refuses to be impressed. "Wilcoxes are better than nothing," says Miss Avery, but "that's all over. . . . A better time is coming now, though you've kept me long enough waiting. In a couple of weeks I'll see your lights shining through the hedge of an evening" (pp. 219–220).

Is the novel's claim, then, that the ways of the Wilcoxes (and the Basts) are necessary but regrettable instruments of human progress, whereas the

Howards and the Schlegels enjoy intrinsically valuable ways of living? Is the deepest suggestion of *Howards End* that Wilcoxes are means but Howards ends? And does the arc of the narrative reproduce this long human trajectory in miniature, sacrificing Henry, Charles, and Leonard so that Margaret, Helen, and Ruth may prevail?

So cold an implication may seem at odds with the warmth of the happy ending—and with Forster's insistence on the unmatched worth of individuals, the paramount importance of personal relations. Yet the final chapter is strikingly rich in imagery of sacrifice. As several critics have noted, it reverberates with the mythology of dying and reviving gods charted by James Frazer in *The Golden Bough* (1890—a book popular with undergraduates at Forster's Cambridge) and wielded to famous literary effect by T. S. Eliot in *The Waste Land* (1922). At the heart of such myths is a sacrificial deity whose violent death—often a dismemberment, as in the Egyptian legend of Osiris—is replicated by the decline of vegetation in autumn and whose rebirth is enacted by earth's quickening in spring. Chapter 44 of *Howards End* opens with Tom's father cutting the big meadow, passing "again and again amid whirring blades and sweet odours of grass, encompassing with narrowing circles the sacred centre of the field" (p. 267). A few lines later, Helen warns Tom that baby "is not to be cut into two or more pieces by the cutter," while a man with a scythe stands close by. Shortly after, the narrator transcribes Margaret's thoughts, somewhat spookily, as, "Leonard was dead; Charles had two years more in prison. One usen't always to see clearly before that time. It was different now" (p. 268). Helen then expresses her affection for the diminished Mr. Wilcox of the present—"I like Henry because he does worry"—and admits that she has started to forget Leonard. Melodramatically, yet in accord with the sacrificial strain of the final scene, she declares, "I tempted him, and killed him" (pp. 268–69).

The intensity of the Wilcoxes' subjugation, and the completeness of success enjoyed by Margaret, Helen, and Ruth, may have discomfited Forster himself in the end. In a famously puzzling diary entry of 1965, he writes first of feeling that *Howards End* is his "best novel," with its fine "range of characters, social sense, wit, wisdom, and colour," then continues, "Have only just discovered why I don't care for it: not a single character in it for whom I care" (quoted in Stallybrass, "Editor's Introduction" to *Howards End* xvii). It is hard to imagine Forster not caring for the Schlegel sisters as he wrote their story: interesting, imperfect, funny, and imbued with his own values, they have struck many readers as two of his most likeable personalities. Yet at moments in the final chapter, they sound uncharacteristically complacent, if still perceptive and sincere. One can imagine how their victory, so strangely won and so costly to others, might put them at a remove from a writer wary of those whom power makes self-assured. One can imagine them losing some of their author's affection in gaining Howards End.

In the novel's denouement, then, Forster seems to have sketched his hopes for the future even while acknowledging his utopia's costs—the kinds of people who would be excluded from it, the values it would suppress. The answer to "Who shall inherit England?" implies an answer to the follow-up, "And who shall not?" Yet to think of *Howards End* as a utopian fiction is to recognize that Trilling's question, framed as it is in national terms, is finally too limiting. Forster's feeling for his country ran deep, sometimes clashing with his internationalism, and Englishness is a serious matter in *Howards End*. Yet the novel's conclusion holds out a vision of what may be best for human beings generally, not just for one nation or one people. Forster takes his epigraph from a "sermon" by Margaret:

> Only connect the prose and the passion, and both will be exalted, and human love will be seen at its height. Live in fragments no longer. Only connect, and the beast and the monk, robbed of the isolation that is life to either, will die. (p. 150)

In context, the exhortation pertains to a typically English discomfort with sexuality and the body; but Margaret's language points in many other directions as well, to many variations on the effort to reconcile aspirations toward infinity with the immediacy of earth. One reason *Howards End* has had such enduring appeal, surely, is that it ventures an answer—which readers are invited to dispute, of course—to the enormous question of how life should be lived if it is to be good.

The cultural meanings of this work thus depend, to a degree unusual even for prose fiction, on how things turn out for the characters. Yet there are any number of elements along the way to that culmination that have touched readers' feelings and challenged their intellects over the years— any number of reasons apart from its resonant finale to admire Forster's endlessly inventive novel. To grasp the intricacies of its social vision, one must attend closely to the resolution of the narrative. But one does not go to *Howards End* just for its ending.

# CONTEXTS

"The Embankment, 1900."

# *Money*

What does it mean that Margaret and Helen "stand each year upon six hundred pounds" (p. 51) and that Tibby stands upon £800? What would it mean to have £30,000 (or £1,000,000) a year, as the rich man imagined by the ladies' discussion club in chapter 15 does? And what would Margaret's suggestion of an annual £300 given to "as many poor men" (p. 103) as possible enable? The following survey of money in the Edwardian era offers some help with questions like these.

## Currency

Prior to 1971, the British pound was divided into 20 shillings. Each shilling was worth 12 pence. A price of 3 pounds, 10 shillings, 5 pence might be written £3/10/5 or £3 10s 5d (the d for pence being from the Latin *denarius*). A price of four shillings might be written 4s or 4/-.

## Distribution of Wealth

Edwardian and early Georgian Britain was marked by a staggering concentration of affluence among those at the top of the economic scale and an enormous gap between rich and poor. In a much-read study published in 1905, the Liberal legislator L. G. Chiozza Money calculated that less than 1/30 of the people of the United Kingdom received above 1/3 of the nation's total income (42); recent historiography finds that in 1911–13, the richest 1% owned 69% of the capital—a degree of aggregation probably unmatched in the West of the time and unsurpassed in Britain during the rest of the century

(Thompson 3–4). Further, rising overall prosperity in the Edwardian years failed to translate into gains for the average worker. During the Great Depression, 1873–98, real wages for workers had improved even though profits fell; by contrast, the years 1898–1913 saw real wages remaining static or declining. It was not until 1913 that the average worker's purchasing power had returned to what it had been in 1900 (Havighurst 45).

## Incomes

In 1905, Money (42) provided this overview of the United Kingdom:

- 1,250,000 people in households with an annual income of more than £700
- 3,750,000 people in households with an annual income between £160 and £700
- 38,000,000 people in households with an annual income of less than £160

With £600 and £800 a year, the Schlegel siblings would be among the wealthiest 3% or so of the population. Forster seems to have wanted them to be aware of their privilege but not ostentatiously well off; in successive drafts of *Howards End* he lowered their income from an original £1,200 each for Helen and Margaret and £1,500 for Tibby (Beauman 157).

In early adulthood, Forster lived on the income from two inheritances. His father, who died when he was not yet two, left £7,000 for him and his mother; his aunt Marianne Thornton left him an additional £8,000 on her death in 1887. These together would have brought in about £450 a year if invested conservatively (Beauman 96). In his biography *Marianne Thornton* (1956), Forster notes that the latter legacy enabled him to attend Cambridge, travel, and write.

Forster was always eager to supplement his unearned income with earned. In 1903, he received £12 for teaching a six-lecture course on the Florentine Republic (Beauman 140). In 1914, he became a part-time cataloguer at the National Gallery for £100 a year (Beauman 286). In 1916, he made £4 a month tutoring a Greek businessman in English (*Letters* 234). For his first novel, *Where Angels Fear to Tread*, Forster was offered nothing down; for his fourth, *Howards End*, his advance was £130 (*Selected Letters* 71; Beauman 223). According to Forster himself, the value of his aunt's £8,000 began to decline after World War I, but by that point he was able to support himself by writing: in the wake of the immediate success of 1924's *Passage to India*, he described himself as "famous, wealthy, miserable, physically ugly" (*Marianne Thornton* 289; Beauman 336).

Annual incomes furnish additional insight into Edwardian hierarchies. At the top of the scale in 1911, a highly successful barrister might have made £15,000 or more and a High Court judge £5,000–10,000. The Secretary of State received £5,000, while a Member of Parliament was paid £400—considered adequate only for those legislators who came from the working classes (Havighurst 50).

The architectural historian Stefan Muthesius (44) gives this survey of incomes at the end of the nineteenth century:

- £3,000–£5,000 and higher: knights, peers, judges, merchants, gentlemen
- £1,000–£3,000: leading lawyers, top civil servants, merchants
- £500–£700: lawyers, doctors, top clerks
- £350: higher clerks
- £200: lower clerks, shopkeepers
- £100–150: lowest-paid clerks

Leonard Bast is at the low end of the range for Edwardian clerks. According to John Burnett, "Probably the upper ceiling for very experienced clerks in legal and insurance offices was £500–£600, but the majority rose to no more than £150–£200 . . . : many earned as little as £60 or £80 a year, and though they might dress like a gentleman could scarcely live like one" (185). Indeed, poorer clerks were paid less than some skilled laborers (Thompson 6). According to Helen, her gift of £5,000 would, if accepted, bring Leonard £150 annually—just enough to keep up middle-class appearances and just below the level at which income tax would be collected (£160 a year).

Further down the scale, pay was appalling. According to Jack London in *The People of the Abyss* (1903, excerpted later in Contexts), a telephone girl might, after five years at her job, make £1 a week; the average weekly wage of common laborers other than dockers was 16s and of dockers 8–9s. Women made coats for less than 1s a day and trouser finishers earned 3–4s a week—that is, £7–£17 annually. Nearly 1.3 million Londoners survived on a family income of 21s weekly or less (London 109–11).

## Expenses

Such low wages meant that many workers were just getting by, or not getting by. London calculates that the telephone girl making £1 weekly would require 18s weekly to live, with no margin "for clothes, recreation, or sickness"; on a wage of 11s, the beginner in this line of work would find meeting even basic needs a struggle. Estimating rent, food, coal, and soap for a family of five at roughly 21s weekly, London implies that many of the 1.3 million people mentioned above were doing without basic necessities (110, 108). In *How the Labourer Lives*, Benjamin Seebohm Rowntree and May Kendall calculate that a similar income (£1/0/6) in 1913 would barely support two adults and three children, and this only if the family consumed very little tea and no eggs, butter, or butcher's meat (Wilson 55). Leonard Bast worries about the extravagance of 2s for a concert and must spend a penny for gas to prepare the evening meal; one indignity complained of by poorer Londoners in the period was that coin-operated gas often ran out with the food half-cooked.

In *The People of the Abyss*, London calculates the rent paid by the poor family of five at 6s a week, or about £16 annually. The low-paid clerk making £100–150 a year might have a five- to six-room house outside the city costing £12–30 in annual rent (Muthesius 44); for the same price, a clerk choosing to live in town might get two or three rooms (Burnett 197). The higher clerk making £350 a year might spend £40–60 annually for a seven- to eight-room house and keep one or two servants, while the merchant having £1,000–£3,000 each year might rent a fifteen-room house at £100 a year and keep a butler, two maids, a cook, and a governess (Muthesius 44). When Forster and his mother took a suburban semi-detached house in 1904, they paid £55 annual rent for a drawing room, a dining room, two larger bedrooms, attic bedrooms for two maids, and a small study (Beauman 155).

What did other goods and services cost? At the turn of the century, a set of inexpensive furniture outfitting a prosperous working-class home could be had for about £13 (Burnett 170). In 1898, Forster contemplated adding to his undergraduate possessions a chest of drawers at 15–17s (*Selected Letters* 18). In 1912, he bought a deck chair for his journey to India at either 4s for plain or 11s for reclining (Beauman 251); the same year, he paid £17/10/0 for a portrait of himself by his friend Roger Fry (Furbank 206). In *Howards End*, Dolly complains that accepting Miss Avery's present of an enamel pendant from fashionable Bond Street, price above £5, would have required inviting the giver to Evie's wedding.

When *Howards End* was published, it came out at 6s, a standard price for the first release of a serious novel (Feltes 90); other sorts of books could sell for half that amount. In 1893, the annual fee for the young Forster's day school was £18; in 1899, Forster hired a bicycle in Salisbury for 2s per half day; in 1907, he felt himself to be spending freely in staying at a hotel in the Lake District for 12s daily (Beauman 54; *Selected Letters* 30, 89). The price of 2s is not only what Leonard Bast pays for a good seat at a Beethoven performance but also what an aunt of Forster's paid to see a play in 1897 (*Selected Letters* 16). And in 1919, Forster was given a ticket to a highly exclusive musical performance in which the audience (including countesses and duchesses) "sat upon exquisite gilt chairs"; the price of that ticket was £1/1/0 (*Selected Letters* 305).

# *Early Reviews of* Howards End

Readers have been attracted to many aspects of *Howards End.* Some have admired the dignity and tenderness of the bond between Margaret and Helen or praised Forster's gift for social comedy. Others seem to relish the sheer atmosphere of civilization conjured in the novel—to enjoy inhabiting, for a while, an environment in which artistic, intelligent people take frank delight in art and intelligence. Still others point to Forster's command of surprise (the skillful lead-up to the revelation of Helen's pregnancy, for instance) or his willingness to let characters develop, as real people do, in unanticipated as well as predictable ways. For many, however, what remains most miraculous is Forster's sheer prowess with language—his ability to draw together a hundred textual filaments with a phrase like "the heart of a man ticking fast in his chest" (p. 102) or to convey depths of awkwardness by following "It's an appalling umbrella. It must be mine," from Helen, with the narrator's, "But it was not" (p. 35). The following selections give a good sense of what caught the attention of the novel's first reviewers: its philosophy, its originality, its observational acuity, its emotional truth.

## Anonymous

*An influential weekly, the* Times Literary Supplement *began in 1902 as a section of the* Times, *a national paper, but was published independently starting in 1914. Its reviews were unsigned until 1974.*

**from the *Times Literary Supplement* (27 October 1910)**

Mr. E. M. Forster has now done what critical admirers of his forego-
ing novels have confidently looked for—he has written a book in
which his highly original talent has found full and ripe expression.
Neither of its three clever, imperfect, slightly baffling predecessors
was quite at unity with itself. In each case there was an uncertainty of
attack and a want of harmony in the method which prevented an
exceptionally fine sense of character from making its proper effect.
All this is put right in *Howard's End*. Here Mr. Forster has finally got
his method under control, and has seized his idea in a grasp that completely encircles it; so that the peculiar freshness and individuality of
his gift can now be properly seen and understood. It is in the first
place securely founded, this gift, upon a power of generalization
which holds the tightly-handled plot compactly together. But Mr.
Forster works from the centre outwards, and reaches the graces and
humours of the surface of his story with a mind quite clear as to the
structure beneath. His generalization starts from the everlasting
opposition of the two types which between them hold civilized life
together, the people who are not interested in "personal relations" but
who alone make the world practically habitable for the other type, the
people who are not interested in the thing done but only in the human
beings who do it. The Wilcox family stand for the first, English, honest, unimaginative, exasperating, and the Schlegel family for the second, of mixed blood and restless brains and hampering imaginations,
certainly not less exasperating, the Wilcoxes being those who deal in
realities without understanding them, the Schlegels those understand
realities without dealing in them. The Schlegels, indeed, must do all
the understanding, and the question is whether they can understand
enough for both and so effect an alliance with the Wilcoxes, instead
of standing aside and making fun of them. Margaret Schlegel makes
the attempt and dares a compromise: "More and more," she says, "do
I refuse to draw my income and sneer at those who guarantee it."
Helen, her sister, is *intransigeante*,[1] and faces the disaster to which her
consistency brings her. Mr. Forster seizes the very essence of the
contrast, and again and again pierces his material, with the sharpest
needles, at the exact psychological point. It is another question
whether the actual incidents of the story, apart from the perfect justice
of the psychology, are well invented and disposed; and here we could

[1]French: unwilling to compromise.

make some criticisms. But we are dealing with a very remarkable and original book, and we will not linger over faults which do not touch its central virtue. Nor need more be said of the character drawing than that it has all the light shrewdness we have seen before in this writer's work, with the added clarity of practice. What gives Mr. Forster's writing its quite unique flavour is something more than this. It is the odd charming vein of poetry which slips delicately in and out of his story, showing itself for a moment in the description of a place or a person, and vanishing the instant it has said enough to suggest something rare and romantic and intangible about the person or the place. It is a refinement which belongs to realism, not romance, for it is simply due justice done to an element in life too momentary and swift for most realism, so called, to overtake. But where quick-fingered lightness and deftness are demanded there Mr. Forster never fails; and he has caught in this book a sensitive reflection of life on which he is very heartily to be congratulated.


**Anonymous**

> *Published 1827–1916, the* Standard *was a daily newspaper oriented toward businessmen.*

### from the *Standard* (28 October 1910)

Mr. Forster's work—*Howard's End* is Mr. Forster's fourth novel—occupies a niche entirely by itself in the house of contemporary fiction. It is not like anything else that is being done, and everything that he writes develops his original statement consistently and clearly. The secret of his original statement may be found in the title of his last novel, *The Room with a View*, in the motto to his new story "Only Connect . . . ," and in the name of a delightful short story that he wrote some time ago, *The Celestial Omnibus*. There is a Room—a Room described with minuteness, accuracy, and a remarkable feeling for the salient things in it; but it is "a Room with a View." [. . .] There is an Omnibus, with all its everyday complement of absurd persons, wisps of straw from the stables, and the daily paper in the hands of its passengers; but the Omnibus is Celestial. Most novelists would have us to understand that we reach heaven by getting as far from earth as possible. Mr. Forster's philosophy is that heaven is all about us and the vision of it is granted only to those who will catch up their piece of earth in both their hands and go bravely forward. It is this doctrine of courage and common sense that gives Mr. Forster's book so compelling a fascination, and he has never before vindicated both his message and his method so ably as in his new novel. In its broadest outline the subject of *Howard's End* is the all-pervading influence of Place, and it is curious to note that this has been the subject of several recent novels. But Mr. Forster develops his theme beyond its ordinary range. In his other novels—especially in *The Longest Journey*—the influence of place has been felt, but now it is the faith, the creed, the gospel of the persons of his story. Every one is tested by the walls, the chimneys, the garden of *Howard's End*. Do they see, do they understand, can they connect? The Willcox family has the house in its possession. Mrs. Willcox (the most arresting and subtle character in all Mr. Forster's gallery) does understand and dies, leaving the place to the one person who shares her knowledge. But the Wilcoxes—good, honest, stubborn, blind—cling to their possession, and during the rest of the book we see the house quietly, subtly, actively, setting to work to deliver itself into the hands of its proper possessor. When the book is closed the reader glances apprehensively about him—regards his tables and chairs with alarm, invests the meanest lodging with terribly secret activity.

One can fancy only too easily the way that such a theme would have been treated by other writers. There would be great slabs of scenery, the house would be drawn again and again, every actor in the comedy would have passed sniffing about the garden and exclaiming in emphatic asides that he always felt so odd in that part of the country and he really did not know what was happening to him. Mr. Forster emphasises nothing; he draws the house in several sharp, startling lines, and then leaves it to his readers. He makes no statement, and he flings his characters from place to place, from incident to incident, from life to death, from death to immortality with an apparent indifference. It seems possible, as we read, that anything may happen to any one, and that there are no rules or laws at all—and then, at the end, "Only Connect . . ." Mr. Forster whispers, and everything falls into its place and the ordinary certainty of life is revealed.

There are a great many other things in the book. The characters of Margaret and Helen, Mrs. Willcox, Mr. Willcox, and Leonard, are wonderfully rendered, and there are scenes—the coming of Margaret to Howard's End, Leonard's death, Margaret's motor drive through the country—that are unforgettable. Mr. Forster's humour, too, is quite unlike anyone else's humour, and it is always surprising and unforeseen. With this book he seems to us to have arrived, and, if he never writes another line, his niche should be secure.

## R. A. Scott-James (1878–1959)

*Founded in 1846 with Charles Dickens as editor, the* Daily News, *a Liberal-inflected paper, carried contributions from important progressive-minded literati. The journalist and literary critic R. A. Scott-James promoted a number of key modernist writers during his long career.*

### from the *Daily News* (7 November 1910)

"Only connect . . ." is Mr. Forster's motto. It is because he has taken this motto not only for his book but also for his method of work that he has achieved the most significant novel of the year. Those who seek to express a philosophic view of life in fiction generally strain their characters till they are puppets of their philosophy. Those, on the other hand, who are content to trace individual characters realistically are in danger at all times of losing the scheme and purpose of their work. It is because they do not "connect"; because to write a novel near to nature on the one hand, and true to the larger vision on the other requires tremendous labour of thought making perception and wisdom fruitful; the fitting of the perception of little things with the perception of universal things; consistency, totality, *connection.* Mr. Forster has written a *connected* novel.

Mr. Forster's method is a sort of bridge between that of Mr. Conrad and that of Mr. Galsworthy.[1] The former, I am told, starts the making of a story with an incident which impressed itself on his imagination, and round this primary situation the story is hinged; the latter, starting with a generalization, selects facts which illustrate it. Both methods are legitimate, and the one by Mr. Conrad, the other by Mr. Galsworthy, have been successfully used. But who could say of *Howard's End* that the one method or the other had been adopted?

---

[1]Joseph Conrad (1857–1924), illustrious Polish-born writer of novels in English; John Galsworthy (1867–1933), English novelist and playwright.

The novel rises like a piece of architecture full-grown before us. It is all bricks and timber, but it is mystery, idealism, a far-reaching symbol.

### House and Home

And as it happens Howard's End, from which the title is taken, is itself a house. Though the scene is only occasionally placed in this old house, with its wych-elm, its garden, and its Hertfordshire environment, Howard's End is always the background of the story. It is always there as a soft refrain which comes back and back amid a hundred new situations. This house itself is a sort of symbol of everything in England, old and new, changeless, yet amid flux. It connects in itself two ideas which seem to be sundered as the Poles. First of all it is a *home*. To Mrs. Wilcox, who was born there, it stands for everything personal, intimate, cherished; not merely "bricks and mortar," but a "Holy of Holies into which Howard's End had been transfigured." But in the second place it is property; it is bricks and mortar simply; it is exchangeable for money; it is part of the economic order of things, and has no sacred connection save that which attaches to the "rights of property." For Henry Wilcox, and for Charles, his son, it is no home; it is only a house. "To them Howard's End was a house: they could not know that to her it had been a spirit, for which she sought a spiritual heir."

For Mrs. Wilcox thought she had found a spiritual heir to her home in Margaret Schlegel; and she had indicated her wishes in a little pencil note which the Wilcoxes ignored.

> May they not have decided even better than they supposed? Is it credible that the possessions of the spirit can be bequeathed at all? Has the soul offspring? A wych-elm tree, a vine, a wisp of hay with dew on it—can passion for such things be transmitted where there is no bond of blood? No, the Wilcoxes are not to be blamed. The problem is too terrific, and they could not even perceive a problem.

If Margaret Schlegel stands for the refinement which has survived culture, the personal force which combines intellect, perception, and charm, her sister Helen is more truly the antithesis to the Wilcoxes, or, to be precise, the eldest son Charles Wilcox. Helen is all that which is known as "temperament." With what vivacity Mr. Forster makes her talk, with what high spirits and impulsive generosity she always acts!

She does not see so clearly as Margaret does the danger of the Schlegel life, which is all ideas, enlightenment, and fineness, the danger that it may become "sloppy." For a moment Helen had responded to the lure of the Wilcox energy, the pushful, practical, masterful makers of the world, the people who lived "the outer life of 'telegrams and anger.'" She had responded, in her impulsive, slightly hysterical way, at the touch of a younger Wilcox, but she shrank away again to a set-tled hostility against it; whereas to Margaret this life—the life of "telegrams and anger"—"was to remain a real force. She could not despise it, as Helen and Tibby affected to do. It fostered such virtues as neatness, decision, and obedience, virtues of the second rank, no doubt, but they have formed our civilization. They form character, too; Margaret could not doubt it: they keep the soul from becoming sloppy. How dare Schlegels despise Wilcoxes, when it takes all sorts to make a world?"

### Poetry and the Economic Basis

For Mr. Forster does not let us forget that even Helen Schlegel, with all her indifference to material things, with her recklessness, her generos-ity, her habit of taking not thought, has a secured income of six hun-dred a year. And that is the great difference between her and Mr. Bart, the miserable little clerk, who yearned after the infinite, but was by pressure of poverty and social pretensions compelled to yearn even more after his lost umbrella. Helen is willing to do anything for the squalid Mr. Bart, because he is unfortunate, and because he has ideals. But Margaret is more practical without suffering loss on the finer side.

> The imagination (she says) ought to play upon money and realize it vividly, for it's the—the second most important thing in the world. It is so slurred over and hushed up, there is so lit-tle clear thinking—oh, political economy, of course, but so few of us think clearly about our own private incomes, and admit that independent thoughts are in nine cases out of ten the result of independent means. Money: Give Mr. Bart money, and don't bother about his ideals. He'll pick up those for himself.

Margaret, then, does not give rein to her bias. It is Helen who is the *extreme* of the spiritual life, plunging into it like a gambler, seeing the moment but not seeing whither it leads. And her antithesis is the brutal Charles, who stands equally recklessly on his right of property—on the speed of his motor-cars, the decisiveness of his actions, the effectiveness of his anger and his telegrams. He is all prose, and goes to prison; Helen is all passion, and has a bastard child. But Margaret has her feet at least firmly planted on the earth, and she is able to make a success of marriage with Henry Wilcox.

> Only connect! That was the whole of her sermon. Only connect the prose and the passion, and both will be exalted, and human love will be seen at its height. Live in fragments no longer. Only connect, and the beast and the monk, robbed of the isolation that is life to either, will die.

In thus drawing together one or two of the threads with which the story supplies us, I may seem to have emphasized too much the theoretical or philosophical side of this novel. A philosophical novel it is, but its fineness as philosophy is just that which would have delighted the late William James.[2] At all points it is life itself, experience itself, which is the touchstone and the fabric of Mr. Forster's theory. No cut-and-dried view of life, no summary of society, but a consciousness of the infinitely variable thing that is human nature, obedient to no laws but the laws of personality. If personality dwindles into a piece of mechanism in Charles Wilcox and diffuses itself into a lost aspiration in Mr. Bast, it is even so the product, albeit a wrecked product, of the millions of personal forces that have made England. Each of these persons whom he shows to us is pathetically individual—pathetically, because it is hardly possible to be otherwise when you expose a limited human soul in the naked light of the whole universe; and it is for this reason that Mr. Forster, vainly holding up before us an ethical ideal with hopeful intention, is often depressing to a bewildering extent. Yet the persons are too human to affect us long in this way. Charles is real enough to be hateful. Which of us has not known a Tibby, self-possessed, unbiased in his narrow intellectual freedom, unaware of the world, and scornful of it? Mrs. Munt, the fussy aunt, is an admirable intrusion of comedy. Poor, squalid Mr. Bast, with his drunken "Jacky," his poverty, his democratic gentility, and his one romance in life, is an exquisite piece of diabolical character-drawing. And there is Evie, and Dolly, and the sweet Miss Avery;

---

[2]Hugely influential American psychologist and philosopher (1842–1910), elder brother of the novelist Henry James and the diarist Alice James.

and permeating the book, like Howard's end itself, is the simple, dignified, homely figure of Mrs. Wilcox, whose personality haunts us even as the genius of the house seems to take wings of fancy in Mr. Forster's hands, and put us among fantastic, other-worldly things. "Couldn't you and I camp out in this house for the night?" cries Helen, inflamed with fancies which its owners, who hated her, could never have understood.

> "Because my plans——"
> "——Which you change in a moment."
> "Then because my life is great, and theirs are little," said Helen, taking fire. I know of things they can't know of, and so do you. We *know* that there's poetry. They can only take them on hearsay. We know this is our house, because it feels ours. Oh, they may take the title deeds and the doorkeys, but for this one night we are at home."
> "It would be lovely to have you once more alone," said Margaret. "It may be a chance in a thousand."
> "Yes, and we could talk." She dropped her voice. "It won't be a very glorious story. But under that wych-elm——"

There is life, imagination, and the very flame of action giving quality to this novel over and above the technique with which it is built up and the wisdom with which it is informed.

## Arnold Bennett (1867–1931)

*The New Age, a literary magazine, was an important forum for debates about modernism in the arts and other early twentieth-century issues such as women's suffrage, spiritualism, and Guild socialism (which advocated workers' enjoyment of profits through trade guilds). Arnold Bennett was one of those Virginia Woolf would dismiss as "materialists"—novelists who missed the pith of life because they were caught up with descriptions of trivial things—in her 1919 essay "Modern Fiction." Bennett's suggestion that* Howards End *is too careful to stand as "first-class literature" needs to be weighed against his own reputation for writing with sales in mind; his novel* Clayhanger, *also 1910, was preferred by some readers.*

## from *The New Age* (12 January 1911)

Now I am in a position to state that no novel for very many years has been so discussed by the *élite* as Mr. Forster's *Howard's End*. The ordinary library reader knows that it has been a very considerable popular success; persons of genuine taste know that it is a very considerable literary achievement; but its triumph is that it has been mightily argued about during the repasts of the *élite*. I need scarcely say that it is not Mr. Forster's best book; no author's best book is ever the best received—this is a rule practically without exception. A more curious point about it is that it contains a lot of very straight criticism of the *élite*, or at any rate of the first census of the *élite*. And yet this point is not very curious either. For the *élite* have no objection whatever to being criticised. They rather like it, as the alligator likes being tickled with peas out of a pea-shooter. Their hides are superbly impenetrable. And I know not which to admire the more, the American's sensitiveness to pea-shooting, or the truly correct Englishman's indestructible indifference to it. Mr. Forster is a young man. I believe he is still under thirty, if not under twenty-nine. If he continues to write one book a year regularly, to be discreet and mysterious, to refrain absolutely from certain themes, and to avoid a too marked tendency to humour, he will be the most fashionable novelist in England in ten years time. His worldly prospects are very brilliant indeed. If, on the other hand, he writes solely to please himself, forgetting utterly the existence of the *élite*, he may produce some first-class literature. The responsibilities lying upon him at this crisis of his career are terrific. And he so young too!

# Leonard's Reading

Leonard Bast wants to better himself through his reading in two senses. Seeking food for his imagination and his intellect, he also hopes that absorbing the right books will make him a person of culture and taste. The cruel truth that Forster illuminates is that knowing which books are the right ones is almost impossible unless one is part of a social set that credibly decides which books fit the bill. As Londoners in the vanguard or near-vanguard of intellectual life, the Schlegels would have found Leonard's reading a thoroughly mixed bag: none of it was cutting-edge in the first years of the twentieth century, but whereas George Meredith and Henrik Ibsen could be respected for their artistry and their questioning of social conventions, the best-selling Marie Corelli would have been abominated. Excerpted here are four books that, revered by Leonard, offer a window into his convictions and desires.

## John Ruskin (1819–1900)

*No art historian has ever commanded a broader audience than John Ruskin. One of the most famous British authors of the nineteenth century and an inspiration to workers' movements in the twentieth, he produced nearly forty volumes of criticism in which he introduced leading painters, fueled a Gothic revival in architecture, denounced capitalist greed, and lamented the ecological devastation wrought by industry. In "The Nature of Gothic," the most famous section of* The Stones of Venice, *he proposes that the moral character of a society can be discerned from its artistic culture. Leonard is reading another section, on the religious architecture of Torcello (like Murano, an island in the Venetian Lagoon).*

from *The Stones of Venice* (1851–1853)

## Chapter II.

### Torcello

§ I. Seven miles to the north of Venice, the banks of sand, which near the city rise little above low-water mark, attain by degrees a higher level, and knit themselves at last into fields of salt morass, raised here and there into shapeless mounds, and intercepted by narrow creeks of sea. One of the feeblest of these inlets, after winding for some time among buried fragments of masonry, and knots of sunburnt weeds whitened with webs of fucus,[1] stays itself in an utterly stagnant pool beside a plot of greener grass covered with ground ivy and violets. On this mound is built a rude brick campanile,[2] of the commonest Lombardic type, which if we ascend towards evening (and there are none to hinder us, the door of its ruinous staircase swinging idly on its hinges), we may command from it one of the most notable scenes in this wide world of ours. Far as the eye can reach, a waste of wild sea moor, of a lurid ashen grey; not like our northern moors with their jet-black pools and purple heath, but lifeless, the color of sackcloth, with the corrupted sea-water soaking through the roots of its acrid weeds, and gleaming hither and thither through its snaky channels. No gathering of fantastic mists, nor coursing of clouds across it; but melancholy clearness of space in the warm sunset, oppressive, reaching to the horizon of its level gloom. To the very horizon, on the north-east; but, to the north and west, there is a blue line of higher land along the border of it, and above this, but farther back, a misty band of mountains, touched with snow. To the east, the paleness and roar of the Adriatic, louder at momentary intervals as the surf breaks on the bars of sand; to the south, the widening branches of the calm lagoon, alternately purple and pale green, as they reflect the evening clouds or twilight sky; and almost beneath our feet, on the same field which sustains the tower we gaze from, a group of four buildings, two of them little larger than cottages (though built of stone, and one adorned by a quaint belfry), the third an octagonal chapel, of which we can see but little more than the flat red roof with its rayed tiling, the fourth, a considerable church with nave and aisles, but of which, in like manner, we can see little but the long central ridge and lateral

[1]Seaweed.
[2]Bell-tower.

slopes of roof, which the sunlight separates in one glowing mass from the green field beneath and grey moor beyond. There are no living creatures near the buildings, nor any vestige of village or city round about them. They lie like a little company of ships becalmed on a far-away sea.

§ II. Then look farther to the south. Beyond the widening branches of the lagoon, and rising out of the bright lake into which they gather, there are a multitude of towers, dark, and scattered among square-set shapes of clustered palaces, a long and irregular line fretting the southern sky.

Mother and daughter, you behold them both in their widow-hood,—TORCELLO and VENICE.

Thirteen hundred years ago, the grey moorland looked as it does this day, and the purple mountains stood as radiantly in the deep distances of evening; but on the line of the horizon, there were strange fires mixed with the light of sunset, and the lament of many human voices mixed with the fretting of the waves on their ridges of sand. The flames rose from the ruins of Altinum,[3] the lament from the multitude of its people, seeking, like Israel of old, a refuge from the sword in the paths of the sea.

The cattle are feeding and resting upon the site of the city that they left; the mower's scythe swept this day at dawn over the chief street of the city that they built, and the swathes of soft grass are now sending up their scent into the night air, the only incense that fills the temple of their ancient worship. Let us go down into that little space of meadow land.

§ III. The inlet which runs nearest to the base of the campanile is not that by which Torcello is commonly approached. Another, somewhat broader, and overhung by alder copse, winds out of the main channel of the lagoon up to the very edge of the little meadow which was once the Piazza of the city, and there, stayed by a few grey stones which present some semblance of a quay, forms its boundary at one extremity. Hardly larger than an ordinary English farmyard, and roughly enclosed on each side by broken palings and hedges of honeysuckle and briar, the narrow field retires from the water's edge, traversed by a scarcely traceable footpath, for some forty or fifty paces, and then expanding into the form of a small square, with buildings on three sides of it, the fourth being that which opens to the water. Two of these, that on our left and that in front of us as we

---

[3]Town destroyed by Attila, leader of the Huns, in 452. Its inhabitants fled to Torcello and other islands in the Venetian Lagoon.

approach from the canal, are so small that they might well be taken for the out-houses of the farm, though the first is a conventual building, and the other aspires to the title of the "Palazzo publico,"[4] both dating as far back as the beginning of the fourteenth century; the third, the octagonal church of Santa Fosca, is far more ancient than either, yet hardly on a larger scale. Though the pillars of the portico which surrounds it are of pure Greek marble, and their capitals are enriched with delicate sculpture, they, and the arches they sustain, together only raise the roof to the height of a cattle-shed; and the first strong impression which the spectator receives from the whole scene is, that whatever sin it may have been which has on this spot been visited with so utter a desolation, it could not at least have been ambition. Nor will this impression be diminished as we approach, or enter, the larger church to which the whole group of building is subordinate. It has evidently been built by men in flight and distress, who sought in the hurried erection of their island church such a shelter for their earnest and sorrowful worship as, on the one hand, could not attract the eyes of their enemies by its splendor, and yet, on the other, might not awaken too bitter feelings by its contrast with the churches which they had seen destroyed. There is visible everywhere a simple and tender effort to recover some of the form of the temples which they had loved, and to do honor to God by that which they were erecting, while distress and humiliation prevented the desire, and prudence precluded the admission, either of luxury of ornament or magnificence of plan. [. . .]

§ VIII. Let us consider a little each of these characters in succession; and first (for of the shafts enough has been said already), what is very peculiar to this church, its luminousness. This perhaps strikes the traveller more from its contrast with the excessive gloom of the Church of St. Mark's;[5] but it is remarkable when we compare the Cathedral of Torcello with any of the contemporary basilicas in South Italy or Lombardic churches in the North. St. Ambrogio at Milan, St. Michele at Pavia, St. Zeno at Verona, St. Frediano at Lucca, St. Miniato at Florence, are all like sepulchral caverns compared with Torcello, where the slightest details of the sculptures and mosaics are visible, even when twilight is deepening. And there is something especially touching in our finding the sunshine thus

[4]Italian: public building, town hall. (Actually "Palazzo Pubblico.")

[5]The cathedral of Venice, one of the most famous churches in the world and the subject of analysis by Ruskin and scores of other critics.

freely admitted into a church built by men in sorrow. They did not need the darkness; they could not perhaps bear it. There was fear and depression upon them enough, without a material gloom. They sought for comfort in their religion, for tangible hopes and promises, not for threatenings or mysteries; and though the subjects chosen for the mosaics on the walls are of the most solemn character, there are no artificial shadows cast upon them, nor dark colors used in them: all is fair and bright, and intended evidently to be regarded in hopefulness, and not with terror.

## George Meredith (1828–1909)

*His most celebrated work of poetry, "Modern Love," is quoted in* Howards End *(p. 254), but George Meredith was yet more famous for fictions whose mix of irony and sincerity left some readers bewildered and others exhilarated. In 1910, he remained a touchstone of the art, one reviewer praising* Howards End *as reminiscent of his work (if not quite as flawless); by 1927, however, Forster could declare that Meredith was "not the great name he was twenty or thirty years ago, when much of the universe and all Cambridge trembled" (*Aspects of the Novel *62). The following section of* The Ordeal of Richard Feverel, *which resonates with Leonard's own tale of walking at night, comes very late in the novel. Traveling in the German Rhineland, Feverel has learned that his wife, back in England, is to have their child. The bearer of the news is his father, Sir Austin; Lady Judith is Richard's married traveling companion; Clare is a recently deceased cousin.*

### from *The Ordeal of Richard Feverel* (1859)

Hence, fantastic vapours! What are ye to this? Where are the dreams of the Hero when he learns that he has a child? Nature is taking him to her bosom. She will speak presently. Every domesticated boor in these hills can boast the same, yet marvels the Hero at none of his visioned prodigies as he does when he comes to hear of this most common performance. A father? Richard fixed his eyes as if he were trying to make out the lineaments of his child.

Telling Austin he would be back in a few minutes, he sallied into the air, and walked on and on. "A father!" he kept repeating to himself: "a child!" And though he knew it not, he was striking the key-notes of Nature. But he did know of a singular harmony that suddenly burst over his whole being.

The moon was surpassingly bright: the summer air heavy and still. He left the highroad and pierced into the forest. His walk was rapid: the leaves on the trees brushed his cheeks; the dead leaves heaped in the dells noised to his feet. Something of a religious joy—a strange sacred pleasure—was in him. By degrees it wore: he remembered himself: and now he was possessed by a proportionate anguish. A father! he dared never see his child. And he had no longer his phantasies to fall upon. He was utterly bare to his sin. In his troubled mind it seemed to him that Clare looked down on him—Clare who saw him as he was—and that to her eyes it would be infamy for him to go and print his kiss upon his child. Then came stern efforts to command his misery and make the nerves of his face iron.

By the log of an ancient tree half-buried in dead leaves of past summers, beside a brook, he halted as one who has reached his journey's end. There he discovered he had a companion in Lady Judith's little dog. He gave the friendly animal a pat of recognition, and both were silent in the forest-silence.

It was impossible for Richard to return; his heart was surcharged. He must advance, and on he footed, the little dog following.

An oppressive slumber hung about the forest-branches. In the dells and on the heights was the same dead heat. Here where the brook tinkled it was no cool-lipped sound, but metallic, and without the spirit of water. Yonder in a space of moonlight on lush grass, the beams were as white fire to sight and feeling. No haze spread around. The valleys were clear, defined to the shadows of their verges; the distances sharply distinct; and with the colours of day but slightly softened. Richard beheld a roe moving across a slope of sward far out of rifle-mark. The breathless silence was significant, yet the moon shone in a broad blue Heaven. Tongue out of mouth trotted the little dog after him; couched panting when he stopped an instant; rose wea-riedly when he started afresh. Now and then a large white night-moth flitted through the dusk of the forest.

On a barren corner of the wooded highland looking inland stood grey topless ruins set in nettles and rank grass-blades. Richard mechanically sat down on the crumbling flints to rest, and listened to the panting of the dog. Sprinkled at his feet were emerald lights: hundreds of glow-worms studded the dark dry ground.

He sat and eyed them, thinking not at all. His energies were expended in action. He sat as a part of the ruins, and the moon turned his shadow westward from the South. Overhead, as she declined, long ripples of silver cloud were imperceptibly stealing towards her. They were the van of a tempest. He did not observe them, or the leaves beginning to chatter. When he again pursued his course with his face set to the Rhine, a huge mountain appeared to rise sheer over him, and he had it in his mind to scale it. He got no nearer to the base of it for all his vigorous outstepping. The ground began to dip; he lost sight of the sky. Then heavy thunder-drops struck his cheek, the leaves were singing, the earth breathed, it was black before him and behind. All at once the thunder spoke. The mountain he had marked was bursting over him.

Up started the whole forest in violet fire. He saw the country at the foot of the hills to the bounding Rhine gleam, quiver, extinguished. Then there were pauses; and the lightning seemed as the eye of Heaven, and the thunder as the tongue of Heaven, each alternately addressing him; filling him with awful rapture. Alone there—sole human creature among the grandeurs and mysteries of storm—he felt the representative of his kind, and his spirit rose, and marched, and exulted, let it be glory, let it be ruin! Lower down the lightened abysses of air rolled the wrathful crash: then white thrusts of light were darted from the sky, and great curving ferns, seen steadfast in pallor a second, were supernaturally agitated and vanished. Then a shrill song roused in the leaves and the herbage. Prolonged and louder it sounded, as deeper and heavier the deluge pressed. A mighty force of water satisfied the desire of the earth. Even in this, drenched as he was by the first outpouring, Richard had a savage pleasure. Keeping in motion, he was scarcely conscious of the wet, and the grateful breath of the weeds was refreshing. Suddenly he stopped short, lifting a curious nostril. He fancied he smelt meadow-sweet. He had never seen the flower in Rhineland—never thought of it; and it would hardly be met with in a forest. He was sure he smelt it fresh in dews. His little companion wagged a miserable wet tail some way in advance. He went on slowly, thinking indistinctly. After two or three steps he stooped and stretched out his hand to feel for the flower, having, he knew not why, a strong wish to verify its growth there. Groping about, his hand encountered something warm that started at his touch, and he, with the instinct we have, seized it, and lifted it to look at it. The creature was very small, evidently quite young. Richard's eyes, now accustomed to the darkness, were able to discern it for what it was, a tiny leveret, and he supposed that the dog had probably frightened its dam just before he found it. He put the little thing on one hand in his breast, and stepped out rapidly as before.

The rain was now steady; from every tree a fountain poured. So cool and easy had his mind become that he was speculating on what kind of shelter the birds could find, and how the butterflies and moths saved their coloured wings from washing. Folded close they might hang under a leaf, he thought. Lovingly he looked into the dripping darkness of the coverts on each side, as one of their children. Then he was musing on a strange sensation he experienced. It ran up one arm with an indescribable thrill, but communicated nothing to his heart. It was purely physical, ceased for a time, and recommenced, till he had it all through his blood, wonderfully thrilling. He grew aware that the little thing he carried in his breast was licking his hand there. The small rough tongue going over and over the palm of his hand produced this strange sensation he felt. Now that he knew the cause, the marvel ended; but now that he knew the cause, his heart was touched and made more of it. The gentle scraping continued without intermission as on he walked. What did it say to him? Human tongue could not have said so much just then.

A pale grey light on the skirts of the flying tempest displayed the dawn. Richard was walking hurriedly. The green drenched weeds lay all about in his path, bent thick, and the forest drooped glimmeringly. Impelled as a man who feels a revelation mounting obscurely to his brain, Richard was passing one of those little forest-chapels, hung with votive wreaths, where the peasant halts to kneel and pray. Cold, still, in the twilight it stood, rain-drops pattering round it. He looked within, and saw the Virgin holding her Child. He moved by. But not many steps had he gone ere his strength went out of him, and he shuddered. What was it? He asked not. He was in other hands. Vivid as lightning the Spirit of Life illumined him. He felt in his heart the cry of his child, his darling's touch. With shut eyes he saw them both. They drew him from the depths; they led him a blind and tottering man. And as they led him he had a sense of purification so sweet he shuddered again and again.

When he looked out from his trance on the breathing world, the small birds hopped and chirped; warm fresh sunlight was over all the hills. He was on the edge of the forest, entering a plain clothed with ripe corn under a spacious morning sky.

## Robert Louis Stevenson (1850–1894)

*The popular author of novels such as* Treasure Island *(1883) and* The Strange Case of Dr. Jekyll and Mr. Hyde *(1886), Robert Louis Stevenson also published nonfiction, including the essay collection excerpted here,* Virginibus Puerisque and Other Papers *(1881). When Leonard says, "I felt like R. L. S. You probably remember how in 'Virginibus—'" (p. 97), he is likely thinking of "Walking Tours," but the title piece (Latin: "For Girls and Boys") also comments on Leonard's situation in pondering the hard realities of married life. Both articles were originally published in 1876, but the text given here comes from the 1881 collection.*

## Virginibus Puerisque (1881)

[. . .] The fact is, we are much more afraid of life than our ancestors, and cannot find it in our hearts either to marry or not to marry. Marriage is terrifying, but so is a cold and forlorn old age. The friendships of men are vastly agreeable, but they are insecure. You know all the time that one friend will marry and put you to the door; a second accept a situation in China, and become no more to you than a name, a reminiscence, and an occasional crossed letter, very laborious to read; a third will take up with some religious crotchet[1] and treat you to sour looks thenceforward. So, in one way or another, life forces men apart and breaks up the goodly fellowships forever. The very flexibility and ease which make men's friendships so agreeable while they endure, make them the easier to destroy and forget. And a man who has a few friends, or one who has a dozen (if there be anyone so wealthy on this earth), cannot forget on how precarious a base his happiness reposes; and how by a stroke or two of fate—a death, a few light words, a piece of stamped paper, a woman's bright eyes—he may be left, in a month, destitute of all. Marriage is certainly a perilous remedy. Instead of on two or three, you stake your happiness on one life only. But still, as the bargain is more explicit and complete on your part, it is more so on the other; and you have not to fear so many contingencies; it is not every wind that can blow you from your anchorage; and so long as Death withholds his sickle, you will always have a friend at home. People who share a cell in the Bastile,[2] or are thrown together on an uninhabited isle, if they do not immediately

---

[1] Peculiar idea.

[2] La Bastille, famous prison in Paris whose storming on 14 July 1789 launched the French Revolution.

fall to fisticuffs, will find some possible ground of compromise. They will learn each other's ways and humours, so as to know where they must go warily, and where they may lean their whole weight. The discretion of the first years becomes the settled habit of the last; and so, with wisdom and patience, two lives may grow indissolubly into one.

But marriage, if comfortable, is not at all heroic. It certainly narrows and damps the spirits of generous men. In marriage, a man becomes slack and selfish, and undergoes a fatty degeneration of his moral being. It is not only when Lydgate misallies himself with Rosamond Vincy, but when Ladislaw marries above him with Dorothea, that this may be exemplified.[3] The air of the fireside withers out all the fine wildings of the husband's heart. He is so comfortable and happy that he begins to prefer comfort and happiness to everything else on earth, his wife included. Yesterday he would have shared his last shilling; to-day "his first duty is to his family," and is fulfilled in large measure by laying down vintages and husbanding the health of an invaluable parent. Twenty years ago this man was equally capable of crime or heroism; now he is fit for neither. His soul is asleep, and you may speak without constraint; you will not wake him. It is not for nothing that Don Quixote was a bachelor and Marcus Aurelius[4] married ill. For women, there is less of this danger. Marriage is of so much use to a woman, opens out to her so much more of life, and puts her in the way of so much more freedom and usefulness, that, whether she marry ill or well, she can hardly miss some benefit. It is true, however, that some of the merriest and most genuine of women are old maids, and wives who are unhappily married, have often most of the true motherly touch. And this would seem to show, even for women, some narrowing influence in comfortable married life. But the rule is none the less certain: if you wish the pick of men and women, take a good bachelor and a good wife.

I am often filled with wonder that so many marriages are passably successful, and so few come to open failure, the more so as I fail to understand the principle on which people regulate their choice. I see women marrying indiscriminately with staring burgesses[5] and ferret-faced, white-eyed boys, and men dwell in contentment with noisy

---

[3]Four characters from George Eliot's *Middlemarch* (1871).

[4]Roman emperor and Stoic philosopher (121–80) who, like Cervantes' Don Quixote (1605), was associated with high ideals. Faustina the Younger, the wife of Marcus Aurelius, was accused of heinous crimes by some Roman commentators (as imperial spouses often were), but the marriage was reportedly happy.

[5]Town officials; here indicating respectable older citizens.

scullions,[6] or taking into their lives acidulous vestals.[7] It is a common answer to say the good people marry because they fall in love; and of course you may use and misuse a word as much as you please, if you have the world along with you. But love is at least a somewhat hyperbolical expression for such lukewarm preference. It is not here, anyway, that Love employs his golden shafts; he cannot be said, with any fitness of language, to reign here and revel. Indeed, if this be love at all, it is plain the poets have been fooling with mankind since the foundation of the world. And you have only to look these happy couples in the face, to see they have never been in love, or in hate, or in any other high passion, all their days. When you see a dish of fruit at dessert, you sometimes set your affections upon one particular peach or nectarine, watch it with some anxiety as it comes round the table, and feel quite a sensible disappointment when it is taken by some one else. I have used the phrase "high passion." Well, I should say this was about as high a passion as generally leads to marriage. [. . .]

## Walking Tours (1881)

[. . .] Now, to be properly enjoyed, a walking tour should be gone upon alone. If you go in a company, or even in pairs, it is no longer a walking tour in anything but name; it is something else and more in the nature of a picnic. A walking tour should be gone upon alone, because freedom is of the essence; because you should be able to stop and go on, and follow this way or that, as the freak takes you; and because you must have your own pace, and neither trot alongside a champion walker, nor mince in time with a girl. And then you must be open to all impressions and let your thoughts take colour from what you see. You should be as a pipe for any wind to play upon. "I cannot see the wit," says Hazlitt, "of walking and talking at the same time. When I am in the country I wish to vegetate like the country,"[1]— which is the gist of all that can be said upon the matter. There should be no cackle of voices at your elbow, to jar on the meditative silence of the morning. And so long as a man is reasoning he cannot surrender himself to that fine intoxication that comes of much motion in the

---

[6]Menial servants.

[7]Sour virgins.

---

[1]From "On Going on a Journey" (1822), by William Hazlitt.

open air, that begins in a sort of dazzle and sluggishness of the brain, and ends in a peace that passes comprehension. [. . .]

In the course of a day's walk, you see, there is much variance in the mood. From the exhilaration of the start, to the happy phlegm of the arrival, the change is certainly great. As the day goes on, the traveller moves from the one extreme towards the other. He becomes more and more incorporated with the material landscape, and the open-air drunkenness grows upon him with great strides, until he posts along the road, and sees everything about him, as in a cheerful dream. The first is certainly brighter, but the second stage is the more peaceful. A man does not make so many articles towards the end, nor does he laugh aloud; but the purely animal pleasures, the sense of physical wellbeing, the delight of every inhalation, of every time the muscles tighten down the thigh, console him for the absence of the others, and bring him to his destination still content.

Nor must I forget to say a word on bivouacs. You come to a milestone on a hill, or some place where deep ways meet under trees; and off goes the knapsack, and down you sit to smoke a pipe in the shade. You sink into yourself, and the birds come round and look at you; and your smoke dissipates upon the afternoon under the blue dome of heaven; and the sun lies warm upon your feet, and the cool air visits your neck and turns aside your open shirt. If you are not happy, you must have an evil conscience. You may dally as long as you like by the roadside. It is almost as if the millennium[2] were arrived, when we shall throw our clocks and watches over the housetop, and remember time and seasons no more. Not to keep hours for a lifetime is, I was going to say, to live for ever. You have no idea, unless you have tried it, how endlessly long is a summer's day, that you measure out only by hunger, and bring to an end only when you are drowsy. I know a village where there are hardly any clocks, where no one knows more of the days of the week than by a sort of instinct for the fête on Sundays, and where only one person can tell you the day of the month, and she is generally wrong; and if people were aware how slow Time journeyed in that village, and what armfuls of spare hours he gives, over and above the bargain, to its wise inhabitants, I believe there would be a stampede out of London, Liverpool, Paris, and a variety of large towns, where the clocks lose their heads, and shake the hours out each one faster than the other, as though they were all in a wager. And all these foolish pilgrims would each bring his own misery along with

[2]Radical transformation of the world.

him, in a watch-pocket! It is to be noticed, there were no clocks and watches in the much-vaunted days before the flood.[3] It follows, of course, there were no appointments, and punctuality was not yet thought upon. "Though ye take from a covetous man all his treasure," says Milton, "he has yet one jewel left; ye cannot deprive him of his covetousness."[4] And so I would say of a modern man of business, you may do what you will for him, put him in Eden, give him the elixir of life—he has still a flaw at heart, he still has his business habits. Now, there is no time when business habits are more mitigated than on a walking tour. And so, during these halts, as I say, you will feel almost free. [. . .]

## Richard Jefferies (1848–1887)

*Richard Jefferies, a journalist and novelist, was best known for his depictions of agricultural life and the English countryside. Many of his writings could be the "something of Richard Jefferies" (p. 98) inspiring Leonard's night walk, but the first chapter of his widely loved autobiography, excerpted here, seems an especially strong contender by virtue of its testimony to the need to be not "always in one place."*

## from *The Story of My Heart* (1883)

### Chapter 1

The story of my heart commences seventeen years ago. In the glow of youth there were times every now and then when I felt the necessity of a strong inspiration of soul-thought. My heart was dusty, parched for want of the rain of deep feeling; my mind arid and dry, for there is a dust which settles on the heart as well as that which falls on a ledge. It is injurious to the mind as well as to the body to be always in one place and always surrounded by the same circumstances. A species of thick clothing slowly grows about the mind, the pores are choked, little habits become a part of existence, and by degrees the mind is

---

[3]Survived by those on Noah's ark (Genesis 6–8).
[4]From *Areopagetica* (1644), by John Milton. (The original has "bereave" instead of "deprive.")

inclosed in a husk. When this began to form I felt eager to escape from it, to throw it off like heavy clothing, to drink deeply once more at the fresh fountains of life. An inspiration—a long deep breath of the pure air of thought—could alone give health to the heart.

There was a hill to which I used to resort at such periods. The labour of walking three miles to it, all the while gradually ascending, seemed to clear my blood of the heaviness accumulated at home. On a warm summer day the slow continued rise required continual effort, which carried away the sense of oppression. The familiar everyday scene was soon out of sight; I came to other trees, meadows, and fields; I began to breathe a new air and to have a fresher aspiration. I restrained my soul till I reached the sward of the hill; psyche, the soul that longed to be loose. I would write psyche always instead of soul to avoid meanings which have become attached to the word soul, but it is awkward to do so. Clumsy indeed are all words the moment the wooden stage of commonplace life is left. I restrained psyche, my soul, till I reached and put my foot on the grass at the beginning of the green hill itself.

Moving up the sweet short turf, at every step my heart seemed to obtain a wider horizon of feeling; with every inhalation of rich pure air, a deeper desire. The very light of the sun was whiter and more brilliant here. By the time I had reached the summit I had entirely forgotten the petty circumstances and the annoyances of existence. I felt myself, myself. There was an intrenchment on the summit, and going down into the fosse[1] I walked round it slowly to recover breath. On the south-western side there was a spot where the outer bank had partially slipped, leaving a gap. There the view was over a broad plain, beautiful with wheat, and inclosed by a perfect amphitheatre of green hills. Through these hills there was one narrow groove, or pass, southwards, where the white clouds seemed to close in the horizon. Woods hid the scattered hamlets and farmhouses, so that I was quite alone.

I was utterly alone with the sun and the earth. Lying down on the grass, I spoke in my soul to the earth, the sun, the air, and the distant sea far beyond sight. I thought of the earth's firmness—I felt it bear me up; through the grassy couch there came an influence as if I could feel the great earth speaking to me. I thought of the wandering air— its pureness, which is its beauty; the air touched me and gave me something of itself. I spoke to the sea: though so far, in my mind I saw

---

[1]Ditch or pit.

it, green at the rim of the earth and blue in deeper ocean; I desired to have its strength, its mystery and glory. Then I addressed the sun, desiring the soul equivalent of his light and brilliance, his endurance and unwearied race. I turned to the blue heaven over, gazing into its depth, inhaling its exquisite colour and sweetness. The rich blue of the unattainable flower of the sky drew my soul towards it, and there it rested, for pure colour is rest of heart. By all these I prayed; I felt an emotion of the soul beyond all definition; prayer is a puny thing to it, and the word is a rude sign to the feeling, but I know no other.

By the blue heaven, by the rolling sun bursting through untrodden space, a new ocean of ether every day unveiled. By the fresh and wandering air encompassing the world; by the sea sounding on the shore—the green sea white-flecked at the margin and the deep ocean; by the strong earth under me. Then, returning, I prayed by the sweet thyme, whose little flowers I touched with my hand; by the slender grass; by the crumble of dry chalky earth I took up and let fall through my fingers. Touching the crumble of earth, the blade of grass, the thyme flower, breathing the earth-encircling air, thinking of the sea and the sky, holding out my hand for the sunbeams to touch it, prone on the sward[2] in token of deep reverence, thus I prayed that I might touch to the unutterable existence infinitely higher than deity.

With all the intensity of feeling which exalted me, all the intense communion I held with the earth, the sun and sky, the stars hidden by the light, with the ocean—in no manner can the thrilling depth of these feelings be written—with these I prayed, as if they were the keys of an instrument, of an organ, with which I swelled forth the notes of my soul, redoubling my own voice by their power. The great sun burning with light; the strong earth, dear earth; the warm sky; the pure air; the thought of ocean; the inexpressible beauty of all filled me with a rapture, an ecstasy, an inflatus.[3] With this inflatus, too, I prayed. Next to myself I came and recalled myself, my bodily existence. I held out my hand, the sunlight gleamed on the skin and the iridescent nails; I recalled the mystery and beauty of the flesh. I thought of the mind with which I could see the ocean sixty miles distant, and gather to myself its glory. I thought of my inner existence, that consciousness which is called the soul. These, that is, myself—I threw into the balance to weigh the prayer the heavier. My strength of body, mind and soul, I flung into it; I put forth my strength; I wrestled

[2]Grassy area.
[3]Inspiration.

and laboured, and toiled in might of prayer. The prayer, this soul-emotion was in itself—not for an object—it was a passion. I hid my face in the grass, I was wholly prostrated, I lost myself in the wrestle, I was rapt and carried away.

Becoming calmer, I returned to myself and thought, reclining in rapt thought, full of aspiration, steeped to the lips of my soul in desire. I did not then define, or analyse, or understand this. I see now that what I laboured for was soul-life, more soul-nature, to be exalted, to be full of soul-learning. Finally I rose, walked half a mile or so along the summit of the hill eastwards, to soothe myself and come to the common ways of life again. Had any shepherd accidentally seen me lying on the turf, he would only have thought that I was resting a few minutes; I made no outward show. Who could have imagined the whirlwind of passion that was going on within me as I reclined there! I was greatly exhausted when I reached home. [. . .]

# The Condition of England

The Edwardians were highly conscious of living in a time of transition. New technologies were beginning to alter daily experience; newly formidable competitors and unsettling international events were raising doubts about how long Britain could maintain its commercial and political supremacy. Meanwhile, social investigators such as Charles Booth, L. G. Chiozza Money, and Benjamin Seebohm Rowntree were raising awareness of the miserable conditions of the least fortunate and of gross inequalities in the distribution of wealth. Some of the texts excerpted here provide empirical findings on the state of Britain; all of them, like *Howards End*, ask what kinds of people and what sets of values ought to shape Britain's destiny in the years to come.

## Edward Carpenter (1844–1929)

*Edward Carpenter influenced Forster both personally and through his books. Veering wide of social norms by living with a male romantic partner, Carpenter provided a vivid counterweight to the homophobia Forster partly internalized; writing in support of a range of views outside the Victorian-Edwardian mainstream, he prompted readers to reconsider topics such as homosexuality, socialism, vegetarianism, pacifism, and simple living. Excerpted from the characteristic title essay of* Civilisation: Its Cause and Cure *are the beginning and two passages falling near the close. Both speak to the feeling for the earth that suffuses* Howards End.

## from *Civilisation: Its Cause and Cure* (1889)

We find ourselves to-day in the midst of a somewhat peculiar state of society, which we call Civilisation, but which even to the most optimistic among us does not seem altogether desirable. Some of us, indeed, are inclined to think that it is a kind of disease which the various races of man have to pass through—as children pass through measles or whooping cough; but if it is a disease, there is this serious consideration to be made, that while History tells us of many nations that have been attacked by it, of many that have succumbed to it, and of some that are still in the throes of it, we know of no single case in which a nation has fairly recovered from and passed through it to a more normal and healthy condition. In other words the development of human society has never yet (that we know of) passed beyond a certain definite and apparently final stage in the process we call Civilisation; at that stage it has always succumbed or been arrested.

Of course it may at first sound extravagant to use the word disease in connection with Civilisation at all, but a little thought should show that the association is not ill-grounded. To take the matter on its physical side first, I find that in Mullhall's Dictionary of Statistics the number of accredited doctors and surgeons in the United Kingdom is put at over 23,000. If the extent of the nation sickness is such that we require 23,000 medical men to attend to us, it must surely be rather serious! And *they* do not cure us. Wherever we look to-day, in mansion or in slum, we see the features and hear the complaints of ill-health; the difficulty is really to find a healthy person. The state of the modern civilised man in this respect—our coughs, colds, mufflers, dread of a waft of chill air, &c.—is anything but creditable, and it seems to be the fact that, notwithstanding all our libraries of medical science, our knowledges, arts, and appliances of life, we are actually less capable of taking care of ourselves than the animals are. Indeed, talking of animals, we are—as Shelley I think points out—fast depraving the *domestic* breeds.[1] The cow, the horse, the sheep, and even the confiding pussy-cat, are becoming ever more and more subject to disease, and are liable to ills which in their wilder state they knew not of. And finally the savage races of the earth do not escape the baneful influence. Wherever Civilisation touches them, they die like flies from the small-pox, drink, and worse evils it brings along with it; and often its mere contact is sufficient to destroy whole races.

---

[1]"A Vindication of Natural Diet" (1813), by the Romantic poet and essayist Percy Bysshe Shelley.

But the word Disease is applicable to our social as well as to our physical condition. For as in the body disease arises from the loss of the physical unity which constitutes Health, and so takes the form of warfare or discord between the various parts, or of the abnormal development of individual organs, or the consumption of the system by predatory germs and growths; so in our modern life we find the unity gone which constitutes true society, and in its place warfare of classes and individuals, abnormal development of some to the detriment of others, and consumption of the organism by masses of social parasites. If the word disease is applicable anywhere, I should say it is—both in its direct and its derived sense—to the civilised societies of to-day.

Again, mentally, is not our condition anything but satisfactory? I am not alluding to the number and importance of the lunatic asylums which cover our land, nor to the fact that maladies of the brain and nervous system are now so common; but to the strange sense of mental unrest which marks our populations, and which amply justifies Ruskin's cutting epigram: that our two objects in life are, "Whatever we have—to get more; and wherever we are—to go somewhere else."[2] This sense of unrest, of disease, penetrates down even into the deepest regions of man's being—into his moral nature—disclosing itself there, as it has done in all nations notably at the time of their full civilisation, as the sense of Sin. All down the Christian centuries we find this strange sense of inward strife and discord developed, in marked contrast to the naive insouciance of the pagan and primitive world; and, what is strangest, we even find people glorying in this consciousness—which, while it may be the harbinger of better things to come, is and can be in itself only the evidence of loss of unity and therefore of ill-health, in the very centre of human life. [. . .]

\* \* \*

And now, by way of a glimpse into the future—after this long digression what is the route that man will take?

This is a subject that I hardly dare tackle. "The morning wind ever blows," says Thoreau, "the poem of creation is uninterrupted—but few are the ears that hear it."[3] And how can we, gulfed as we are in this present whirlpool, conceive rightly the glory which awaits us? No limits that our present knowledge puts need alarm us; the impossibilities will yield very easily when the time comes; and the anatomical dif-

---

[2] Slightly misquoted from part 2 of John Ruskin's "Fiction, Fair and Foul" (1880).
[3] *Walden* (1854), by Henry David Thoreau.

ficulty as to how and where the wings are to grow will vanish when they are felt sprouting!

It can hardly be doubted that the tendency will be—indeed is already showing itself—towards a return to nature and community of human life. This is the way back to the lost Eden, or rather forward to the new Eden, of which the old was only a figure. Man has to undo the wrappings and the mummydom of centuries, by which he has shut himself from the light of the sun and lain in seeming death, preparing silently his glorious resurrection—for all the world like the funny old chrysalis that he is. He has to emerge from houses and all his other hiding places wherein so long ago ashamed (as at the voice of God in the garden) he concealed himself—and Nature must once more become his home, as it is the home of the animals and the angels. [. . .]

*     *     *

And when the Civilisation-period has passed away, the old Nature-religion—perhaps greatly grown—will come back. This immense stream of religious life which beginning far beyond the horizon of earliest history has been deflected into various metaphysical and other channels—of Judaism, Christianity, Buddhism, and the like—during the historical period, will once more gather itself together to float on its bosom all the arks and sacred vessels of human progress. Man will once more *feel* his unity with his fellows, he will feel his unity with the animals, with the mountains and the streams, with the earth itself and the slow lapse of the constellations, not as an abstract dogma of Science or Theology, but as a living and ever-present fact. Ages back this has been understood better than now. Our Christian ceremonial is saturated with sexual and astronomical symbols; and long before Christianity existed, the sexual and astronomical were the main forms of religion. That is to say, men instinctively felt and worshipped the great life coming to them through Sex, the great life coming to them from the deeps of Heaven. They deified both. They placed their gods—their own human forms—in sex, they placed them in the sky. And not only so, but wherever they felt this kindred human life—in the animals, in the ibis, the bull, the lamb, the snake, the crocodile; in the trees and flowers, the oak, the ash, the laurel, the hyacinth; in the streams and water-falls, on the mountainsides or in the depths of the sea—they placed them. The whole universe was full of a life which, tho' not always friendly, was *human* and kindred to their own, *felt* by them, not reasoned about, but simply perceived. To the early man the notion of his having a separate individuality could only with difficulty occur; hence he troubled himself not with the suicidal questionings concerning the whence and whither which now vex the modern mind. For what causes these questions to be asked is simply the wretched feeling of isolation, actual or prospective, which man necessarily has when he contemplates himself as a separate atom in this immense universe—the gulf which lies below seemingly ready to swallow him, and the anxiety to find some mode of escape. But when he feels once more that he, that *he* himself, is absolutely indivisibly and indestructibly a part of this great whole—why then there is no gulf into which he can possibly fall; when he is sensible of the fact, why then the *how* of its realization, tho' losing none of its interest, becomes a matter for whose solution he can wait and work in faith and contentment of mind. The Sun or Sol, visible image of his very Soul, closest and most vital to him of all mortal things, occupying the illimitable heaven, feeding all with its life; the Moon, emblem and nurse of his own reflective thought, the conscious Man, measurer of Time, mirror of the Sun; the planetary passions wandering to and fro, yet within bounds; the starry destinies; the changes of the earth, and the seasons; the upward growth and unfoldment of all organic life; the emergence of the perfect Man, towards whose birth all creation groans and travails—all these things will return to become realities, and to be the frame or setting of his supra-mundane life. The meaning of the old religions will come back to him. On the high tops once more gathering he will celebrate with naked dances the glory of the human form and the great processions of the stars, or greet the bright horn of the young moon which now after a hundred centuries comes back laden with such wondrous associations—all the yearnings and the dreams and the wonderment of the generations of mankind—the worship of Astarte and of Diana, of Isis[4] or the Virgin Mary; once more in sacred groves will he reunite the passion and the delight of human love with his deepest feelings of the sanctity and beauty of Nature; or in the open, standing uncovered to the Sun, will adore the emblem of the everlasting splendor which shines within. The same sense of vital perfection and exaltation which can be traced in the early and pre-civilisation peoples—only a thousand times intensified, defined, illustrated and purified—will return to irradiate the redeemed and delivered Man.

---

[4]Astarte was a goddess in numerous ancient Mediterranean religions; Diana was an ancient Roman goddess and Isis an ancient Egyptian one.

## Jack London (1876–1916)

*In 1902, the American journalist and fiction writer Jack London investigated the notorious slums of London's East End, not only interviewing inhabitants but also disguising himself as one of the poorest of the poor in order to glimpse the area's ways from the inside. He published his findings a year later in a book he prized above all his others. The following excerpt conveys his concern—shared by many others of his time—that conditions in large towns and cities (where prospects of employment continued to draw people away from the country) were inflicting terrible damage on bodies and souls.*

## from *The People of the Abyss* (1903)

My first impression of East London was naturally a general one. Later the details began to appear, and here and there in the chaos of misery I found little spots where a fair measure of happiness reigned,—sometimes whole rows of houses in little out-of-the-way streets, where artisans dwell and where a rude sort of family life obtains. In the evenings the men can be seen at the doors, pipes in their mouths and children on their knees, wives gossiping, and laughter and fun going on. The content of these people is manifestly great, for, relative to the wretchedness that encompasses them, they are well off.

But at the best, it is a dull, animal happiness, the content of the full belly. The dominant note of their lives is materialistic. They are stupid and heavy, without imagination. The Abyss seems to exude a stupefying atmosphere of torpor, which wraps about them and deadens them. Religion passes them by. The Unseen holds for them neither terror nor delight. They are unaware of the Unseen; and the full belly and the evening pipe, with their regular "arf an' arf,"[1] is all they demand, or dream of demanding, from existence.

This would not be so bad if it were all; but it is not all. The satisfied torpor in which they are sunk is the deadly inertia that precedes dissolution. There is no progress, and with them not to progress is to fall back and into the Abyss. In their own lives they may only start to fall, leaving the fall to be completed by their children and their childen's children. Man always gets less than he demands from life; and so little do they demand, that the less than little they get cannot save them.

---

[1] Half-and-half, a mix of porter and ale or of other malt liquors.

At the best, city life is an unnatural life for the human; but the city life of London is so utterly unnatural that the average workman or workwoman cannot stand it. Mind and body are sapped by the undermining influences ceaselessly at work. Moral and physical stamina are broken, and the good workman, fresh from the soil, becomes in the first city generation a poor workman; and by the second city generation, devoid of push and go and initiative, and actually unable physically to perform the labour his father did, he is well on the way to the shambles at the bottom of the Abyss.

If nothing else, the air he breathes, and from which he never escapes, is sufficient to weaken him mentally and physically, so that he becomes unable to compete with the fresh virile life from the country hastening on to London Town to destroy and be destroyed.

Leaving out the disease germs that fill the air of the East End, consider but the one item of smoke. Sir William Thisleton-Dyer, curator of Kew Gardens,[2] has been studying smoke deposits on vegetation, and, according to his calculations, no less than six tons of solid matter, consisting of soot and tarry hydrocarbons, are deposited every week on every quarter of a square mile in and about London. This is equivalent to twenty-four tons per week to the square mile, or 1248 tons per year to the square mile. From the cornice below the dome of St Paul's Cathedral was recently taken a solid deposit of crystallized sulphate of lime. This deposit had been formed by the action of the sulphuric acid in the atmosphere upon the carbonate of lime in the stone. And this sulphuric acid in the atmosphere is constantly being breathed by the London workmen through all the days and nights of their lives.

It is incontrovertible that the children grow up into rotten adults, without virility or stamina, a weak-kneed, narrow-chested, listless breed, that crumples up and goes down in the brute struggle for life with the invading hordes from the country. The railway men, carriers, omnibus drivers, corn and timber porters, and all those who require physical stamina, are largely drawn from the country; while in the Metropolitan Police there are, roughly, 12,000 country-born as against 3000 London-born.

So one is forced to conclude that the Abyss is literally a huge man-killing machine, and when I pass along the little out-of-the-way streets with the full-bellied artisans at the doors, I am aware of a greater sorrow for them than for the 450,000 lost and hopeless

[2]The Royal Botanic Gardens, on the south side of the Thames in the London suburbs.

wretches dying at the bottom of the pit. They, at least, are dying, that is the point; while these have yet to go through the slow and preliminary pangs extending through two and even three generations.

And yet the quality of the life is good. All human potentialities are in it. Given proper conditions, it could live through the centuries, and great men, heroes and masters, spring from it and make the world better by having lived.

## G. Lowes Dickinson (1862–1932)

*In 1934, Forster published a biography of Goldsworthy Lowes Dickinson, a longtime friend and fellow alumnus of the Cambridge Apostles (see p. xvi). A founder of the liberal* Independent Review, *Dickinson also published several books, among them* A Modern Symposium, *which draws its title from the famous work by Plato in which friends debate the nature of love. In Dickinson's updating, fictional representatives of various Edwardian positions (a Tory, a Liberal, a Socialist, an anarchist, a scientist, and so on) defend their most basic beliefs while gathered at a country estate. Reprinted here—for their way of speaking to the Wilcox-Schlegel opposition, the links between culture and social class, and the ideal of communion with nature—are passages from speeches by Philip Audubon, a man of business; Aubrey Coryat, a poet; and Sir John Harington, a man of leisure. Ellis, Allison, Wilson, Remenhem, and Cantilupe are other participants.*

### from *A Modern Symposium* (1905)

[AUDUBON:] "[. . .] From the earliest days I can remember I realized what the nature of this world really is. And all experience has confirmed that first intuition. That other people don't seem to have it, too, is a source of constant amazement to me. But really, and without wishing to be arrogant, I believe the reason is that they choose to be duped and I don't. They intend, at all costs, to be happy, or interested, or whatever it is that they prefer to call it. And I don't say they are not wise in their generation. But I'm not made like that; I just see things as they are; and I see that they're very bad—a point in which I differ from the Creator.

"Well, now, to come to to-night's discussion, and my attitude towards it. You have assumed throughout, as, of course, you were bound to do, that things are worth while. But if they aren't, what becomes of all your aims, all your views, all your problems and disputes? The basis on which you are all agreed, however much you may differ in detail, is that things can be made better, and that it's worth while to make them so. But if one denies both propositions, what happens to the superstructure? And I do deny them; and not only that, but I can't conceive how any one ever came to accept them. Surely, if one didn't approach the question with an irrational bias towards optimism, one would never imagine that there is such a thing as progress in anything that really matters. Or are even we here impressed by such silly and irrelevant facts as telephones and motorcars? Ellis, I should think, has said enough to dispel that kind of illusion; and I don't want to labour a tedious point. If we are to look for progress at all we must look for it, I suppose, in men. And I have never seen any evidence that men are generally better than they used to be; on the contrary, I think there is evidence that they are worse. But anyhow, even granting that we could make things a bit better, what would be the use of doing it in a world like this? If the whole structure of the universe is bad, what's the good of fiddling with the details? You might as well waste your time in decorating the saloon of a sinking ship. Granting that you can improve the distribution of property, and raise the standard of health and intelligence and all the rest of it, granting you could to-morrow introduce your socialist state, or your liberal state, or your anarchical co-operation, or whatever the plan may be—how would you be better off in anything that matters? The main governing facts would be unaltered. Men, for example, would still be born, without being asked whether they want it or no. And that alone, to my mind, is enough to condemn the whole business. I can't think how it is that people don't resent more than they do the mere insult to their self-respect involved in such a situation. Nothing can cure it, nothing can improve it. It's a fundamental condition of life. [. . .]"

[CORYAT:] "[. . .] Of course the things really are bad that you say are bad. But they're so good as well! I mean—well, the other day I read one of those dreadful articles—at least, of course they're very useful I suppose—about the condition of the agricultural labourer. Well, then I took a ride in the country, and saw it all in its setting and complete, with everything the article had left out; and it wasn't so bad after all. I don't mean to say it was all good either, but it was just wonderful. There were great horses with shaggy fetlocks resting in green fields, and cattle wading in shallow fords, and streams fringed with willows, and little cheeping birds among the reeds, and larks and cuckoos and thrushes. And there were orchards white with blossom, and little gardens in the sun and shadows of clouds brushing over the plain. And the much-discussed labourer was in the midst of all this. And he really wasn't an incarnate grievance! He was thinking about his horses, or his bread and cheese, or his children squalling in the road, or his pig and his cocks and hens. Of course I don't suppose he knew how beautiful everything was; but I'm sure he had a sort of comfortable feeling of being a part of it all, of being somehow all right. And he wasn't worrying about his condition, as you all worry for him. I don't mean you aren't right to worry, in a way; except that no one ought to worry. But you oughtn't to suppose it's all a dreadful and intolerable thing, just because you can imagine something better. That, of course, is only one case; but I believe it's the same everywhere; yes, even in the big cities, which, to my taste, look from outside much more repulsive and terrible. There's a quality in the inevitable facts of life, in making one's living, and marrying and producing children, in the ending of one and the beginning of another day, in the uncertainties and fears and hopes, in the tragedies as well as the comedies, something that arrests and interests and absorbs, even if it doesn't delight. I'm not saying people are happy; sometimes they are and sometimes they aren't. But anyhow they are interested. And life itself is the interest. And that interest is perennial, and of all ages and all classes. And if you leave it out you leave out the only thing that counts. That's why ideals are so empty; just because, I mean, they don't exist. And I assure you—now I'm going to confess—that often, when I come away from some meeting or from reading some dreadful article on social reform, I feel as if I could embrace everything and every one I come across, simply for being so good as to exist—the 'bus-drivers, the cabmen, the shop-keepers, the slum-landlords, the slum-victims, the prostitutes, the thieves. There they are, anyhow, in their extraordinary setting, floating on the great river of life, that was and is and will be, itself its own justification, through whatever country it may flow. And if you don't realize that—if you have a whole community that doesn't realize it—then, however happy and comfortable and equitable and all the rest of it you make your society, you haven't really done much for them. Their last state may even be worse than the first, because they will have lost the natural instinctive acceptance of life, without learning how to accept it on the higher plane.

"And that is why—now comes what I really do care about, and what I've been wanting to say—that is why there is nothing so important for the future or the present of the world as poetry. Allison, for instance, and Wilson would be different men if only they would read my works! I'm not sure even, if I may say so, that Remenham himself wouldn't be the better." Remenham, however, smilingly indicated that he had read them. Whereat Coryat rather comically remarked, "Oh, well! Yes! Perhaps then my poetry isn't quite good enough. But there's Shakspere, and Milton, and—I don't care who it is, so long as it has the essential of all great poetry, and that is to make you feel the worth of things. I don't mean by that the happiness, but just the extraordinary value, of which all these unsolved questions about Good and Evil are themselves part. No one, I am sure, ever laid down a great tragedy—take the most terrible of all, take 'Lear'—without an overwhelming sense of the value of life; life as it is, life at its most pitiless and cruel, with all its iniquities, suffering, perplexity; without feeling he would far rather have lived and had all that than not have lived at all. But tragedy is an extreme case. In every simpler and more common case the poet does the same thing for us. He shows us that the lives he touches have worth, worth of pleasure, of humour, of patience, of wisdom painfully acquired, of endurance, of hope, even I will say of failure and despair. He doesn't blink anything, he looks straight at it all, but he sees it in the true perspective, under a white light, and seeing all the Evil says nevertheless with God, 'Behold, it is very good.' You see," he added, with his charming smile, turning to Audubon, "I agree with God, not with you. And perhaps if you were to read poetry . . . but, you know, you must not only read it; you've got to feel it."

"Ah," said Audubon, "but that I'm afraid is the difficulty."

"I suppose it is. Well—I don't know that I can say any more."

And without further ado he dropped back into his seat.

[HARINGTON:] "[. . .] Life as such is neither good nor bad, and Audubon's undistinguishing censure is surely as much out of place as Coryat's undistinguishing approval. Life is raw material for the artist, whether he be the private man carrying out his own destiny, or the statesman shaping that of a nation. The end of the artist in either case is the good life; and on his own conception of that will depend the value of his work.

"[. . .] All of you, I think, except Cantilupe, have assumed that the good life, whatever it may be, can be attained by everybody; and that society should be arranged so as to secure that result. That is, in fact, the democratic postulate, which is now so generally accepted not only in this company but in the world at large. But it is that postulate that I dispute. I hold that the good life must either be the privilege of a few, or not exist at all. The good life in my view, is the life of a gentleman. That word, I know, has been degraded; and there is no more ominous sign of the degradation of the English people. But I use it in its true and noble sense. I mean by a gentleman a man of responsibility; one who because he enjoys privileges recognizes duties; a landed proprietor who is also, and therefore, a soldier and a statesman; a man with a natural capacity and a hereditary tradition to rule; a member, in a word, of a governing aristocracy. [. . .] you cannot revolutionize classes and their relations without revolutionizing culture. It is idle to suppose you can communicate to a democracy the heritage of an aristocracy. You may give them books, show them pictures, offer them examples. In vain! The seed cannot grow in the new soil. The masses will never be educated in the sense that the classes were. You may rejoice in the fact, or you may regret it; but at least it should be recognized. For my own part I regret it, and I regret it because I conceive that the good life is the life of the gentleman.

"From this it follows that my ideal of a polity is aristocratic. For a class of gentlemen presupposes classes of workers to support it. And these, from the ideal point of view, must be regarded as mere means. I do not say that that is just; I do not say it is what we should choose; but I am sure it is the law of the world in which we live. Through the whole realm of nature every kind exists only to be the means of supporting life in another. Everywhere the higher preys upon the lower; everywhere the Good is parasitic on the Bad. And as in nature, so in human society. Read history with an impartial mind, read it in the white light, and you will see that there has never been a great civilization that was not based upon iniquity. [. . .]

"For Democracy—note it well—destroys greatness in every kind, of intellect, of perception, as well as of character. And especially it destroys art, that reflection of life without which we cannot be said to live. For the artist is the rarest, the most choice of men. His senses, his perception, his intelligence have a natural and inborn fineness and distinction. He belongs to a class, a very small, a very exclusive one. And he needs a class to appreciate and support him. No democracy has ever produced or understood art. [. . .]"

## C. F. G. Masterman (1873–1927)

*A Liberal journalist and Member of Parliament, C. F. G. Masterman published numerous books and articles designed to heighten public awareness of the perils confronting the British nation. In* The Condition of England, *his most famous work, he describes both with sweep and in detail the very different situations of the country's several economic classes; the effects of technological progress on literature, science, and religion; and the challenges of the immediate future. The first selection is from a chapter on the affluent and socially prominent, the second from one on the toiling masses, the third from one on science.*

## from *The Condition of England* (1908)

### from Chapter II, The Conquerors

The most obvious increase of this waste comes from the "speeding up" of living which has taken place in all classes in so marked a fashion within a generation. The whole standard of life has been sensibly raised, not so much in comfort as in ostentation. And the result is something similar to that in the insane competition of armaments which takes place amongst the terrified nations of the world. One year ten huge ironclads[1] confront twenty. A decade after, fifteen huge ironclads of another type have replaced the first: to be confronted again by thirty of the new floating castles. So many millions have been thrown to the scrap heap. The proportion of power has remained unaffected. It is the same in the more determined private competition for supremacy in a social standard. Where one house sufficed, now two are demanded; where a dinner of a certain quality, now a dinner of a superior quality; where clothes or dresses or flowers, now more clothes, more dresses, more flowers. It is waste, not because fine clothes and rare flowers and pleasant food are in themselves undesirable, but because by a kind of parallel of the law of diminishing returns in agriculture, additional expenditure in such directions fails to result in correspondent additions of happiness. In many respects, indeed, the effect is not only negatively worthless, but even positively harmful. Modern civilisation in its most highly organised forms has elaborated a system to which the delicate fibre of body and mind is

---

[1]Warships protected by iron or steel plates.

unable to respond. And the result is the appearance (whimsical enough to Carlyle's spectators "beyond the region of the fixed stars"[2]) of a society expending half its income in heaping up the material of disease, to which the other half of its income is being laboriously applied for remedy.

But the general effect (to the above-mentioned dispassionate spectators) is of an extravagance of wealth and waste which is only not insolent because it is for the most part unconscious, the sport of blind forces rather than the deliberate defiance of the limits of human endeavour. It is not insolence or—as it might have appeared in the olden days—a determination to rival the fabled immortals, which has charged all our high roads with wandering machines racing with incredible velocity and no apparent aim. Many (such as W. E. Henley) demand "Speed in the face of the Lord."[3] Others are inflamed with the desire for "driving abroad in furious guise," as an escape from the *ennui* of a life which has lost its savour; as in the tortured and bored procession in old Rome, for the "easier and quicker" passing of the "impracticable hours."[4] But a large proportion of those who have employed motor cars in habitual violation of the speed limit, and in destruction of the amenities of the rural life of England, have done so either because their neighbours have employed motor cars, or because their neighbours have not employed motor cars; in an effort towards equality with the one, or superiority over the other. When every man of a certain income has purchased a motor car, when life has become "speeded up" to the motor-car level, that definite increase of expenditure will be accepted as normal. But life will be no happier and no richer for such an acceptance; it will merely have become more impossible for those who (for whatever reason) are unequal to the demands of such a standard. And the same is true of the multiplication of meals; of the rise in the price of rent in certain districts of London, for example, because every one wants to live there; of numberless exactions

---

[2]In *The French Revolution* (1837), Thomas Carlyle wrote of Louis XV, "His wide France, look at it from the Fixed Stars (themselves not yet Infinitude), is no wider than thy narrow brickfield." In the geocentric astronomy of Ptolemy (127–45), the stars (whose relative positions do not change) are fixed in a sphere beyond that of the (position-shifting) planets.

[3]*Song of Speed* (1903).

[4]In "Obermann Once More" (1867), Matthew Arnold writes of the bored Roman nobleman who "drove abroad, in furious guise, / Along the Appian way. // He made a feast, drank fierce and fast, / And crown'd his hair with flowers— / No easier nor no quicker pass'd / The impracticable hours."

and extortions which have grown up in a society whose members are "like wealthy men who care not how they give."[5]

## from Chapter IV, The Multitude

THE Multitude is the People of England: that eighty per cent. (say) of the present inhabitants of these islands who never express their own grievances, who rarely become articulate, who can only be observed from outside and very far away. It is a people which, all unnoticed and without clamour or protest, has passed through the largest secular change of a thousand years: from the life of the fields to the life of the city. Nine out of ten families have migrated within three generations: they are still only, as it were, commencing to settle down in their new quarters, with the paint scarcely dry on them, and the little garden still untilled. How has the migration affected them? How will they expand or degenerate in the new town existence, each in the perpetual presence of all? That is a question of as profound interest in answering as it is difficult to answer. The nineteenth century—in the life of the wage-earning multitudes—was a century of disturbance. The twentieth promises to be a century of consolidation. What completed product will emerge from its city aggregation, the children of the crowd? You must learn of them to-day, as I have said, from outside: from the few observers who have lived amongst them and recorded their experience; from the very few representative men, with articulate utterance, which they have flung up from amongst themselves. You must examine masses of documents and statistics embodied in Government publications, or tentative efforts towards a sociology: recording how they live, and eat and drink, and obtain shelter, and marry and are given in marriage; the particulars of their upbringing, how they seek or elude religions and charity, and escape from the laws which are passed for their protection, and enjoy and suffer, and live and die. The mass of this chaotic and undigested evidence waits for the observer who will create from it some general picture of the life of the English people. And when all these statistics and cold facts are assimilated, there yet remains the further inquiry of the temper and spirit of a race subjected to such forces; hampered and limited by the narrow walls between which they labour and endure. [. . .]

---

[5]In "Tithonus" (1833), by Alfred, Lord Tennyson, the title character recalls how his lover, the goddess of dawn, granted him immortality "with a smile, / Like wealthy men who care not how they give."

England at once, under such an analysis, separates itself into divergent parts. There is rural England, still largely unaffected by modern science and invention, except by the loss of population, drained away; the agricultural labourers, the fishermen, and the artisans of the sleeping provincial towns. There is urban England in hastily created industrial centres, vocal with the clanging of furnaces and the noise of the factories; but still a population in manageable aggregation, set in open spaces, never far from green fields under a wide sky. And there is London: a population, a nation in itself; breeding, as it seems, a special race of men; which only is also produced, and that in less intensive cultivation, in the few other larger cities—Glasgow, Manchester, Liverpool—where the conditions of coagulation offer some parallels to this monster clot of humanity. Everywhere, indeed, this million-peopled, exaggerated London sets at defiance the generalisations drawn from the normal town areas. House rent is immensely higher. The mean weekly price for two rooms in London is six shillings, in the provinces a little more than one half; for four rooms the variation is between nine shillings in the one, five shillings in the other. A portion of this surplus is the booty of more highly paid labour. The greater part vanishes in the increased value of the land, heaped up by the mere fact of aggregation, and flowing away into the pockets of many affluent and fortunate persons.

## from Chapter VII, Science and Progress

SUCH appear some, at least, of the characteristics of the various classes of Society to-day in England. In general material condition there is little to excite foreboding. A proportion of the population is raised well above the privations of poverty larger than ever before in history. Extravagance and a longing for pleasure and excitement are common to all classes. The aggregation of plenty is such as the Old World has never before seen. The vision, as a whole, is of a laborious energetic race, deserting the countryside for the cities, and there heaping up wealth, which is shared, in some degree, by all but the poorest. If anything is wrong in material conditions it is in the apparatus, not of accumulation, but of distribution. An altogether inadequate proportion of this accumulation is the absolute possession of a tiny class which sits secure upon the summit. In heavy tolls levied upon labour in the form of royalties and the monopoly rents of land, in inherited fortune which reaps its interest from remote regions and foreign kingdoms, in unusual profit of industrial investment through times of trade "boom," in financial speculation and all the various special advantage of business, commerce, and manufacture in this free market of England, there is being concentrated in few hands vast and ever-increasing fortune. Security accepted as normal, comfort more widely spread than ever before, and a standard of extravagance and display which would have astonished all previous ages, characterise the heart of the Empire at the height of its material greatness. "Situate at the entering of the sea," with a population exceeding Scotland or Ireland, and the revenues of many European States, the greatest city of that Empire is taking toll from the industry of all the world. In the midst of which outward evidence of attainment sounds almost unnoticed the complaining of a poverty more degraded and intolerable than in many less successful lands: whose misery is intensified by its conjunction in adjacent cities with a people evidently given up to the arts of enjoyment, and finding an ever-increasing plenty inadequate to its ever-increasing demand.

And always the hope is latent that "something will turn up" which will solve all the unfortunate social problems, and make every one happy and content. Sometimes it is to be the advance of mechanical discovery, sometimes a new spirit of kindliness and patience: sometimes fuller conquests of trade or commerce or Imperial dominion; but always the bringing in from outside of a *Deus ex machina*[6] which will supplement nobody's loss with everybody's gain. The advance in acquisition during a century of invention has been so astonishing, the progress of whole classes from a low-grade, comfortless, ignorant life into a highly-paid, skilled, intelligent working-people so remarkable, that to many the continuance of such a process seems inevitable. Amelioration is to come as a legitimate child of the forces of change, and without effort or sacrifice is to reveal a continuous process of uplifting. Certainly by all material and tangible tests—income, prices, security, comfort, addition to leisure and wages—the bulk of the people of this country have advanced so incredibly since the "Hungry Forties"[7] that the

---

[6]"God out of a machine" (Latin), an artifice that turns up at the last moment to solve all problems.

[7]The 1840s, a period of widespread misery and economic depression brought on partly by bad harvests in Britain and Ireland.

reality of those days would appear to the present generation but as bad dreams. They cannot believe that these things were actually enacted upon these islands less than eighty years ago. The Report of the Royal Commission on Children's Labour in the Factories,—the most sensational blue-book of the century,—for example, would seem rather to refer to the Spaniards in the West Indies or the administration of King Leopold in the Congo than to the solid ground and pleasant airs of England.[8] And in every kind of material test—fall of pauperism, fall of the death-rate, decline of infectious and poverty diseases—or increase of wages, shortening of hours of labour, fall in prices; or, again, spread of education and of means of recreation, improvement in houses and in the sanitation of cities, the offering of opportunities of advancement: in all these the advance has been so amazing that there would seem to be no place for the pessimist who would prophesy coming disaster.

It is rather in the region of the spirit that the doubts are still disturbing. Fulness of bread in the past has been accompanied with leanness of soul. And the modern prophet is still undecided whether this enormous increase of life's comforts and material satisfactions has revealed an equal and parallel advance in courage and compassion and kindly understandings. The nations, equipped with ever more complicated instruments of warfare, face each other as armed camps across frontiers mined and tortured with the apparatus of destruction. A scared wealthy and middle class confronts a cosmopolitan uprising of the "proletariat," whose discontent it can neither appease nor forget. The industrious populations which have been swept into masses and congestions by the new industry has not yet found an existence serene, and intelligible, and human. No one, to-day, looking out upon a disturbed and sullen Europe, a disturbed and confident America, but is conscious of a world in motion: whither, no man knows.

---

[8]The first report by the Royal Commission on the Employment of Children in Factories (1833) detailed miserable conditions and led to legislation that, among other provisions, limited to 8 hours the workday of those aged 9–13 years. A second commission in 1843 documented long hours and unsafe conditions in other industries and in mines. In British opinion, Spanish rule in the Caribbean and Belgian rule in the Congo epitomized brutal exploitation.

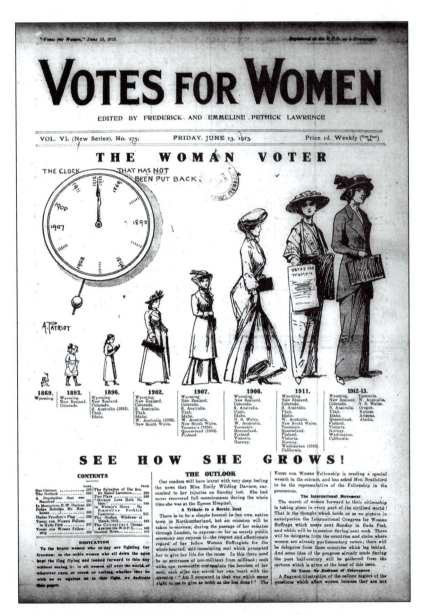

Cover of *Votes for Women*, paper of the
Women's Social and Political Union, 13 June 1913.

## Elizabeth Robins (1862–1952)

*In the play* Votes for Women, *which premiered in 1907, the actress and feminist Elizabeth Robins combined a romantic plot with representations of suffragists speaking heroically before public crowds. The same year, Robins released a novelistic adaptation,* The Convert. *The following passage, which showcases the passion and rhetorical agility of the fictional Ernestine Blunt, indicates how the suffrage question links several matters in* Howards End: *relations between men and women, Wilcox values and Schlegel values, the exploitation of labor, and manners' connection to power.*

### from *The Convert* (1907)

"Be quiet, while I tell you something. You men have taught us that women can get a great deal by coaxing, often far more than we deserve! But justice isn't one of the things that's ever got that way. Justice has to be fought for. Justice has to be won."

Howls and uproar.

"You men—" (it began to be apparent that whenever the roaring got so loud that it threatened to drown her, she said, "You men—" very loud, and then gave her voice a rest while the din died down that they might hear what else the irrepressible Ernestine had to say upon that absorbing topic). "You men discovered years ago that you weren't going to get justice just by deserving it, or even by being men, so when you got tired of asking politely for the franchise, you took to smashing windows and burning down Custom Houses, and over-turning Bishops' carriages;[1] while *we*, why, we haven't so much as upset a curate off a bicycle!"

Others might laugh, not Ernestine.

"You men," she went on, "got up riots in the streets—*real* riots where people lost their lives. It may have to come to that with us. But the Government may as well know that if women's political freedom has to be bought with blood, we can pay that price, too."

Above a volley of boos and groans she went on, "But we are opposed to violence, and it will be our last resort. We are leaving none of the more civilized ways untried. We publish a great amount of literature—I hope you are all buying some of it—you can't understand our movement unless you do! We organize branch

---

[1]Both the palace of the Bishop and the Custom House were burned in the Bristol Riots of 1831, which broke out after the House of Lords rejected a bill that would have expanded suffrage.

unions and we hire halls—we've got Somerset Hall to-night, and we hope you'll all come and bring your friends. We have very interesting debates, and *we* answer questions, politely!" she made her point to laughter. "We don't leave any stone unturned. Because there are people who don't buy our literature, and who don't realize how interesting the Somerset Hall debates are, we go into the public places where the idle and the foolish, *like that man just over there!*— where they may point and laugh and make their poor little jokes. But let me tell you we never hold a meeting where we don't win friends to our cause. A lot of you who are jeering and interrupting now are going to be among our best friends. *All* the intelligent ones are going to be on our side."

Above the laughter, a rich groggy voice was heard, "Them that's against yer are all drunk, miss' (hiccup). 'D—don't mind 'em!"

Ernestine just gave them time to appreciate that, and then went on—"Men and women were never meant to fight except side by side. You've been told by one of the other speakers how the men suffer by women more and more underselling them in the Labour market—"

"Don't need no tellin'."

"Bloody black-legs!"[2]

"Do you know how that came about? I'll tell you. It's come about through your keeping the women out of your Unions. You never would have done that if they'd had votes. You saw the important people ignored them. You thought it was safe for you to do the same. But I tell you it *isn't ever* safe to ignore the women!"

High over the groans and laughter the voice went on, "You men have got to realize that if our battle against the common enemy is to be won, you've got to bring the women into line."

"What's to become of chivalry?"

"What *has* become of chivalry?" she retorted; and no one seemed to have an answer ready, but the crowd fell silent, like people determined to puzzle out a conundrum.

"Don't you know that there are girls and women in this very city who are working early and late for rich men, and who are expected by those same employers to live on six shillings a week? Perhaps I'm wrong in saying the men expect the women to live on that. It may be they *know* that no girl can—it may be the men know how that struggle ends. But do they care? Do *they* bother about chivalry? Yet they

[2]Scabs; strike-breakers.

and all of you are dreadfully exercised for fear having a vote would unsex women. We are too delicate—women are such fragile flowers." The little face was ablaze with scorn. "I saw some of those fragile flowers last week—and I'll tell you where. Not a very good place for gardening. It was a back street in Liverpool. The 'flowers'" (oh, the contempt with which she loaded the innocent word!)—"the flowers looked pretty dusty—but they weren't quite dead. I stood and looked at them! hundreds of worn women coming down steep stairs and pouring out into the street. What had they all been doing there in that—garden, I was going to say!—that big grimy building? They had been making cigars!—spending the best years of their lives, spending all their youth in that grim dirty street making cigars for men. Whose chivalry prevents that? Why were they coming out at that hour of the day? Because their poor little wages were going to be lowered, and with the courage of despair they were going on strike. No chivalry prevents men from getting women at the very lowest possible wage— (I want you to notice the low wage is the main consideration in all this)—men get these women, that they say are so tender and delicate, to undertake the almost intolerable toil of the rope-walk. They get women to make bricks. Girls are driven—when they are not driven to worse—they are driven to being lodging-house slaveys or over-worked scullions. *That's* all right! Women are graciously permitted to sweat over other people's washing, when they should be caring for their own babies. In Birmingham"—she raised the clear voice and bent her flushed face over the crowd—"In Birmingham those same 'fragile flowers' make bicycles to keep alive! At Cradley Heath we make chains. At the pit brows we sort coal. But a vote would soil our hands! You may wear out women's lives in factories, you may sweat them in the slums, you may drive them to the streets. You *do*. But a vote would unsex them."

Her full throat choked. She pressed her clenched fist against her chest and seemed to admonish herself that emotion wasn't her line.

"If you are intelligent you know as well as I do that women are exploited the length and the breadth of the land. And yet you come talking about chivalry! Now, I'll just tell you men something for your future guidance." She leaned far out over the crowd and won a watchful silence. *"That talk about chivalry makes women sick."* In the midst of the roar, she cried, "Yes, they mayn't always show it, for women have had to learn to conceal their deepest feelings, but depend on it that's how they feel."

Then, apparently thinking she'd been serious enough, "There might be some sense in talking to us about chivalry if you paid our taxes for us," she said; while the people recovered their spirits in roaring with delight at the coolness of that suggestion.

"If you forgave us our crimes because we are women! If you gave annuities to the eighty-two women out of every hundred in this country who are slaving to earn their bread—many of them having to provide for their children; some of them having to feed sick husbands or old parents. But chivalry doesn't carry you men as far as that! No! No further than the door! You'll hold that open for a lady and then expect her to grovel before such an exhibition of *chivalry*! We don't need it, thank you! We can open doors for ourselves."

# England and Germany

Following the unification of its several states into the German Empire in 1871, Germany undertook a massive program of modernization that soon made it Great Britain's most fearsome commercial competitor. It also began to build up its military forces and, starting in the 1880s, extended its imperial reach into Africa and the Pacific. By the end of the century, Germany's threat to British interests was being trumpeted by an array of influences on public opinion, from Lord Northcliffe's *Daily Mail* to the sensational "invasion novels" that imagined Britain assaulted by foreign powers. The selections given here register anxiety about German prospects and values in different ways; against both German militarism and British instigators of war, *Howards End* defends the kind of enlightened cosmopolitanism evoked by J. A. Hobson in *Imperialism* (see pp. 357–61).

## E. E. Williams (1866–1935)

*In 1887, British authorities began requiring that German imports be labeled "Made in Germany," on the assumption that consumers would resist the inferior wares. By the turn of the century, however, German manufactures had become so identified with quality that some British makers were falsely affixing the label to their own goods. Meanwhile, shares of world commerce had shifted: in 1870, England's portion of global industrial production was 32%, Germany's 13%; by 1913, England's had diminished to just 14% while Germany's had risen to 16% (Umbach 120). E. E. Williams was one of several polemicists urging the British to learn from German business practices.*

## from *"Made in Germany"* (1896)

The Industrial Supremacy of Great Britain has been long an axiomatic commonplace; and it is fast turning into a myth, as inappropriate to fact as the Chinese Emperor's computation of his own status. This is a strong statement. But it is neither wide nor short of the truth. The industrial glory of England is departing, and England does not know it. There are spasmodic outcries against foreign competition, but the impression they leave is fleeting and vague. The phrase, "Made in Germany," is raw material for a jape at the pantomime, or is made the text for a homily by the official guardians of some particular trade, in so far as the matter concerns themselves. British Consuls, too, send words of warning home, and the number of these is increasing with significant frequency. But the nation at large is yet as little alive to the impending danger as to the evil already wrought. The man in the shop or the factory has plenty to say about the Armenian Question and the House of Lords,[1] but about commercial and industrial matters which concern him vitally he is generally much less eloquent. The amount of interest evinced by the amateur politician seems invariably to advance with the remoteness of the matter from his daily bread. It is time to disturb the fatal torpor: even though the moment be, in one sense, unhappily chosen. The pendulum between depression and prosperity has swung to the latter, and manufacturers and merchants are flushed with the joyful contemplation of their orderbooks. Slackness has given way to briskness; the lean years have been succeeded by a term of fat ones. The prophet of evil commands his most attentive audiences when the times are with him. When they are good—though the good be fleeting—his words are apt to fall unheeded. [. . .]

England could not hope for an eternal monopoly of the world's manufactures; and industrial growths abroad do not of necessity sound the knell of her greatness. But she must discriminate in her equanimity. And most certainly she must discriminate against Germany. For Germany has entered into a deliberate and deadly rivalry with her, and is battling with might and main for the extinction of her supremacy.

In estimating England's industrial position, regard must also be had to her function as the world's middleman. Not only is she a man-

---

[1]The question of self-determination for the Armenian people became an important topic in international affairs after the Congress of Berlin in 1878. In the 1890s, a number of Liberal politicians, especially Lord Rosebery (Prime Minister 1894–95), sought reform or even abolition of the House of Lords. The veto power of the Lords was eventually curtailed by the Parliament Act of 1911.

ufacturer for other peoples: she is likewise their agent for distribution. There is scarce a nation—certainly not one of any importance—which does not come to England to buy goods sent in for sale from elsewhere. She sells those nations hams from her Colonies, coffee from Arabia, gloves from France, currants from Greece, cotton from America—in fact it would be hard to name an article produced abroad which is not on sale in those universal market-places, the Mersey and the Thames.[2] In this retail business, also, the Germans are setting themselves to beat us; and South Americans are already buying their Irish linen through Hamburg houses. If there be an advance in this form of competition on the part of Germany, we shall lose the little benefit accruing from the German export trade; for in all other respects it is wholly baneful to us.

## The German Revolution

Up to a couple of decades ago, Germany was an agricultural State. Her manufactures were few and unimportant; her industrial capital was small; her export trade was too insignificant to merit the attention of the official statistician; she imported largely for her own consumption. Now she has changed all that. Her youth has crowded into English houses, has wormed its way into English manufacturing secrets, and has enriched her establishments with the knowledge thus purloined. She has educated her people in a fashion which has made it in some branches of industry the superior, and in most the equal of the English. Her capitalists have been content with a simple style, which has enabled them to dispense with big immediate profits, and to feed their capital. They have toiled at their desks, and made their sons do likewise; they have kept a strict controlling hand on all the strings of their businesses; they have obtained State aid in several ways—as special rates to shipping ports; they have insinuated themselves into every part of the world—civilised, barbarian, savage—learning the languages, and patiently studying the wants and tastes of the several peoples. Not content with reaping the advantages of British colonisation— this was accomplished with alarming facility—Germany has "protected" the simple savage on her own account, and the Imperial Eagle now floats on the breezes of the South Sea Islands, and

[2]Major rivers of Liverpool and London.

droops in the thick air of the African littoral.[3] Her diplomatists have negotiated innumerable commercial treaties. The population of her cities has been increasing in a manner not unworthy of England in the Thirties and Forties. Like England, too, she is draining her rural districts for the massing of her children in huge factory towns. Her yards (as well as those of England) too, are ringing with the sound of hammers upon ships being builded for the transport of German merchandise. Her agents and travellers swarm through Russia, and wherever else there is a chance of trade on any terms—are even supplying the foreigner with German goods *at a loss*, that they may achieve their purpose in the end. In a word, an industrial development, unparalleled, save in England a century ago, is now her portion. A gigantic commercial State is arising to menace our prosperity, and contend with us for the trade of the world. It is true that this mad rush towards industrialism does not meet with universal approval; and the Agrarian Party is energetic in its denunciation of the ruin wrought thereby to Germany as an agricultural State. But its protests have nothing availed it yet, nor are ever likely to avail it anything.

## Made in Germany

The phrase is fluent in the mouth: how universally appropriate it is, probably no one who has not made a special study of the matter is aware. Take observations, Gentle Reader, in your own surroundings: the mental exercise is recommended as an antidote to that form of self-sufficiency which our candid friends regard as indigenous to the British climate. Your investigations will work out somewhat in this fashion. You will find that the material of some of your own clothes was probably woven in Germany. Still more probable is it that some of your wife's garments are German importations; while it is practically beyond a doubt that the magnificent mantles and jackets wherein her maids array themselves on their Sundays out are German-made and German-sold, for only so could they be done at the figure. Your governess's *fiancé* is a clerk in the City;[4] but he also was made in Germany. The toys, and the dolls, and the fairy books which your children maltreat in the nursery are made in Germany: nay, the material of your favourite (patriotic) news-

[3]The African coast; an eagle was featured on the coat of arms of the German Empire. Germany's "South Seas" protectorate in 1896 was German New Guinea; other Pacific territories would soon include the Caroline Islands and part of Samoa. In Africa, Germany's colonies included Cameroon, South West Africa, German East Africa, and Togoland.

[4]The City of London, the business heart of Greater London.

paper had the same birthplace as like as not. Roam the house over, and the fateful mark will greet you at every turn, from the piano in your drawing-room to the mug on your kitchen dresser, blazoned though it be with the legend, *A Present from Margate.*[5] Descend to your domestic depths, and you shall find your very drain-pipes German made. You pick out of the grate the paper wrappings from a book consignment, and they also are "Made in Germany." You stuff them into the fire, and reflect that the poker in your hand was forged in Germany. As you rise from your hearthrug you knock over an ornament on your mantelpiece; picking up the pieces you read, on the bit that formed the base, "Manufactured in Germany." And you jot your dismal reflections down with a pencil that was made in Germany. At midnight your wife comes home from an opera which was made in Germany, has been here enacted by singers and conductor and players made in Germany, with the aid of instruments and sheets of music made in Germany. You go to bed, and glare wrathfully at a text on the wall; it is illuminated with an English village church, and it was "Printed in Germany." If you are imaginative and dyspeptic, you drop off to sleep only to dream that St. Peter (with a duly stamped halo round his head and a bunch of keys from the Rhineland) has refused you admission into Paradise, because you bear not the Mark of the Beast[6] upon your forehead, and are not of German make. But you console yourself with the thought that it was only a Bierhaus[7] Paradise any way; and you are awakened in the morning by the sonorous brass of a German band.

## Elizabeth von Arnim (1866–1941)

*In 1905, Forster lived at Nassenheide, Pomerania, where he tutored the children of the Prussian Count Henning August von Arnim and his Australian-born wife, Elizabeth. Though today Elizabeth is most remembered as the author of* The Enchanted April *(1922), when she and Forster became friends she was best known for the book whose first chapter is excerpted here, a classic for British garden lovers. The work bespeaks not*

[5]Resort town in Kent.
[6]Revelations 13:11–18 describes a deceiving beast who "causeth all . . . to receive a mark in their right hand, or in their foreheads: And that no man might buy or sell, save he that had the mark, or the name of the beast, or the number of his name."
[7]Beer hall.

*only the love of nature she and Forster shared but also—in its arch depiction of German marital owls and of her own husband as the "Man of Wrath"—a view of German manners that would lead her to more stinging anti-German satire in* The Caravaners *(1909) and to what some dubbed sheer anti-German propaganda in* Christine *(1917).*

### from *Elizabeth and Her German Garden* (1898)

*May 7th.*—I love my garden. I am writing in it now in the late afternoon loveliness, much interrupted by the mosquitoes and the temptation to look at all the glories of the new green leaves washed half an hour ago in a cold shower. Two owls are perched near me, and are carrying on a long conversation that I enjoy as much as any warbling of nightingales. The gentleman owl says 🎵, and she answers from her tree a little way off, 🎵, beautifully assenting to and completing her lord's remark, as becomes a properly constructed German she-owl. They say the same thing over and over again so emphatically that I think it must be something nasty about me; but I shall not let myself be frightened away by the sarcasm of owls.

This is less a garden than a wilderness. No one has lived in the house, much less in the garden, for twenty-five years, and it is such a pretty old place that the people who might have lived here and did not, deliberately preferring the horrors of a flat in a town, must have belonged to that vast number of eyeless and earless persons of whom the world seems chiefly composed. Noseless too, though it does not sound pretty; but the greater part of my spring happiness is due to the scent of the wet earth and young leaves.

I am always happy (out of doors, be it understood, for indoors there are servants and furniture), but in quite different ways, and my spring happiness bears no resemblance to my summer or autumn happiness, though it is not more intense, and there were days last winter when I danced for sheer joy out in my frost-bound garden in spite of my years and children. But I did it behind a bush, having a due regard for the decencies.

There are so many bird-cherries round me, great trees with branches sweeping the grass, and they are so wreathed just now with white blossoms and tenderest green, that the garden looks like a wedding. I never saw such masses of them; they seem to fill the place. Even across a little stream that bounds the garden on the east, and right in the middle of the cornfield beyond, there is an immense one, a picture of grace and glory against the cold blue of the spring sky. [. . .]

From nearly all the windows of the house I can look out across the plain, with no obstacle in the shape of a hill, right away to a blue line of distant forest, and on the west side uninterruptedly to the setting sun—nothing but a green, rolling plain, with a sharp edge against the sunset. I love those west windows better than any others, and have chosen my bedroom on that side of the house so that even times of hair-brushing may not be entirely lost; and the young woman who attends to such matters has been taught to fulfill her duties about a mistress recumbent in an easy-chair before an open window, and to not profane with chatter that sweet and solemn time. This girl is grieved at my habit of living almost in the garden, and all her ideas as to the sort of life a respectable German lady should lead have got into a sad muddle since she came to me. The people round about are persuaded that I am, to put it as kindly as possible, exceedingly eccentric, for the news has traveled that I spend the day out of doors with a book, and that no mortal eye has ever yet seen me sew or cook. But why cook when you can get someone to cook for you? And as for sewing, the maids will hem the sheets better and quicker than I could, and all forms of needlework of the fancy order are inventions of the Evil One for keeping the foolish from applying their hearts to wisdom.

We had been married five years before it struck us that we might as well make use of this place by coming down and living in it. Those five years were spent in a flat in a town, and during their whole interminable length I was perfectly miserable and perfectly healthy, which disposes of the ugly notion that has at times disturbed me that my happiness here is less due to the garden than to a good digestion. And while we were wasting our lives there, here was this dear place, with dandelions up to the very door, all the paths grass-grown and completely effaced, in winter so lonely, with nobody but the north wind taking the least notice of it, and in May—in all those five lovely Mays—no one to look at the wonderful bird-cherries and still more wonderful masses of lilacs, everything glowing and blowing, the Virginia creeper madder every year until at last, in October, the very roof was wreathed with blood-red tresses, the owls and the squirrels and all the blessed little birds reigning supreme, and not a living creature ever entering the empty house except the snakes, which got into the habit during those silent years of wriggling up the south wall into the rooms on that side whenever the old housekeeper opened the windows. All that was here,—peace, and happiness, and a reasonable life,—and yet it never struck me to come and live in it. [. . .]

My other half being indulgent, and with some faint thought perhaps that it might be as well to look after the place, consented to live in it, at any rate for a time; whereupon followed six specially blissful weeks from the end of April into June, during which I was here alone, supposed to be superintending the painting and papering, but, as a matter of fact, only going into the house when the workmen had gone out of it.

How happy I was! I don't remember any time quite so perfect since the days when I was too little to do lessons and was turned out with sugar on my eleven-o'clock bread and butter onto a lawn closely strewn with dandelions and daisies. The sugar on the bread and butter has lost its charm, but I love the dandelions and daisies even more passionately now than then, and never would endure to see them all mown away if I were not certain that in a day or two they would be pushing up their little faces again as jauntily as ever. During those six weeks I lived in a world of dandelions and delights. The dandelions carpeted the three lawns—they used to be lawns, but have long since blossomed out into meadows filled with every sort of pretty weed—and under and among the groups of leafless oaks and beeches were blue hepaticas, white anemones, violets, and celandines in sheets. The celandines in particular delighted me, with their clean, happy brightness, so beautifully trim and newly varnished, as though they too had had the painters at work on them. Then, when the anemones went, came a few stray periwinkles and Solomon's-seal, and all the bird-cherries blossomed in a burst. And then, before I had a little got used to the joy of their flowers against the sky, came the lilacs—masses and masses of them, in clumps on the grass, with other shrubs and trees by the side of walks, and one great continuous bank of them half a mile long right past the west front of the house, away down as far as one could see, shining glorious against a background of firs. When that time came, and when, before it was over, the acacias all blossomed too, and four great clumps of pale, silvery-pink peonies flowered under the south windows, I felt so absolutely happy, and blest, and thankful, and grateful, that I really cannot describe it. My days seemed to melt away in a dream of pink and purple peace. [. . .]

The first part of that time of blessedness was the most perfect, for I had not a thought of anything but the peace and beauty all round me. Then he appeared suddenly who has a right to appear when and how he will, and rebuked me for never having written, and when I told him that I had been literally too happy to think of writing, he seemed to take it as a reflection on himself that I could be happy alone. I took him round the garden along the new paths I had had made, and showed him the acacia and lilac glories, and he said that it was the purest selfishness to enjoy myself when neither he nor the offspring were with me, and that the lilacs wanted thorough pruning. I tried to appease him by offering him the whole of my salad and toast supper which stood ready at the foot of the little veranda steps when we came back, but nothing appeased that Man of Wrath, and he said he would go straight back to the neglected family. So he went; and the remainder of the precious time was disturbed by twinges of conscience (to which I am much subject) whenever I found myself wanting to jump for joy. I went to look at the painters every time my feet were for taking me to look at the garden; I trotted diligently up and down the passages; I criticised and suggested and commanded more in one day than I had done in all the rest of the time; I wrote regularly and sent my love; but I could not manage to fret and yearn. What are you to do if your conscience is clear and your liver in order and the sun is shining?

## Rudyard Kipling (1865–1936)

*Seeking reparations for damage to foreign nationals' property during Venezuela's civil war, Britain, Germany, and Italy instituted a naval blockade against that country in 1902. The poet and fiction writer Rudyard Kipling published "The Rowers" in protest against this alliance, recalling German sympathy for the Dutch-descended Boers, Britain's most recent military opponents. (Printing the poem on 22 December 1902, The New York Times applied this headnote: "In 'The Rowers' Britons Are Reminded of the Anglophobia in Germany During the Boer War.") The poem exemplifies Kipling's brand of patriotism as well as his tendency to focus on the workers, civil servants, and soldiers who kept the British Empire running.*

## The Rowers (1902)

The banked oars fell an hundred strong,
    And backed and threshed and ground;
But bitter was the rowers' song
    As they brought the war-boat round.

They had no heart for the rally and roar
    That makes the whaleback smoke

When the great blades cleave and hold and leave
    As one on the racing stroke.

They sang: "What reckoning do ye keep,
    And steer her by what star,
If we come unscathed from the Southern deep
    To be wrecked on a Baltic bar?

"Last night ye swore our voyage was done,
    But seaward still we go;
And ye tell us now of a secret vow
    Ye have made with an open foe:

"That we must lie off a lightless coast
    And haul and back and veer
At the will of the breed that have wronged us most
    For a year and a year and a year.

"There was never a shame in Christendie[1]
    They laid not to our door:
And ye say we must take the Winter sea,
    And safe with them once more!

"Look south, the gale is scarce o'er past
    That stripped and laid us down
When we stood forth, but they stood fast
    And prayed to see us drown.

"The dead they mocked are scarcely cold;
    Our wounds are bleeding yet;
And ye tell us now that our strength is sold
    To help them press for a debt!

"'Neath all the flags of all mankind
    That use upon the seas,
Was there no other fleet to find,
    That ye strike hands with these?

[1]Christendom.

"Of evil times that men could choose
 On evil fate to fall,
What brooding judgment let ye loose
 To pick the worst of all;

"In sight of peace from the narrow seas,
 O'er half the world to run
With a cheated crew to league anew
 With the Goth and the shameless Hun?"[2]

---

[2]"Goth" and "Hun"—from Germanic and Central Asian tribes of the era of the Roman Empire—were often used by the British to suggest barbarism. "Hun" became an especially popular slur during World War I.

# West Africa and Imperialism

Though mentioned only briefly, the Imperial and West African Rubber Company plays an important thematic role in *Howards End*. In connecting the Wilcox family's Britain-building virtues to the imperialist "destroyer" who (in the narrator's telling) makes the earth "grey" (p. 258), it poses the broad question of culture's debt to barbarism in the more specific terms of Britain's reliance on exploitation overseas. The first two selections here argue for government support of British commercial interests in West Africa; the latter two come from general critiques of imperialism. (A stunning imaginative rendering of the British presence in West Africa from a native point of view may be found in Chinua Achebe's novel *Things Fall Apart*, published in 1958.)

### Mary Kingsley (1862–1900)

*In 1893 and again in 1894–95, Mary Kingsley undertook an extraordinary project for a single woman of that era: journeying through West Africa to gather impressions for a travel narrative (and fish specimens for the British Museum). The first book based on her explorations,* Travels in West Africa *(1897), was sensationally popular in its time and has recently been rediscovered by literary critics. The second, excerpted here, combines personal recollections with scholarship and polemic: critiquing the relatively centralized British colonial administration, Kingsley argues for a system that would vest authority in business organizations and native rulers. Although she stresses her partisanship on behalf of the British people and British trade, Kingsley at times evinces unusual respect for African customs and cultural difference.*

from *West African Studies* (1899)

## Commerce in West Africa

The vast regions of Africa from 30° N. to 20° S., have long been known not to possess a climate suitable for colonising in. "Men's blood rapidly putrifies under the tropic zone." "Tropical conditions favour the growth of pathogenic bacteria"—a rose called by another name. Anyhow, not the sort of country attractive to the father of a family to found a home in. Yet, as in spite of this, European nations are possessing themselves of this country with as much ardour as if it were a health resort and a gold mine in one, it is plain they must have another reason, and this reason is in the case of Germany and England primarily commercial pressure.

These two Teutonic nations have the same habit in their commercial production that they have in their human production,—the habit of overdoing it for their own country; and just as Lancashire,[1] for example, turns out more human beings than can comfortably exist there, so does she turn out more manufactured articles than can be consumed there; and just as the surplus population created by a strong race must find other lands to live in, so must the surplus manufactures of a strong race find other markets; both forms of surplus are to a strong race wealth.

The main difference between these things is that the surplus manufactured article is in no need of considering climate in the matter of its expansion. It stands in a relation to the man who goes out into the world with it akin to that of the wife and family to the colonist; the trader will no more meekly stand having his trade damaged than the colonist will stand having his family damaged; but at the same time, the mere fact that the climate destroys trade-stuff is, well, all the better for trade, and trade, moreover, leads the trader to view the native population from a different standpoint to that of the colonist. To that family man the native is a nuisance, sometimes a dangerous one, at the best an indifferent servant, who does not do his work half so well as in a decent climate he can do it himself. To the trader the native is quite a different thing, a customer. A dense native population is what the trader wants; and on their wealth, prosperity, peace and industry, the success of his endeavours depends.

Now it seems to me that there are in this world two classes of regions attractive to the great European manufacturing nations, Eng-

---

[1]County in northwest England famed for textile manufactures.

land and Germany, wherein they can foster and expand their surplus production of manufactured articles. (1) Such regions as India and China. (2) Such regions as Africa. The necessity of making this division comes from the difference between the native populations. In the first case you are dealing with a people who are manufacturers themselves, and you are selling your goods mainly against gold. In the second the people are not manufacturers themselves except in a very small degree, and you are selling your goods against raw material. In a bustling age like this there seems to be a tendency here and in Germany to value the first form of market above the second. I fail to see that this is a sound valuation. The education our commerce gives will in a comparatively short time transform the people of the first class of markets into rival producers of manufactured articles wherewith to supply the world's markets. We by our pacification of India have already made India a greater exporter than she was before our rule there. If China is opened up, things will be even worse for England and Germany; for the Chinese, with their great power of production, will produce manufactured articles which will fairly swamp the world's markets; for, sad to say, there is little doubt but they can take out of our hands all textile trade, and probably several other lines of trade that England, Germany, and America now hold. [. . .]

The case of the second class of markets—the tropical African—is different. Such markets are of enormous value to us; they are, especially the West African ones, regions of great natural riches in rubber, oil, timber, ivory, and minerals from gold to coal. They are in most places densely populated with customers for England's manufactured goods. The advantages of such a region to a manufacturing nation like ourselves are enormous; for not only do we get rid there of our manufactured goods, but we get, what is of equal value to our manufacturing classes, raw material at a cheap enough rate to enable the English manufacturers to turn out into the markets of the civilised world articles sufficiently cheap themselves to compete with those of other manufacturing nations.

The importance to us of such markets as Africa affords us seems to me to give us one sufficient reason for taking over these tropical African regions. I do not use the word justification in the matter, it is a word one has no right to use until we have demonstrated that our interference with the native population and our endeavours for our own population have ended in unmixed good; but it is a sound reason, as good a reason as we had in overrunning Australia and America. Indeed, I venture to think it is a better one, for the possession of a great market enables thousands of men, women and children to live in comfort and safety in England, instead of going away from home and all that home means; and this commercial reason,—for all its not having a high falutin sound in it,—is the one and only expansion reason we have that in itself desires the national peace and prosperity of the native races with whom it deals.

It seems to me no disgrace to England that her traders are the expanding force for her in Africa. There are three classes of men who are powers to a State—the soldier, the trader, and the scientist. Their efforts, when co-ordinated and directed by the true statesman—the religious man in the guise of philosopher and poet—make a great State. Being English, of course modesty prevents my saying that England is a great State. I content myself by saying that she is a truly great people, and will become a great State when she is led by a line of great statesmen—statesmen who are not only capable, as indeed most of our statesmen have been, of seeing the importance of India and the colonies, but also capable of seeing the equal importance to us of markets.

England's democracy must learn the true value of the markets that our fellow-countrymen have so long been striving to give her, and must appreciate the heroism those men have displayed, only too often unrequited, never half appreciated by the sea-wife, who "breeds a breed of rovin' men and casts them over sea." Those who go to make new homes for the old country in Australia and America do not feel her want of interest keenly; but those heroes of commerce who go to fight and die in fever-stricken lands for the sake of the old homes at home, do feel her want of interest.

## E. D. Morel (1873–1924)

*E. D. Morel, a journalist and Liberal politician, pressed the British government to intervene against the brutal treatment of Africans (in the rubber industry and other enterprises) in the Congo Free State ruled by Belgium's King Leopold II (sovereign 1865–1909). In* Affairs of West Africa, *Morel joins Kingsley (to whom he dedicates the book) in urging stronger state support of British business interests in the region; in the excerpt given here, he describes rubber collecting in Nigeria. The Niger Coast, Lagos, and Gold Coast protectorates were established by the British—with various degrees of violence—in the years just prior to Morel's writing.*

from *Affairs of West Africa* (1902)

## Rubber-collecting in Nigeria

I have already briefly alluded to the vegetable products of Nigeria. The collection of rubber, however, presents many features of interest, and deserves more extended treatment.

Of late years the West African rubber industry has grown enormously. In some cases the increase has been phenomenal. The Niger Coast Protectorate and the Gold Coast have within the space of six years more than doubled their rubber exports. The performance of Lagos has been still more remarkable, although unfortunately the wastefulness, or perhaps it would be fairer to say the lack of scientific knowledge on the part of the natives in tapping the trees and vines, has led to a notable falling off in production during the last three years. It seems evident that Western Africa may in time rival Brazil as the rubber-producing country of the world.

The rubber found in West Africa is of various kinds. The place of honour, so far as our own Colonies are concerned, may be given to the rubber-tree properly so-called, *Kickxia Africana* (the "Ere" or "Ireh" of the natives), and a beautiful tree it is, springing up clean and smooth to a height of sixty feet. Then come various species of *Ficus*, and last, but not least, the *Landolphias*, or rubber-vines.

In Nigeria rubber is found, roughly speaking, from Abutshi, 120 miles up the river Niger, as far as Jebba on the Niger and Yola on the Binue. We will suppose that a rubber-collecting expedition has been decided upon by the inhabitants of some village fifteen or twenty miles from the river side (rubber in Nigeria is scarce on the actual river banks).

Soon after dawn all the available men and women gather together—a light-hearted, jabbering crowd. Extraordinary animation reigns throughout the village. The ground is strewn with the implements necessary to the rubber-collector's art, and with the victuals essential to the sustenance of his body while the work is being pursued. They include such varied articles as calabashes, "matchets,"[1] knives, dried yam in bags, and fresh water in bottles which once contained that delectable, throat-peeling liquid known as Hamburg gin. Mingled with them, in apparently hopeless confusion, numerous spears and flint-lock guns lie scattered. There is generally something or other on the prowl in an African forest in the shape of leopards, or

---

[1]Machetes.

"humans," or spirits—and it is just as well to be prepared for any emergency. Hence these warlike accompaniments, calculated to deceive the inexperienced into a belief that raiding and not rubber is in question.

Through the village and beyond it, passing plantations of millet, yams, Indian corn and cassava, winds the caravan, until the fringe of the forest looms near. Then, abruptly parting with the bright sunlight and the waving fields, we plunge headlong into an atmosphere of gloomy, fantastic weirdness, and disappear amid the silent shadows of the giant trees. [. . .]

No sooner has the member of a caravan—every one acts, as a rule, independently of his fellow—pitched upon a spot which seems propitious, than down comes the load off his head. A little preliminary in the shape of refreshment is ever conducive to good labour, so recourse is had to the *ci-devant*[2] gin-bottle and the dried yams. These inner cravings having been satisfied, the rubber-collector makes with his "matchet" a number of transverse incisions in the bark of an adjacent rubber-tree, or vine, as the case may be; hangs his calabashes (empty gourds) beneath the cruel rent, sees that the sap is running; looks round for more trees, makes more incisions, hangs up more calabashes; and then, feeling fully satisfied with his labours, casts himself down upon the ground and lies there awhile, heedless of the crawling legions of the insect fraternity. Every now and then he will lazily rise and make the round of the trees he has tapped, to assure himself that the sap is flowing freely into the calabashes. A really good workman will collect three or four pounds of rubber a day, so that, taking an average of, say, two pounds for each individual, a caravan numbering one hundred and fifty souls will gather a considerable quantity of the stuff in a comparatively short time. The sap is then boiled in an iron pot to make it coagulate, salt and lime being sometimes added to help the process of solidification. It is then rolled into balls. When the calabashes are full the homeward march begins.

The home-coming of the caravan is marked by congratulations on the part of those who stayed behind, and every proud owner of a calabash or two of rubber recounts to the members of an admiring household the wild and terrible adventures (in the shape of spooks, leopards, and what not) which have befallen him in the forest.

The last stage in the business, so far as the native is concerned, has then to be carried out. The rubber having been collected, it must be

[2]Former (French: formerly).

sold. So off goes the collector to the nearest trading station with the spoil. Now, if the commercial ways of the Heathen Chinee are dark, the ways of the Heathen son of Ham[3] are much the same on occasion. The rubber, he knows, is bought by weight. Primitive reasoning convinces him that if he rolls his rubber round a stone or bullet, not only will the ball weigh more, but he will be able to make more balls out of the rubber he has collected. The consequence is that the European trader, when he cuts the rubber ball in two (being used to these little pranks), frequently comes across a stone, bullet, or other heavy substance embedded in the centre, to the unbounded astonishment, needless to remark, of our friend the collector, who cannot for the life of him understand who placed it there, and asserts, with much emphasis and gesticulation, that only a ju-ju[4] or spirit of the most depraved character could have played an honest man so low-down a trick.

When the rubber has finally passed into the white trader's hands, after the preliminary native preparation, it is still found to contain a large proportion of water (about 10 per cent.) and emits a most disagreeable odour. This water has to be ejected before the rubber is fit for the European market. The balls or cakes are therefore placed in a pressing machine, resembling an ordinary mangle,[5] then cleaned of the impurities which may still remain, and finally cut into strips, soaked in sea-water to prevent "sweating," and shipped in wooden casks.

The rubber trade of Nigeria is only in its infancy, and the advent of competitive private enterprise into the Niger territories should have the effect of stimulating the industry to a notable extent.

The unfortunate destruction of the rubber trees and vines in the Lagos forests has been instrumental in producing a *furor* of restrictive legislation on the part of the authorities. There is grave doubt as to whether this method of approaching the subject is not mistaken and likely to defeat its own ends. It is incongruous, to say the least of it, to first of all encourage the native to exploit a new product, to give him no scientific instruction or training in the process, and then, when the inevitable happens, to express great indignation at his villainous capacity for mischief, and frame legislation calculated to interfere with his free use of his own property! It is not the general custom of the native to destroy a product out of which he makes money. In the

---

[3]African or dark-skinned person; from the legend that descendants of Noah's son Ham (Genesis 9:19–27) populated Africa and parts of the Middle East.

[4]Magic or spirit associated with a physical object.

[5]Machine for pressing laundry.

case of the oil-palm, in the usage of which they have been long accustomed, the native chiefs themselves legislate against over-tapping, witness the "porroh" of the Mendis.[6] It is a matter of instruction. It is
notorious that the crisis in the Lagos rubber industry is entirely attrib-
utable to the gross foolishness displayed by the authorities in the first
instance in not taking the necessary means to teach the natives the art
of rational production. What is wanted is the creation of small centres
of instruction in every district, where the natives could come for information, where various products could be shown, tested and com-
mented upon. The official in charge would have no powers whatever
conferred upon him in a political sense, but would be connected, of
course, with the Government. His duty would be that of instructor,
supervisor, guide, and assistant. He would certainly be welcomed by
the chiefs, so long as they were assured that his *rôle* was entirely
divorced from political designs. The experience would cost very little,
and the benefits accruing therefrom, both as regards the perfecting of
existing native industries and the stimulation of new ones, would be
considerable, and would do away with the necessity, or alleged necessity, of subsequent legislation of an irritating character. A little more
of that sort of thing and a little less blood-letting and "murder of
native institutions," as Miss Kingsley used to put it, in order to improve
them, would be very desirable.

## J. A. Hobson (1858–1940)

*J. A. Hobson was one of the leading Liberal thinkers of his day, an econ-
omist who criticized laissez-faire policies and an internationalist who
stressed the need for cooperation among governments. In his most
famous work, excerpted here, he argues that imperialism resulted not
only from Europe's drive to find new markets and new sources of raw
materials but also from its pursuit of fresh venues for capital investment.
In the following selection, Hobson distinguishes between legitimate colonialism and dangerous imperialism, and between a "humane cosmopolitanism" stressing bonds that transcend nation and an "anarchic
cosmopolitanism" of private enterprise. As the critic Mary Ellis Gibson
has suggested, this latter distinction may explain why Forster sometimes*

[6]Among the Mende people of Sierra Leone, regulation of commerce was within the
purview of the secret male society of the Poro.

*associates cosmopolitanism with the cultured openness of the Schlegel sisters, at other times with the flattening of life brought on by modern nomadism and Wilcoxian imperialists (107–9).*

## from *Imperialism* (1902)

It is a debasement of this genuine nationalism, by attempts to overflow its natural banks and absorb the near or distant territory of reluctant and unassimilable peoples, that marks the passage from nationalism to a spurious colonialism on the one hand, Imperialism on the other.

Colonialism, where it consists in the migration of part of a nation to vacant or sparsely peopled foreign lands, the emigrants carrying with them full rights of citizenship in the mother country, or else establishing local self-government in close conformity with her institutions and under her final control, may be considered a genuine expansion of nationality, a territorial enlargement of the stock, language and institutions of the nation. Few colonies in history have, however, long remained in this condition when they have been remote from the mother country. Either they have severed the connection and set up for themselves as separate nationalities, or they have been kept in complete political bondage so far as all major processes of government are concerned, a condition to which the term Imperialism is at least as appropriate as colonialism. The only form of distant colony which can be regarded as a clear expansion of nationalism is the self-governing British colony in Australasia and Canada, and even in these cases local conditions may generate a separate nationalism based on a strong consolidation of colonial interests and sentiments alien from and conflicting with those of the mother nation. [. . .]

Colonialism, in its best sense, is a natural overflow of nationality; its test is the power of colonists to transplant the civilisation they represent to the new natural and social environment in which they find themselves. We must not be misled by names; the "colonial" party in Germany and France is identical in general aim and method with the "imperialist" party in England, and the latter is the truer title. Professor Seeley well marked the nature of Imperialism. "When a State advances beyond the limits of nationality its power becomes precarious and artificial. This is the condition of most empires, and it is the condition of our own. When a nation extends itself into other territories the chances are that it cannot destroy or completely drive out, even if it succeeds in conquering, them. When this happens it has a great and permanent difficulty to contend with, for the subject or rival nationalities cannot be properly assimilated, and remain as a permanent cause of weakness and danger."[1]

The novelty of the recent Imperialism regarded as a policy consists chiefly in its adoption by several nations. The notion of a number of competing empires is essentially modern. The root idea of empire in the ancient and medieval world was that of a federation of States, under a hegemony, covering in general terms the entire known or recognised world, such as was held by Rome under the so-called *pax Romana*.[2] When Roman citizens, with full civic rights, were found all over the explored world, in Africa and Asia, as well as in Gaul and Britain, Imperialism contained a genuine element of internationalism. With the fall of Rome this conception of a single empire wielding political authority over the civilised world did not disappear. On the contrary, it survived all the fluctuations of the Holy Roman Empire. Even after the definite split between the Eastern and Western sections had taken place at the close of the fourth century, the theory of a single State, divided for administrative purposes, survived. Beneath every cleavage or antagonism, and notwithstanding the severance of many independent kingdoms and provinces, this ideal unity of the empire lived. It formed the conscious avowed ideal of Charlemagne, though as a practical ambition confined to Western Europe. Rudolph of Habsburg not merely revived the idea, but laboured to realise it through Central Europe, while his descendant Charles V. gave a very real meaning to the term by gathering under the unity of his imperial rule the territories of Austria, Germany, Spain, the Netherlands, Sicily, and Naples. In later ages this dream of a European Empire animated the policy of Peter the Great, Catherine, and Napoleon. Nor is it impossible that Kaiser Wilhelm III. holds a vision of such a world-power.[3]

Political philosophers in many ages, Vico, Machiavelli, Dante, Kant,[4] have speculated on an empire as the only feasible security for peace, a hierarchy of States conforming on the larger scale to the feudal order within the single State.

[1]John Robert Seeley, *The Expansion of England*, 1883.

[2]Latin: "Roman peace," referring to a long era in the history of the Roman Empire, 27 BCE–180 CE.

[3]A misprint for Wilhelm II, ruler of the German Empire 1888–1918.

[4]Giambattista Vico (1668–1744); Niccolò Machiavelli (1469–1527); Dante Alighieri (1265–1321); Immanuel Kant (1724–1804).

Thus empire was identified with internationalism, though not always based on a conception of equality of nations. The break-up of the Central European Empire, with the weakening of nationalities that followed, evoked a new modern sentiment of internationalism which, through the eighteenth century, was a flickering inspiration in the intellectual circles of European States. "The eve of the French Revolution found every wise man in Europe—Lessing, Kant, Goethe, Rousseau, Lavater, Condorcet, Priestley, Gibbon, Franklin[5]—more of a citizen of the world than of any particular country. Goethe confessed that he did not know what patriotism was, and was glad to be without it. Cultured men of all countries were at home in polite society everywhere. Kant was immensely more interested in the events of Paris than in the life of Prussia. Italy and Germany were geographical expressions; those countries were filled with small States in which there was no political life, but in which there was much interest in the general progress of culture. The Revolution itself was at bottom also human and cosmopolitan. It is, as Lamartine said, 'a date in the human mind,' and it is because of that fact that all the carping of critics like Taine[6] cannot prevent us from seeing that the character of the men who led the great movements of the Revolution can never obliterate the momentous nature of the Titanic strife. The soldiers of the Revolution who, barefooted and ragged, drove the insolent reactionaries from the soil of France were fighting not merely for some national cause, but for a cause dimly perceived to be the cause of general mankind. With all its crudities and imperfections, the idea of the Revolution was that of a conceived body of Right in which all men should share."[7]

This early flower of humane cosmopolitanism was destined to wither before the powerful revival of nationalism which marked the next century. Even in the narrow circles of the cultured classes it easily passed from a noble and a passionate ideal to become a vapid senti-

[5]Figures representing the thought and achievements of the Enlightenment from Germany (Gotthold Lessing, 1729–81; Kant; Johann Wolfgang von Goethe, 1749–1832), France (Jean Jacques Rousseau, 1712–78; Nicolas de Caritat, Marquis de Condorcet 1743–94), Switzerland (Johann Kaspar Lavater, 1741–1801), England (Joseph Priestley, 1733–1804; Edward Gibbon, 1737–94), and the United States (Benjamin Franklin, 1706–90).

[6]In his *Origines de la France Contemporaine* (Origins of Contemporary France), 1875–93, the French critic and historian Hippolyte Taine maintained a skeptical stance on the French Revolution. In 1847, the French poet Alphonse de Lamartine had published a celebratory history of the Girondins, a doomed moderate political faction in the Revolution.

[7]Quoting William Clarke in the *Progressive Review*, February 1897.

mentalism, and after the brief flare of 1848[8] among the continental populace had been extinguished, little remained but a dim smouldering of the embers. Even the Socialism which upon the continent retains a measure of the spirit of internationalism is so tightly confined within the national limits, in its struggle with bureaucracy and capitalism, that "the international" expresses little more than a holy aspiration, and has little opportunity of putting into practice the genuine sentiments of brotherhood which its prophets have always preached.

Thus the triumph of nationalism seems to have crushed the rising hope of internationalism. Yet it would appear that there is no essential antagonism between them. A true strong internationalism in form or spirit would rather imply the existence of powerful self-respecting nationalities which seek union on the basis of common national needs and interests. Such a historical development would be far more conformable to laws of social growth than the rise of anarchic cosmopolitanism from individual units amid the decadence of national life.

Nationalism is a plain highway to internationalism, and if it manifests divergence we may well suspect a perversion of its nature and its purpose. Such a perversion is Imperialism, in which nations trespassing beyond the limits of facile assimilation transform the wholesome stimulative rivalry of varied national types into the cut-throat struggle of competing empires.

## Leonard Woolf (1880–1969)

*While Leonard Woolf and Forster did not become close friends until a few years after the publication of* Howards End, *they knew each other at Cambridge and shared many beliefs—in the importance of social tolerance and free inquiry, for example. Having joined the British colonial administration in Ceylon in 1904, Woolf soon turned against imperialism; returning to England in 1911, he commenced a writing career. Reflecting both diligent research and a passionate belief in international cooperation and justice,* Empire and Commerce *exemplifies the style of thinking Forster held in highest regard.*

---

[8]A series of revolutions, inspired by democratic ideals, swept across European states (and Brazil) in that year. Most were quickly suppressed.

from *Empire and Commerce in Africa* (1920)

## PART III. CHAPTER II.

### The Future of Africa

[. . .] In the last chapter I have attempted to trace the general effects of European policy in Africa. In my judgment those effects have been almost wholly evil. The European went into Africa about forty years ago desiring to exploit it and its inhabitants for his own economic advantage, and he rapidly acquired the belief that the power of his State should be used in Africa to promote his own economic interests. Once this belief was accepted, it destroyed the idea of individual moral responsibility. The State, enthroned in its impersonality and a glamour of patriotism, can always make a wilderness and call it peace, or make a conquest and call it civilization. The right of Europe to civilize became synonymous with the right of Europe to rob or to exploit the uncivilized. The power of each European State was applied ruthlessly in Africa. In bitter competition with one another, they partitioned territory which belonged to none of them. By fraud or by force the native chiefs and rulers were swindled or robbed of their dominions. Any resistance by the inhabitants to the encroachments either of individual Europeans or of European States was treated as "rebellion," and followed by massacres known as wars or punitive expeditions. In this process tribe was used against tribe and race against race, and wherever any native administration existed it was destroyed.

This work was accomplished by men who were not more rapacious or evil than the ordinary man; it was accomplished by men often of ideals and great devotion, but who accepted a political dogma, namely, that their actions were justified by the right and duty of the European State to use its power in Africa for the economic interests of its European subjects. Just in the same way those who burnt and tortured heretics were probably no more cruel or evil than the majority of their fellows; they were men of ideals and great devotion who accepted the religious dogma that it was the right and duty of the Church to torture men's bodies for the sake of their souls.

The dogma of economic imperialism prevailed with the aid of modern rifle and gun. The slaughter of the most warlike Africans encouraged the survivors to submit, and peace descended upon the greater part of Africa. The first stage of economic imperialism was accomplished, and the European looked round and openly proclaimed that the work he had done was good. The reason which he gave and gives for this opinion is interesting and deserves a little examination. The policy of conquest and partition which we have described is usually defended on two grounds: first, that it was inevitable; and secondly, that it eventually substituted a system of law and order for one of lawless barbarism. [. . .]

Life in Africa during the first fifty years of the nineteenth century was undoubtedly ugly and cruel and bloody. But its misery was not, like that of civilization, organized or continual. This fact accounts for the contradictory descriptions and estimates of it which we find in the works of travellers and missionaries. The villages and country of the Congo, which the civilization introduced by King Leopold subsequently converted into a desert, seemed to Coquilhat when he visited them in 1883 to be idyllic, the inhabitants prosperous, peaceful, and happy. On the other hand, men like Grenfell, who knew and denounced the atrocities perpetrated by European economic imperialism in the Belgian Congo, furnish evidence of the horrors of barbarism which preceded them.[1]

It is, however, for our purpose unnecessary to attempt any accurate comparison between the misery of African savagery and the misery of European exploitation. Even if we admit that the atrocities of the first far outweigh the atrocities of the second, and that Europe has given to Africa the inestimable gift of law and order, this is no justification of the system of conquest, partition, and economic exploitation which we have examined. When Europeans are forced to defend the evil that they have done in Africa by pleading that the evil has been less than that done by the savage rulers and the Arab slave traders whom they have destroyed, their case must be a singularly weak one. Economic imperialism stands self-condemned if the only thing which it can say for itself is that the present conditions in British East Africa, for instance, are rather better than they were when Captain Lugard led his expedition into Uganda.[2] [. . .]

Much of the criticism of the international solution of the problem of Africa seems to me justified. The ultimate beliefs and desires which create that problem are economic and social. They are part of that system upon which European society is now based, and which we call

[1]Camille-Aimé Coquilhat (1853–91) was a Belgian soldier who became an administrator of the Congo; George Grenfell (1849–1906) was a British missionary and explorer.

[2]F. D. Lugard (1858–1945), a main target of Woolf's critique in *Empire and Commerce*, was instrumental in opening Uganda to British trade and colonization between 1890 and 1900.

for short the capitalist system. The capitalist system is not the creation, nor does it consist, of "capitalists." It is created by and consists of the beliefs and desires, the subconscious social philosophy, of the millions who are born and die in European cities and villages. We who are part of those millions accept our knowledge and our ideals as instinctively and automatically as the mouse-hunting cat; but, being human beings, we thereby in the process create a society and social philosophy whose effects are felt far beyond the boundaries of Europe. It is dangerous to attempt to define in a sentence or two anything so complicated and subconscious as this social philosophy. But its essence undoubtedly consists in the domination of men and their society by economic ideals. Whatever be the cause, it is certain that at no time in the history of the world has there existed a society of human beings dominated by such a universal economic passion as ours is. It is the passion of buying cheap and selling dear. The commodities which we desire to sell dear and to buy cheap differ from person to person: some of us deal in wheat and cotton goods, others in labour, others in the product of the intellect or imagination. But in all these transactions, which fill nine-tenths of our lives, we accept unconsciously the same principle, ideal, and even obligation: to make a profit out of cotton goods or labour or stocks and shares or works of art or historical investigation, by selling in the dearest and buying in the cheapest market.

The application of this principle to the relations of Europeans to Africans is undoubtedly the fundamental cause of the African problem. Europe has treated the African and his land simply as something to make a profit out of, something which it could buy very cheap and sell very dear. In the process different parts of Europe and different Europeans have struggled and fought and swindled one another for possession of this valuable prize. But merely to stop this economic struggle in so far as it is carried on by groups organized in nations will not change Europe's relations with Africa, which are based upon economic exploitation. You may substitute international control for national imperialism, and you will still find, if the economic beliefs and desires of Europe continue the same, that the struggle for the economic exploitation of the African is now carried on by international instead of national groups.

Thus we are forced to the conclusion that if the European State is to become an instrument for good rather than of evil in Africa, the economic beliefs and desires of Europeans must suffer a change. [. . .]

# *Culture and Bloomsbury*

One of the noblest elements in the lives of the Schlegel siblings is their pleasure in the arts—something important to Forster's Cambridge friends and to the Bloomsbury Group, with which he would soon become more intimate. Like other fictions by Bloomsbury writers, however, *Howards End* ultimately poses hard questions about culture's benefits and costs. In Leonard Bast's efforts to educate himself, and in the Schlegels' impatience with what they consider the banality of his reading, Forster shows how culture can divide class from class as well as unite soul with soul. Nor does he make matters easier by having the Schlegel sisters abandon the world of clever urbanites up on the latest books and music for a more bucolic, perhaps less intellectually vibrant, existence. The first two selections given here assert the value of culture and aesthetic engagement; the second two, from Bloomsbury novels, express greater anxiety about culture's effects.

## Matthew Arnold (1822–1888)

*Proposing culture as an antidote to the spiritual barrenness of an age dominated by money and machinery,* Culture and Anarchy *can be seen as an early document in the pitting of art against commerce that would reach its height under modernism. Yet as* Howards End *indicates, Matthew Arnold's brand of idealism was showing signs of wear by the beginning of the twentieth century. The dream of a society in which culture elevates all classes certainly hovers in the background of Forster's story of refined Schlegels and business-driven Wilcoxes, but it is also put into question by Leonard Bast, who leads Margaret to think, "Culture had worked in her own case, but during the last few*

*weeks she had doubted whether it humanized the majority, so wide and
so widening is the gulf that stretches between the natural and the philosophic man, so many the good chaps who are wrecked in trying to cross
it" (p. 94). The selection here is from the beginning of chapter 1.*

## from *Culture and Anarchy* (1882)

### Chapter I.
### Sweetness and Light

The disparagers of culture make its motive curiosity; sometimes, indeed,
they make its motive mere exclusiveness and vanity. The culture which is
supposed to plume itself on a smattering of Greek and Latin is a culture
which is begotten by nothing so intellectual as curiosity; it is valued
either out of sheer vanity and ignorance or else as an engine of social and
class distinction, separating its holder, like a badge or title, from other
people who have not got it. No serious man would call this *culture*, or
attach any value to it, as culture, at all. To find the real ground for the
very different estimate which serious people will set upon culture, we
must find some motive for culture in the terms of which may lie a real
ambiguity; and such a motive the word *curiosity* gives us.

I have before now pointed out that we English do not, like the foreigners, use this word in a good sense as well as in a bad sense. With us
the word is always used in a somewhat disapproving sense. A liberal
and intelligent eagerness about the things of the mind may be meant by
a foreigner when he speaks of curiosity, but with us the word always
conveys a certain notion of frivolous and unedifying activity. [. . . Yet]
as there is a curiosity about intellectual matters which is futile, and
merely a disease, so there is certainly a curiosity,—a desire after the
things of the mind simply for their own sakes and for the pleasure of
seeing them as they are,—which is, in an intelligent being, natural and
laudable. Nay, and the very desire to see things as they are implies a balance and regulation of mind which is not often attained without fruitful
effort, and which is the very opposite of the blind and diseased impulse
of mind which is what we mean to blame when we blame curiosity.
Montesquieu says: "The first motive which ought to impel us to study is
the desire to augment the excellence of our nature, and to render an
intelligent being yet more intelligent."[1] This is the true ground to assign

---

[1]From the "Discours sur les motifs qui doivent nous encourager aux science" (1725),
by the Baron de Montesquieu (Gregor 199).

for the genuine scientific passion, however manifested, and for culture, viewed simply as a fruit of this passion; and it is a worthy ground, even though we let the term *curiosity* stand to describe it.

But there is of culture another view, in which not solely the scientific passion, the sheer desire to see things as they are, natural and proper in an intelligent being, appears as the ground of it. There is a view in which all the love of our neighbour, the impulses towards action, help, and beneficence, the desire for removing human error, clearing human confusion, and diminishing human misery, the noble aspiration to leave the world better and happier than we found it,—motives eminently such as are called social,—come in as part of the grounds of culture, and the main and pre-eminent part. Culture is then properly described not as having its origin in curiosity, but as having its origin in the love of perfection; it is *a study of perfection*. It moves by the force, not merely or primarily of the scientific passion for pure knowledge, but also of the moral and social passion for doing good. As, in the first view of it, we took for its worthy motto Montesquieu's words: "To render an intelligent being yet more intelligent!" so, in the second view of it, there is no better motto which it can have than these words of Bishop Wilson: "To make reason and the will of God prevail!"[2] [. . .]

The moment this view of culture is seized, the moment it is regarded not solely as the endeavour to see things as they are, to draw towards a knowledge of the universal order which seems to be intended and aimed at in the world, and which it is a man's happiness to go along with or his misery to go counter to,—to learn, in short, the will of God,—the moment, I say, culture is considered not merely as the endeavour to *see* and *learn* this, but as the endeavour, also, to make it *prevail*, the moral, social, and beneficent character of culture becomes manifest. The mere endeavour to see and learn the truth for our own personal satisfaction is indeed a commencement for making it prevail, a preparing the way for this, which always serves this, and is wrongly, therefore, stamped with blame absolutely in itself and not only in its caricature and degeneration. But perhaps it has got stamped with blame, and disparaged with the dubious title of curiosity, because in comparison with this wider endeavour of such great and plain utility it looks selfish, petty, and unprofitable.

[2]From the "Sacra Privata" of the Anglican Bishop Thomas Wilson (1781). The later quote from Wilson is from the same work (Super 418).

And religion, the greatest and most important of the efforts by which the human race has manifested its impulse to perfect itself,—religion, that voice of the deepest human experience,—does not only enjoin and sanction the aim which is the great aim of culture, the aim of setting ourselves to ascertain what perfection is and to make it prevail; but also, in determining generally in what human perfection consists, religion comes to a conclusion identical with that which culture,—culture seeking the determination of this question through *all* the voices of human experience which have been heard upon it, of art, science, poetry, philosophy, history, as well as of religion, in order to give a greater fulness and certainty to its solution,—likewise reaches. Religion says: *The kingdom of God is within you*; and culture, in like manner, places human perfection in an *internal* condition, in the growth and predominance of our humanity proper, as distinguished from our animality. It places it in the ever-increasing efficacy and in the general harmonious expansion of those gifts of thought and feeling, which make the peculiar dignity, wealth, and happiness of human nature. As I have said on a former occasion:[3] "It is in making endless additions to itself, in the endless expansion of its powers, in endless growth in wisdom and beauty, that the spirit of the human race finds its ideal. To reach this ideal, culture is an indispensable aid, and that is the true value of culture." Not a having and a resting, but a growing and a becoming, is the character of perfection as culture conceives it; and here, too, it coincides with religion.

And because men are all members of one great whole, and the sympathy which is in human nature will not allow one member to be indifferent to the rest or to have a perfect welfare independent of the rest, the expansion of our humanity, to suit the idea of perfection which culture forms, must be a *general* expansion. Perfection, as culture conceives it, is not possible while the individual remains isolated. The individual is required, under pain of being stunted and enfeebled in his own development if he disobeys, to carry others along with him in his march towards perfection, to be continually doing all he can to enlarge and increase the volume of the human stream sweeping thitherward. And here, once more, culture lays on us the same obligation as religion, which says, as Bishop Wilson has admirably put it, that "to promote the kingdom of God is to increase and hasten one's own happiness."

But, finally, perfection,—as culture from a thorough disinterested study of human nature and human experience learns to conceive it,— is a harmonious expansion of *all* the powers which make the beauty

---

[3]In *A French Eton* (1864).

and worth of human nature, and is not consistent with the over-development of any one power at the expense of the rest. Here culture goes beyond religion, as religion is generally conceived by us. [. . . A]bove all in our own country has culture a weighty part to perform, because here that mechanical character, which civilisation tends to take everywhere, is shown in the most eminent degree. Indeed nearly all the characters of perfection, as culture teaches us to fix them, meet in this country with some powerful tendency which thwarts them and sets them at defiance. The idea of perfection as an *inward* condition of the mind and spirit is at variance with the mechanical and material civilisation in esteem with us, and nowhere, as I have said, so much in esteem as with us. The idea of perfection as a *general* expansion of the human family is at variance with our strong individualism, our hatred of all limits to the unrestrained swing of the individual's personality, our maxim of "every man for himself." Above all, the idea of perfection as a *harmonious* expansion of human nature is at variance with our want of flexibility, with our inaptitude for seeing more than one side of a thing, with our intense energetic absorption in the particular pursuit we happen to be following. So culture has a rough task to achieve in this country. Its preachers have, and are likely long to have, a hard time of it, and they will much oftener be regarded, for a great while to come, as elegant or spurious Jeremiahs[4] than as friends and benefactors. That, however, will not prevent their doing in the end good service if they persevere.

## G. E. Moore (1873–1958)

*G. E. Moore, a professor, was one of the former members or "angels" who attended meetings of the Cambridge Apostles (see p. xvi). His* Principia Ethica *(Foundations of Ethics) was the Apostles' philosophical bible. In the book's most famous pages, presented here, he follows an exhaustive critique of major approaches to ethics with a surprisingly blunt declaration that the two most valuable things in life must be human intimacy and aesthetic experience. This privileging of friendship and art was manifest in the life and writings of the Bloomsbury Group, which included several Apostles, and it inflects the Schlegels' conduct of existence—including their love of a "little Ricketts picture" (p. 35; for an illustration by Ricketts, see p. 371)—in* Howards End.

---

[4]Prophets (from the Old Testament figure associated with the books of Jeremiah and Lamentations).

## from *Principia Ethica* (1903)

If, now, we use this method of absolute isolation, and guard against these errors, it appears that the question we have to answer is far less difficult than the controversies of Ethics might have led us to expect. Indeed, once the meaning of the question is clearly understood, the answer to it, in its main outlines, appears to be so obvious, that it runs the risk of seeming to be a platitude. By far the most valuable things, which we know or can imagine, are certain states of consciousness, which may be roughly described as the pleasures of human intercourse and the enjoyment of beautiful objects. No one, probably, who has asked himself the question, has ever doubted that personal affection and the appreciation of what is beautiful in Art or Nature, are good in themselves; nor, if we consider strictly what things are worth having *purely for their own sakes*, does it appear probable that any one will think that anything else has *nearly* so great a value as the things which are included under these two heads. I have myself urged [. . .] that the mere existence of what is beautiful does appear to have *some* intrinsic value; but I regard it as indubitable [. . .] that such mere existence of what is beautiful has value, so small as to be negligible, in comparison with that which attaches to the *consciousness* of beauty. This simple truth may, indeed, be said to be universally recognised. What has *not* been recognised is that it is the ultimate and fundamental truth of Moral Philosophy. That it is only for the sake of these things—in order that as much of them as possible may at some time exist—that any one can be justified in performing any public or private duty; that they are the *raison d'être*[1] of virtue; that it is they—these complex wholes[2] *themselves*, and not any constituent or characteristic of them—that form the rational ultimate end of human action and the sole criterion of social progress: these appear to be truths which have been generally overlooked.

That they are truths—that personal affections and aesthetic enjoyments include *all* the greatest, and *by far* the greatest, goods we can imagine, will, I hope, appear more plainly in the course of that analysis of them, to which I shall now proceed.

---

[1]French: reason for existing.

[2]Moore defines complex wholes (which he also calls "organic unities") as "wholes which possess the property that their value is different from the sum of the values of their parts" (29).

Charles Ricketts, illustration for *Daphnis and Chloe*, 1893.

## Leonard Woolf (1880–1969)

*In this novel, Harry Davis, a lawyer's son and an art student, is in love with brilliant, beautiful Camilla Lawrence (based on Virginia Stephen, who in 1912 had married Leonard Woolf). Though Camilla and Harry respect each other intellectually, she finds she does not love him; in the first passage here, she and her sister Katharine (based on Virginia's sister Vanessa) discuss the prospect of marriage before her feelings are quite definite. Meanwhile, Harry has been fanning the affections of a suburban girl named Gwen Garland by encouraging her to read advanced books. The second and third passages are set at a suburban garden party where Gwen meets Camilla, then overhears her rival's verdict on a life lacking real engagement with art and ideas. (Emily is a sister of Gwen's devoted to charity work; The Poor Dear Things are aid recipients; Mrs. Brown is a local widow; Macausland is a local cleric.) The novel bears comparison to* Howards End *for its portrait of two intelligent sisters and its sometimes anguished grappling with confusions enmeshing the cultured, the would-be cultured, and those who care for culture not at all. Its eventual crisis, though different in specifics from Leonard Bast's, is brought on by Gwen's reading.*

### from *The Wise Virgins* (1914)

Harry, even when he was in it, always retained the first impression which the Lawrence circle gave him: interminable talk and silences in very comfortable chairs. These epicures[1] in the art of emotions and the emotions of art had emancipated themselves from the convention that there are some things that men and women cannot talk about, and they had done this so successfully that a stranger might at first have been led to conclude from their practice that those are the only things that men and women of intelligence can talk about. Such a conclusion would have been hasty. It was perhaps their weakness, at any rate intellectually, that they never did those things—but then they never did anything. In the mornings Camilla painted, and Katharine retired to a room called the study, in which, it was understood, she was writing a book. It was quite obvious to those who knew them that Katharine should have been in the studio and Camilla in the study. Mr Lawrence was—or rather imagined that he was—daily in the only place in which he could suitably have been, the British Museum. Actually on the five days out of the seven which made up

[1]Persons of refined tastes.

their "working" week he spent the hours between ten and eleven of the morning deciding that he could study Byzantine art as well in his arm-chair as in a museum, and between eleven and one he did so.[2]

The centre of the circle was Horton Street, but from time to time that centre shifted to a little house among downs, fields, and trees in Kent. To sit in the arm-chairs in Kent was the final sign that you were in the innermost circle. This sign came to Harry about a week after the river party at Maidenhead.

"I've asked Harry to come down with us on Friday," said Camilla to Katharine on the Thursday. "I suppose you don't mind."

It was one o'clock, and Camilla had come into the study. The floor was littered with innumerable sheets of white paper; in the centre Katharine was sitting in an arm-chair with a pen in her hand and a sheet of white paper on a book upon her knees. She bit the end of the pen, wrinkled her forehead, and looked up dubiously at Camilla.

"You'll have to decide, you know" she said judicially, "whether you are or are not going to marry Harry."

Camilla walked over to the window and leaned upon the window-sill, looking down into the quiet street. The world of actual things which she looked at—the trees heavy now with their summer leaves, the dingy iron palings, the heat beating up from the strip of polished asphalt road, the draggled old woman tottering along on the opposite pavement—seemed for the moment so much more real to her than herself and Harry and marriage. Katharine's remark sounded absurd; she could not seriously think of it. Other people married, but one did not marry—not people one knew—oneself.

"He hasn't asked me to marry him," she said.

"I didn't say he had. But he will. I give him two or three weeks, possibly less, if he sees much of you down there."

Camilla came and sat on the arm of Katharine's chair. Her eyes wandered to the window, her hands smoothed Katharine's hair.

"Do you think I ought to marry anyone, dearest?" she asked.

"I don't think anyone ought to marry you," Katharine laughed.

"Why?"

"Well, he would have to be very much in love with you, and—"

"There's no reason in nature, is there, why he shouldn't be that?"

"No, that's just it, just what I'm telling you, if you'll only listen. He would be; you would always want him to be; you'd insist on it,

---

[2]By the turn of the century, the British Museum in Bloomsbury housed hundreds of artifacts from the Eastern Roman, or Byzantine, Empire (330–1453).

and so he probably would be. You're attractive enough, of course—
to some people."

"Well, what more could you want? I seem to be made for marriage. Attractive: love therefore enduring until death do us part. *Mens
sana in corpore sano*;[3] so that all the marriage service can be read
without blushes. And a mind on wings! Katharine, I'm simply made
for marriage."

"It's never any good talking to you, Camilla; you never listen to a
word one says. I never said you ought not to marry: I said no one ought
to marry you. You can't marry a man without his marrying you."

"Pooh, you old raven, sitting there croaking your nevermore at
me.[4] All that applies probably to every woman who has married since
Eve, or who hasn't. You admit that I'm simply the ideal woman for
marriage, so why go on croaking your nevermore at me?"

"I imagine a husband might not always be content merely to be in
love with you. It isn't a normal male idea of the ideal wife."

"Ah—yes, I see; you mean I couldn't be in love with anyone?
Wouldn't that show I'm a normal woman? But do you honestly think
I'm as cold as all that, Katharine dearest? You know I love you far
more than you love me."

"That's hardly the point we were talking about, is it?"

"But I'm not cold, am I? I couldn't be so very attractive if I were.
I'm very affectionate, you know that, don't you? I like silk and kisses
and soft things and strokings. I was told the other day that I was like
hills with virgin snow on them; but that's nonsense, isn't it?"

"It does sound like it, certainly. But that wasn't what I said."

"But you haven't been in love; no one has ever seen you luxuriat-
ing, you old raven. Yet you don't think yourself an icefield."

"I shall marry, however, and I shall be in love with my husband,"
said Katharine with impassive conviction, and it was quite clear that
she would be. Camilla looked at her. Her face was already like that of
a mother's; her own would always retain something of the virgin's.

"Women don't fall in love till afterwards," she said thoughtfully,
"and after all, I am a woman."

*   *   *

Gwen had read Dostoevsky's *Idiot* and several other books which
Harry had sent her, but there had been few opportunities for talking
alone to Harry since the day of the river party. She was not at all sure

---

[3]Latin: a sound mind in a sound body.
[4]Referring to "The Raven," by Edgar Allan Poe (1845).

that the books had thrown any light for her upon the problems that he had presented her with, and there were many things which she would have liked to talk to him about. She had begun unconsciously to regard him as a sort of oracle upon life. She looked forward to chances of meeting him, and was invariably disappointed by meeting him where it was impossible to put to him the problems which he had helped to call into existence. Her feeling of discontent and her irritation with the aimlessness of her life in Richstead had grown more distinct and frequent, but neither Dostoevsky nor Mr Bernard Shaw[5] nor Meredith nor Mr Conrad, who formed the mental tonic which the young man prescribed, seemed to provide any cure for that uncomfortable state of mind. This state of mind, common to the young of all ages since Ecclesiastes,[6] has at the present time no name; the old-fashioned young men and women of the 'nineties would certainly have diagnosed it in Gwen as weltschmerz.[7] It was, however, another kind of schmerz from which Gwen was suffering at the present moment. She looked at Camilla.

"Is that Miss Lawrence?" she asked Harry.

"Yes; how do you know that?"

"Oh, Hetty told May that she was coming with you today." There was a pause. "She's very beautiful," Gwen went on.

"Do you think so?"

"Yes, I suppose she's very clever too. She looks as if she were."

Harry glanced across at Camilla, who was absorbed in Ethel's account of The Poor Dear Things. He smiled. "It depends on what you mean by clever."

"Oh, you know what I mean," Gwen said impatiently. "All your family are clever, and we aren't. We are just ordinary, stupid people. You talk to Miss Lawrence, I'm sure, in quite a different way from what you talk to—to—well, Ethel. *I* can't even understand *The Egoist*."[8]

"And Miss Lawrence can't understand the binomial theorem, and *I* can't understand you or Mrs Brown, though I love you both very dearly."

"You're sneering and laughing at me now," said Gwen.

---

[5]Fyodor Dostoevksy (1821–81), Russian novelist; George Bernard Shaw (1856–1950), Irish playwright and essayist.

[6]Old Testament book whose speaker reflects on the meaninglessness of life, as in 1.2, "Vanity of vanities, saith the Preacher, vanity of vanities; all is vanity" (King James Version).

[7]Apathy, world-weariness (German: world-pain); coined by the German writer Jean Paul in his novel *Selina* (1810).

[8]An 1879 novel by George Meredith; Forster discusses its plot in *Aspects of the Novel* (1927).

Harry was astonished to see that there were almost tears in her eyes. "What nonsense, Gwen," he said. "You think much too much about cleverness and stupidity. 'Be good, sweet maid, and let who can be clever.'[9] Nobody could call you stupid. If you're going to take *The Egoist* as a test—good Lord! nobody ever has understood it. A lot of gibberish. Nobody can understand it, because Meredith didn't understand it himself—he never took the trouble to think clearly. And as for Miss Lawrence, I don't suppose she has ever read it."

"I wonder if you mean that. I want to ask you about things so much, but—but it's so difficult here, and then you seem so sneering sometimes."

"I don't mean to be; but, look here, we can't talk in this place. You're going to Eastbourne, aren't you, for the summer, when mother and Hetty go? I shall be coming down then and we'll settle the universe there. Let's go and hear what Ethel is telling Miss Lawrence now."

\* \* \*

"[. . .] but the girls, the poor pale-eyed girls of Richstead, I pity them. After all, the mothers have their children, and the men their work; but imagine those poor Miss Garlands waiting, waiting for those abominable young men in straw hats and that disgusting clergyman to come up and ask them to marry them."

Gwen jumped up, her one idea to get away from those terrible voices and words. There were tears in her eyes. Camilla and Harry were on the other path, separated from her only by a single row of rhododendrons. If she moved they might see her; they would know that she had heard from the tears on her flaming cheeks. She sat down again, bitterly determined to listen to the verdict and sentence to the end.

"Do you know, Camilla, I think most of them are thoroughly happy," she heard Harry say. "That's the worst of it."

"I don't believe it, I can't believe so badly of humanity. They are bored to death. They simply don't know what to do with themselves. They are lost and they know it. You can see it in those fluttering blue eyes of Miss Garland. Heavens! how bored those eyes are with life. They are just like the pathetic, stupid eyes of one of those little squat toy-dogs belonging to some old maid; you know the kind, it sits on a chair and looks at you; it's been dandled and over-fed and nursed through life, and has never been allowed to run about or bark or smell

[9]From "A Farewell" by Charles Kingsley (1858): "Be good, sweet maid, and let who will be clever; / Do noble things, not dream them, all day long: / And so make life, death, and that vast for-ever / One grand, sweet song."

at other dogs; it does not know what on earth it all means or what on earth it wants, and so it sits up round a committee table for Poor Dear Things, and begs. Good God! why don't they break out?"

Harry laughed, and at the sound Gwen crouched down almost against the arm of the seat. "Now you're going to abuse men," she heard him say; "I know you are, Camilla. One can always hear it in a woman's voice a sentence ahead at least, when she's going to slang men."

"Well, it does make me almost hate men. The injustice of it. It is their fault. And look at them, those imbecile, cackling young men and that gross clergyman. They've got the range of the world. They've been to Eton and Oxford and Cambridge."

"No, no, not Eton. Don't make them out worse than they are; Dulwich[10] possibly."

"Well, Dulwich then. Your Miss Garland never went to Dulwich. So she's uneducated, purposeless, sterile—and all for them. And there she is, waiting, waiting, and, now she's done for, has to console herself with committees and crèches, having lost all hope of ever being turned into a Mrs Brown, and burying four out of five and a husband. And she'll be expected to envy her younger sister when she's chosen to satisfy the desires of a middle-aged clergyman."

Harry laughed again. "You're a prophetess, Camilla. Why, that's just what is happening, I believe."

"Loathsome, horrible! I think I shall go, Harry—into a nunnery. I can creep off by a back way."

"I'll come with you—even into the nunnery. We'll walk over the common to Silvertown, and then you can take the tube from there."

Gwen listened to their footsteps as they walked away. She did not move. Her face was still hot with shame and pain. How could people be so horrible, so cruel! She hated Camilla, she hated Harry, but still more she hated Mr Macausland. They must have known that she was there and could hear them; they had done it deliberately in order to hurt her. And she had liked Harry! He had seemed more than usually kind to her on the lawn not an hour ago. She wanted to cry; it was with an effort that she kept her tears back. She sat numbed, weary; her head ached. It wasn't true what they had said, she wouldn't have it true—and then every now and again came a horrible sinking sensation in her heart. Was it perhaps true?

[10]Eton and Dulwich were public schools (see notes to pp. 168–69).

## Virginia Woolf (1882–1941)

*The following scenes from Virginia Woolf's debut novel take place at a resort in a fictional English colony on the South American coast; the characters are all English tourists. In the first scene, which transpires around a tea table, the heroine Rachel Vinrace's feelings about Edward Gibbon's massive* Decline and Fall of the Roman Empire *(1776–88) meet with disapproval from a young intellectual named St. John Hirst. This leads Mrs. Thornbury, an older lady, to a defense of the less cultured country aristocracy that may be compared to Forster's esteem for those who live close to the earth. In the second scene, Rachel sits with Hirst's friend Terence Hewet—the two are falling in love—on the edge of a sea-side cliff. Woven into their conversation are two of Woolf's favorite themes: relations between the arts and the consequences of differences between women's education and men's.*

## from *The Voyage Out* (1915)

"I give you up in despair," he said. He meant it lightly, but she took it seriously, and believed that her value as a human being was lessened because she did not happen to admire the style of Gibbon. The others were talking now in a group about the native villages which Mrs. Flushing ought to visit.

"I despair too," she said impetuously. "How are you going to judge people merely by their minds?"

"You agree with my spinster Aunt, I expect," said St. John in his jaunty manner, which was always irritating because it made the person he talked to appear unduly clumsy and in earnest. "'Be good, sweet maid'—I thought Mr. Kingsley and my Aunt were now obsolete."[1]

"One can be very nice without having read a book," she asserted. Very silly and simple her words sounded, and laid her open to derision.

"Did I every deny it?" Hirst enquired, raising his eyebrows.

Most unexpectedly Mrs. Thornbury here intervened, either because it was her mission to keep things smooth or because she had long wished to speak to Mr. Hirst, feeling as she did that all young men were her sons.

"I have lived all my life with people like your Aunt, Mr. Hirst," she said, leaning forward in her chair. Her brown squirrel-like eyes became even brighter than usual. "They have never heard of Gibbon. They only care for their pheasants and their peasants. They are great

[1]See p. 376.

big men who look so fine on horseback, as people must have done, I think, in the days of the great wars. Say what you like against them—they are animal, they are unintellectual; they don't read themselves, and they don't want others to read, but they are some of the finest and the kindest human beings on the face of the earth! You would be surprised at some of the stories I could tell. You have never guessed, perhaps, at all the romances that go on in the heart of the country. Those are the people, I feel, among whom Shakespeare will be born if he is ever born again. In those old houses, up among the Downs——"

"My Aunt," Hirst interrupted, "spends her life in East Lambeth[2] among the degraded poor. I only quoted my Aunt because she is inclined to persecute people she calls 'intellectual,' which is what I suspect Miss Vinrace of doing. It's all the fashion now. If you're clever it's always taken for granted that you're completely without sympathy, understanding, affection—all the things that really matter. Oh, you Christians! You're the most conceited, patronising, hypocritical set of old humbugs in the kingdom! Of course," he continued, "I'm the first to allow your country gentlemen great merits. For one thing, they're probably quite frank about their passions, which we are not. My father, who is a clergyman in Norfolk, says that there is hardly a squire in the county who does not——"

"But about Gibbon?" Hewet interrupted. The look of nervous tension which had come over every face was relaxed by the interruption.

\* \* \*

Raising his eyes Hewet observed her head; she had taken her hat off, and the face rested on her hand. As she looked down into the sea, her lips were slightly parted. The expression was one of childlike intentness, as if she were watching for a fish to swim past over the clear red rocks. Nevertheless her twenty-four years of life had given her a look of reserve. Her hand, which lay on the ground, the fingers curling slightly in, was well shaped and competent; the square-tipped and nervous fingers were the fingers of a musician. With something like anguish Hewet realised that, far from being unattractive, her body was very attractive to him. She looked up suddenly. Her eyes were full of eagerness and interest.

"You write novels?" she asked.

For the moment he could not think what he was saying. He was overcome with the desire to hold her in his arms.

[2] Area of London south of the Thames.

"Oh, yes," he said. "That is, I want to write them."

She would not take her large grey eyes off his face.

"Novels," she repeated. "Why do you write novels? You ought to write music. Music, you see"—she shifted her eyes, and became less desirable as her brain began to work, inflicting a certain change upon her face—"music goes straight for things. It says all there is to say at once. With writing it seems to me there's so much"—she paused for an expression, and rubbed her fingers in the earth—"scratching on the matchbox. Most of the time when I was reading Gibbon this afternoon I was horribly, oh infernally, damnably bored!" She gave a shake of a laughter, looking at Hewet, who laughed too.

"*I* shan't lend you books" he remarked.

"Why is it," Rachel continued, "that I can laugh at Mr. Hirst to you, but not to his face? At tea I was completely overwhelmed, not by his ugliness—by his mind." She enclosed a circle in the air with her hands. She realised with a great sense of comfort how easily she could talk to Hewet, those thorns or ragged corners which tear the surface of some relationships being smoothed away.

"So I observed," said Hewet. "That's a thing that never ceases to amaze me." He had recovered his composure to such an extent that he could light and smoke a cigarette, and feeling her ease, became happy and easy himself.

"The respect that women, even well-educated, very able women, have for men," he went on. "I believe we must have the sort of power over you that we're said to have over horses. They see us three times as big as we are or they'd never obey us. For that very reason, I'm inclined to doubt that you'll ever do anything even when you have the vote." He looked at her reflectively. She appeared very smooth and sensitive and young. "It'll take at least six generations before you're sufficiently thick-skinned to go into law courts and business offices. Consider what a bully the ordinary man is," he continued, "the ordinary hard-working, rather ambitious solicitor or man of business with a family to bring up and a certain position to maintain. And then, of course, the daughters have to give way to the sons; the sons have to be educated; they have to bully and shove for their wives and families, and so it all comes over again. And meanwhile there are the women in the background. . . . Do you really think that the vote will do you any good?"

"The vote?" Rachel repeated. She had to visualise it as a little bit of paper which she dropped into a box before she understood his question, and looking at each other they smiled at something absurd in the question.

"Not to me," she said. "But I play the piano. . . . Are men really like that?" she asked, returning to the question that interested her. "I'm not afraid of you." She looked at him easily.

"Oh, I'm different," Hewet replied. "I've got between six and seven hundred a year of my own. And then no one takes a novelist seriously, thank heavens."

# Works Cited
in This Edition

Beauman, Nicola. *Morgan*. London: Hodder and Stoughton, 1993.

Burnett, John. *A Social History of Housing 1815–1970*. Newton Abbot, U.K.: David and Charles, 1978.

Feltes, N. N. *Modes of Production in Victorian Novels*. Chicago: University of Chicago Press, 1986.

Forster, E. M. *Abinger Harvest and England's Pleasant Land*. London: André Deutsch, 1996.

———. "Appendix: Rooksnest." In *Howards End*. London: Edward Arnold, 1973, 341–51.

———. *Aspects of the Novel, and Related Writings*. London: Edward Arnold, 1974.

———. *The Longest Journey*. London: Edward Arnold, 1984.

———. *The Manuscripts of* Howards End. London: Edward Arnold, 1973.

———. *Marianne Thornton*. London: André Deutsch, 2000.

———. *A Room with a View*. London: Edward Arnold, 1977.

———. *Selected Letters of E. M. Forster*. Ed. Mary Lago and P. N. Furbank. Vol. 1. Cambridge, MA: Harvard University Press, 1983.

———. *Two Cheers for Democracy*. London: Edward Arnold, 1972.

———. *Where Angels Fear to Tread*. London: Edward Arnold, 1975.

Furbank, P. N. *E. M. Forster: A Life*. New York: Harcourt Brace Jovanovich, 1978.

Gibson, Mary Ellis. "Illegitimate Order: Cosmopolitanism and Liberalism in Forster's *Howards End*." *ELT* 28 (1985): 106–23.

Gregor, Ian. "Notes." In *Culture and Anarchy*. By Matthew Arnold. Indianapolis, IN: Bobbs-Merrill, 1971, 177–250.

Havighurst, Alfred F. *Britain in Transition: The Twentieth Century*. Chicago: University of Chicago Press, 1979.

Hubbard, Elbert. *Little Journeys to the Homes of Eminent Artists*. Vol. 1. East Aurora, NY: Roycrofters, 1902.

London, Jack. *The People of the Abyss*. New York: Macmillan, 1903.

Moore, G. E. *Principia Ethica*. Cambridge, U.K.: Cambridge University Press, 1903.

Money, L. G. Chiozza. *Riches and Poverty*. London: Methuen, 1905.

Muthesius, Stefan. *The English Terraced House*. New Haven, CT: Yale University Press, 1982.

Olson, Jeane N. "The 'Noble Peasant' in E. M. Forster's Fiction." *Studies in the Novel* 20 (1988): 389–403.

Stallybrass, Oliver. "Editor's Introduction." In *Howards End*. By E. M. Forster. London: Edward Arnold, 1973, vii–xix.

———. "Editor's Introduction." In *The Manuscripts of* Howards End. By E. M. Forster. London: Edward Arnold, 1973, vii–xviii.

———. "Notes." In *Howards End*. By E.M. Forster. London. Edward Arnold, 1973.

Super, R. H. "Critical and Explanatory Notes." In *Culture and Anarchy*. By Matthew Arnold. Ann Arbor, MI: University of Michigan Press, 1965, 357–486.

Thompson, Paul. *The Edwardians: The Remaking of British Society*. 2nd ed. London: Routledge, 1992.

Tinkler, Penny. *Smoke Signals: Women, Smoking, and Visual Culture*. Oxford, U.K.: Berg, 2006.

Trilling, Lionel. *E. M. Forster*. Norfolk, CT: New Directions, 1943.

Umbach, Maiken. "The Deutscher Werkbund, Globalization, and the Invention of Modern Vernaculars." In *Vernacular Modernism*. Ed. Maiken Umbach and Bernd Hüppauf. Stanford, CA: Stanford University Press, 2005, 114–40.

Wilson, A. N. *After the Victorians*. New York: Farrar, Straus and Giroux, 2005.

Yeats, William Butler. *Collected Poems*. New York: Collier, 1989.

# Further Reading

## E. M. Forster's Writings

*The Abinger Edition of E. M. Forster.* 20 vols. London: Edward Arnold, 1972–1984, and London: André Deutsch, 1996–2004. (Includes most of the individual volumes of Forster listed under Works Cited in This Edition.)

*Commonplace Book.* London: Scolar, 1978.

*Interviews and Recollections.* New York: St. Martin's, 1993.

*Selected Letters.* 2 vols. Cambridge, MA: Harvard University Press, 1983–85.

## Biographical Studies

Beauman, Nicola. *Morgan.* London: Hodder and Stoughton, 1993.

Furbank, P. N. *E. M. Forster: A Life.* New York: Harcourt Brace Jovanovich, 1978.

King, Francis. *E. M. Forster and His World.* London: Thames and Hudson, 1978.

Lago, Mary. *E. M. Forster: A Literary Life.* New York: St. Martin's, 1995.

## Critical Studies

Beer, J. B. *The Achievement of E. M. Forster.* London: Chatto and Windus, 1962.

Born, Daniel. "Private Gardens, Public Swamps: *Howards End* and the Revaluation of Liberal Guilt." *Novel* 25 (1992): 141–59.

Bradshaw, David, ed. *The Cambridge Companion to E. M. Forster.* Cambridge, U. K.: Cambridge University Press, 2007.

Brooker, Peter, and Peter Widdowson. "A Literature for England." In *Englishness: Politics and Culture 1880–1920*. Ed. Robert Colls and Philip Dodd. London: Croom Helm, 1986, 116–63.

Cavaliero, Glen. *A Reading of E. M. Forster*. Totowa, NJ: Rowman and Littlefield, 1979.

Colmer, John. *E. M. Forster: The Personal Voice*. London: Routledge and Kegan Paul, 1975.

Crews, Frederick C. *E. M. Forster: The Perils of Humanism*. Princeton, NJ: Princeton University Press, 1962.

Das, G. K., and John Beer, eds. *E. M. Forster: A Human Exploration*. New York: New York University Press, 1979.

Dowling, David. *Bloomsbury Aesthetics and the Novels of Forster and Woolf*. New York: St. Martin's, 1985.

Firchow, Peter. "Germany and Germanic Mythology in *Howards End*." *Comparative Literature* 33 (1981): 50–68.

Gardner, Philip. "E. M. Forster and the Possession of England." *MLQ* 42 (1981): 166–83.

———, ed. *E. M. Forster: The Critical Heritage*. London: Routledge and Kegan Paul, 1973.

Hall, Mary Katherine. "The Reification of High Culture in Merchant-Ivory's *Howards End*." *Literature Film Quarterly* 31 (2003): 221–26.

Hoy, Pat C. "The Narrow, Rich Staircase in Forster's *Howards End*." *Twentieth Century Literature* 31 (1985): 221–35.

Langland, Elizabeth. "Gesturing Toward an Open Space: Gender, Form, and Language in *Howards End*." In *Out of Bounds*. Ed. Laura Claridge and Elizabeth Langland. Amherst, MA: University of Massachusetts Press, 1990, 252–67.

Levenson, Michael. "Liberalism and Symbolism in *Howards End*." *Papers on Language and Literature* 21 (1985): 295–316.

Martin, Richard. *The Love That Failed*. The Hague: Mouton, 1974.

Martin, Robert K., and George Piggford, eds. *Queer Forster*. Chicago: University of Chicago Press, 1997.

May, Brian. *The Modernist as Pragmatist*. Columbia, MO: University of Missouri Press, 1997.

McConkey, James. *The Novels of E. M. Forster*. Ithaca, NY: Cornell University Press, 1957.

McDowell, Frederick P. *E. M. Forster*. Rev. ed. Boston: Twayne, 1982.

————. *E. M. Forster: An Annotated Bibliography of Writings about Him*. De Kalb, IL: Northern Illinois University Press, 1976.

Medalie, David. *E. M. Forster's Modernism*. Houndmills, U. K.: Palgrave, 2002.

Rosecrance, Barbara. *Forster's Narrative Vision*. Ithaca, NY: Cornell University Press, 1982.

Stewart, Garrett. "The Foreign Offices of British Fiction." *MLQ* 61 (2000): 181–206.

Stone, Wilfred. *The Cave and the Mountain*. Stanford, CA: Stanford University Press, 1966.

Summers, Claude J. *E. M. Forster: A Guide to Research*. New York: Garland, 1991.

————. *E. M. Forster: Literature and Life*. New York: Ungar, 1983.

Trilling, Lionel. *E. M. Forster*. Norfolk, CT: New Directions, 1943.

White, Leslie. "Vital Disconnection in *Howards End*." *Twentieth Century Literature* 51 (2005): 43–63.

Widdowson, Peter. *E. M. Forster's* Howards End. London: Chatto and Windus, 1977.

Wilde, Alan. *Art and Order*. New York: New York University Press, 1964.

Wright, Anne. *Literature of Crisis, 1910–22*. New York: St. Martin's, 1984.